# SYMBOL TO VORTEX

# SYMBOL TO VORTEX

## POETRY, PAINTING AND IDEAS,
### 1885–1914

Alan Robinson

St. Martin's Press     New York

© Alan David Robinson 1985

St. Martin's Press, Inc., 175 Fifth Avenue, New York, NY 10010
Printed in Hong Kong
Published in the United Kingdom by The Macmillan Press Ltd.
First published in the United States of America in 1985

Quotes from previously unpublished letters by Ezra Pound, copyright © 1985 by the Trustees of the Ezra Pound Literary Property Trust; used by permission of New Directions Publishing Corp., agents for the Trustees.

ISBN   0–312–78188–1

**Library of Congress Cataloging in Publication Data**

Robinson, Alan.
    Symbol to vortex.

    Includes bibliographical references and index.  1. Symbolism (Art movement).  2. Abstract expressionism.  3. Arts – Philosophy.  4. Aesthetics,  Modern – 19th  century.  5. Aesthetics, Modern – 20th century.  6. Pound, Ezra, 1885–1972 – Aesthetics.
I. Title.
NX600.S95R62   1985        700        83–24449
ISBN 0–312–78188–1

*To my father and in memory of my mother*

# Contents

Divergent responses of German Romantic philosophy to
the Enlightenment's despiritualisation of nature: the
Idealism of Kant and Hegel; the empathetic, animistic
aesthetics of Schopenhauer. Abstract expressionism of
music.
'Empathetic' and 'abstract expressionist' Symbolism.

Re-establishment in *fin de siècle* of anti-materialist aesthetics. Abstract expressionist Symbolism of Watts, Image
and early Yeats. Empathetic Symbolism evolved by
Moore, MacColl and several New English Art Club
painters.
Symons's poetic experimentation with both approaches
and occasional 'objectivist' poems. His subsequent animistic aesthetics: all art-forms the non-discursive communication of noumenal 'rhythm'.

Empathetic Symbolist poetry consolidated by Hulme

and Flint. Hulme's relativist critique of Idealism; his Lippsian, Bergsonian empathetic aesthetic.

Hulme's shift in aesthetic outlook rooted in Tory polemic of 1911, influenced by *Action française* and paralleled by English Nietzschean radical Right.

Abstract expressionist and empathetic Symbolism of pre-war movements in visual arts. Empathetic animism (influentially epitomised by Bergsonism) the unifying tendency of Futurism, German Expressionism and Imagism/Vorticism.

Pound's quest for symbolic vehicle for religious poetry of his planned animistic, anti-materialist Renaissance: initially in Celtic, then in Classical metamorphic mythology, finally in Stilnovism.

His hermetic, Symbolist poetics, cognate with Yeats's post-1903 position and transcendentalist animism of contemporary visual arts: poetry a talismanic 'equation', channelling psychic energy through language to generate archetypal states of consciousness and, as basis of *Cantos*, *forma* of Unity of Culture.

Practical details of Pound's planned Renaissance. Search for patronage on *quattrocento* model for high-quality periodical and College of the Arts/London 'Vortex'.

Symbolist poetics of Pound's pre-Imagist phase maintained throughout Imagism/Vorticism.

His Imagist poetry characterised by empathetic and abstract expressionist Symbolism; objectivist reorientation initiated by H.D.

# List of Plates

# Preface

There is, I contend, an unbroken continuity in *avant-garde* aesthetics from the *fin de siècle* to Vorticism. To demonstrate this requires an unusually broad-based investigation; I seek therefore to bring to light the striking congruity of the art and literature of the period, emphasising the pervasive transcendentalism which present-day critics have undervalued. Developing this approach, I argue further for a radical reinterpretation of the relationship between Yeats and Pound.

The characteristic tendency in aesthetics from the 1890s to the First World War was to regard all the art-forms as complementary expressions of the same anti-materialist sensibility. Artists and writers voiced this in a stylistic register whose metaphysical connotations have been neglected by later literary and art-historians, enabling them to reduce discussion of the pre-war movements to matters of technique. The period is accordingly treated as a chaos of heterogeneous and apparently disparate '-isms'. I venture to challenge the adequacy of this wholly formalistic approach and hence to reveal instead of confusing divergence a shared post-Impressionist ideology.

On the basis of manifestos and articles published in the many 'little magazines' I seek to demonstrate the period's veritable saturation in an animistic aesthetics. This developed from the anti-positivist revolution of the *fin de siècle* into the syncretic assimilation of Bergsonism, Theosophism and pantheism which characterised the literary and artistic *avant-garde* in the late Edwardian era.

Pound's adherence to this aesthetic consensus means that modern accounts of Imagism/Vorticism in poetry (the terms are inter-changeable) misinterpret its aesthetic in attempting to present it as breaking with Symbolism and looking forward formalistically to the *Cantos.* Far from marking a reorientation, as the received critical view has proposed, Pound's aesthetic in this period is, I argue, completely cognate with the transcendentalist animism which characterised several major movements in the contemporary visual arts. And, while previous critics have maintained that Pound was reacting unreservedly against Yeats, the development suggested here is rather that Pound reproduces the pattern of Yeats's own post-1903 aesthetic and psychological theories.

A. R.

# Acknowledgements

I should like to express gratitude to the following, who have generously in various invaluable ways smoothed the path of my research: Mr David Auchterlonie; Mr Alfred C. Edwards; Mrs Valerie Eliot; Professor Ian Fletcher; Dr I. H. C. Fraser; Mr Alister Kershaw; Mr James Laughlin; Mrs Ianthe Price; the staffs of the Bodleian Library; Faber & Faber Ltd (particularly Miss Connie Whittaker); the Houghton Library, Harvard; the Humanities Research Center, Texas (particularly Ms Ellen S. Dunlap); New Directions Publishing Corporation (particularly Ms Peggy Fox).

My sincere thanks are due to the British Academy, whose timely and munificent grant relieved completely the burden of copyright fees.

Last but by no means least I should like to thank my long-suffering supervisor, Dr John Kelly, for his humour and forbearance during this long disease, my thesis; my examiners, Professors Richard Ellmann and Samuel Hynes, who proffered valuable advice; Professor Ernst Honigmann, who manfully read the entire typescript and suggested useful improvements; Mrs Margaret Palmer, who successfully transformed my graffiti into an attractive typescript; and, above all, my wife, Elaine, who gave not only extensive practical assistance but, more crucially, the loving support which alone enabled me to complete this project.

T. S. Eliot manuscript material used by permission of Mrs Valerie Eliot.

Copyright material from the manuscript collections of the Humanities Research Center, the University of Texas at Austin, appears with the permission of the University of Texas and the appropriate copyright-holders: Professor Samuel Hynes; Mr Alister Kershaw, the literary executor of Richard Aldington; Mrs Ianthe Price and Dr O. Flint, the children of F. S. Flint.

Further copyright material quoted by permission of the Houghton Library, Harvard University, and of Keele University Library.

# Abbreviations and Notes on the Text

The place of publication of books cited is London unless otherwise specified. The following authors are identified by surname only: T. E. Hulme, George Moore, Ezra Pound, Edward Storer, Arthur Symons, W. B. Yeats.

The following abbreviations are employed in text and notes. References to *CJ*, *FS*, *Spec*, *WdB* and *WWR* are made in the text wherever convenient.

| | |
|---|---|
| *CJ* | Immanuel Kant, *Critique of Judgement*, trs. J. C. Meredith (Oxford, 1952). |
| *FS* | T. E. Hulme, *Further Speculations*, ed. Samuel Hynes (Minneapolis, 1955). |
| HRC, Texas | Humanities Research Center, the University of Texas at Austin. |
| NEAC | New English Art Club |
| NKV | Neue Künstlervereinigung |
| *Spec* | T. E. Hulme, *Speculations*, ed. Herbert Read, 2nd edn (1936). |
| *WdB* | Friedrich Nietzsche, *Werke in drei Bänden*, ed. Karl Schlechta, 6th edn (1969; repr. Frankfurt-am-Main, Berlin and Vienna, 1976–9). |
| *WWR* | Arthur Schopenhauer, *The World as Will and Representation*, (1819; 2nd, enlarged edn, 1844), trs. E. F. J. Payne, 2 vols (Indian Hills, Colorado, 1958). |

*Abbreviations used in relation to material at HRC, Texas*

| | |
|---|---|
| ALI | autograph letter initialled |
| ALS | autograph letter signed |
| AMS | autograph manuscript |

APCS        autograph postcard signed
TLS         typed letter signed
TMS         typed manuscript
TS with A
additions   typescript with autograph additions

The following works by Pound and Yeats, cited in more than one chapter, are referred to by title only (in an abbreviated form where this is indicated in square brackets). The editions cited are as follows.

*Pound*

*Collected Early Poems of Ezra Pound*, ed. Michael John King (1977). [*Early Poems.*]
*Collected Shorter Poems*, 2nd edn (1968). [*Shorter Poems.*]
*Gaudier-Brzeska: A Memoir* (1916), enlarged edn 1970 (paperback repr. New York, 1974). [*Gaudier-Brzeska.*]
*Guide to Kulchur* (1938; repr. 1966).
*Literary Essays of Ezra Pound*, ed. T. S. Eliot, paperback edn (1960). [*Literary Essays.*]
*Patria Mia and The Treatise on Harmony* (1962). [*Patria Mia.*]
*Pound/Joyce. The Letters of Ezra Pound to James Joyce; with Pound's Essays on Joyce*, ed. Forrest Read (1968). [*Pound/Joyce.*]
*The Selected Letters of Ezra Pound 1907–1941*, ed. D. D. Paige, paperback edn (New York, 1971). [*Letters.*]
*Selected Prose 1909–1965*, ed. William Cookson (1978). [*Selected Prose.*]
*The Spirit of Romance*, revised edn (1952). [*Spirit of Romance.*]
*The Translations of Ezra Pound*, enlarged edn (1970). [*Translations.*]

*Yeats*

*Autobiographies* (1955).
*Essays and Introductions* (1961).
*Explorations* (1962).
*The Letters of W. B. Yeats*, ed. Allan Wade (1954) [*Letters.*]
*Letters to the New Island*, ed. Horace Reynolds (1934).
*Memoirs*, ed. Denis Donoghue (1972).
*Uncollected Prose by W. B. Yeats*, ed. John P. Frayne and Colton Johnson, 2 vols (1970 and 1975). [*Uncollected Prose.*]

*The Variorum Edition of the Plays of W. B. Yeats*, ed. Russell K. Alspach (1966). [*Variorum Plays*.]

*The Variorum Edition of the Poems of W. B. Yeats*, ed. Peter Allt and Russell K. Alspach (New York, 1957). [*Variorum Poems*.]

For all works to which the above conventions do not apply, full details are given on the first reference in each chapter, with abbreviation as convenient on subsequent reference.

# 1 The Perceiving Imagination

The problem confronting the literary historian of a period as eclectic and cosmopolitan as the early twentieth century is as daunting as that which James expressed in the Preface to *Roderick Hudson*: 'Really, universally, relations stop nowhere, and the exquisite problem of the artist is eternally but to draw, by a geometry of his own, the circle within which they shall happily *appear* to do so.'[1] The radius of my circle extends to Romanticism, that nebulous phenomenon which, although the origin of the themes of all later chapters, can here only be treated in a simplified schema, whose aims and scope I shall now clarify.

My prime objective is to establish a philosophical model and a vocabulary for later discussions. The use of aesthetic theory enables me to abbreviate my exposition and to take a representative cross-section of complex problems otherwise requiring extensive illustration. An examination of German Romantic aesthetics has two further advantages for my later argument. First, it rehearses conveniently a variety of responses to the crisis of a desacralised world, which was repeated in an accentuated form in the late nineteenth century. The Romantic search for a compensatory animistic cosmology, giving primacy to the artistic imagination as an intuitive means of access to noumena or things-in-themselves, forms a paradigm and in many cases an influential source for the Modernist generation. Secondly, it raises as a corollary the crucial problem of how such insights may be embodied in art, anticipating strikingly the concerns of Symbolism and Imagism. Some general considerations will serve to introduce these technical issues.

The central question in the Romantic period was the relationship between man and his environment. The Enlightenment had provoked a crucial change in *Weltanschauung*. Rational and scientific inquiry could no longer support the traditional view of nature as a vast system of interrelated beings and the belief that it embodied a 'locus of meaning' which could be read from it. Through man's increasing rational self-possession nature was desacralised; mechanist, atomistic and utilitarian philosophy regarded it simply as 'objectified' fact, completely divorced from man and merely the field of his potential activity or dominion. The concomitant stress on individual liberty from external laws of necessity argued so ably by Kant simply accentuated the disjunction between man and now-inanimate nature. This diremption of subjective consciousness and environment could only be bridged by what the individual, creative imagination contributed to perception. It thus assumed unprecedented importance as the sole remaining guarantor of man and nature's spiritual significance. Of the resulting epistemological strategies which were adopted in the Romantic period to reaffirm the spiritual congruity of man and nature, two – the Idealist and the empathetic – form the principal subject of this chapter.

The central theme of Hegelian Idealism is the desire to repossess a potentially alien world by subsuming it within the subjective consciousness (by regarding both as evolving towards self-conscious identity with the indivisible cosmic mind), reasserting its spiritual quality at the expense of its ontological autonomy. The major alternative to this representative Idealist approach was the Romantic revival of Spinozist pantheism and Neoplatonic animism, for which Schopenhauer's empathetic aesthetics provides a representative paradigm.

My exposition of these divergent epistemologies begins with the relevant ideas of the seminal figure of German Romantic philosophy: Kant.

## I  *KANT*

In the *Critique of Pure Reason* (1781, 1787) Kant contended that in the mind there exist *a priori* 'forms' of perception, namely space and time, to which all experience must conform. These are *logically*, not temporally, prior to experience; not its cause, but the basis of its ordered existence. This unavoidable mental framework renders all experience of merely provisional validity. For, being unable to move outside the subjective conditions of perception, one apprehends merely phenomenal appearances, and not *noumena* or *things-in-themselves*.

Kant analyses the epistemological process in terms of increasing hierarchical complexity. Sense-data are translated by the *imagination* into ordered experiential images or representations. These are then correlated conceptually by the *understanding*. But, although the understanding's aetiological inquiry presupposes that every event must depend on a preceding cause, it never considers whether these disparate causative relationships bear witness to an underlying, unconditioned rationale. *Reason*, however, is only satisfied with the absolute determination of all particulars by necessary *a priori* laws or noumenal Ideas, rather than the relative validity of the understanding's mechanistic generalisations, which derive from the world of sense and are thus conditioned by our subjective 'forms' of perception.

Kant concludes that reason's deductive aspirations are chimerical, for one can have no *knowledge* of what lies outside possible experience, which therefore must remain theoretically indeterminable. Nevertheless reason's teleological quest is subjectively necessary; man cannot accept the absurd contingency which a world devoid of supersensible purpose would imply.

Kant's dissatisfaction with a purely mechanistic cosmology was developed in the *Critique of Judgement* (1790). There he maintained that, although the realm of Ideas or things-in-themselves is unverifiable, its hypothetical existence might nevertheless receive intuitive confirmation. Hence man's delight in the *beautiful* in nature. For the intricate organisation of certain natural forms compels us to judge that their parts depend on some supersensible causality, on an Idea of the whole, validating our rational hypothesis that nature is not just a mechanistic aggregate. Of greater interest than this formalistic aesthetic, however, is Kant's complementary account of the *sublime* in nature, which lays more weight on the *imagination*.

The fundamental distinction between the beautiful and the sublime is that the formlessness of the latter apparently frustrates our rational quest for evidence of noumenal purposiveness. Yet paradoxically it also arouses pleasure. The solution to this peculiarity is that the *object* which for convenience' sake we term sublime is really a catalyst which leads us to discover a rational, noumenal sublimity *in our own mind*: 'For the sublime . . . cannot be contained in any sensuous form, but rather concerns ideas of reason, which, although no adequate presentation of them is possible, may be excited and called into the mind by that very inadequacy itself which does admit of sensuous presentation' (*CJ*, 92).

Kant offers two examples of this process. First, beyond a certain point (as in viewing the multitude of stars) our comprehension is frustrated in its desire to synthesise a manifold of representations into the intuitive whole which reason requires. From this momentary disappointment arises a profound appreciation of our rational faculty, whose Ideas so exceed the capacity of our sensibility. Secondly, our initial, terrified helplessness in the face of powerful natural forces reveals our ability to elevate ourselves rationally above the vicissitudes of physical experience and thus to an intuitive awareness of our inner moral superiority.

Kant summarises his views thus: the sublime 'is an object (of nature) the *representation of which determines the mind to regard the elevation of nature beyond our reach as equivalent to a presentation of ideas*' (*CJ*, 119). In other words our inability to extend our imagination to an adequate intuition of the natural object, which reason leads us to attempt, and consequent vivid intuition of hitherto unrealised depths in our mind leads us to *regard* this stimulating object as a presentation of something supersensible, without our being able to effectuate this presentation *objectively*. For the intuitive imagination the object becomes a symbolic embodiment of the world of Ideas. This is the heart of Kant's thought on aesthetics and he goes on to employ this notion of the sublime eliciting intuitive awareness of supersensible Ideas as the basis of an analogy with artistic creation.

He defines the mark of genius as 'soul' (*Geist*), which he describes as the faculty of presenting *aesthetic ideas*:

> by an aesthetic idea I mean that representation of the imagination which induces much thought, yet without the possibility of any definite thought whatever, i.e. *concept*, being adequate to it, and which language, consequently, can never get quite on level terms with or render completely intelligible. – It is easily seen, that an aesthetic idea is the counterpart (pendant) of a *rational idea*, which, conversely, is a concept, to which no *intuition* (representation of the imagination) can be adequate. (*CJ*, 175–6).

The effect of 'aesthetic ideas' in Kant's account clearly anticipates that of literary symbols. What his theory lacks, however, is detailed explanation of how aesthetic ideas might be embodied in a work of art. He was aware of the problem of finding a formal equivalent to communicate emotion, as the following quotation prefiguring Eliot's 'objective correlative' indicates:

> genius properly consists in the happy relation . . . enabling one to find out ideas for a given concept, and, besides, to hit upon the *expression* for them – the expression by means of which the subjective mental condition induced by the ideas as the concomitant of a concept may be communicated to others. . . . For to get an expression for what is indefinable in the mental state accompanying a particular representation and to make it universally communicable – be the expression in language or painting or statuary – is a thing requiring a faculty for laying hold of the rapid and transient play of the imagination, and for unifying it in a concept . . . that admits of communication without any constraint of rules. (*CJ*, 179–80).

But his suggested instances of this process are disappointing. For example, he develops the notion of an *aesthetic attribute* which differs from a logical attribute in that it expresses derivatives of the object and its affinities to other concepts, instancing lamely Jupiter's eagle and Juno's peacock. His explanation of their effect is, however, a model of insight. They do not, he claims,

> represent what lies in our concepts of the sublimity and majesty of creation, but rather something else – something that gives the imagination an incentive to spread its flight over a whole host of kindred representations that provoke more thought than admits of expression in a concept determined by words. They furnish an *aesthetic idea*, which serves the above rational idea as a substitute for logical presentation, but with the proper function, however, of animating the mind by opening out for it a prospect into a field of kindred representations stretching beyond its ken. (*CJ*, 177–8)

The acuteness of his analysis lies in the suggestion that the aesthetic process is that of imaginative, analogical association, in which the reader is inspired by his intuitive response to the aesthetic object to explore in a non-conceptual manner hitherto unrealised aspects of his own subconsciousness. The aesthetic object is the constant stimulus to this process (and to that degree its external embodiment) but the result is potentially as indefinite or polysemous as the range of subjective responses. The images the mind produces do not need to be visualised in detail, yet create cumulatively a more profound internal impression than a series of assigned statements could attain: 'give the imagination an impetus to bring more thought into play in the matter, though in an undeveloped manner, than allows of being brought within the embrace of a concept, or, therefore, of being definitely formulated in language'. (*CJ*, 178).

In succeeding chapters I shall examine alternative literary strategies of creating such an autonomous entity which would stimulate the perceiver to experience a mental state similar to that which underlay its creation. Kant's explanation of the possibility of non-discursive, symbolic communication remains the central theme of Modernist aesthetics.

## II   *THE POST-KANTIANS*

Two major and divergent developments from Kant now demand attention. Schopenhauer's modification of Kant led to empathetic theory, Hegel's to absolute Idealism.

### (a) *Schopenhauer*

Schopenhauer's philosophy, like Kant's, is grounded in perceptual interaction with the external world. Our epistemology is, he maintains, primarily causative: we apprehend discrete objects through their action upon us as 'representations', that is, perceptual images, rather than in their essential nature as things-in-themselves.

Such phenomenal apprehension is, however, a partial distortion of experience. For, in performing a motor activity, the knowing subject is able not only to perceive his own body as phenomenon like any other representation, but at the same time to be directly, non-perceptually aware of this as manifesting an act of will. The connection between the representation and the inner awareness is not causative: they are simply different *aspects* of the same activity, the one objectifying the other (*WWR*, I, 99–100). The perceiver must therefore either assume that the apparent uniqueness of one representation – the self – derives merely from his privileged knowledge of it as both phenomenon and noumenon, or that the self is indeed essentially different from all other representations, which would accordingly be reduced to mere phantoms (an attitude which Schopenhauer terms 'theoretical egoism' – *WWR*, I, 103–4; see also I, 370, 375–6).

In adopting the former conclusion Schopenhauer makes his most important innovation: a relocation of the Kantian noumenon. Far from belonging to a supersensible world of which we can have no knowledge, the noumenal lies within all phenomenal representations, a realisation forestalled only by our customary perceptual attitude. A materialistic cosmology is therefore inadequate, as Schopenhauer emphasises in his remarks on scientific, aetiological investigation, or what he terms 'the *principle of sufficient reason*' (*WWR*, I, 124; emphasis added).

Despite regarding scientific inquiry into our environment as indispensable, Schopenhauer insists that it never penetrates beyond the connection and interrelation of representations. As with human personality, there remains an essential quiddity which external analysis is powerless to explain. For aetiology is concerned merely with the phenomenal appearance of varying states of an object in space and time. It can demonstrate the cause for a particular action, but not the principle for the object's acting in general; the noumenal beginning of this chain of causes and effects can never be reached (*WWR*, II, 172–3). Only by introspection can we understand what this groundless residuum might be, terming it 'will' on the analogy of our own self-consciousness.

Being indivisible and thus beyond the possibility of plurality, the will lies outside the forms of perception: space and time. It may therefore only be perceived indirectly when objectified through the '*principium individuationis*' into myriad phenomena, at different grades ranging from blind natural forces to man. These grades correspond to Platonic Ideas, existing beyond the innumerable transient manifestations through which alone they are apprehensible (*WWR*, I, 129). To perceive the Ideas requires a profound reorientation of our consciousness. For the intellect is only concerned with relations between things, rather than their inner essence (*WWR*, II, 283–8). It is, however, possible temporarily to free oneself from the practically orientated will, by concentrating intense contemplative attention on an individual object. In such absorption one no longer perceives 'the individual thing as such, but the *Idea*, the eternal form, the immediate objectivity of the will at this grade' (*WWR*, I, 178–9).[2]

The Schopenhauerian Idea might perhaps be described as the seagullness of a seagull, the snakeness of a snake, or, in more conventional language, the quintessential, unchanging nature of any thing which is realised or objectified in its various external manifestations. Schopenhauer's analogy is between the character of a man or animal as revealed in its actions and the essential quality of natural phenomena. Wave-forms change, but we have an inner notion of what a wave is which enables us to recognise the common element which underlies the superficially differing examples, just as we refer a man's many actions back to the same familiar character:

> When clouds move, the figures they form are not essential, but indifferent to them. But that as elastic vapour they are pressed together, driven off, spread out, and torn apart by the force of the wind, this is their nature, this is the essence of the forces that are objectified in them, this is the Idea.   (*WWR*, I, 182)

> [The Idea] is the peculiar *character* of the thing, and thus the complete expression of the essence that exhibits itself to perception as object.   (*WWR*, II, 364)

Chapters 2 and 5 will demonstrate how this empathetic register became a commonplace in the post-Impressionist [3] polemic against the dispassionate superficiality of Impressionism.

Schopenhauer's aesthetic is elucidated by the remarkably similar views of Hopkins, whose term 'inscape' (which corresponds to the Schopenhauerian 'Idea') has been defined as follows:

> I infer that '*in*-scape' is the outward reflection of the *inner* nature of a thing, or a sensible copy or representation of its individual essence; and thus I define it as the unified complex of those sensible qualities of an object that strike us as inseparably belonging to and most typical of that object, so that through the knowledge of this unified complex of sense-data we may gain an insight into the individual essence of the object. [4]

Through contemplation Hopkins believed that we experience first in intuitive perception the sensuous individuality of the object – its 'inscape' – and then its 'instress', the inner force which gives the object its actuality. Instress is not a sensible quality and is also used by Hopkins to refer to the unique impression which this specifically individual object makes on the percipient – what Lipps would term 'empathy'.

Schopenhauer expressly distinguished his own outlook from pantheism, such as that of Scotus Erigena (Hopkins's mentor), for whom every single thing is a theophany, as this belief, he claimed, extended beyond the boundaries of experience in postulating that God and not the will is the thing-in-itself, the indwelling essence, of all things (*WWR*, II, 643–4). His Modernist interpreters conveniently forgot such niceties, and later chapters will record Schopenhauer's syncretic assimilation to pantheism and Neo-platonic and Bergsonian animism.

The importance for my inquiry of Schopenhauer's empathetic aesthetics lies accordingly in his relocation of Kant's things-in-themselves within the phenomenal world. In so doing Schopenhauer revalidated the spiritual cosmology discredited by the Enlightenment: everything, if perceived with disinterested contemplation, revealed an inherent noumenal essence and hence became again an object of potential reverence. His arguments were to prove indispensable to the Modernist reaction against material-ism, being utilised for example by Symons, the *Blaue Reiter* painters, and (mediated by Bergson) the Futurists and Vorticists, to establish the metaphysical, empathetic aesthetics which characterised all pre-war *avant-garde* movements (save Cubism) in painting and poetry.

The alternative to this empathetic perceptual relationship is a purely expressionist aesthetic. And indeed Schopenhauer maintains that the difference between music and all other art forms is along these lines. The crucial distinction is that apart from occasional languid attempts at genre painting, music is non-representational and hence abstract. It neither wishes nor is able to depict the external world; its realm is that of pure emotions. In Schopenhauerian language, the other arts by depicting individual things attempt to stimulate in us knowledge of the Ideas which objectify the will. Music, however, bypasses the representation of phenomena and thus the Ideas *immediately* to objectify the will itself. It therefore has no necessary reference to the external world but directly expresses emotion in what might later have been termed an 'archetypal' state (*WWR*, I, 261).[5] The attempt to emulate in literature this property of music is the basis of 'abstract expressionist Symbolism'.

(b) *Hegel*

Hegel's philosophy, the culmination of German Romanticism, became in the influential misreading of Villiers the Bible of Mallarméan Symbolism, attractive by virtue of its arrogantly uncompromising Idealism. His solution to the problem of man's apparent disjunction from nature is intentionally conceptual. The universe is, he claims, a manifestation of rational necessity and is posited by what he terms *Geist*, an absolute spiritual principle. In order to exist *Geist* requires an object for its consciousness and so must project itself into finite individuals. This embodiment negates *Geist*'s own nature but is an essential preliminary to self-realisation, for through the unfolding of the historical process *Geist* achieves reconciliation with its own spiritual essence. Gradually finite creatures attain self-conscious awareness of their own rationality (culminating with man) and hence of their identity with the underlying spiritual principle of the universe, whose vehicles they are. The corporeal is thus transcended by the philosophical consciousness in the synthesis of a higher spiritual unity with *Geist*.

Hegel regarded the exclusively rational character of this doctrine as its strength; such a theoretical attitude to nature is, however, limited. For his strictly hierarchical view of natural phenomena and their general inferiority to the mind and all its creations leads him to place little value on either animal life or natural beauty. His interest is solely for what *reflects* the human mind and he has little respect for the autonomous existence of unmediated nature. The goal of the spirit is self-realisation, liberation from external contingency. Spiritless nature can only stimulate this, he claims, once it has, as a work of art, been moulded by the reflective consciousness which in this way subjects to its control the alien external world. [6] All nature aspires towards the condition of self-conscious spirit but can never attain it. The mind must impress itself on the environment to make this worthy of attention: no longer does it merely contribute to what it perceives, but rather *only* what it contributes gives the perceived its value.

He writes, 'for man, all reality must come through the medium of perception and ideas, and only through this medium does it penetrate the heart and the will. Now here it is a matter of indifference whether a man's attention is claimed by immediate external reality or whether this happens in another way, namely through pictures, symbols, and ideas containing in themselves and

portraying the material of reality'.⁷ This explanation of the
aesthetic response is clearly inadequate as an attitude to the natural
world which only appears significant in so far as it approximates to
an artistic image. He has completely reduced its ontological status
to the point where a mere simulacrum of reality would suffice for
ordinary experience. If what we perceive is only valuable after
being mentally transmogrified, the need for such a prior process is
clearly a disadvantage. It would be better if we lived in a purely
mental world; perception becomes a tiresome prelude to the
conceptual realm. His attitude is not solipsistic; external 'reality'
does exist; but the world of art because artificial is paradoxically
more 'real' than everyday nature.⁸

While related to Neoplatonism, this clearly foreshadows the
hermetically intellectual world of late Mallarmé, as does Hegel's
general contention that art is merely a vehicle for expressing the
highest truths known to man, which may be more adequately
conveyed in philosophical thought than the sensuous form to which
art is shackled. This, he insists, is the condition of the present,
Romantic art, which is more concerned with spiritual content than
its formal realisation:

> For at the stage of romantic art the spirit knows that its truth does
> not consist in its immersion in corporeality; on the contrary, it
> only becomes sure of its truth by withdrawing from the external
> into its own intimacy with itself and positing external reality as an
> existence inadequate to itself. Even if, therefore this new content
> too comprises in itself the task of making itself *beautiful*, still
> beauty in the sense hitherto expounded remains for it something
> subordinate, and beauty becomes the *spiritual* beauty of the
> absolute inner life as inherently infinite spiritual subjectivity.
>
> But therefore to attain its infinity the spirit must all the same
> lift itself out of purely formal and *finite* personality into the
> *Absolute*; i.e. the spiritual must bring itself into representation as
> the subject filled with what is purely substantial and, therein, as
> the willing and self-knowing subject.⁹

From this it is but a step to conclude that, as art and the external
world are significant only as reflectors of self-conscious spirit, it is
better to dismiss them altogether and live as though mental life was
the *ens realissimum*, and indeed this extreme form of Idealism found
ready advocates in the *fin de siècle*.

To complete the foundation for later chapters I must now outline schematically how these empathetic, expressionist and Idealist approaches were realised in the divergent tendencies of Symbolism.

## III   *EMPATHETIC AND ABSTRACT EXPRESSIONIST SYMBOLISM*

Although several interpretations of this complex and multifaceted phenomenon are possible, the term Symbolism will be employed throughout my argument to denote the stylistic and perceptual attitudes exemplified by Verlaine from about 1866 to 1884 and by Mallarmé after his metaphysical crisis of 1866–9. Let me elucidate the reasons for this selective focus.

My prime concern is with the influence of French Symbolism in England. In the 1890s this was almost exclusively restricted to Verlaine and Mallarmé. The former inspired many imitators, most notably Symons and Dowson, of those mellifluent lyrics in *Poèmes saturniens, Fêtes galantes* and *Romances sans paroles* (*abstract expressionist Symbolism*) which subordinate the referential qualities of language to an interest, inspired by music, in the potential of subliminal, non-discursive communication through phonological patterning, synaesthesia, and the subtle, rhythmic modulation of their *vers impairs*.

Verlaine's other influential technique, which I shall term *empathetic Symbolism*, is inspired by empathetic interaction with the environment. The resulting spiritual harmony between poet and perceived is conveyed through a technique of *méprises*: naturally incontiguous or physically impossible juxtapositions of images or phenomena emphasise the deliquescence of his consciousness with the hitherto external world, in which both relinquish their customary opposition or distinction. The formerly independent phenomena of the environment are thus transformed from a literal scene into a metaphorical correlative which reflects their new imaginary status.

Comparison with an empathetic Symbolist painter, van Gogh, will perhaps clarify this point. In *Wheatfield with Crows* (1890), for example (see Plate 1), the subject of the painting is neither the field itself, nor van Gogh, but rather the intense emotional *relationship* between the two. This powerful empathetic mood is conveyed by the representational distortions which the scene undergoes on canvas, which force the spectator to regard the painting not as literal mimesis, but rather as a symbolic embodiment of a mental state. The startling *méprises* of Verlaine's poetry likewise dictate a metaphorical rather than a referential reading: the setting of the poem has been transformed by the empathetic imagination into a symbolic articulation of the mood which it inspires in the poet.

Many of Symons's poems attempt to emulate this procedure; it was to become Pound's principal Imagist technique.

Mallarmé's influence was more complicated, being restricted to his early poetry and his late aesthetic speculations. Combining a partial grasp of Hegelian Idealism with (Neo)platonism, the later Mallarmé desired to break away completely from the phenomenal world towards a poetry of absolute metaphysical purity (which was first influential in England only after the First World War). This late poetry sought, by subtly generating the illusion of physical evanescence, to elicit from their gross physical manifestation the ideal essences of phenomena.

Mallarmé's aesthetic speculations on how this might be accomplished overlap with the 'abstract expressionist' variety of Symbolism. For the increasing effacement of the physical world in his later poetry was accompanied by a complementary quest for stylistic impersonality, which would restore the purity of the Absolute. While refining language from its customary denotative, referential functions, therefore, Mallarmé also abjured the desire for self-expression. The otherwise unattainable world of Ideas would then, he hoped, be evoked by the unpredictable interaction of the words themselves and the suggestive *mise en page*. Rhetorical control passed accordingly from the poet to the poem's language itself, entailing 'la disparition élocutoire du poëte, qui cède l'initiative aux mots, par le heurt de leur inégalité mobilisés'.[10]

It was the poetry of Mallarmé's early years and that transitional work, 'Hérodiade', which principally attracted Yeats. It seems likely that his limited command of French precluded his adopting the later poetry as a stylistic model. Nevertheless, I shall argue, one should not underestimate Yeats's considerable indebtedness to the aesthetic speculations, as opposed to the poetry, of later Mallarmé. These (as mediated by Symons) are, I believe, reflected in Yeats's essays on Symbolism in *Ideas of Good and Evil*[11] (discussed in Chapter 6 apropos hermetic theories of language) and in isolated abstract expressionist poems (examined in Chapter 2) in *The Wind Among the Reeds*.

The reader may now turn with some relief from this theoretical prolegomenon to its detailed realization in the anti-materialist movements in painting and poetry in England from the *fin de siècle* to the First World War.

# 2 Symbolism, Impressionism and 'Exteriority'

Chapter 1 offered a critical vocabulary and a philosophical model for empathetic and abstract expressionist Symbolism. This dual perspective will now be utilised to investigate the immediate context of ideas and influences for the period 1908–14 on which this study focuses. The key theme is the determined rejection of the dispassionate objectivity of the prevailing Naturalist aesthetic and consequent emergence of the varieties of anti-materialist aesthetics which dominated all pre-war movements in art and poetry.

My account concentrates on the literary impact of developments in the visual arts. There are two reasons for this approach: first, its anticipation of my analysis of Imagism/Vorticism as a movement intended to unite all the arts; secondly, the widespread and reiterated emphasis in the 1890s on innovations in both art and literature as complementary expressions of the same anti-materialist sensibility. I make no pretence to an all-inclusive survey of art-criticism in the 1890s; this would lead me far from the continuum of aesthetic theory which I am tracing.[1] Instead my inquiry is mainly restricted to writers of acknowledged stature, such as Yeats, Symons and Moore, and to artists or minor literary figures with whom they enjoyed friendships and who were in a position to influence the formation of their ideas – for example, Selwyn Image, Walter Sickert, D. S. MacColl and Wilson Steer. Only incidental treatment is devoted to technical innovations in painting, for these were almost entirely ignored by the literary figures under discussion.

Several external factors precipitated the aesthetic revolution of the 1890s. In the post-Romantic world varieties of nature mysticism had assumed the role of a surrogate religion. A more popular specific for agnosticism was, however, a secular faith in indefinite human perfectibility, derived either from evolutionary positivism or historical theories based on still rudimentary sociological investigation. The widespread mid-Victorian conviction that social problems

15

would be eradicated necessarily as the result of advances in science and industry (losing its hold as optimistic dreams remained unrealised at the end of the century), provoked an artistic reaction against middle-class complacency, accompanied by aesthetic revulsion from the vulgarity of contemporary taste. The widespread cultivation of a Baudelairean, dandy-like aloofness was an individualistic assertion of the artist's singularity in a world of bourgeois mediocrity and utilitarian practicality. Flamboyant nonconformism was the social counterpart of the supposed 'Idealist' philosophies adopted by many French Symbolists, which in practice were generally reducible to detached slogans justifying the uniqueness of personal perception. [2]

In England Idealism tended to reflect more narrowly anxiety about the loss of religious assurances; the creation of an alternative world of the imagination fulfilled an emotional need in the spiritual vacuum produced by nineteenth-century materialism. Herbert Spencer offered a reformulation of d'Holbach's mechanistic universe, all the more devastating and apparently irrefutable in its determinism for the intervening growth in scientific expertise, while urban and industrial expansion literalised the worst nightmares of the Romantics, creating squalor, isolating man from the natural world and further fragmenting society. The higher criticism of the Bible undermined the confidence of those hitherto able to maintain their religious faith, while geological and astronomical discoveries cast scriptural truth further into question. Man's moral dignity demanded that he devise an emotionally and imaginatively satisfying alternative which would restore some significance to existence.

The resulting anti-materialism found divergent expression in the Oxford neo-Hegelian movement, culminating in the Idealism of Bosanquet and Bradley; the strengthening of the Anglo-Catholic ritualistic faction within the Church of England (although this had a detrimental effect on popular religious faith); and the many conversions to Catholicism during the 1890s. Less orthodox and more fashionable solutions were offered by the Theosophical Society founded in New York in 1875 to propagate the doctrines of 'Esoteric Buddhism', which soon expanded in England, where its monthly, *Lucifer*, began publication in 1877. [3] A comparable appeal was exercised by the Society for Psychical Research (founded in 1882), whose surprisingly extensive membership combined professional psychologists, men of letters, artists, politicians and socialites. It answered the requirements of scientific research in an era which scarcely distinguished psychology from spiritualism, catering at the same time for a more intangible emotional need for spiritual reassurance.[4] The general predisposition towards mysticism found its rallying-point and unifying ideology with the advent of Bergsonism in Edwardian England, discussed in later chapters.

In the arts the unprepossessed vision which was the original ideal of Realism as much as of Romantic transcendentalism received its *reductio ad absurdum* in documentary Naturalism. Excitingly novel spontaneity and unpremeditation was replaced by microscopic, all-inclusive accuracy defended as sincere depiction of unvarnished reality. The Realist enterprise was encouraged by the conviction that there was no longer a higher reality beyond phenomenal facts: that the contingency of everyday existence concealed no essential significance unattainable by empirical investigation. The result was frequently an art of the eye, of *appearances*, befitting an age whose faith in the ultimate sufficiency of science restricted 'reality' to the observable and objectively verifiable. It was accordingly not surprising that the late-nineteenth-century revolt against material-ism should reject an aesthetic committed to what Schopenhauer had termed 'the principle of sufficient reason', the cataloguing of observable relationships between phenomena, in favour of a more essential art of noumena or things-in-themselves. Yeats's charac-teristically hierophantic summary captures the spirit of the age:

> Those among the younger generation whose temperament fits them to receive first the new current, the new force, have grown tired of the *photographing* of life, and have returned by the path of symbolism to *imagination* and *poetry*, the only things which are ever permanent.[5]

Having mapped the salient contours of the anti-materialist terrain, I shall now survey more closely the evolution of the various transcendentalist aesthetics. By way of introduction let me reiterate my earlier schematisation of Romantic aesthetics into Idealist and empathetic. This broad classification enables an initial discrimi-nation to be made between the various anti-materialist tendencies of the English *avant-garde* in the 1890s.

The fundamental aim of the Idealist approach, exemplified by Yeats, Watts and Image, was to supplant the contemporary world with a more congenial and autonomous world of the imagination. The empathetic, by contrast, exemplified by Symons and many

New English Art Club painters, evolved from a critique of the dispassionate, scientific detachment of French Impressionist painting, via advocacy of a sympathetic interaction with the external world, towards the unequivocally animistic aesthetic which was to characterise all pre-war movements in painting and poetry, with the exception of Cubism.

Requesting the reader's willing suspension of disbelief at the outset, therefore, I hope by the end of the chapter to have dispelled any confusion which my initially bewildering categorisation may have aroused.


## I  *IDEALISM*

With the exception of Naturalists, and of 'activists' such as Kipling, most late nineteenth-century artists found refuge from contemporary materialism and drabness in the creative imagination. The English Impressionists, discussed in section II, accommodated the urban world by depicting it with imaginative suggestivity. A more extreme alternative, exemplified by the second phase of Pre-Raphaelite painting, was to reject the contemporary world altogether, turning instead to time-and-space exoticism: in Rossetti's case to early Italian iconography, in Burne-Jones's to Greek, Norse and Celtic legends, with heavy debt to Morris. The continuity with Symbolism of this search in mythologies for otherwise unavailable formal vehicles for imaginative expression is demonstrated by Watts, who created his own allegorical figures. The escapism of Yeats's youthful recourse to Spenserian pastoral and Indian mysticism similarly led via changing conceptions of Celtic mythology towards Symbolism.

Yeats's uncompromising anti-materialism, depending on analogies among all the art forms, emphasises the bewilderingly diverse manifestations scientific Naturalism was felt to assume in the late nineteenth century. His onslaught against Huxley's materialist agnosticism was accompanied by sorties on a wide front against what he regarded as its literary and artistic counterparts. Shaw, the later dramas of Ibsen, Symons's impressionism, the paintings of Bastien-Lepage and Carolus-Duran (here echoing Moore and Sickert) were rejected in favour of a chimerical world of 'style' and heroic passion, whose touchstones were such diverse phenomena as the majestic demeanour of Maud Gonne, and the idealised grandeur of figures in the paintings of Blake and Rossetti and in Villiers's *Axël*. [6] To further the realisation of this 'new religion, almost an infallible Church of poetic tradition', Yeats attempted to persuade his father's former colleague from the Brotherhood, Nettleship, to continue painting in the then unfashionable Pre-Raphaelite mode, even planning in 1890 an article on Nettleship for the *Art Review* (together with 'an article on Blake and his anti-materialist Art') and considering editing a book of his designs. [7]

I believe that Yeats's Symbolist formulations derive principally from a native tradition of aesthetic thought rather than French importations, and that, as one might expect from a former art student whose father and brother were both painters, contemporary pronouncements about the visual arts were a significant influence. [8] Important but unfamiliar [9] articles by Watts and Image appeared at the beginning of the 1880s which foreshadow Yeats's Symbolist position and suggest vividly the ambience in which his views were formed.

Watts's 'The Present Conditions of Art' was undoubtedly received as an important theoretical manifesto. It appeared in the prestigious *Nineteenth Century*; as late as 1900 Symons gave it special commendation. [10] It seems unlikely that Yeats, whose father, beginning as a second generation Pre-Raphaelite, laboriously copied Watts's technique of figure-painting, [11] would have failed to hear of this article and its successors in the *Magazine of Art* [12] in 1888 and 1889 (the period when Yeats, living in Bedford Park, was associating with Morris). In 1896 Yeats included Watts in his multi-genre Who's Who of the Symbolist Movement and in his 1906 lecture, 'The Ideal in Art', presented Watts sympathetically, as he had earlier Blake, as one forced into the role of hierophant by his lack of a mythology or symbolism shared with his audience which would have formed the basis for a popular, imaginative art. [13]

The first part of Watts's article adduces familiar arguments to justify art to a utilitarian audience for whom it represented merely a frivolous diversion. He attacks the hard-headed pragmatism which sees 'beauty' as irrelevant because commercially unrewarding, hoping to reawaken in the masses the instinctive aesthetic sensibility which, like Morris, he believed to have been a common heritage in ancient and medieval times. [14] Watts then outlines a more personal conception of the artist's role. To communicate directly with his audience the artist should preferably take his subjects from the age, but in any case take 'the impress of its life'. But the contemporary urban world is so denuded of 'beauty' that the artist, unable to find there appropriate materials for self-expression, must instead either 'invent his language' or imitate past glories. The origins of Watts's own allegorical paintings are apparent. Yet, despite Watts's belief that art must withdraw from an aesthetically incompatible external world, it remained for him nevertheless the repository and safeguard of man's moral sensibility. For, as Arnold had suggested, in an agnostic world the arts assumed the unprecedented importance of a surrogate religion: 'ministers of the most divine part of our natures'.[15]

In Watts's view the character of painting was well-defined: it could not depict contemporary ugliness and should not descend to historical or anecdotal painting which merely served the analytical reason esteemed by positivism. It was instead a vehicle for the presentation of what Kant had termed 'aesthetic ideas', stimulating the spectator's *imagination* through the evocation of an alternative mode of reality.[16]

This argument is elaborated in 'The Aims of Art'. Watts maintains that Michelangelo's prophets and sybils in the Sistine Chapel, Phidias's 'Pallas Athene', and the Sphinx 'call up profoundly religious feelings'. Accordingly, 'It is not merely upon association with what is usually implied by the term religion that effects of this kind must depend, but upon an appeal to the spiritual side of man's nature.' Such works justify the claim of art, like poetry, to be regarded as a 'religious cult', for they embody the aspirations of man's 'divine faculty' of 'Imagination'. It seems therefore likely, he continues, that an appeal to man's spiritual instincts stronger than through dogmatic utterances may be made 'by impressive symbols of the mysteries that surround human life from its beginning to its close'. Art's function, therefore, is to appeal through the imagination to man's irrepressible religious yearnings, satisfying those elements of his personality neglected in a pragmatic, materialist society. The similarity with Yeats's later comments on Blake is obvious.[17]

Watts again offers an impressive restatement of Kantian doctrine, which also anticipates strikingly Yeats's theories of the 'Great Memory' and the 'Moods':

There is . . . an innate poetic sense in almost all, varying in degree, and acted upon unequally in individuals. Perceptions and emotions are shut up within the human soul, sleeping and unconscious, till the poet or the artist awakens them. Nature is full of similes – symbols and parables to the eye of faith, poetic suggestions to the poetic sensibility. Where the expression of these is vague, as in music, the utterance will be differently construed, and in the art that would be suggestive rather than representative of material fact, very various emotions and definitions may be conveyed.

After this remarkable assertion Watts qualified his fervour for 'that divine gift imagination' by the bathetic addition that of course art is not exclusively devoted to such serious pursuits, a reservation forgotten in his concluding stress on the mission of art as 'the discernment of truth and beauty, . . . the arousing of man's imagination, . . . the widening of the span of this celestial region'. His failure of nerve culminated in the despondent 'More Thoughts on our Art of To-Day',[18] but Watts had already described with impressive conviction a viable role for art as the symbolic evocation of that 'mystery' neglected by contemporary materialism.

His beliefs were echoed in Image's articles in the *Century Guild Hobby Horse*, which established the broad policy of that magazine. Through his father's interest or that of Morris, Yeats was probably acquainted with Image's views in periodical form;[19] he certainly discussed them at Rhymers' Club meetings and at the house which Image shared with Johnson, finding Image's conversation initially not extreme enough in its 'Pre-Raphaelitism' to satisfy absolutely his fanatical requirements.[20]

Like Watts, Image attempted to justify art to a utilitarian audience on the grounds that it gave access to the higher 'world of imagination', whose satisfaction and development was as important to man's well-being as material considerations.[21] Yet to restrict one's enjoyment to the appreciation of its verisimilitude was to lose most of this imaginative stimulus: 'For Art though it is based on Nature, and is for ever returning to Nature for inspiration, is not an imitation of Nature, but a co-existent world for us with influences and charms of its own.'[22] In Image's view art created an autonomous, self-referential world, deriving from the artist's imaginative transformation of his perceptual experience, but not simply an accurate transcription of external reality. It should depict only what the imagination fixed upon in the external world to transmute into the timeless 'world of our imaginative life'. For art, as evidencing the painter's *creative* idea and selection and touch and tone', was to be distinguished from 'the mechanical reproduction of Nature, Photography'.[23]

The brunt of Image's polemic was directed against a series of articles by Francis Bate, later published as a pamphlet, entitled 'The Naturalistic School of Painting' (his term for Impressionism).[24] As Secretary of the New English Art Club (NEAC), the most radical group of English painters, Bate found a ready audience; the pamphlet, originally published in December 1886, had already run into a second edition in 1887. Their disagreement thus requires detailed attention, particularly as Bate summarises usefully the prevailing distortion of French Impressionism: its scientific exactitude in capturing superficial appearances and exclusion of imaginative or spiritual qualities.

As Bate vacillates irritatingly, but in a manner characteristic of the period, between alternative interpretations of 'impression', his usage demands careful discrimination. One sense is in the epigraph chosen from the transcendentalist Emerson: 'When we speak of Nature . . . we have a distinct, but most poetical, sense in the mind. We mean the integrity of impression made by manifold natural objects.'[25] The initial definition is accordingly the artist's subjective perception of the external world, so that painting is not just a matter of objective, photographic transcription but instead records an emotional response. On this basis Impressionists such as Sickert, Symons and Moore discriminated their imaginative work from the photographic art of Bastien-Lepage, the Newlyn School or Zola. Ignoring the implications of his epigraph, however, Bate's positivist enthusiasm for the greater representational accuracy now attainable in painting led him to forget the imaginative element in Impressionism. Instead he employed the word with the more neutral meaning of 'sense-impression'. For, in explaining the advances in representational fidelity of the painters of the 'naturalistic school', Bate argues that 'The first impression of a picture must as nearly as possible be as the first impression of nature', forestalling a subjectivist reading by adding that the first impression of any scene is that of light, succeeded by colour, then perhaps by form and texture, where 'impression' must be synonymous with 'sense-datum'.[26] Emphasis on imaginative engagement disappears from Bate's account, leaving the caricature of Impressionism which lasted in England until the First World War.

He holds in principle that 'In nature dwells the spirit of all poetry', but in practice eschews any attempt to communicate emotional interaction with the external world. The limited aspiration of art, he suggests, is the capture of fleeting appearances and atmospheric effects – that instantaneous recording of light which characterised French Impressionism. Any more ambitious aims are dismissed as either unrealisable or irrelevant:

> The province of the painter's art is first to reflect nature: To transcribe it upon canvas, or what not, accurately. . . . The painters of the Naturalistic School . . . hold that in the accurate representation of nature, is represented also all the beauty and poetry of art.[27]

Bate's neutral formulations inescapably suggest a dispassionate photographic realism. By a semantic shift which accompanied a change in artistic sensibility his terminology became susceptible to a pejorative interpretation: 'Our pictures should be accurate reflections of the *appearance* of Nature, not copies of a part of it, but reflections of the appearance of the whole of it.' What he intended to say was that the painter's close dependence on observation of natural effects should be borne out in the technique of his work: just as in actual life one can tell from the quality of light and the length and direction of cast shadows the time of day, so this should be possible in accurate painting.[28] It was an attempt to establish textbook principles for painting based on scientific data. His excitement at the French Impressionists' capture of light (his comments read as an unnerving gloss on Monet's later *Haystacks* and Rouen Cathedral series, denigrated by both Moore and MacColl) leads Bate to reduce his Emersonian painter to a dispassionate mirror. 'Reflections' replace the earlier 'impressions', while the understandable if unfortunate stress on 'appearance' was to be interpreted (by Moore, and later by the Expressionists and English post-Impressionist[29] critics, as explained in Chapter 5) as describing an art concerned exclusively with the superficial aspects of objects rather than their inner nature, and hence seen in Schopenhauerian terms as neglecting the thing-in-itself, the essential haecceity of an object, in favour of its representation or external husk. Bate confirmed his allegiances by choosing for his concluding article an epigraph by Herbert Spencer on 'the science of appearances'.[30] If Image forced art into an Idealist mould, Bate reduced it to optics.

Image's rejoinder anticipates directly the anti-Impressionist polemic of Roger Fry and Desmond MacCarthy, and Pound's distinction of Vorticism from Impressionism (examined in Chapters 5 and 8). Bate's definition of art as '*only* an accurate reflection of natural appearances' was, Image argued, in fact a more appropriate definition of Science, whose object was 'to discover, and present . . . the facts of Nature as they are in themselves, unaffected by human imagination or feeling', the very qualities which radically distinguished art from both nature and science. Thus

> to render a painting . . . perfectly a work of Art . . . it should be the product of a man's imaginative and emotional faculties working out their pleasure amid the experiences supplied to them by Nature; not in the least only reflecting these experiences . . . but creating out of these experiences a world of their own, the degree of whose coincidence with the actual appearances of the Natural world is to depend on the man's choice, guided by an instinct for what is sufficient to carry his meaning. . . . Nature . . . supplies Art with a store-house . . . of raw-material, of symbols, from which she may by selection and creative combinations give expression to her own imaginative and emotional experiences.[31]

In England in the 1890s this conception of the autonomy of art found its closest literary equivalent in Yeats's Symbolist poetry. Yeats is a resolutely individual figure whom it is refreshingly, if frustratingly, difficult to classify. My present aim of demonstrating the continuity of aesthetics in England from the *fin de siècle* to the First World War does not allow sufficient space to do justice to his varied poetic output in the 1890s. My account will therefore be restricted to an examination of the difference between two varieties of abstract expressionist Symbolism in his poetry: that which was influenced by the visual arts, and a primarily linguistic variety (arguably inspired by Verlaine and Mallarmé) which has, I feel, been undervalued by many of his critics.

The former tendency drew on Yeats's fascination with such powerful allegorical and Symbolist painters as Blake, Watts, Burne-Jones, Moreau and Puvis. It is reflected in such poems as 'Michael Robartes asks Forgiveness because of his Many Moods' and 'The Secret Rose',[32] which gather a visually impressive assemblage of mythological or allegorical figures and landscapes in a manner intended to evoke cumulatively an aura of sublimity or ecstasy. It is a technique which relies primarily on visual, iconographic effects rather than on imaginative suggestion through abstract, non-referential use of language.

Consider as a representative example of this style 'Michael Robartes remembers Forgotten Beauty',[33] which comprises a decorative, Pre-Raphaelite panoply of evocative images of beauty, remoteness and transience. Yeats ensures their suggestive impact by introducing beauty as 'long faded from the world', establishing an atmosphere of romance. This intimation of piquant inaccessibility is then reinforced by the incantatory repetition of mellifluently vague epithets such as 'dream-heavy' and the syntactic iteration of 'flame on flame', 'deep on deep', 'Throne over throne', whose receding perspective draws the reader into the imaginative world of the poem, to envelop him with the mysterious aura which is its theme.

This combination of visual montage with complementary verbal emphasis is paralleled in 'The Secret Rose', in which the rose is initially described as 'Far-off, most secret, and inviolate'. The superlative of 'secret' and the absolute adjective 'inviolate' prepare the reader for the ineffable or the ideal, which the poem's iconography then symbolises. (Lack of space precludes an account of Yeats's pervasive use in the 1890s of the esoteric iconography of the Cabbala and Golden Dawn ritual.[34])

The distinction between this iconographic approach and Yeats's more exclusively linguistic abstract expressionist Symbolism is particularly obvious in 'Michael Robartes bids his Beloved be at Peace', a poem unusual in combining the alternative strategies.[35]

Yeats's customary occult symbolism surfaces in the cardinal points, but the esoteric significance of 'the Shadowy Horses' is subsumed in more powerfully indefinite emotional evocation. The reader's interest concentrates on the suggestive resonances of 'Shadowy' and 'Disaster', whose portentousness but lack of assignment (the average reader might perhaps associate them tentatively with the horsemen of the Apocalypse) stimulates flights of reverie. The poem's language itself enforces a figurative reading, fusing the physically denotative with the atmospherically abstract. Consider the initial description of the horses: 'their long manes a-shake,/ Their hoofs heavy with tumult, their eyes glimmering white'. One is struck immediately by the verbal character of the epithets, suggesting a wilful, perhaps minatory vigour. At the same time the sensuousness of the phrases implies an imaginative interpretation: the second line pivots on the noun 'tumult', which redirects attention from an initially physical reading towards suggestion of the mental disturbance that is the poem's theme. Only gradually does one suspect the origins of the imagery in the experience of physical love: the 'long manes' of the horses bear an uneasy and ill-defined relation to the lover's sheltering hair of line 10. One level of suggestion intimates accordingly that the physical consummation of sex is somehow equivalent to or inextricable from universal apocalypse, a theme prominent elsewhere in *The Wind Among the Reeds*.

Yeats achieves a similar blend of esotericism and emotional suggestivity in another poem also reminiscent of Joyce's 'I hear an army . . .', 'The Valley of the Black Pig'.[36] Here Yeats is, I feel, less successful. He depends more on the ready-made emotive counters of legendary or mythological material in lines 5 and 6 and the impressive but cryptic sonorities of Golden Dawn ritual in the final line. Nevertheless the opening lines do create a vivid impression of potential energy accumulating like a natural force (imaged as ominous precipitation and swirling, on which is superimposed retrospectively the disembodied tension of purely implicit throwing-arms), released with frightening impersonality as a messianic irruption. The poem leaves ultimately a vague sense of that rhythmic interplay between consolatory but escapist lassitude and frenetic, disquieting activity that is both desired and feared, which permeates all aspects of Yeats's thinking in the 1890s.

I indicated earlier Yeats's mastery of poetic rhythms and verbal patterning and it is this aural aspect of his poetry which approximates most closely to the linguistic experimentation of French Symbolism. Thus the allegory of 'The Travail of Passion'[37] and the flaccid, stylised diction of the last line are relieved by the delightful assonance of the words themselves, whose capacity to insinuate themselves into the memory, largely detached from any semantic convention, was, one suspects, the predominant factor in their selection by Yeats: 'Lilies of death-pale hope, roses of passionate dream'. The prime reason for this memorable effect is rhythmic. The caesura divides the line into two syntactically identical phrases, creating the expectation of a rhythmic congruity which is denied by the syllabic asymmetry. The extra syllable of the second phrase forces the reader to dwell lingeringly on the polysyllabic 'passionate', establishing an aura of languor with the falling cadence which concludes the poem. Thus in itself the rhythmic disposition of the phrases aids their interpretation: there is an apparent semantic equation between the two parts of the line, but the added syllable hints at a development which confirms one reading of the poem. If one ventures an interpretation of the poem's overall import, there is a suggested analogy between the 'travail' of sexual initiation and Christ's passion, each concluding in a form of ecstasy or apotheosis. The lilies are thus in a sense identical with the roses as images for two different conditions of the same personality: the anxious anticipation of innocence which preceded the forbidding acquaintance with 'an immortal passion' breathing 'in mortal clay' and the composed reverie which follows experience.

A more striking example of Yeats's symbolic qualities than this rather overwrought poem is provided by the revised version of 'The Indian to His Love'.[38] The early poem 'Ephemera' had with disconcerting blatancy employed the natural world, in the Romantic convention, as a sympathetic metaphor for the lovers' faded passion.[39] With impressive subtlety the 1895 revisions to 'The Indian to His Love' break away from this Romantic tradition to evoke an ideal Symbolist landscape which is indivisible from an abstract mental state. The excision of the vapid second stanza concentrated attention on the visual qualities of the poem; but these in turn were transformed from their originally decorative, Pre-Raphaelite specificity to become less denotative and correspondingly more evocative. In line 3, for example, the phrase 'in crimson feather' becomes 'on a smooth lawn'. This provides just enough visual detail to stimulate the imagination, but its primary impact is aural within the sound pattern of long, languid vowels relieved by the counterpoint effect of the alliteration on dentals and labials. The mellifluent, incantatory quality of the stanza's delivery already suggests a mental state. This evocation is aided by the unrealistic, ambiguous description (signalled by 'dreams' in line 1) of the island whose 'great boughs' assume a retrospective aura of insubstantiality or mirage as they 'drop tranquillity', an ideal rather than a physical attribute. Similarly the originally decorative epithet 'enamelled' reinforces the unnaturalness of the setting, for it reflects an imaginative interpretation of the light glinting on the waves, rather than a neutrally detached description.

The succeeding stanzas of the poem maintain this emotional suggestiveness, largely by the extension of sound-patterns. The long vowel of 'moor' in line 6 undergoes variation in 'our', 'lonely' and 'woven', then modulates into the 'Murmuring' of lines 8 and 10, the repetition emphasising the narcotic effect. Critical isolation of such sound-patterns indicates that the words at one level do actually operate in an abstract, semantically unconventional fashion; logic denies any connection between the verbs 'moor' and 'murmur', but these are nevertheless unavoidably related by the alternative, non-discursive system of musicality which the poem establishes. The revised version of the final stanza resumes this alternation of dentals, labials and long vowels (to which sibilants are now added) which carries the semantic burden of the poem, culminating in the euphonious but logically problematic 'When eve has hushed the feathered ways, / With vapoury footsole by the water's drowsy blaze'. These lines are perhaps the closest Yeats came to late Mallarméan Symbolism. The epithet 'feathered' is indefinitely resonant – suggesting the visual aspect of leafy fronds, the delicate motion and fragility of the vegetation, the tactile sensation produced by ferns or similar plants, and the cushioning effect of luxuriant grass. Without requiring one to choose among these various readings, the epithet also suggests an ethereality developed by the phrase 'vapoury footsole', which picks up from line 18 the theme of ghosts, but at the same time leads one to regard the present scene as unstable, potentially deliquescent, or liable to be consumed by the setting sun, which itself is given an unwonted quality of strangeness. For, although the phrase 'the water's drowsy blaze' is logically explicable as the reflection of the rays in the sea, the poem's linguistic technique fuses the two incompatible entities into a surreal watery flame, lulling one into conviction of the imaginative existence of this unnatural effect through the cumulative and irrational power of the sound-patterns. My point is therefore that although the lines are logically analysable one's reading of the poem is not in discursive terms. The poem's primary impact is aural and rhythmic, the falling cadence of the final line again supported subtly by a syllabic asymmetry following the caesura after 'footsole'. On later readings one explores the various connotations of the words, without feeling the need to establish one uniquely valid interpretation, which the figurative quality and incompatibility on a literal level of the images in any case forbid. Instead one confronts a poem of abstract expressiveness akin to music, whose various un-paraphrasable meanings are inextricable from their verbal embodiment and whose purposely unrealised, non-discursive import is established by a phonetic pattern which challenges and overcomes the conventional referentiality of language.

Beside this Idealist aesthetic, there developed another alternative to the dispassionate objectivity of Naturalism. Laying equal stress on the creative imagination, but advocating not the sublimation of the external world but rather its sympathetic interpretation, the English Impressionist aesthetic, by virtue of its reciprocal perceptual relationship, preluded empathic post-Impressionism.

## II *IMPRESSIONISM*

On purely technical grounds the naturalistic perfection of French Impressionism offered its emulators the prospect of only banal imitation; the quest for alternatives led to Cézanne's concern with solidity and structure, and Seurat's carefully composed, almost statuesque scenes, in contrast with the casual, fortuitous immediacy of Impressionist landscape. The emotional intensity of van Gogh heralded an equally significant concern with empathic expressionism. Monet, castigated in England for dispassionate superficiality, offers in the transition from his early landscapes to the contemplative stasis of *Les Nymphéas: série de paysages d'eau* (begun 1897; first part exhibited in 1900; continued 1903–8; second series exhibited in 1909) a striking paradigm for the general movement towards an art revealing meditative interaction with the external world instead of recording the contingent transience of momentary effects of light and fortuitous groupings of people or objects, arbitrarily glimpsed and frozen in unnaturally eternalised instantaneity. [40]

All art – and Monet's was no exception – must of course reflect to some degree its creator's sensibility; what was disconcerting in French Impressionism to an English audience accustomed to the Northern Romantic tradition was the monotonous, unaccented brilliance of the canvases, which with their intentional randomness, unselectivity and lack of compositional emphasis suggested an accompanying emotional detachment. The frequent analogies drawn by English critics with photographic verism were apposite, for Impressionist cityscapes do bear a recognisable debt to the dispassionate cropping of the camera lens. This intuitive sense of similarity conditioned a value-judgement, disparaging Impressionism for lack of imaginative involvement in perception.

In the following discussion my emphasis lies on the subjectivist character of English Impressionism and the polemical tactics adopted to distinguish it from both the dispassionate superficiality of the French variety and the photographic literalness of the English naturalist painters. The section concludes by analysing some striking anticipations of the post-Impressionist, empathetic aesthetic.

As indicated in the previous section, there were several varieties of 'Impressionism' in England. In 1891 D. S. MacColl conveniently listed three: Impressionism 'in the sense of Velasquez – truth, that is, to a refined vision of the object'; 'in the sense of Caran d'Ache's *plein-air*-ist who lays in his landscape with a pail of violet paint, and proceeds to paint *what he sees, as he sees it*, with such sincerity to his temperament that a haystack becomes a three-decker'; and, finally, 'in the most proper sense, as the effort to catch and render fleeting and transitory things'.[41] Of the third, essentially French, variety there was little evidence in England. Instead attention focused on the contrast between the type of dispassionate, scientific objectivity exemplified in Bate's account, and Whistler's more lyrical version.

In contrast with Bate's concern for accurate reflection of appearances of nature and atmospheric conditions (inspired by the French vogue for *pleinairisme*, in which the artist painted his canvas on the spot out of doors), Whistler's technique already indicated the subjectivist nature of his variety of Impressionism. On evening walks he would memorise a scene, transferring to canvas after an interval of time its salient features as he recollected them. Topographical fidelity was irrelevant; instead the external setting offered merely a point of departure for the composition of a harmony or arrangement in colour. Imagination rather than observation was the essence of his art.

Lack of interest in representational fidelity *per se* was a disconcerting innovation, as the Whistler *vs* Ruskin trial demonstrated. In an arresting exchange Whistler explained his aims in *Nocturne in Blue and Silver*:

> I did not intend it to be a 'correct' portrait of the bridge. It is only a moonlight scene and the pier in the centre of the picture may not be like the piers at Battersea Bridge as you know them in broad daylight. As to what the picture represents that depends upon who looks at it.[42]

Whistler's courageously innovative proposition was that the content or 'meaning' of a picture was determined by what response the suggestive work stimulated in the imagination of the individual

spectator. As Symons repeatedly stressed, Whistler's art of evocation rather than transcription or anecdote paralleled the transition in poetry from Parnassianism to (Verlaine's) Symbolism.

Whistler took as axiomatic that the value of a painting did not lie
in extraneous criteria but depended exclusively on its pictorial
qualities. In thus outlining the theoretical basis of abstract expressionism he employed the same analogy as the Symbolist poets
with the non-representational art of music: 'As music is the poetry of
sound, so is painting the poetry of sight, and the subject-matter has
nothing to do with harmony of sound or of colour.'[43]

One must, however, distinguish (see Plates 2 and 3) between those
abstract expressionist Symbolist paintings by Whistler – such as
*Nocturne in Blue and Silver* (c. 1871–2) or *Nocturne in Black and Gold:
The Fire Wheel* (1875) – which in their formal self-sufficiency are
independent of any vestiges of representational elements, and those
empathetic Symbolist, exemplified by *Nocturne in Blue–Green* (1871)
or *Nocturne in Blue and Gold: Old Battersea Bridge* (c. 1872–5), which
are content with imaginatively heightening the depicted scene
through atmospheric suggestivity and compositional emphasis
through tonal planes (what was regarded at the time as Whistler's
'impressionist' style). The difference is that rather than using
elements of the external world as a vehicle for (self-)expression, the
'impressionist' in this acceptation is concerned with imaginative
interaction with the landscape. This emotional engagement is
conveyed through a combination of unusually harmonious tones,
atmospheric vagueness, exceptional compositional selectivity, simplification and planar distortion. These signal its transformation
from literal reality into a metaphorical correlative for the mood
which it has inspired in the painter. My present interest lies not with
Whistler's theoretically abstract aesthetic, but rather with the
gradual development from his subjectivist 'impressionism' of the
explicitly animistic aesthetic of Post-Impressionism.

A surprisingly apposite gloss on the distinction between Bate's
French and Whistler's English Impressionism, noted at the time by
both Steer and MacColl, is provided by Reynolds's *Discourses on
Art.*[44] From a recognisable basis in Neoplatonic aesthetics, Reynolds
moved in the later Discourses to lay more stress, although with some
reservations, on the imagination, that faculty so distrusted by the
Augustans.[45] It was then less an idealising approach to external
reality than the question of subjective perception which concerned
him. In an advanced civilisation only the uncultivated still regarded

an art of deceptive imitation as more desirable than one designed 'to make an *impression* on the imagination and the feeling'.[46] The vulgar delight in a descent to minutiae which Reynolds had earlier deprecated in accordance with Augustan, neoclassical decorum,[47] provoked an attack on the eighteenth-century equivalent of photography:

> If we suppose a view of nature represented with all the truth of the *camera obscura*, and the same scene represented by a great Artist, how little and mean will the one appear in comparison of the other, where no superiority is supposed from the choice of the subject.

The superiority of true landscape-painting over mere imitation derived partly from the literary associations which the painter could evoke, but more importantly in the '*poetical* ability' to make 'the elements sympathise with his subject' by modifying skilfully the representational details of the scene and harmonising its lighting to correspond with an emotional '*impression*'.[48] This suggestion that the difference between an art 'which addresses itself to the imagination' and one 'which is solely addressed to the eye' (Bate's art of 'appearances', or the 'surface' art denigrated by Whistler) was equivalent to that between the 'mechanical' and the 'poetical' was to be reiterated by Whistler and echoed by Sickert and Moore.[49]

The imagination's power to transmogrify landscape justified Whistler's insistence that the contemporary world was a valid artistic theme if handled impressionistically. Rejecting photographic transcription, Whistler modified the urban setting by clothing its repellent squalor in poetic atmosphere; hence his predilection for the ambiguity and suggestive luminosity of twilight or nocturnal scenes:

> When the evening mist clothes the riverside with poetry, as with a veil, and the poor buildings lose themselves in the dim sky, and the tall chimneys become campanili, and the warehouses are palaces in the night, . . . and fairy-land is before us . . . .[50]

*Avant-garde* interest was accordingly directed towards techniques of denotative reticence and imaginative evocation.

Whistler's argument shaped the Preface to the catalogue of the London Impressionists' Exhibition of December 1889 written by

Walter Sickert, a former pupil. Sickert defines the Impressionism of his group largely by elimination, distinguishing it both from the French variety of 'hand-coloured tracings of instantaneous photographs' and above all from objective 'realism': 'It is not occupied in a struggle to make intensely real and solid the sordid or superficial details of the subjects it selects.' Nevertheless, far from ignoring contemporary urban life, Sickert held that London artists should strive 'to render the magic and the poetry which they daily see around them'.[51] The important elements all derived from Whistler: the contrast with photography, the disparagement of superficiality and the argument for transmogrification of such problematical subjects as the cityscape. The perceptual subjectivity at the heart of this approach was supported by Sickert's colleague Wilson Steer, who defined art as 'the expression of an impression seen through a personality'.[52]

In two brief notes in 1890 Sickert had stressed the importance in impressionism of 'mood' and 'selection';[53] deficiency in these was to be the indictment he levelled against painting's fashionable idol, the *pleinairist* Bastien-Lepage, the *bête noire* also of Moore.[54] Sickert carefully balanced his iconoclasm with praise for the traditional work of Millet, whose success lay in a technique resembling Whistler's and Degas's: painting from an image shaped by the memory and avoiding therefore both the technical inconveniences of *pleinairisme* and also its piecemeal transcription of nature. Nothing could be further from the work of 'the modern photo-realist in painting', 'the sterile ideal of the instantaneous camera'.[55]

Further confirmation of the prime importance in English Impressionism of subjectivist perception came from another NEAC painter, Charles Furse, for whom the painter's individuality was revealed in his

> ability to give forth his impressions, not as seen through the lens of the camera, but as abstractions drawn from nature through the subtlety and charm of his mind. It is not the painter's business to record what he sees, but to suggest what he feels.[56]

Having investigated the rejection of dispassionate objectivity by contemporary painters it is now time to examine the influence which their advocacy of subjectivist perception exercised on literary figures. Here I consider George Moore, in the next section Symons, both of whom counted almost as many artists as writers among their associates.

Sickert's group was supported by a journalistic clique, led by Moore and MacColl; although technically shaky, Moore was an extremely useful populariser. An *habitué* of the Hogarth Club, the regular haunt of the NEAC, he was a particular intimate of Steer, who had, however, reservations about Moore's self-absorption and indiscretion.[57] Sickert, whom Moore first met in 1885–6, had scant respect for his knowledge but found endearing his naive, infectious enthusiasm for art and occasional surprising insights, although he was frequently irritated by Moore's characteristic *blague*.[58] This judgement was shared by Will Rothenstein, while MacColl was equally divided between praise for Moore's stylistic verve, which captured the attention of a popular audience; dislike of his obtrusive personality; and scepticism about his cant phraseology and logic in technical argument.[59]

Always suggestible and fickle in his allegiances, Moore had commenced decadent poet, experimenting next with Naturalist novels. In the late 1880s, however, he reacted against the limitations of Naturalism, mounting through his art criticism a campaign against 'exteriority'.[60] It is this final reorientation which renders him of interest for my study, for the opportunism determining Moore's protean aesthetic ensures that he is an accurate pointer to shifts in general sensibility.

With the exception of a single unsympathetic article, Moore's art criticism has received no close scrutiny.[61] It is nevertheless of considerable representative importance. I shall argue that the salient theme, symptomatic of the age, is the rejection of French Impressionism as alien to a native tradition of poetised landscape.

It is vital to disengage this aspect of Moore's writings on Impressionism from its distracting involvement in the contemporary debate about artistic freedom in subject-matter. Under Degas's influence Sickert had become the first English artist to depict interiors of London music-halls, which, like the music-hall itself (chiefly patronised by the lower classes), were unacceptable in polite circles and delicate enough to arouse the opposition of the NEAC hanging-committee.[62] Music-hall became an emblem for artistic freedom in subject-matter and consequently a Bohemian cult;[63] music-hall pictures by Sickert and Steer appeared in the first six volumes of the *Yellow Book*, but disappeared after July 1895, following Beardsley's excision from the April 1895 issue. They also had fallen victim to the widespread moral outrage occasioned by the Wilde trial.

The public-relations problem faced by the *avant-garde* was accordingly to dissociate themselves from the opprobrium of Naturalism. Moore's extended apologia arose from the very real threat of being banned by Smith's and the circulating libraries. Arthur Waugh's censure of the current neglect of 'the moral idea' in favour of 'journalistic detail' and 'the fidelity of the *kodak*' is an accurate barometer of opinion; significantly two of his targets were Moore's early idol Swinburne and Moore's novel *A Mummer's Wife*. Like Crackanthorpe, Moore could counter such an indictment only by attempting to discriminate on impressionist lines the *avant-garde* art favoured by his circle from the much-denigrated Naturalism by stressing its imaginative subjectivism rather than slavish literalism.[64]

The strategy adopted by Moore and all the Sickert clique was to thrust the 'naturalist' label onto Bastien-Lepage and his English followers, Clausen and Stanhope Forbes's Newlyn School (for a characteristic example of Forbes's style, see Plate 4), supporting these allegations by attacking on a wider front the dispassionate objectivity of French Impressionism, popularly associated with Realism.

In 'The New Pictures in the National Gallery'[65] Moore introduces as the distinguishing factor of true art what with portentous mystification he terms, but never defines, *'une atmosphère de tableau'*. One needs accordingly to interpret Moore's jargon, but given sympathetic attention his argument becomes clear. He contrasts the shortcomings of *pleinairisme* with a technique which would introduce emotion in depiction through the use of shadow.[66] Just as Reynolds had suggested that one factor in the poetic painting of landscape was skilful employment of light, so Moore maintains that the blank realism of *pleinairisme* should be qualified by atmospheric effects or by painting such subjects indoors in the tradition of the Dutch school with consequent heavy reliance on chiaroscuro.

Moore's touchstone Degas had never favoured the *plein-air* technique, to which his other idol, Manet, had been a late convert. Furthermore, Degas's description of Bastien-Lepage as that 'Bouguereau of naturalism'[67] made Moore even more eager to disavow his own initial affiliations to the Bouguereau/Cabanel school. (In 1873 Moore had studied painting at Julian's Academy, where Bouguereau was a visiting professor.) Thus Moore's ideal, in contrast to 'Bastien-Lepageism', which he defined as 'mechanical drawing and modelling, built up systematically, and into which nothing of the artist's sensibility may enter', was an art, such as that of Degas, Whistler or Sickert, which eschewed 'photographic' 'copying of nature in favour of painting from memory which depended on imagination'.[68] Landscape-painting depended not on representational exactitude, but rather on evoking the emotions of the painter in its imaginative contemplation: in other words, the significance nature held for the Romantic poet or, in Moore's favourite parallel, the Norwich School and Millet. The crucial question was whether a painting rendered 'the spirit and essence of a scene, or merely its *externality*'. Without artistic selection it would be a photograph; with it, it would have '*character* and style', reflecting the artist's 'mind' and 'soul'.[69]

Moore expressed this intuition in vaguely technical terms by praising the 'values' (an alternative to 'chiaroscuro') of the Barbizons and the Dutch in contrast with the unrelieved brilliance of the Impressionist palette, particularly that of Monet. These created an '*atmosphère du tableau*', furnishing the indispensable element of 'mystery' and 'suggestion'.[70] Lack of poetising chiaroscuro indicating the emotional engagement which alone would have made such subjects fit for art reduced paintings inspired by Bastien-Lepage, such as Clausen's *Labourers after Dinner* or Stanhope Forbes's *Forging the Anchor*, to the uncompromising ugliness of 'dry facts' rather than 'passionate impressions'.[71]

The following attack on Monet makes explicit Moore's rejection of French Impressionism as alien to a native tradition of Romantic landscape:

> this ever-changing but ever shallow, brilliant appearance . . . appealing, as it does, almost entirely to the eye, wearies, and, despite our eager admiration, we long for the underlying note of human sympathy which makes nature a mirror for the soul to view itself.[72]

Moore's point is merely Monet's lack of emotional engagement with what he depicts, but already hints at the empathy of Post-Impressionism. Moore made similar comments in distinguishing between Monet's and Sisley's Impressionism. For Sisley, Moore maintains, 'nature is, perhaps, on account of his English origin, something more . . . than a brilliant appearance', approached with 'sympathy', in a 'meditative spirit'.[73] It would be misleading (particularly in the light of his implicit analogy with the Norwich School) to regard Moore as describing anything more than an imaginative impression of landscape (what Reynolds had found in Claude and Salvator Rosa). Nevertheless the register in which this finds expression foreshadows post-Impressionist criticism.

MacColl shared many of Moore's views. Using almost identical vocabulary he also attacked the photographic literalness of the Newlyn School and Fildes[74] and was, like most English critics of the period, sceptical of Monet (described as 'often more experimentalist than successful artist', hinting at an unhealthy scientific preoccupation) and enthusiastic about Degas, particularly for his triumphant handling of artistically delicate motifs.[75] Unlike Moore, however, MacColl does not merely expose the shortcomings of Impressionism on traditional lines, but already adumbrates a post-Impressionist aesthetic. For MacColl was not merely a sounding-board for the *avant-garde*; he was arguably the most innovative and erudite English aesthetician of the 1890s, the subtlety of his ideas now neglected in favour of later formulations by such acknowledged precursors of Modernism as Symons.

It seems that MacColl was among the earliest of Mallarmé's English readers. An article from 1892 reads as a transposition into painting of Mallarméan aesthetics, with some indebtedness to the arabesques of *art nouveau* (probably indirectly via Burne-Jones) in its remarks on line and contour, and to Whistler on colour. MacColl gives an exciting account of the fundamental tenets of Post-Impressionism:

> drawing is at bottom, like all the arts, a kind of gesture, a method of dancing upon paper. The dance may be mimetic; but it is the *verve* of the performance, not the closeness of the imitation, that impresses. . . . The dance must control the pantomime. Rivers and skies and faces are taken up by a painter as illustrations of a mood, and the lines of the image he creates are not meant to reproduce the thing, but to convey what he felt about the thing. . . . Thus, the unbroken sweep of a contour like a bird's flight, will mean one kind of movement of pleasure, the tender approaches of broken lines another, and every touch of the emerging likeness will be a commentary, a confession.

If developed, this perspective would, MacColl perceived, justify a purely formal appreciation of painting:

> In the lines of abstract ornament, you will often get a more
> striking impression of conflict or of repose than from the most
> document-supported picture of battle or of sleep; and it is· this
> element, the music of space and form, that really plays to the
> imagination behind the images that represent person or
> thing. . . . If this is true of form, it is true also of colours.[76]

There were accordingly two main Symbolist threads of opposition to mere imitation in painting: the abstract expressionist, and
the 'impressionist' or empathetic Symbolist. The latter originated in
polemical emphasis on the imaginative interpretation of the
external world rather than its dispassionate transcription. From this
interest in nature as a sympathetic reflection of the mood which it
inspired in the painter, it developed to lay greater stress on an
empathetic relationship with nature perceived as an independently
existing phenomenon with a mysterious life of its own, revealing to
the contemplating artist its essential haecceity, often with animistic
or pantheistic overtones. It is this latter movement towards Post-
Impressionism in England which I shall now examine.

MacColl discovered in Steer's work (van Gogh's would provide
an obvious parallel) an innovative technical response to the external
world, which was to be the principal development of Post-
Impressionism. Steer's freedom of handling in a seascape communicated his emotional engagement by fragmenting the paint
surface and using a thick impasto to suggest his exuberance at 'the
way the charges of light patter and break upon those reflecting
surfaces'. His brush-strokes were not intended to convey form or
texture but rather 'to express by a symbol the vivid life in the sky-
colour, the sea-colour, and the sand-colour, and it is doubtful if the
richness and subtlety of their colour can be conveyed in any other
way'.[77] Neither MacColl nor Steer, unlike the following generation, was introducing any transcendentalist implications into a
technique expressing the painter's emotional response to
the essential quality of a depicted object; but it was an easy step to
extend this register in criticism, or for a mystical painter to utilise a
similar approach as a vehicle for the expression of an epiphanic
insight into the inner nature of an object, or contemplative
awareness of an object as a theophany. That MacColl in his
rejection of superficial Impressionism of the Monet variety in favour

of a more expressionist art marked a transitionary stage prior to Post-Impressionism proper is indicated by his statement that

> It is a commonplace that the effects of light and darkness translate naturally into terms of cheerfulness, mystery, and trouble. It is then no great stretch to suppose it allowable to express by a vivacity or a calm in the handling of a picture the mood of the painter about his subject. Rather, he will be convicted of insensibility and apathy if his technique shows no sympathy with the thing it expresses.[78]

The later 1890s saw increasing importance attached to the artist's imaginative interaction with what he perceived. Furse's 'Letters on Drawing' (1895–6) display already the fundamental elements of the empathetic aesthetic of Post-Impressionism. Sympathetic responsiveness, he argues, prevents anything from being regarded as ugly; only learn to regard it as worthy of attention and

> you will make your drawing vibrant with your knowledge of the *character* of the thing; I mean the *character* of the structure (for it is only through the appreciation of the *character* of the structure that the *soul* or mind of the person is brought within the grasp of the artist)

All things are subject-matter for art provided '*you can find yourself in the thing*' and search lovingly for 'the intimate, subtle essence of the thing', 'its own particular charm, its personal *character*'.[79] The main burden of Furse's argument advocates drawing from an overall impression of an object rather than gradually building up from local detail, but the Schopenhauerian register in which this is phrased indicates how the empathy of Post-Impressionism with its concern for an object's inner essence rather than its superficial representation was a natural development from the polemic between 'impressionism' and photographic Naturalism. By the end of the decade the approach of Bate, Monet, Bastien-Lepage and the Newlyn School had become thoroughly discredited, as evidenced in an article by another NEAC painter, C. J. Holmes, in that Symbolist bastion, the *Dome*. In attempting to transfer to canvas the light and colour of the air, Impressionists such as Monet, Sisley and Pissarro attempted the impossible; their work 'does not aim at design or decorative colour, or at any poetic rendering of things. It is merely a scientific treatise on the possibilities of pigments, and must be judged as such.'[80] Fry and MacCarthy (discussed in Chapter 5) were to utilise exactly this critique of Impressionism.

In summary, therefore, art criticism during the 1890s evidenced a reaction against naturalistic exteriority. Impressionism in the sense of the imaginative transmutation of an object, suggesting the emotions it evoked in the perceiving artist, was opposed to the scientific objectivity of Impressionism in what was understood to be the French sense of a superficial art of appearances. As yet this entailed no mystical implications, but a continuum already existed between an art of imaginative contemplation and the endowment of such an experience with spiritual qualities.

## III   *SYMONS*

Symons's poetic development parallels that in painting from Impressionism to Post-Impressionism, evidencing the imaginative engagement with his subjects of the empathetic Symbolist. His increasingly mystical bias in the later 1890s led Symons to develop from this empathetic poetics an animistic aesthetics which anticipates in striking detail the anti-materialist position common to almost all the pre-war movements in painting and poetry. My discussion concentrates therefore on his best two volumes of poetry, *Silhouettes* (1892) and *London Nights* (1895), and on his metaphysical aesthetics, devoting particular attention to his response to the visual arts.

The first formative influence on Symons was Pater's Hegelian account of the increasing 'complexity' and self-consciousness of the arts, culminating in 'self-analytical' modern literature – 'a consciousness brooding with delight over itself'.[81] In search of poetic models displaying this stylistic modernity Symons turned initially to the sophistication of Meredith's *Modern Love* ('the most "modern" poem we have') and to Browning's lyrics.[82] In Symons's view the most stimulating technical innovation in poetry was Browning's dramatic monologue, which rejected simple narrative in favour of more subtle delineation of mood, making 'the soul the centre of action'. Browning focused instinctively on a moment of peripeteia, provoking a mental revaluation; the perfection of his style consisted 'in the intensity of its expression of a single moment of passion or emotion'. A perfect gloss on the aspirations of Symons's early poetry is provided by his comment that in 'Johannes Agricola' and 'Porphyria's Lover' Browning demonstrated 'a power of conceiving subtle mental complexities with clearness and of expressing them in a picturesque form and in perfect lyric language. Each poem renders a single mood, and renders it completely.' Browning's importance as a stylistic inspiration for 'impressionist' poetry is evident in Symons's enthusiasm for two uncharacteristic poems, the 'strong and suggestive little *pictures, Night and Morning* – each, in twelve or in four lines, a whole life-history'.[83] Browning therefore directed Symons's interest (evidenced in his *Days and Nights*, 1889) towards *moments* of dramatic intensity, sophistication in psychological analysis and, in rare examples, a visually suggestive style.

Following Symons's move to London in 1889 and formative visits to Paris in 1889 and 1890, the latter lasting three months, Browning was supplanted by new influences.[84] Although still focusing on significant moments, Symons no longer depended on the psychologically analytical dramatic monologue but devoted attention instead to the suggestive, 'symbolist' evocation of mood and atmosphere. Without abandoning his definition of modernity as stylistic and emotional complexity, he now found more congenial Verlaine's mellifluent variety, which with its alliteration, assonance, internal rhyme and rhythmic fluidity captured 'la *Nuance*, the last fine shade'.[85] At the same time he sought inspiration in the visual arts, not merely versifying the impressions evoked by a painting, a genre with a venerable history, but instead attempting to reproduce in words the same effect as Impressionist painting.

Symons had met Moore in Paris in 1890 and took rooms in March 1891 in Fountain Court, close to Moore's in King's Bench Walk.[86] The pair became close friends (Symons dedicated *Studies in Two Literatures* to Moore) and Moore probably stimulated Symons's new interest in modern art.[87] In a review of *Impressions and Opinions* Symons demonstrated in a paraphrase of Moore's account of Degas (which he regarded as the most admirable study in the book) that for him the Impressionists' challenging range of subject-matter had become an essential ingredient in modernity.[88] By 1892 Symons was writing what he termed 'Degas poems'.[89]

Symons's article 'Mr Henley's Poetry' is essentially a manifesto in defence of such modernity, advocating in poetry the subjectivist 'impressionism' of Sickert's group of painters: 'Intensely personal in the feeling that transfuses the picture, it is with a brush of passionate impressionism that [Henley] paints . . . London.'[90] In commenting on Henley's first 'London Voluntary' Symons echoed Whistler and Sickert (cf. *supra*, pp. 32–3) with the rhetorical question whether it was not 'almost as fine as a Whistler? – instinct with the same sense of the poetry of cities, the romance of what lies beneath our eyes, if we only have the vision and the point of view'.[91] The comparison was justified. Henley's poem 'To James McNeill Whistler' praised the artist's transmogrification with an 'incantation' of the skeletal hulk of Old Battersea Bridge and its surroundings into the 'enchanted pleasure-house of a Nocturne'.[92] His second and third 'London Voluntaries' depicted the metropolis in the transfiguring light of dawn and sunset. Henley made clear his inspiration by describing the 'fleeting', 'flickering', 'shining' reflections of 'the universal alms of light', and more particularly his debt to Whistler and the London Impressionists by remarking on the 'enchanted lustrousness' and 'mellow magic' which by 'a luminous transiency of grace' rendered the urban squalor unrecognisable.[93] It appears, however, that Henley's influence on Symons was largely confirmation of the artistic validity of urban subject-matter and the *avant-garde* importance of Impressionism, for Symons's response to Impressionism differs markedly in technique from both the sentimental lyricism of 'London Voluntaries' and the physiological sensationalism of some poems from 'In Hospital'.

Instead Symons's impressionist poetry aspired towards an imaginative suggestivity related to French Symbolism. Compare his implicit comparison of Verlaine's originality with Whistler's nocturnes: 'It is a twilight art, full of reticence, of perfumed shadows, of hushed melodies. It suggests, it gives impressions, with a subtle avoidance of any too definite or precise effect of line or colour.' A later article characterised Verlaine's poetry as 'impressionism – sometimes as delicate, as pastoral, as Watteau, sometimes as sensitively modern as Whistler, sometimes as brutally modern as Degas. It is all . . . the suggestion and evocation of sensations . . . .' In Verlaine's significantly named 'Aquarelles', 'the rhythm undulates in a vague, dreamy dance, like the very spirit of the hour and place in certain twilight moods'.[94]

Symons's subjectivist orientation is revealed as early as his 1893 analysis of 'decadence', which in fact describes what he understood by 'modernity': 'an intense self-consciousness, a restless curiosity in research, an over-subtilizing refinement upon refinement, a spiritual and moral perversity'.[95] The two tendencies in the modern movement – 'impressionism' and 'symbolism' – shared this stylistic complexity, expressed in wholly Paterian phraseology: 'To fix the last fine shade, the quintessence of things; to fix it fleetingly; to be a disembodied voice, and yet the voice of a human soul: that is the ideal of Decadence'. What distinguished them was their perceptual attitude to the external world: the former (like French Impressionist painting) sought unprecedented accuracy in depicting appearances, the latter was concerned with things-in-themselves, their essential nature. Both sought 'not general truth merely, but *la vérité vraie*, the very essence of truth – the truth of appearances to the senses, of the visible world to the eyes that see it; and the truth of spiritual things to the spiritual vision'. Impressionism, in the Goncourts as in Verlaine, was 'a desperate endeavour to give sensation, to flash the impression of the moment, to preserve the very heat and motion of life'; Pater and Henley were instanced as English examples. The Symbolist attempted to 'flash upon you the "soul" of that which can be apprehended only by the soul – the finer sense of things unseen, the deeper meaning of things evident'. [96]

Symons's rather undiscriminating choice of examples emphasises his uncertain distinction between 'impressionism' and 'symbolism'. He referred to Maeterlinck's 'symbolistic and impressionistic drama' – the syntactic link between the epithets suggesting that the two approaches were ultimately not exclusive – and explained that Maeterlinck employed an 'effect of atmosphere' to appeal directly to the 'sensations' and nerves. [97] Apparently for Symons there was little distinction between 'sensation' and 'impression'; sense-impressions melted into subjectivist interpretation. *Silhouettes*, the title of Symons's second volume of poetry, alluded to the pantomimic shadow theatre at the Chat Noir; he also applied the word to Verlaine's 'Paysages belges'. [98] The association was that each was an art of suggestion, providing just enough detail to stimulate the imagination of its audience; significantly this was in Symons's account also the technique of Maeterlinck's theatre, described as 'symbolist'. [99] From the very outset, therefore, Symons associated the nuances of his own and Verlaine's 'impressionist' verse with what could be labelled 'symbolism'.

Symons soon encountered problems, however, in his attempts to create a poetic equivalent to Whistler's 'impressionism'. For he lacked the ability to emulate successfully Verlaine's symbolist techniques with the requisite suggestivity and subtlety. His actual poetic practice frequently resembled the perceptual detachment and abhorrent naturalism of French Impressionist painting rather than his desired emotional expressiveness. Several of his poems are close to the perceptual characteristics and technical procedures of French Impressionist canvases, recalling their haphazard inclusiveness and random composition, dependent on momentary glimpses.

Consider the first stanza of 'Going to Hammersmith', which is unrepresentative only in that it depicts actual motion rather than merely the alternating sensations of the light-sensitive retina:

> The train through the night of the town,
>     Through a blackness broken in twain
>         By the sudden finger of streets;
> Lights, red, yellow, and brown,
>     From curtain and window-pane,
>         The flashing eyes of the streets.[100]

Byron, particularly in 'Mazeppa', had been extremely successful at recreating the exhilarating sensation of speed, while Browning's jaunty, staccato rhythms may have influenced Symons's technique, as may Verlaine's mimicry of the discontinuity of Impressionist painting in, for example, 'Walcourt' and 'Simples fresques I'.[101] What is new in this briskly exuberant poem is Symons's fusion of abrupt, verbless syntax mimetic of rapid transit with energetically succeeding visual sensations. The enforced passivity of the traveller shut off from almost all external stimuli forces him to depend exclusively on sight for his contact with the outside world, while the speed of the train and the darkness permit only fleeting glimpses of objects and disconnected aspects of the arbitrarily illuminated cityscape. The perceiver is accordingly detached from what he beholds, deprived of the opportunity for contemplative engagement, regarding all objects with equal and random emphasis in a wholly superficial perspective. One might compare the opening of 'Impression':

> The pink and black of silk and lace,
>     Flushed in the rosy-golden glow
> Of lamplight on her lifted face;
> Powder and wig, and pink and lace,
>
> And those pathetic eyes of hers

or the first line of 'In Bohemia': 'Drawn blinds and flaring gas within'; or these lines from 'At the Stage-door':

> Under the archway, suddenly seen, the curls
> And thin, bright faces of girls,
> Roving eyes, and smiling lips, and the glance. . . .[102]

In each case we are offered a fragmentary vision; synecdochic aspects and glimpses stimulate the imagination to complete the scene. The effect is of immediacy and a skilful reproduction of scintillating, coruscating light, captured in a syntactic fashion resembling the juxtaposed brushstrokes of unmixed colour in Impressionist painting which coalesce in the spectator's sensibility to create the illusion of flickering or carefully discriminated illumination. Yet the transient excitement which the poems stimulate fades, leaving the reader with an uneasy sense of brilliance but ultimate triviality.

The conflict between this approach and Symons's aim of imaginative evocation is pointed by the early 'Under the Cliffs'.[103] In its original version, before Symons excised the mawkish and distractingly contextual third stanza (whose removal, however, exposes damagingly the thinness of his material), the first stanza lamely attempts to suggest a mood of indolence disturbed by an intrusive reflection. Symons emulates Verlaine in interlacing the lines with a pattern of (hopefully hypnotic) syntactic and verbal iteration, the latter centring on 'white', 'pallid', 'whitely', and 'fleet', 'feet', 'footsteps', this metamorphosis in particular suggesting a hallucinatory, dream-like quality in which the landscape melts into his reverie. The conceit of the sun 'walking' on which the stanza turns is nevertheless, one must admit, somewhat forced. This intentionally atmospheric opening is succeeded by an 'impressionist' stanza, which indicates a temporal progression towards sunset, but otherwise hesitates between a purely descriptive and an evocative function comparable with that of the previous stanza:

> Bright light to windward on the horizon's verge;
> To leeward violet shades of thunder black,
> And the wide sea between
> A level stretch of scarcely-varying green
> Far off, the violet tints are on the track
> Of the dim sails that vanish and emerge.

The affective resonances of colours, dependent on their immediate visual impact, cannot be conveyed by language employed in this propositional manner. Instead of striving to reproduce in the very different verbal medium the emotional suggestiveness of colour-harmonies in painting, by creating an alternative linguistic variety of Symbolism, using stylised rhythms and aural patterning to complement the existing emotional resources of language, Symons attempts a literal translation of brush-strokes into words. As a result his transformation of the natural vista into a landscape painting remains merely a descriptive catalogue of its pictorial contents. The effect is to reduce the stanza, like the contemporary conception of French Impressionism, to absolute fidelity to observable phenomena, neutralising the subjective associations which words inevitably bring from earlier linguistic contexts and restricting their connotative resonance in favour of a matter-of-fact, scientific register which, with the exception of the vaguely metaphorical 'on the track' and the poetic 'verge' (occasioned, like the inversion in line 2, by the rhyme-scheme), merely records objectively verifiable data. Symons's aspiration towards a Symbolist technique of leaving (his) emotional attitude implicit, to be suggested by the verbal interplay of the poem, required a linguistic richness beyond that of his jejune, unevocative style.

Dissatisfied with this unrelieved bareness Symons heavily revised the stanza, introducing an emotional resonance absent from the earlier version. The painterly denotative 'violet shades of thunder black' became more suggestively menacing as 'stormy shadows, violet-black', while the mannered colour-contrasts of the final three lines were replaced by subjective interpretation:

> A vast unfurrowed field of windless green;
> The stormy shadows flicker on the track
> Of phantom sails that vanish and emerge.

The revisions establish a more mysterious atmosphere, accentuating the curiously random movement, and introducing metaphorical transformation into the dispassionate rendering, which casts doubt on the nature of what was earlier an unequivocally external scene.

Two other poems further illustrate Symons's empathetic Symbolist attempt to employ landscape as a metaphorical equivalent for a state of consciousness.

In 'For a Picture by Walter Sickert (Hôtel Royal, Dieppe)',

Symons contrasts Sickert's famous rendering of the scene with the despair it engenders in him, expressed in emotionally charged vocabulary which insistently directs our attention from the external panorama to the poet's state of mind:

> The grey-green stretch of sandy grass,
>    Indefinitely desolate;
>    A sea of lead, a sky of slate;
> Already Autumn in the air, alas!
>
> One stark monotony of stone,
>    The long hotel, acutely white,
>    Against the after-sunset light
> Withers grey-green, and takes the grass's tone.
>
> Listless and endless it outlies,
>    And means to you and me no more
>    Than any pebble on the shore:
> But, ah! to see it as with Sickert's eyes![104]

Symons made the landscape's metaphorical function more explicit when he revised the last line to the Paterian 'Or this indifferent moment as it dies', but its imaginative status is assured by the linguistic strategies of the poem. The objectivity of the pictorial vocabulary is tempered by the stylised aesthetic distance established by such features as the heavy alliteration on 'g', 's' and 'a', the calculatedly off-key Verlainian assonance on 'One', 'monotony' and 'stone', and the rhythmic variation produced by the enjambements and the punctuational stress of the semi-colons. The apparently objective recording of visual impressions obliquely intimates decay and despair with the introduction of the metaphorical 'Autumn',[105] the animistic implications of 'desolate', 'Withers' and 'Listless', the subjective tension indicated by 'acutely', and the harsh indifference suggested by the unrelieved solidity of 'lead' and 'slate', which have imaginative associations beyond mere reference to colours from a palette.

A less assured example of this metaphorical technique is provided by 'On the Beach'.[106] This begins promisingly in a sensuous 'impressionist' manner, with a connotative adverb, subdued alliteration, an enjambement which reinforces rhythmically the deliquescence visually suggested by the mist and the epithet 'ghostly', and the subjectivity implicit in 'wane' to hint at an atmospheric and emotional imprecision:

> Night, a grey sky, a ghostly sea,
>   The soft beginning of the rain:
>   Black on the horizon, sails that wane,
> Into the distance mistily.

But Symons feels the need to develop discursively the metaphorical import of the scene by paralleling it with 'The shore-line of infinity' and in the final stanza indicating explicitly the mood which the first stanza had more lyrically and mysteriously evoked.

Despite Symons's admiration for Verlaine, however, he never adequately imitated Verlaine's subtle fusion of his consciousness with the landscape in such poems as 'Paysages tristes' and 'Malines'.[107] Equally Dowson was always more adept than Symons at reproducing Verlainian 'Verses making for mere sound, and music, with just a suggestion of sense, or hardly that. . . .'[108] Only occasionally did Symons approach a lyrical abstract expressionist Symbolism – notably in 'In Fountain Court' – but without Verlaine's profusion of phonetic invention and rhythmic variation in such poems as 'À Clymène', 'Clair de lune', and 'Ariettes oubliées', I–III and v.[109] Instead the reticent detachment of Symons's empathetic Symbolism brought him apparently closer to the objectivist variety of Imagism exemplified by H.D. The difference in aim is that Symons usually attempts to transform the landscape into a symbolic embodiment of his mood. The objectivist variety of Imagism by contrast grants greater prominence to the phenomenal actuality of the external world for its own sake, making the poem's subject not the empathetic engagement of the poet, but rather the mysterious haecceity of the objects depicted.

Two decisive criteria distinguish empathetic Symbolist from objectivist procedures. First, in the former the subject of the poem is the poet's emotional response to the external world: in other words, an affective mood. In objectivist poetry, by contrast, although the poet's imaginative and emotional attitude is implicit in his style, prime attention is devoted to the depicted objects themselves, whose detailed physical configuration frequently assumes importance as a sensuous extension of their inner life. Secondly, in an objectivist poem one confronts a literal rather than a metaphorical scene, which the poet has selected as significant but which he merely presents. The very act of transposing the phenomenal into language itself establishes an aesthetic distance, ensuring that the objects depicted receive unwonted contemplative attention. The objectivist accordingly reduces stylisation to a deceptively straightforward minimum, hoping by this means to allow the objects themselves to stimulate an unpredetermined, fresh response in the reader.

Let me illustrate this crucial distinction by discussing two early poems by Symons which anticipate the objectivist variety of Imagism.

The idiosyncratic 'In Winter', even to the extent of its superfluous narrative coda, foreshadows the early objectivist techniques of Flint and H.D.:

> Pale from the watery west, with the pallor of winter a-cold,
> Rays of the afternoon sun in a glimmer across the trees;
> Glittering moist underfoot, the long alley. The firs, one by one,
> Catch and conceal, as I saunter, and flash in a dazzle of gold
> Lower and lower the vanishing disc: and the sun alone sees
> As I wait for my love in the fir-tree alley alone with the sun.[110]

Aside from the epithet 'a-cold', the poem if unexciting is radically innovative in tendency. Germane in inspiration to Symons's attempts to emulate paintings, it shares neither their mannered idiom nor their metaphorical reading of nature. One finds instead simple denotative statements, the first three lines a verbless series of perceptions, recording primarily visual sense-data but with no hint of empathetic engagement. Symons's gesture of presenting the scene as poetically significant is an assertion of its imaginative potentiality, but his absolutely impersonal description leaves its import for the reader to determine.

This instance of objectivism is unparalleled in its extremity in Symons's work. A more representative example of his position is offered by 'Before the Squall', which is close to Symons's characteristic empathetic Symbolism but which devotes more attention to realising the literal, physical actuality of the scene than to the poet's mood:

> The wind is rising on the sea,
>    White flashes dance along the deep,
> That moans as if uneasily
>    It turned in an unquiet sleep.

Ridge after rocky ridge upheaves
   A toppling crest that falls in spray
Where the tormented beach receives
   The buffets of the sea's wild play.

On the horizon's nearing line,
   Where the sky rests, a visible wall,
Grey in the offing, I divine
   The sails that fly before the squall.[111]

Unlike Symons's empathetic Symbolist work, the scene here is not transformed into a metaphorical correlative. With the exception of the explicit anthropomorphism of lines 3–4 and the more subtle, connotative verb 'dance', Symons's imaginative response remains implicit, effaced beside the physical actuality of the seascape. Stylistic details within the poem nevertheless intimate Symons's empathetic engagement. 'Upheaves' in line 5, 'tormented' in line 7 (if read as a Gallicism) and 'buffets' and 'play' in line 8, which may likewise be interpreted either as physical description or within an emotionally suggestive register, indicate obliquely Symons's empathetic attitude, in a method later employed by H.D.. The poem's rhythms also contribute to this effect. The daring lack of punctuation in the second stanza, for example, both mimes vividly the sea's energy and also, by the pace of delivery it requires from the reader, conveys a sense of the poet's exhilaration at what he beholds. Following this empathetic involvement the deliberately under-stated constatation of the final stanza provides a skilful contrast in tone, the emotional withdrawal satisfyingly completing the poem's formal closure.

The empathetic tendencies inherent in the subjectivism of Symons's 'impressionism' became more pronounced as he moved increasingly towards transcendentalism. In 1895–6 he abandoned the Paterian, sensationalist Epicureanism which had been a factor in his initial adoption of an 'impressionist' aesthetic.[112] His orientation towards mysticism was confirmed by the influence of Yeats, who lived next to Symons in Fountain Court from October 1895 to February or March 1896,[113] and accompanied him to Ireland in summer 1896.

The following year Symons reappraised the evolution of the modern movement: the emerging pattern of the 1890s confirmed a general transition from objective Naturalism to empathetic

Symbolist art. Symons now described Maeterlinck's Symbolist drama as most accurately representing the tendency of the decade; with increasing fervency he saw literature as the harbinger of a mystical revival: 'This old gospel, of which Maeterlinck is the new voice, has been quietly waiting until certain bankruptcies – the bankruptcy of Science, of the Positive Philosophies – should allow it full credit.'[114] The naturalistic element in the modern movement had been generally rejected, conveniently enabling Symons to make decadence, with its unfortunate public associations, a question of linguistic deformation and thus to retitle his final manifesto of the decade *The Symbolist Movement in Literature*.[115] The 1899 definition of Symbolism derives recognisably from the 1893 definition of 'decadence' (that is, 'modernity'):

> this revolt against exteriority, against rhetoric, against a materialistic tradition; . . . this endeavour to disengage the ultimate essence, the soul, of whatever exists and can be realised by the consciousness; . . . this dutiful waiting upon every symbol by which the soul of things can be made visible.[116]

The crucial distinction is that the alternative, 'impressionist' representation of *la vérité vraie* has disappeared; art has become wholly transcendental.

Symons's increasingly mystical concerns focused his attention on an empathetic poetics, centring on dance, which was to lead him towards Symbolist theory. In the early 'Javanese Dancers', with its mimetically sinuous rhythms breaking off in their flow only to reiterate the movement more emphatically, and polysyllabic adverbs of largely atmospheric importance, Symons had evoked a hypnotically erotic impression.[117] He focuses on the expressive qualities of the dance, but at this stage is concerned principally with its seductive implications. One is left with an image of intense physicality, of a dancer who could easily be related to the contemporary fascination with Salome, as in the sinister narcissism of 'La Mélinite: Moulin Rouge'.[118] The later 'To a Dancer' makes explicit the sexual attractions music-hall ballet held for Symons.[119]

By contrast 'Nora on the Pavement' appears free from salacious resonances and voyeurism.[120] The poem's fourth stanza again dwells on the expressive nature of dance, but here there is no design to entice or stimulate; instead Nora is captured in a moment of naïvely unconscious self-expression. The word 'child' is a frequent affectation in Symons's poetry, but here its application to Nora is justified by his sense of her spontaneous escape from the constraints of code-governed behaviour to self-sufficient independence, oblivious of the existence of either spectators or conscious purpose (cf. lines 23–5). Thus in context the numinous register of Symons's rapt 'It is the soul of Nora' appears far from hyperbolical.

The poem falls into two sections. The first three stanzas with their unusually intricate enjambement and sinuous rhythms create a vivid impression of the physical motion of the dance. This is complemented by indications of Symons's emotional engagement, conveyed by a masterly use of assonance, which for once approximates to Verlainian quality, and in a brilliant metrical inventiveness recalling Hopkins in 'See her, but ah! not free her' echoed in the 'may be her' of line 14, which lends to the words themselves an aural symbolism, augmented by the insinuatory repetition of key words and the deliberately restricted rhyme-scheme. Having effected this powerful evocation, in the second half of the poem Symons moves into abstract reflection, dismissing as irrelevant the actual details of the movement. Instead he directs attention to the dance as Nora's sudden rediscovery of her essential being or 'haecceity', conveyed by the stark antithesis between the choreographed patterns of the ballet in the third stanza and the individualist expressiveness of the fourth. Thus, while Nora divines unconscious inner resources, the poet's awareness through her of a more essential nature justifies describing the contemplative interaction the poem records as an epiphany.

Another poem from the same volume further emphasises Symons's Symbolist conception of dance. In 'The Primrose Dance: Tivoli' the ambiguous perceptual impressions created by the motion of the pirouetting dancer's skirt tempt Symons to lose sight of her physical actuality, evoking the illusion of a 'rhythmic flower' or ideal primrose (!) rather than Mallarméan iris.[121] Frank Kermode has traced the contemporary impact on aesthetic theory of the dance of Loïe Fuller. This comprised essentially an art of illuminated drapes in motion in which the figure and personality of the dancer had little importance, using instead optical effects and flowing masses of silk which almost completely disguised the human shape, to create forms imaginatively, animating and organising space, evoking a dream-like ambience in which geometrical space was abolished.[122] This form of dance, conforming in its non-discursive qualities to the ideals of late Mallarméan Symbolism, found a counterpart in Symons's interest in the abstract expressiveness of mime and gesture.

His development of a Symbolist aesthetic began with a reaction resembling Yeats's and Moore's against the superfluity of naturalistic staging; by the turn of the century Symons, like Yeats, was enthusiastic over the work of Gordon Craig.[123] His fascination with the symbolic potential of pantomimic gesture found its desired realisation in Maeterlinck's dramas (some of which were written for marionettes and suggested the use of the mask to generalise or *impersonalise* the actor) and in the statuesque portentousness combined with expressive mobility of feature of Duse's acting-style.[124] The stylised conventionality of both aimed to divert the spectator's attention from irrelevant distractions of external details or stage business towards an empathetic involvement with character or what Symons termed the 'soul', articulated through significantly restricted action in an intuitive, non-discursive fashion. Poetic drama was in this respect a less pure form than pantomime, ballet or the visual arts in that it introduced also the rationalistic element of speech with its inbuilt referential assignment. Symons found his ideal accordingly in the Wagnerian *Gesamtkunstwerk* which complemented the pictorial suggestivity of theatrical gesture and the *mise en scène* with the nearly abstract expressiveness of recitative and visually evocative melody, which offered an interpretative accompaniment to the tableauesque action without descending to discursive elaboration.[125]

Following Kermode, several commentators have explored Symons's interest in dance (see n. 122). My concern is instead to demonstrate how Symons's interest in the non-discursive communication of the dancer – 'her *rhythm* reveals to you the soul of her imagined being'[126] – was elaborated into a generalised theory of transcendentalism in the arts, which anticipates the Bergsonian aesthetics discussed in Chapter 5.

Consider Symons's description of Nora's 'dance-measures':

Leaping and joyous, keeping time alone
With Life's capricious rhythm, and all her own,
Life's rhythm and hers, long sleeping,
That wakes, and knows not why, in these dance-measures.[127]

The assertion is that the dancer acts somehow as the symbolic channel or transmitter of a fundamental 'rhythm' which (although with her own individual emphasis) she shares in common with those who watch her and which could be interpreted as an archetypal state of consciousness or essential spirituality. A brief digression will help interpret the implications of Symons's register.

Yeats's early excitement at the portentous immobility of Florence Farr's acting-style was renewed in 1902 by the Fays' disdain for stage business, denigrated by Yeats as the desire 'to copy at every moment the surface of life, to copy life as [the actor] thinks the eye sees it, instead of being content with the simple and noble forms the heart sees'.[128] The Fays' style resembled the 'rhythmic progression' of gestures in Sarah Bernhardt's acting, an ideal which Yeats further defined as 'the nobler movements that the heart sees, *the rhythmical movements that seem to flow up into the imagination from some deeper life than that of the individual soul*'.[129]

The point I wish to emphasise is that Yeats presents the actor as the symbolic instantiation or momentary channel for a life-force outside the self (presumably the *Anima Mundi*) which he describes in terms of *rhythm* (the phraseology employed later by the Theosophist Kandinsky and Bergsonian animists conscious or otherwise such as Middleton Murry and Roger Fry). The unreserved concurrence of Yeats and Symons in this approach is emphasised by Symons's comment apropos *The Wind Among the Reeds*, 'A lyric . . . is an embodied ecstasy . . . so profoundly personal that it loses the accidental qualities of personality, and becomes a part of the universal consciousness', and his implicit comparison of Yeats's drama with Wagnerian opera, according to which Yeats's characters, like 'disembodied passions', 'speak to one another . . . out of a deeper consciousness than either heart or mind, which is perhaps what we call the soul'.[130]

Symons's first application of this animistic aesthetic was in an account of *Parsifal* which modulates between description of its staging and a more mystical register which found in the 'disembodied ecstasy' of the music and the 'noble rhythm' of the acting 'something of the solemnity of sensation produced by the service of the Mass'. The music, 'like one of the great forces of nature' made abstract pictures, but was itself subordinate to the stage tableaux; the arts combined perfectly to produce a picture impressive 'chiefly by its rhythm, the harmonies of its convention. The lesson of *Parsifal* is the lesson that, in art, rhythm is everything'.[131] Symons found this 'rhythm' in a novel *mise en scène* which clearly captivated him. Like Gordon Craig, the producer of *Parsifal* treated the stage as a pictorial composition, grouping characters into 'masses and pat-terns' or ordered 'lines', whose stylised gestural movements were synchronised and given a hieratic solemnity.[132] Rhythm was, however, not restricted to these compositional relationships recal-ling painterly conventions; for Symons, as for the painters and art critics discussed in Chapter 5, it had transcendental implications.

Thus in a later article Symons wrote,

> That slow rhythm, which in Wagner is like the very rhythm of the world flowing onwards from that first breathing out of chaos, which we hear in the opening notes of the *Ring*, seems to broaden outwards like ripples on an infinite sea, through the whole work of Wagner. Like the few supreme artists, Wagner has found the unity of the cosmos.[133]

The phrase 'the very rhythm of the world', implying a Neoplatonic *Anima Mundi* or *nous*, Schopenhauerian 'will' or Bergsonian *évolution créatrice* behind phenomenal appearances, is arresting. Symons offered an explanatory gloss, probably drawing on Schopenhauer's theory of music as the unmediated expression of the thing in itself, the primal unity of the will:

> Wagner's aim at expressing the soul of things is still further helped by his system of continuous, unresolved melody. The melody which circumscribes itself like Giotto's O [i.e. an inclusive representation of the world] . . . is the whole expression of the subconscious life, saying more of himself than any person of the drama has ever found in his soul.[134]

Symons's assertion was therefore that music expressed the universal noumenal 'rhythm', an approach which he extended to all the arts.

Rodin, in Symon's view, was a 'visionary' who believed in the doctrine of 'correspondences':

> He spies upon every gesture, knowing that if he can seize one gesture at the turn of the wave, he has seized an essential *rhythm* of nature. When a woman combs her hair, he will say to you, she thinks she is only combing her hair: no, she is making a gesture which flows into *the eternal rhythm*, which is beautiful because it lives, because it is part of that geometrical plan which nature is always weaving for us.[135]

(One might compare Yeats's remarks from 1906 on 'A Guitar Player'.[136]) Symons argued that the secret of Rodin's appeal lay in the fact that his figures gave the illusion of not being severed from the 'rhythm of nature', the 'universal life of things', the expressive modelling of the clay appearing to release to the spectator a restless inner life.[137]

The source of Symons's approach was MacColl, who in characterising Turner's painting had remarked on his ability to capture in objects 'their own principle of construction, their private rhythm'. It is probable that MacColl was thinking merely of what Constable, for example, would have understood by being a 'natural' painter, namely studying the peculiarities of an external scene so intimately that one was able to capture its elusive configuration (compare Furse's remarks on drawing – *supra*, p. 39). But the phraseology in which MacColl explained Turner's development of this insight into a compositional harmony of formal motifs of rhythmic movement was readily susceptible to a transcendentalist reading:

> Turner pierced through the bewildering accidents of growth down to character, to a system of curve or cleavage. He could grow trees and rocks from within. Every line of the pines in the great Farnley drawing is a picture-line, but also a tree-line; the tree is more lucidly a tree and a part of the general flow, strain, and pressure of the forces about it than any tree we shall see by going to look for one, because its main motive is disentangled and also reinforced, for it is taken up fugally and echoed all over the picture.[138]

It was an easy step to gloss 'forces' as cosmic 'rhythm' as Bergsonian artists and art-critics would a decade later, by which time MacColl's term 'character' had become the unequivocally noumenal 'soul'.

I wish to emphasise, therefore, that Symons presented art as an expression of noumenal 'rhythm'. His source for this transcendentalist animism may have been Neoplatonic (via Yeats) or Schopenhauerian (via Wagner). The significant point is that he applies this philosophy to art in exactly the same manner as Fry, Murry and the Futurists did Bergsonism, and Kandinsky and Marc Theosophism or pantheism.

In summary, the aesthetic legacy of the 1890s was the replacement of naturalistic objectivity by varieties of anti-materialist transcendentalism. In the visual arts this assumed the form of anticipations of the empathetic, post-Impressionist aesthetic. In poetry two principal alternatives emerged: abstract expressionist Symbolism, and empathetic Symbolism rooted in the contemplative interchange between poet and external world.

# 3 The Movement towards Imagism

My aim in this chapter is twofold: to demonstrate how the empathetic Symbolist poetry of the *fin de siècle* was consolidated into the principal variety of Imagism; and to characterise in detail, apropos Hulme, the empathetic, metaphysical aesthetic whose re-emergence in the 1890s was described in Chapter 2.

At the beginning of Chapter 2 I outlined the increasingly widespread dissatisfaction with materialistic trends in nineteenth-century thought and society. One manifestation of the quest for a spiritually and emotionally reassuring alternative was artistic Idealism. Prolonged into the early twentieth century, this desire to create an imaginary refuge from contemporary materialism resulted at the hands of minor poets in a plethora of pastiche Yeats and pastiche Thompson.

A poetic revaluation was urgently required; it was initiated by Hulme and Flint, the leading figures of the first Imagist group, the 'forgotten school of 1909'.[1] Hulme began by attacking the shortcomings of the English 'Symbolist' epigones, in particular their portentously euphuistic diction. This striving for sublimity, far from accomplishing the desired synaesthetic fusion of the physical and the conceptual, had created merely glittering but meretricious conceits. Hulme's counterblast against such verbose and vacuous Idealism was to re-emphasise the importance of directly verifiable sense perception.

He and Flint joined therefore in insisting that, although Symbolism was concerned with emotional expressionism rather than representational mimesis, it nevertheless required a credible, objective embodiment for the psychic states which were its theme. They moved accordingly from 'Idealism', which had survived into the new century reduced to a facile, sentimental escapism, towards empathetic Symbolism. Consolidated from the work of Symons, this technique of establishing a metaphorical equivalent for empathetic interaction with the external world was to furnish the principal variety of Imagism.

Hulme is, however, less significant as a poet than as an aesthetician. In the previous chapter I examined Symons's evolution towards the animistic, empathetic aesthetic which, I shall argue, provided the unifying tenet of all pre-war movements, save Cubism, in painting and poetry. Symons's sources were probably Neoplatonic or Schopenhauerian. The early twentieth century by contrast found its mentor in Bergson, whose first influential English exponent was Hulme. Hulme's fusion of Bergson's animistic organicism with Lipps's cogent psychological explanation of empathy renders him therefore of central significance to my study. For he provides an indispensable paradigm for the empathetic anti-materialism of Futurism, German Expressionism and Imagism/Vorticism: movements whose intricate interrelationship constitutes the subject of the second half of this study.

A close examination of Hulme's development will reveal how this empathetic aesthetics is indivisible from questions of poetic technique.

## I  THE 'IMAGE', LANGUAGE AND PERCEPTION

Like those of most *avant-garde* movements, the Imagists' programme of self-definition was directed most pointedly against their immediate predecessors. Hulme's efforts to evolve a coherent philosophy of language, in practice extremely trite, were primarily directed towards effecting a definitive break from the stylistic shortcomings of the Nineties poets. The English fascination with but inadequate grasp of French Symbolism had resulted in a fashion for synaesthesia and supposedly evocative imprecision which was frequently no more than portentous obfuscation. To eliminate this facile pseudo-mysticism with its sham depths of significance Hulme advocated a visually denotative rather than connotative use of language. Florid sentimentalism could only be avoided, he felt, by remaining as close as possible to authentic perception, grounding one's work in direct observation of and response to the external world, and attempting to convey these immediately verifiable sense-data in simple, precise diction. This stylistic iconoclasm is inseparable from Hulme's metaphysical anxiety, an examination of which forms accordingly the indispensable prolegomenon to his poetics.

In 1907 Hulme was the melancholy advocate of a sensationalist epistemology, accompanied by philosophical relativism and linguistic scepticism, whose imaginative and emotional insufficiency he perceived, but which appeared nevertheless to be philosophically imperative. His source was not Pater or Symons (although his pessimism was undoubtedly accentuated by the morbid late nineteenth-century *Zeitgeist*) but rather, as Wallace Martin has demonstrated, French empiricist–associationist psychology. Here Hulme found both an analysis and a critique of conceptualisation from its departure-point in the '*image*', which, as a contemporary definition reveals, was synonymous with 'representation' or 'residual sense-datum'.[2]

It had been generally assumed that the main ideological influence on Hulme's poetics was Remy de Gourmont. But Martin has argued convincingly that Hulme's indebtedness is rather to Gourmont's own sources, such as the psychologist Théodule Ribot.[3] Ribot figures in Hulme's neglected 'Plan for a Book on Modern Theories of Art' (*Spec.*, 261–4), the seminal importance of which in elucidating Hulme's development will be reiterated throughout my account. Hulme's familiarity with Ribot's work in 1907 is confirmed by the largest group of his manuscript 'Notes on Language and Style', which in addition to references to Hulme's stylistic experiments during his residence at this period in Belgium contains a reference to Ribot, established by the context as *L'imagination créatrice*.[4]

Ribot distinguished three stages in the development of conceptualisation: (i) lower abstraction, preceding linguistic competence and not employing words, although other signs are used; (ii) an intermediary stage in which the role of language gradually increases; (iii) higher abstractions, where the word alone exists in the mind, its substitution complete. For Hulme the crucial part of Ribot's argument was his examination of higher abstractions which have as defining characteristic 'de n'être plus représentable'.[5] Ribot had earlier emphasised that perception involved selection and that even the '*image*' of an object implied some impoverishment of reality.[6] Now he described a movement away from the *image*, rendering phenomenal reality even more remote. The ideal of symbolical abstraction, Ribot argued, was to act as a short-cut in reasoning, so that as in calculus one was not forced constantly to return to first principles. By abbreviating a potential knowledge to which one could refer if necessary the abstraction was of undoubted value. But there was no necessary guarantee of the existence of such potential knowledge; when assayed, concepts might prove merely fool's gold. Thus in moving away from the data of immediate experience one might ultimately lose touch with reality itself, as the abstractions with which one dealt became worthless counters with no practical basis.[7]

Despite conceding the necessity and the general advantages of conceptualisation therefore, Ribot presented its advanced development as a dangerous rarefaction of phenomenal life: the '*image*' and the abstraction were ultimately antagonistic. On this basis he ventured a bold psychological classification: men of abstraction or men of imagination. All artists are taken as belonging to the imaginative type: 'Tous rêvent une œuvre organique, vivante, donc *complexe*.' By contrast abstractionists, such as scientists and philosophers, reject this phenomenal plenitude. Ribot concludes in phrases which underline his proximity to Romantic organicism:

L'abstrait est un cadavre. Il serait moins pittoresque, mais plus juste de dire un squelette; car une abstraction scientifique est la charpente osseuse des phénomènes.

Donc, au fond, l'antagonisme de l'image et de l'idée, c'est celle du tout et de la partie.[8]

Hulme was to discover with some relief the transcendentalist counterbalance which Bergson offered to Ribot's implicit anti-intellectualism; but before this his wholly destructive relativism was reinforced by Jules de Gaultier's journalistic *Le Bovarysme*, of which Hulme wrote, 'I cannot express how intensely I admire the logical consistency with which it is all worked out' (*FS*, 23).[9]

Like Ribot, Gaultier emphasises man's ability to abstract from the heterogeneity of the phenomenal world and thus to communicate through signs, written and verbal, corresponding to his mental *images*. Held as irrefragable, these concepts provide the valuable aid of an 'algebraic short-cut'; but, being in most cases unverifiable, unlike experiential knowledge acquired from perception, they exact in return the price of possible deception.[10]

After a somewhat meretricious and wholly derivative extension

onto a metaphysical plane of his thesis of man's delusion,[11] Gaultier
completed his critique of conceptualisation by rehearsing Bergson's
linguistic scepticism without the redeeming addition of 'intuition'.
He argues that the constant flux of sensations may be perceived only
in an artificial state of arrest. The arbitrariness of this stabilisation
renders all truths and categories provisional. He points out that
subsequent analysis often reveals scientific hypotheses as illusory; the
attempts of the Romantic philosophers to subsume fluid reality
under a single immutable concept are similarly misguided. There
are no absolute values; 'truths' are merely relativist groupings of
elements into social placebos which may at any stage be decomposed
and differently recomposed to fulfil a new pragmatic need.[12]

The epistemology which imposed itself on Hulme was accordingly characterised by a reluctance to abstract from ostensively
verifiable sense-data or *images*, accompanied by a relativist distrust of
the distortions of conceptual language. He expressed this position in
'Cinders', and 'The New Philosophy' and 'Searchers after Reality.
II. Haldane', articles published in summer 1909, at the height of the
'forgotten school' period. There is an obvious debt to Gaultier's
insistence on the pragmatic relativity of 'truths' and his attack on the
Romantics' attempt to reduce contingent reality to a single artificial
concept:

> All is flux. The moralists, the capital letterists, attempt to find a
> framework outside the flux, a solid bank for the river, a pier rather
> than a raft. Truth is what helps a particular sect in the general
> flow.   (*Spec*, 222)[13]

Doubts that abstraction resulted in more than empty hypostatisation of supposed realities were reinforced by scepticism about the
adequacy of language itself. In 'Cinders' a chess-board metaphor is
used to illustrate the artificially neat intellectual grid which
language imposes on the 'cinder-heap' of reality (*Spec*, 218, 219, 221
§2–3).[14] Although of indispensable practical utility the abstract
signs or 'counters' of language were a disturbingly insufficient
shorthand for the full complexity of experience, their selectivity
leaving 'an ungritlike picture of reality' (*Spec*, 224, 230–1). Hulme's
provisional solution to this dilemma was to advocate returning to
visually denotative language, necessarily closer to the 'grit' of
perceptual experience, the *image*.

## II   *EMPATHETIC AESTHETICS*

My concern hitherto has been with Hulme's philosophical relativism. I now wish to show how the empathetic philosophy of Bergson and Lipps offered a positive corrective to Hulme's pessimistic sensationalism and the mechanistic model of experience he derived both from associationist psychology and from scientific determinism. [15]

Hulme's temperamental scepticism rendered him reluctant to espouse any position without qualification, an ambivalence accentuated by his evident delight in dialectical argument. It seems probable that Lipps's chief attraction for Hulme was his ability to give intuition or empathy a psychological rather than a necessarily mystical justification. Nevertheless this instinctive reserve was temporarily outweighed by Hulme's undoubtedly sincere exhilaration at Bergson's apparent refutation of scientific determinism. I believe therefore, despite the jocular dismissiveness of some of his prose statements and poetry, that from 1907 to 1912 Hulme did genuinely adopt a transcendentalist aesthetics; the crucial point about the 'forgotten school of 1909' is just this continuum with the 1890s. [16]

Hulme's ideological vacillation makes it absolutely imperative, as I shall demonstrate, to adopt a rigorously chronological approach to his work. The explanation of Hulme's supposed self-contradiction (as, notoriously, in his account of Romanticism) lies in the confused sense of chronology which besets his commentators, who juxtapose conflicting pronouncements without indicating that these are from different, self-contained phases of Hulme's development. [17] The crucial point to grasp is that all the aestheticians who guided Hulme during his poetic career espoused an empathetic theory of art.

Wallace Martin has distinguished three Hulmes: 'a pre-1907 empiricist, a 1907–12 Bergsonian, and a post-1912 reactionary'. [18] In Chapters 4 and 5 I offer a more precise characterisation of the third Hulme, analysing the Conservative politics which determined his rejection of Bergsonism, and his art-criticism. Here my objective is to rescue the middle Hulme from his biographers, both of whom by transferring back in time Hulme's post-1911 views drastically undervalue the impact on him of Bergson's philosophy, which was coextensive with Hulme's poetic career. [19]

The facts surrounding Hulme's venture into poetry are familiar and need only be briefly recalled. Having first felt the impulse to write poetry in 1907,[20] in 1908 Hulme joined the staid and socialite Poets' Club, where he delivered his 'Lecture on Modern Poetry' (discussed below), the best surviving guide to his poetics. Galvanised by Flint's criticism, however, Hulme came to regard the Poets' Club as dilettante and broke away[21] to form his own *avant-garde* 'Secession Club', which held its first meeting on 25 March 1909. Members of the group included Flint, Edward Storer, Francis Tancred, Florence Farr, Joseph Campbell, Ernest Rhys and Ernest Radford.[22] Pound was introduced at the fourth meeting, on 22 April, a few days after the publication of *Personae*. Weekly meetings continued throughout the spring and summer of 1909, before this 'forgotten school' was dissolved after a brief resumption in the autumn.

This was the crucial period of Hulme's influence, conducted through conversation and example, the exact scope of which is rendered difficult to assess by later misrepresentation. It seems incontestable, however, that it was Hulme who introduced the notion of the 'image' and provided the theoretical lead for the group's experiments.[23] Earlier efforts to reconstruct what went on at these meetings, and the views which Hulme expounded, have been vitiated by the imprecision of commentators. I shall now show why one must remain alert to the chronological fluctuations in Hulme's ideas if he is not to be misinterpreted.

Consider as a representative example of critical distortion Alun Jones's article 'Imagism: A Unity of Gesture'. Discussing Hulme's approach at the 1909 meetings, Jones writes,

> Hulme, beginning negatively with a feeling of dissatisfaction with existing poetry and feeling the need for the expression of a new and more intense sensibility, looked for a more formal poetic structure. Like Cézanne he felt the need 'to make of impressionism something solid and durable like old art'.[24]

Jones's argument is flawed damagingly in that the reference he cites is from a lecture given by Hulme in January 1914. There is no mention of Cézanne in Hulme's work before 'Romanticism and Classicism' (1912), where a reference makes clear that his interpretation of Cézanne had been guided by Maurice Denis's exposition in *Théories, 1890–1910* (1912).[25] There is no mention of geometric 'solidity' in Hulme's writings before 1914; the context of the remark

Jones quotes from *Speculations* places almost beyond doubt Hulme's indebtedness to Metzinger's *Du Cubisme*, which was first published in 1912.[26] At the time of his association with the 'forgotten school' Hulme's poetics were based on the 'Impressionism' of Whistler, not on any Post-Impressionist (see *infra*, p. 71).

Similar misrepresentation occurs at the end of Jones's article. He claims that in the 'original phase' of Imagism 'In many ways Hulme was trying to achieve in poetry that stark directness of statement that he had seen his friend Jacob Epstein achieve in stone.' In fact, as Jones himself told us in his earlier book, Hulme only met Epstein in 1912.[27] He continues,

> The art that he admired was essentially non-naturalistic, exemplified particularly by such works as Epstein's 'Rock-drill' and Gaudier-Brzeska's 'Red Dancer' [*sic*]. . . . But whereas it is possible to argue for abstract art as being impersonal and autonomous, a complete fusion of form and content, the argument cannot be transferred too easily to poetry.[28]

To put the facts straight: Epstein's *Rock Drill* dates from 1913–16 and Gaudier-Brzeska's *Red Stone Dancer* from 1913. Gaudier settled in London in 1911 and was active as a sculptor only from 1912 to 1914.[29] Hence the undisputed fact that from 1912–13 Hulme exclusively admired abstract art is misleadingly carried back to the 'forgotten school' period, when his views on art were by contrast empathetic.

In his book Jones abets further confusion by maintaining that Hulme 'was not in sympathy with the ideas of Lipps except in so far as he saw the origins of romanticism in art and life to lie revealed in the work of Lipps and his colleagues'.[30] Nothing could be further from the truth. Only when Hulme discovered Worringer's *Abstraction and Empathy* did he question the adequacy of Lipps's work. And, although it has recently been maintained erroneously that Hulme heard Worringer lecture in Berlin in winter 1911–12,[31] this aesthetic reorientation was in fact only completed when from December 1912 until probably May 1913 Hulme lived in Berlin.[32]

The result of the chronological blurring exemplified by Jones has been that no critic to date has realised the central relevance to Hulme's poetic theory of the authors represented in the 'Plan for a Book on Modern Theories of Art'. Not surprisingly there is no mention of Worringer, an omission particularly striking in section

5(d), which discusses the German 'historical, sociological school' and the 'art of *primitive people*'. Lipps, by contrast, far from being denigrated as Jones would suggest, has two chapters out of the total of nine devoted to his 'great book' and is described as 'the greatest writer on aesthetics'. I shall now explain exactly why Hulme, enmeshed in linguistic scepticism and scientific determinism, found the empathetic theories of Bergson and Lipps so attractive.

Just as Kant had tried to reconcile belief in individual freedom and self-determination with the rigidity of phenomenal laws, so Bergson denied the validity of determinism by appealing to a fundamental, noumenal self which retained the autonomy and the mystery of the individual, irreducible personality. Like Schopenhauer, he extended this belief in essential quiddity or 'character' from the individual to the whole phenomenal world. Whether one accorded him total credence, or merely regarded his philosophy as a suggestive mythology with the inner logic and coherence of a work of art, the adulation Bergson received in early-twentieth-century Europe made him into a social institution. Riding the contemporary tidal wave of anti-materialism, he gave vivid expression to hitherto unformulated general aspirations and stands out as the leading exponent in a revival of Romantic organicism.

His recurrent theme is that our intelligence, in both its pragmatic outlook and its attempt to represent experience discursively, constantly distorts the true nature of reality. Hence our perception is limited to the data required for a practical response, while even our self-knowledge is restricted to the superficial personality which is engaged in activity. To illustrate the limitations of this motor-based consciousness, he frequently instances Zeno's paradox, which confuses the single, indivisible progression which constitutes a movement with the indefinitely divisible ground which the moving object covers.[33] Scientific observation, he insists, is unable to come to terms with the essential character of movement. It depends on the seizure and juxtaposition of momentary positions of objects. The intervals between these mental photographs may be made almost infinitesimal, but none the less these intervals are elided. Change is only noticed when observable conditions are sufficiently different to be regarded as a new 'state'.[34] The reality of science is thus static; it cannot comprehend continuous duration. It is accordingly totally incompatible with the character of phenomenal life which is constant development: the indeterminate evolution of nature is paralleled by that of the human personality, whose intentions are clarified only in their realisation.[35]

The illusion that reality comprises a series of discrete, juxtaposed entities rather than an indivisible flow is accentuated by the exigencies of language.[36] As a social convention it is directed towards what is universal in human experience, and for the purposes of practical communication this is an advantage. Correspondingly, however, language is unable to convey the unique configuration of each personality, for its inflexible terminology reduces the distinctively individual to the lowest common factor, and the discreteness of its components imposes an arbitrary and misleading fixity on the delicately fugitive modulations of our mental life (cf. Hulme's remarks on the chess-board, p. 62 *supra*).[37] The curious atomistic man of associationist psychology results from the belief that linguistic symbols denote actual rather than arbitrarily fixed entities.[38] The dense intricacy of our subconscious life is incommensurate with language.

This radical anti-intellectualism is, however, counterbalanced by Bergson's reformulation of how absolute rather than merely relative knowledge is possible. An effort of introspection will, Bergson insists, circumvent the distortions inherent in motor-based perception and perpetuated in language. In this fashion we can rediscover our fundamental, noumenal self, which lies buried beneath a crust of automatic, unreflecting responses designed for practical needs, and a layer of apparently disjunct mental states.[39] Like Schopenhauer, Bergson extends this approach to the mechanistic model of experience proposed by scientific aetiology, what Schopenhauer had termed 'the principle of sufficient reason'. Only a radical reorientation of our perception can, he argues, free the intellect from the will's service, where it is content to catalogue relations between objects rather than their inner essence.[40] Thus Bergson defines the artist as someone liberated in one of his senses from the normally practical bias of consciousness and who accordingly possesses the faculty of disinterested contemplation.[41] The artists' genius is their ability to perceive things *in themselves*, not merely superficial phenomena: 'Quand ils regardent une chose, ils la voient pour elle, et non plus pour eux.'[42] Bergson therefore reasserts Schopenhauer's conviction of the mysterious, quasi-spiritual nature of phenomenal life and his belief that sympathetic identification with a creature enables one to penetrate to its essential 'character'.

But 'intuition' is not something restricted to the artist alone. It serves, Bergson argues, as the basis of philosophical method[43] and indeed is the prerequisite for all profound human interaction:

> Mais ce qui est proprement [la personne], ce qui constitue son essence, ne saurait s'apercevoir du dehors, étant intérieur par définition, ni s'exprimer par des symboles, étant incommensurable avec toute autre chose. Description, histoire et analyse me laissent ici dans le relatif. Seule, la coïncidence avec la personne même me donnerait l'absolu.
>
> Il suit de là qu'un absolu ne saurait être donné que dans une *intuition*, tandis que tout le reste relève de l'*analyse*. Nous appelons ici intuition la *sympathie* par laquelle on se transporte à l'intérieur d'un objet pour coïncider avec ce qu'il a d'unique et par conséquent d'inexprimable.[44]

But Bergson offers no correspondingly trenchant explanation of how the impasse of language may be avoided. Before considering this question of expression, however, where predictably Bergson sought confirmation in Symbolist practice, I shall pause to examine Lipps's complementary analysis of non-discursive, symbolic communication, the lucid rationality of which undoubtedly helped to convince Hulme of the validity of Bergson's faith in 'intuition'.

Lipps argues that aesthetic experience occurs through the process of *Hineinleben*, of 'living oneself into' an object through 'self-abandonment' and corresponding imaginative expansion of one's personality.[45] The crucial element is the spiritual *interaction* between percipient and perceived. This is reflected in, but not restricted to, involuntary imitation of the perceived characteristics of the object, which in the appreciation of the plastic arts will probably be physically expressed (compare Berenson's emphasis on 'tactile values') but may remain purely intuitive and unrealised.

He elucidates how such intuitive communication takes place. One's knowledge of another person is necessarily based on extrapolation from one's own personality, utilising the outward signs and gestures of that person – expressions of emotion and movements. If I feel pain, I instinctively utter a sound. If I later hear a sound similar to that with which I expressed my own emotion, then

> I reexperience this emotion, not as an associated idea, but directly *in* the sound.

This seems at first sight merely immediate *sympathetic imagin-*

*ation*. It is actually more. I don't merely have the idea that the emotion is the cause of the sound, but rather I *experience* it. I reproduce it inwardly and do so the more reliably and completely the more I am inwardly wholly absorbed in the sound. I am impelled to celebrate with the rejoicer, to harmonize inwardly with his exultation. And I actually do so if nothing prevents my total self-abandonment to what I hear. This situation, this rejoicing with the joyful expression one hears, may be termed . . . empathy.[46]

The external gestures and activity of the other creature are thus not a 'sign' but a 'symbol' in that they express its character directly, not through external association.[47] The important element is the indivisibility of the process. There is no conscious intellectual link of the gesture to an external meaning. In so far as we respond empathetically to the gesture it *is* for us its meaning, its total and adequate embodiment. To elucidate how we can experience character and emotion through empathy he gives the example of mourning:

The connection between the gesture of mourning and mourning itself . . . is quite *peculiar* and not further *describable* . . . the relationship between the two [may be described] as a sort of *identity* which nevertheless has nothing in common with *logical* identity. The mourning 'manifests' itself and its manifestation *is* the gesture, or this is mourning made manifest. The gesture *is* accordingly mourning, admittedly not mourning in itself, but mourning *manifested*. This is curious, for in other respects the gesture and the mourning are totally incomparable things. Nevertheless this extraordinary state of affairs explains how an inward essence can be contained in a gesture, and generally in the sensuous appearance of an individual; how the body and soul of an individual appear fused together.[48]

Contemplation is thus not merely passive, but an exchange with what we perceive. It differs from mimicry which is conscious repetition of the actions of another, in that we identify immediately with the perceived. We instinctively strive to reproduce the perceived action and

this striving is *immediately connected* to the optical perception, immediately given *in and with it,* so that for my consciousness the optically perceived movement immediately *includes* the striving.

Thus the striving is *objectified* . . . .

Nevertheless the striving doesn't stop being *my* striving nor being felt by me as such. But it is this very same striving which I feel in the optically perceived movement . . . as something immediately belonging to it. . . . In general terms, I feel myself *in a perceived object* striving to complete a movement.[49]

Thus although the activity is our own it appears in contemplative experience as an indivisible extension of the character of the perceived. Through this interaction we experience our own response as the expression of the perceived's character; the division between percipient and perceived elides into fusion. Such pure empathy is, however, rare, and usually remains unrealised, for our rational consciousness normally intervenes to remind us of the disjunction between us and the perceived object.[50]

Hulme's problem, given his linguistic scepticism, was therefore to translate the aesthetic of intuition he derived from Bergson and Lipps into a correspondingly non-discursive literary medium.


## III    *POETIC TECHNIQUE*

In moving from empathetic theory to technical considerations Hulme presents the reader with a minefield of contradictions. His 'Lecture on Modern Poetry' is a confused manifesto, adapting the vigorous polemics of the French Post-Symbolist critics to the situation on this side of the Channel.[51] But, despite his attempt to break free from the Nineties poets, Hulme succeeds only in echoing them or substituting a reductively inadequate poetics.

The 'Lecture' reads in many respects as a reprise of Symons's 'Mr Henley's Poetry' and 'The Decadent Movement in Literature'. Hulme praises the 'jerky rhythms of Henley' and from his relativist position akin to Symons's Paterian sensationalism argues that the characteristic of 'modern' poetry (resembling Symons's Paterian stress on the self-consciousness of modernity) is to have become 'definitely and finally introspective and [deal] with expression and communication of momentary phases in the poet's mind'. Thus the 'mystery of things' is no longer perceived directly as action 'but as an impression, for example Whistler's pictures. . . . What has found expression in painting as Impressionism will soon find expression in poetry as free verse.' As in Symons's Verlainian 'impressionism', the aim of poetry in Hulme's account is to communicate 'some vague mood'.[52]

The apparent distinction is Hulme's advocacy of free verse (Symons had drawn the line at *vers libéré*) but here Hulme's tendentiousness merely results in inconsistencies.[53] His aim is to distinguish his new programme from English 'Symbolism', the constant target of his stylistic criticism, as I indicated earlier apropos poetic diction. To do so he draws on a distinction established by Ribot between two imaginative types: the 'diffluent' or Symbolist, and the 'plastic'.[54]

The diffluent imagination, arising from sentiments not sensations,

> dédaigne la représentation nette et lumineuse du monde extérieur; elle la remplace par une sorte de musique qui aspire à exprimer l'intimité mobile et fugitive de l'âme humaine. C'est l'école du *sujet* 'qui ne veut connaître que la série fuyante de ses états d'âme'. Pour cela, elle use d'une imprécision naturelle ou artificielle; tout flotte dans un rêve, . . . bref, tous les caractères vagues et instables de l'état affectif pur et sans contenu.[55]

It employs images which are described as 'des abstraits, au sens rigoureux, c'est-à-dire des extraits, des simplifications de la donnée sensorielle. Elles agissent, moins par une influence directe que par évocation, suggestion, sous-entendus; elles laissent entrevoir, transparaître: on peut à juste titre les appeler des "idées crépusculaires.".'[56] The plastic imagination is by contrast that of perceptual immediacy:

> celle qui a pour caractères propres la netteté et la précision des formes – plus explicitement: celle dont les matériaux sont des *images* nettes (quelle qu'en soit la nature) se rapprochant de la perception, donnant l'impression de la réalité, et où prédominent les *associations à rapports objectifs*, déterminables avec précision . . . c'est une imagination *extérieure*, issue de la sensation plus que du sentiment et qui a besoin de s'objectiver.[57]

Ribot's classification held obvious attractions for Hulme. In associating the plastic imagination with the perceptual concreteness of the *image* it dovetailed with his linguistic scepticism, distrust of conceptualisation and stress on the visually ostensive quality of language. Yet there was an unacknowledged inconsistency in Hulme's position, revealed if one considers Bergson's proposed method of conveying empathetic 'intuition'. Given the falsification and distortion inherent in language, how can one communicate in a non-discursive fashion? The solution was to suggest 'indirectement par des images', rejecting 'des concepts raides et tout faits' for 'des représentations souples, mobiles, presque fluides, toujours prêtes à se mouler sur les formes fuyantes de l'intuition'.[58] The proximity of the last phrase to the idea of free verse will not have gone unnoticed. And indeed Bergson's literary ideal of Symbolist poetry complemented the connotative qualities of *images* with those of metrical fluidity.

Bergson had argued that the only way to bypass the confusions of spatial analysis and the practical, motor-based consciousness was through contemplative empathy or 'intuition'. The corollary was that because of the similar distortions of language any form of communication must be sympathetic rather than conceptual and hence evoke in one's auditor an intuitive harmony with one's state of mind. This appeal to the inarticulate subconscious implied the use of a purely affective symbolic medium:

> la plupart des émotions sont grosses de mille sensations, sentiments ou idées qui les pénètrent: chacune d'elles est donc un état unique en son genre, indéfinissable, et il semble qu'il faudrait revivre la vie de celui qui l'éprouve pour l'embrasser dans sa complexe originalité. Pourtant l'artiste vise à nous introduire dans cette émotion si riche, si personnelle, si nouvelle, et à nous faire éprouver ce qu'il ne saurait nous faire comprendre. Il fixera donc, parmi les manifestations extérieures de son sentiment, celles que notre corps imitera machinalement, quoique légèrement, en les apercevant, de manière à nous replacer tout d'un coup dans l'indéfinissable état psychologique qui les provoqua.[59]

This stress on 'unconscious imitation' is obviously akin to Lipps's analysis of empathy. In the plastic or performative arts or in everyday behaviour the phenomenon was straightforward; the problem was how to realise this effect in an inherently inadequate linguistic medium. Bergson was clear on what the natue of this objective correlative or symbolic stimulus should be:

Le poète est celui chez qui les sentiments se développent en *images*, et les *images* elles-mêmes en paroles, dociles au rythme, pour les traduire. En voyant repasser devant nos yeux ces *images*, nous éprouverons à notre tour le sentiment qui en était pour ainsi dire l'équivalent émotionnel; mais ces *images* ne se réaliseraient pas aussi fortement pour nous sans les mouvements réguliers du rythme, par lequel notre âme, bercée et endormie, s'oublie comme en un rêve pour penser et pour voir avec le poète.[60]

The crucial point is that Bergson insists that the conceptual distortions of language must be circumvented by non-discursive suggestion, and that for this purpose although perceptual *images* are obviously selected rather than concepts even they require the support of the other affective resources – particularly those of rhythm – which written communication must substitute for the contextual aid of what Searle would term the 'speech act'.

The element of rhythmic fluidity was of obvious importance in Symbolist poetics, for it shared the Bergsonian aim of affective, subliminal communication by suggestion. Yeats's familiar comments provide an apposite gloss:

The purpose of rhythm . . . is to prolong the moment of contemplation . . . by hushing us with an alluring monotony, while it holds us waking by variety, to keep us in that state of perhaps real trance, in which the mind liberated from the pressure of the will is unfolded in symbols.

. . . we would cast out of serious poetry those energetic rhythms, as of a man running, which are the invention of the [practically oriented] will . . . and . . . seek out those wavering, meditative, organic rhythms, which are the embodiment of the imagination.[61]

Given Hulme's Bergsonian linguistic scepticism one grasps immediately why he should argue strenuously for the importance of free verse. It is therefore puzzling that he should then turn round and dismiss the poetic function of rhythm. The reason lies, I believe, in his muddled attempt to dissociate himself from the English Nineties poets, and especially their most eminent representative, Yeats, whose Shakespeare Head *Collected Works* were in press at the time of Hulme's 'Lecture'. This required him to eliminate ruthlessly those aspects of Bergson's poetics which resembled the diffluent imagination and musicality of Symbolism (and hence Yeats), retaining only those compatible with a vaguely 'plastic' imagination.

Hulme's attempted debunking of Yeats, signposted in the 'Notes on Language and Style', is implicit in the iconoclastic, but somewhat disingenuous dismissal of transcendentalism which introduces the 'Lecture' (*FS*, 98, 67). It emerges undisguised in Hulme's bold distinction between two sorts of verse: that which is 'read' and that which is 'chanted' (the latter unavoidably associated with Yeats and Florence Farr). This, declares Hulme unwarrantedly, requires regular metre; the former 'method of recording impressions by visual images in distinct lines' does not. It will be obvious that Hulme is suggesting ridiculously a necessary correlation between a fixed verse-form and inflexible metrical monotony. His all-exclusive classification is thus regular metre versus free verse and visual images. The special pleading, already disquieting, now approaches farce. For, having argued for metrical freedom (following both Kahn and Bergson), Hulme in the interests of his attack on Yeats then dismisses the effect of rhythm, and indeed all the aural qualities of poetry, as irrelevant:

> The effect of rhythm, like that of music, is to produce a kind of hypnotic state [Bergson's 'rêve', Yeats's 'trance'], during which suggestions of grief or ecstasy are easily and powerfully effective. . . . This is for the art of chanting, but the procedure of the new visual art is just the contrary. It depends for its effect not on a kind of half sleep produced, but on arresting the attention, so much so that the succession of visual images should exhaust one.
>
> Regular metre to this impressionist poetry is cramping, jangling, meaningless, and out of place. Into the delicate pattern of images and colour it introduces the heavy, crude pattern of rhetorical verse.    (*FS*, 73–4; cf. 75)

Even within this quotation Hulme's divided aims are painfully apparent. The 'new visual art' is described as being 'delicate', but nevertheless 'exhausting'. Clearly he is determined to proclaim that it will be a dynamic rejoinder to the 'hypnotic' Nineties ('soporific' would doubtless be closer to his intention). Its distinctively poetic qualities are, however, conspicuous by their absence. One learns that its metre will not be 'hypnotic' but otherwise its role is seemingly ineffectual or aesthetically neutral. The desire to attack Yeats has led Hulme to sacrifice wilfully a major connotative element in poetry, dismissing categorically the possibility that rhythm could help to evoke the 'vague mood' he desires to communicate. Hulme's obsession with the ostensive qualities of the *image*, divorced from its affective context, has been made the basis of a theoretical and reductively sterile poetics:

> [Poetry] is not a counter language, but a visual concrete one. It is a compromise for a language of intuition which would hand over sensations bodily. It always endeavours to arrest you, and to make you continuously see a physical thing, to prevent you gliding through an abstract process.   (*FS*, 10)

There is in Hulme's theory nothing to distinguish poetry from prose; his only criterion of excellence is sincerity: the ability to avoid 'counters', 'clichés', 'catchwords' or 'reflex speech', the automatic and second-hand in diction, which he links to the Nineties poets. (For detailed treatment of this point see my 'New Sources for Imagism'.[62])

The result is a truncated Symbolist aesthetic: 'Say the poet is moved by a certain landscape, he selects from that certain images which, put into juxtaposition in separate lines, serve to suggest and to evoke the state he feels' (*FS*, 73). Presumably, if one compares the quotation on p. 74 *supra*, this would resemble a cinematographic impressionism, intentionally discordant and with an absurd hypertrophy in its visual aspects.[63] The linguistic quest for the immediacy of the perceptually proximate *image* leads bizarrely to a poetry which, in theory at least, comprises merely visual montage: recalling, like some of Symons's poetry, the perceptual characteristics of French Impressionism.

Nevertheless, like Symons's, Hulme's conception of 'impressionist' poetry was not restricted to this sensationalist immediacy, but gave equal weight to subjectivist, empathetic perception. This was, however, accompanied by self-conscious insecurity about literature, which led Hulme to belittle what he regarded as Yeats's extravagant pronouncements and probably contributed to his premature abandonment of poetry.[64] Characteristically his records of epiphanic experiences are qualified by diffidence or reticence in maintaining their validity.

Hence in considering the question of inspiration Hulme is

sceptical, emphasising the artificiality and in many cases the factitiousness of literature:

> The beauty of London only seen in detached and careful moments, never continuously, always a conscious effort. . . . Life as a rule tedious, but certain things give us sudden lifts. Poetry comes with the jumps. . . . The moments of ecstasy.
>     Literature, like memory, selects only the vivid patches of life.   (*FS*, 99)

Hulme is outlining what might be termed a poetics of epiphanies; yet he is honest enough to admit that such moments are rare.

Conceding the artistic validity of epiphanies, but obsessed by their ephemerality, in his poetry Hulme constantly undercuts the sublime moment, while in his 'Notes' belittling the practical importance of such numinous experience (see, for example, *FS*, 95). 'Drink' (*FS*, 99–100) is a pastiche of just such fulsome emotions, hinting that the afflatus of the literary man and the drunkard result from similar artificial intoxication. This distrust of unqualified emotionality and his philosophical relativism determined Hulme's notorious rejection of the extravagant 'capital letterism' of Romanticism (the cosmic Idealism of Hegel, Schelling, Coleridge and Shelley) for the stylistic 'sincerity' underlying 'fancy' which denotes crisp precision in linguistic usage and the ability to create vivid images (*Spec*, 126–38). His belief that 'beauty may be in small, dry things' corresponds to a Schopenhauerian position restricting poetry to an empathetic interaction with the phenomenal world:

> wherever you get an extraordinary interest in a thing, a great zest in its contemplation which carries on the contemplator to accurate description . . . there you have sufficient justification for poetry.   (*Spec*, 131)

> I am using contemplation here just in the same way that Plato used it, only applied to a different subject; it is a detached interest. 'The object of aesthetic contemplation is something framed apart by itself and regarded without memory or expectation, simply as being itself, as end not means, as individual not universal'.   (*Spec*, 136)

In the 'Lecture' he states expressly, 'the first time I ever felt the necessity or inevitableness of verse, was in the desire to reproduce the peculiar quality of feeling which is induced by the flat spaces and wide horizons of the virgin prairie of western Canada' (*FS*, 72). He is surely describing a numinous experience.

His most comprehensive statements of his poetic aim in the years 1907–12 emphasise the contemplative isolation of the aesthetic object: 'Dome of Brompton in the mist. Transfer that to art. Dead things not men as the material of art. Everything for art is a thing in itself, cf. the café at Clapham as a thing in itself' (*FS*, 82). Hulme's phraseology derives from Bergson's Schopenhauerian definition of the artist, as paraphrased in 'Bergson's Theory of Art'.[65] The following section elaborates the poetic treatment of such an epiphanic moment. The allusion in its title to Ribot indicates Hulme's determination to avoid the stylistic extravagances he associated with the Symbolist, diffluent imagination and which was reflected in the ironic tone of his poetry:

### Example of Plastic Imagination

The two tarts walking along Piccadilly on tiptoe, going home, with hat on back of head. Worry until could find the exact model analogy that will reproduce the extraordinary effect they produce. Could be done at once by an artist in a blur. The air of absolute detachment, of being things in themselves. . . . Disinterestedness, as though saying: We may have evolved painfully from the clay, and be the last leaf on a tree. But now we have cut ourselves away from that. We are things-in-themselves. We exist out of time.   (*FS*, 82)

The delicate poise of Hulme's position is confirmed by the self-conscious diffidence of 'Autumn', 'Above the Dock' and 'The Man in the Crow's Nest' in which the sea and the heavens are cosily domesticated whereas in a Romantic lyric they might inspire unqualified, sublime exaltation (*Spec*, 265, 266; *FS*, 214).[66] An examination of the evolution of 'A City Sunset' reveals Hulme's stylistic wrestling with another empathetic moment.

All versions depend on the perception of an imaginative identity between the sunset and a seductive woman. In the two versions which Jones prints, 'Sunset' and 'Sunset (II)' Hulme draws a contrast between a fiery and a more tranquil sunset.[67] The draft of the second stanza of 'Sunset' in Hulme's 'Free Verse' notebook (now in Keele University Library) is markedly more diffuse. After the first two lines it reads,

> As a ship from the sea
> With spread sail. dull red
> Shadow'd sharp under the haven's hill
> A ship of embassy. long desired
> That quiet, into cool harbour glides
> In the time of long shadows
> + creeping light.

The somewhat rank alliteration in the third line is pruned back with the substitution of 'against the darkening sky' for 'under the haven's hill'. The attempt in line 4 to evoke connotations of vague yearning is discarded. What remains is purely visual and is made more compact. The descriptive 'glides' is dropped from line 5, leaving the image simply presented, and the periphrastic lines 6 and 7 are reduced to 'At eve' and 'After work' – a literal example of the 'crepuscular spirit' being made more precise.

In the next version the maritime section has disappeared and Hulme focusses exclusively on the *city* sunset, introducing the suggestion that the poet's subjective impression of early evening derives from an imaginative association of the sunset with the prostitutes who appear at the same time. This draft is similar to 'A City Sunset', reprinted by Hynes (*FS*, 214–15) from *For Christmas MDCCCCVIII*.[68] Differences between the manuscript and the printed version are again in the direction of simple visual presentation. The first three lines of the manuscript read,

> Earth seducing. with high conceits
> is the sunset. thaumaturgic. presenting
> at the end of westward streets . . .

In the printed version the connotative 'thaumaturgic' with its Symbolist associations has disappeared and the syntactic link which 'presenting' effected with lines 4–7 is excised, leaving the images juxtaposed. Hulme's less felicitous early style survives in the vagueness of 'with high conceits', 'troubling strangely' and 'alien to long streets' (in the manuscript this is the more incisive 'in the street's mud') and the feebly erotic allusiveness of lines 6–7, which jar with the more striking 'fretted city roofs' in which the epithet implies an imaginative identity between the 'dress' of the sky, the soliciting woman and the decaying cityscape.

The final version, perhaps Hulme's best poem, completes the process of concision:

### Sunset

> A coryphée, covetous of applause,
> Loth to leave the stage,
> With final diablerie, poises high her toe.
> Displays scarlet lingerie of carmin'd clouds,
> Amid the hostile murmur of the stalls.

(*FS*, 219)

The form of the earlier versions had been an implicit simile, but this is now indicated by the title alone. The mere association of the sunset and the woman (now dancer rather than prostitute) is replaced by superimposition, which fuses the two into a single image. The result, ironically in view of Hulme's attack on Symbolism, is a deceptively subtle blend of a mental state with what becomes an equivocally 'external' scene. Contemplation and interpretation combine in a witty imaginary landscape, which offers a metaphorical correlative for the poet's empathetic perception.

In revising his poems Hulme eliminated similes, creating superposition instead of comparison. In line 3 of 'Autumn (II)', for instance, 'seemed' becomes 'were'; line 6 of 'The Embankment', 'The old star-eaten blanket of the sky', is a reduction of the less arresting 'Somewhere the gods (the blanket-makers in the prairie of cold)/Sleep in their blankets.'[69] In 'Susan Ann and Immortality' Hulme's distillation of an earlier draft leaves the essence of the experience which forms the basis of a perceptual equation. Hulme wrote originally, 'Till she thinks the earth is the sky'. In his final draft he extends this confused intimation to its logical outcome in the woman's blurred perception:

> Till the earth was sky,
> Sky that was green,
> And brown clouds passed
> Like chestnut leaves along the ground.

The simile framework (she thinks . . . ) is dismantled, leaving merely the stark statement of identity – 'the earth was sky'. One might compare H.D.'s more skilful handling of a similar perception in 'Oread'.[70]

This removal of the intermediate mental stages in the simile, what could be described as a poetic syllogism, results in daring juxtapositions. Without proceeding so far as parataxis, Hulme nevertheless melts links in the chain of mental associations, leaving disjunct statements which the reader must himself expand to discover their original intuitive connection:

> the black cliffs of your shoe . . .
> cambric surf all foamed with lace . . .
> So see I, her white cloud petticoat,
> Clear Valenciennes, meshed by twisted cowls,
> Rent by tall chimneys, torn lace, frayed and fissured.[71]

These lines stand out against frequently lax use of language: the second example comes from a stanza which contains the vacuous 'My dreaming languorous voyage'. Hulme fought against this limp emotionalism to develop an empathetic Symbolist technique, a sort of metaphoric rhyme which transforms simile into synonymity in associative short-cuts. This innovative method of assembling images (which the Nineties poets had not fully grasped in French Symbolism) was further developed by the later Imagists and assures the historical importance of Hulme's minor poetic experiments, which have otherwise been inexplicably overvalued.

## IV  *FLINT*

The essential continuity of the 'forgotten school' with the 1890s is confirmed by Flint, whose early work is significant chiefly for his response to Symbolism. His own position is established in a fascinating paper, 'Of the thing called "symbolism" & other considerations', delivered to a poetry discussion-group in April 1907.[72] Flint notes that all their group, largely under Symons's influence, instinctively adopt a supposedly 'symbolist' style as the appropriate mode for *avant-garde* poetry (what Flint termed 'the new poetry of mood and emotion'). But in practice they reduce 'symbolism' to a stylistic mannerism, combining limp synaesthesia with vaguely transcendental intimations. To instance this 'incompleteness of thought', 'incoherency' and near meaninglessness he cites,

> Beloved: where shall we end? . . .
> A void firmament thy love, and mine
> Unending wave on wave of foaming wine.
> Beloved: we have no end.

Flint's reading of Mallarmé (he translates selectively from the response to Huret's *Enquête*[73]) enabled him to cast a cold eye on such pastiche late Symons. He was, however, equally dissatisfied with the increasing obliquity and tenuity of Mallarmé's later style, whose flaw, in Flint's view, lay in pursuing imaginative evocation so absolutely as to lose touch completely with phenomenal reality.

Flint's poetic ideal was accordingly determined by the need to reconcile his instinctive anti-materialism with his distrust of the hermetic aspects of Symbolism:

> I have come to judge poetry by the amount of elemental ache in it, of a kind of cosmic consciousness; I seek to find in it a new opening of the eyes on the world, a new Renascence of Wonder. This, of need, must be suggested, must be the esoteric, or 'symbolistic', part of the poem; but along with it . . . must go a body, an outward form, a portrayal of sensorial objects, a picture, that is, which will be the vehicle of an emotion more or less apparent according to the sensibility of the reader.

Like Hulme, therefore, Flint is closer to an empathetic than an Idealist poetics, which would respond emotionally and imaginatively to the external world, restoring its spiritual significance without neglecting its physical actuality. In practice this implied adopting an empathetic Symbolist technique in which, to use Pound's phrase, 'the natural object is always the *adequate* symbol',[74] without proceeding as far as objectivism. For poetry in Flint's account was almost exclusively a matter of conveying the poet's emotional experience.

Although Flint added that the finest example of his poetic ideal was Yeats, his admiration was far from unreserved. In reviewing a reissue of *Poems* (1895) he criticised the artist Yeats's 'complicat[ion] by a mystic philosopher, pleasing himself in a somewhat arid symbolism', unfavourably contrasting the 'brooding subtlety' of 'The Two Trees' and the 'Rose' poems with 'the perfect imaginative emotional simplicity' of *The Countess Kathleen* and *The Land of Heart's Desire*.[75] He reinforced the point by dismissing Yeats's account of the magical properties of symbols, while praising Yeats's own exemplification both in his poetry and in the quotation chosen from Burns of 'emotional' symbolism (which Flint terms 'abstract' symbolism as opposed to 'concrete', or Yeatsian 'intellectual', symbolism).[76] Flint's lack of sympathy with Yeats's Neoplatonic theories (unlike Pound, as discussed in Chapter 6), which he branded as 'philosophy', led him to restrict Symbolism to a rather effete Romanticism.[77] He would have profited from a more vigorous curb to the instinctive mawkishness which devalued both his poetry and criticism.

Thus he praises the 'abstract symbolism' of Shelley's 'Euganean Hills' on largely sentimental grounds:

> the spirit of the place and Shelley's emotion act and interact one on the other until one has that image of perfect poetry: a man and his frailty and desires amid the mystery and wonder of Nature, crying out his trouble like the song in the night of some melancholy beautiful bird.[78]

Flint's principal critical criterion of excellence is affective: each re-reading of Yeats's poetry provided him with a voluptuous escapism in which he seemed

> to penetrate deeper into the emotional mystery of life; one's spirit is steeped in the waters of Eden and made clean and invested with the poet's robe of beauty, so that one becomes unfit for the grimy brutality and carking ugliness of the world's nightmarish present.[79]

This aesthetic revulsion from the ugliness of urban life, and his instinctive need for an anti-materialist cosmology frequently tempted Flint to overvalue stylistically worthless literature from a sentimental sympathy with its theme.[80] It is largely because of this continually resurfacing emotionalism which effectively nullified his technical experimentation and wide reading that Flint remains a minor poet.

The main area of Flint's experimentation concerned the role of what he termed 'cadence'.[81] Unlike Hulme, with his insensitivity to metre, Flint fully grasped the importance to a Symbolist technique of free verse. In 'Of the thing called "symbolism"' he wrote 'Language, indeed, is a very crude thing – a very clumsy pair of forceps with which to grasp and show those subtle things, emotions; and therefore there must be suggestion, and rhythms also: for all emotions are rythmic [*sic*]'. The burden of his early review articles is accordingly a programmatic defence of the poet's need for flexible techniques of 'subtle rhythms and broken cadences' to convey 'the brief fragments of his soul's music'.[82] One quotation will do duty for all:

> A poet should listen to the individual rhythm within him before he turns, if ever, to the accepted form. He should not be content to grind an iambic barrel-organ, for instance. Beauty, emotion, and supple rhythm are the essentials of good poetry.[83]

The final sentence encapsulates the nature and the limitations of Flint's aesthetic, comprising the late nineteenth-century criterion of 'Beauty', metrical freedom, and his affective touchstone. In practice: imaginative indeterminacy in emotional suggestion and – escapism.

The dominant theme of Flint's poetry is the need to assert his imaginative detachment from the depressing ugliness of London. He survives its constricting soullessness only by ruralist nostalgia, like the Georgians, or by subjecting it to aesthetic transformation. The appealing 'A Song of Change' represents this strategy, relating how in the poet's imagination the 'god return[s] to his gaze' and he escapes to a rich mythical world only to return from this ideal beauty to mundane reality and the malignant intrusion of decay and death.[84] Here the fantasy borders on an imaginative metamorphosis similar to Pound's early poetry, and indeed 'Palinode' (1907) resembles Pound's 'La Fraisne' in its attempted evocation of an imaginative experience of suggestive mystical significance at variance with the hostile everyday world.[85]

Flint's idiom resembles that of Pound's early poetry, emphasising their common reliance on the Pre-Raphaelites and the Nineties poets, above all Yeats. The principal difference is that Flint's work is also influenced by French Symbolism, frequently yoked by violence with pastiche Yeats. Despite Flint's advocacy of free verse, many poems are in regular stanzaic forms, gesturing like Symons's in the direction of Symbolist suggestivity mainly through enjambement and aural patterning with pronounced assonance and alliteration, and also by somewhat facile synaesthesia.[86] To catalogue stylistic characteristics in this fashion appears reductive, but the procedure is in fact invited by the derivativeness of Flint's early poems which frequently dissolve into their sources.

In 'Distance' and 'Sketch', for example, Flint depends on Pre-Raphaelite iconography to create a religious aura and mystical significance for meetings with his lover.[87] This temperamental need, like Pound's, to redeem the modern world by transforming it into something rich and strange, underlay his many imitations of Yeats. The Yeatsian aspirations of the sequence 'In the Net of the Stars' are revealed (like Pound's 'Laudantes Decem') in the titles of the individual poems.[88] Flint's 'He thinks of Her Lineage', for example, draws on such poems as 'He remembers Forgotten Beauty' but relies on *assertions* of the ethereality and the supernatural quality of his lover rather than creating any technical effects of strangeness. Thus the poem remains a series of referential statements productive merely of a decorative patina. Similarly, in 'He sings a Song in the Garden of Night' images of cosmic magnitude or sublimity are crudely linked with the lover in the hope, to put it bluntly, that some of the assumed imaginative power will rub off.[89] The metaphors remain contiguous rather than fused, however; their attempts at introducing the portentous, factitious:

> O Love, your little bosoms are
> More to me than the death of a star . . .
> In the white lilies of your limbs
> Is woven the frenzy of the winds
> That blow upon earth's mountain wings. . . .
> And dim eternities lie pressed
> Between my breast and your white breast.

The last two lines above are a particularly striking example of the fashionable tendency of English 'Symbolist' epigones to attempt effecting an aura of mystery by employing abstract vague immensities as concrete nouns with the resulting incongruity which Flint had himself criticised. One stanza of the poem breaks free from this pattern, however:

O Love, I think within your eyes
Is the hush that follows the night's outcries
On silent lakes where brood the stars
Between the dreaming nenuphars.

By developing the metaphor into an extended and suggestive
panorama, aided by the enjambement, assonance and sound play
on sibilants and fricatives, and languid rhythms, Flint atmospherically evokes a mood. The choice of 'nenuphars' indicates his French
inspiration here;[90] and indeed this alternation between French and
pastiche Nineties Symbolism is the most distinctive quality of his
poetry.

The salient example is 'Monody':

Along the road the wind is blowing red
Rose petals and they wed
The brown-grey sand.
In my hand
I hold the roses, and –
Alas! their root was buried
In the heart
Of all my hope.
My blood had coloured them.
I shaped them when –
Past many a horoscope,
Starred
On the roof of space, –
The ship of earth was ferried
Across the pool of night.

Now on the windy hill I stand,
Red roses in my hand,
And the root withered in my heart.

Along the road the wind is blowing red
Rose petals and they wed
The brown-grey sand.
The roses of my hope and heart dispart.[91]

Most of the poem is inspired by Verlaine, with its deliberately
restricted vocabulary, conscious repetitions, and sound-play.

Consider the subconscious patterns and associations established in the opening lines: road–red–rose, wind–wed, sand–hand–hold– and, roses–root, heart–hope. Here the alliteration and assonance counterpoint the rhyme scheme to create a rhythmic sinuosity whose suggestiveness complements the colour-contrasts and controlled, objective presentation. But this style jars gratingly with the obtrusive, detachable conceit in lines 10–15, which is purely a feeble decoration in the cosmic, pseudo-mystical, 'Symbolist' idiom one finds also in early Pound, particularly in the contemporaneous *A Lume Spento* (1908). Compare Flint's 'Stellar', which even falls back on exclamation marks as necessary intensifiers for its desired aura of sublimity.[92] When Flint, like Pound, was able to ditch this derivative style the result was the empathetic Symbolist technique of allowing the external scene to stand as an implicit metaphor for the poet's mental state.

The mingling of France and Yeats (in this case largely of poetic *topoi*) is again apparent in 'The Mask of Gold. ii At a Concert' which begins with bitter-sweet Verlainian melancholia (probably inspired by *Fêtes galantes*) associating autumnal decay with sobbing violins and the ineffectual consolation of a flute. Imagine the reader's surprise therefore at the concluding stanza:

> Loosen your long gold hair, and let it flow
> About me, sweet; for I would fain forget –
> My head upon your breast, eyes dim and wet –
> What you and I may know and do not know.[93]

Appropriately this Nineties luxuriance in sexual and intellectual passivity introduces the final poem of the sequence, 'His Plea', which in conception is close to Yeats's 'He wishes his Beloved were Dead' and is replete almost to the point of caricature with the mannerisms of the period – the limp emotionality, the flowing, perfumed, amber hair, and eyes with a glint of chrysoprase.[94]

Flint is at his most original and significantly his most successful in isolated poems inspired by French Symbolism, which with reticent objectivity employ a distinctly visualised external scene as an equivalent for his state of mind. These correspond to his empathetic Symbolist ideal of emotional suggestivity firmly grounded in the representation of phenomenal reality and anticipate Pound's Imagist procedures.

'Unto us a Child is Born' is obscure partly because of the careless state in which Flint has abandoned the working-out of his ideas and partly because of a genuinely suggestive imaginative power. The poem's theme is that he and his wife's inherited 'primeval' desire for children is threatened by their other inheritance, the industrial world. Parental responsibility to provide for their child necessitates abandoning their cherished elemental world of the imagination for the materialist world which alone will provide a living. Overall the poem is an artistic failure, with a certain wilful preciosity and attempted portentousness which sometimes falls flat. The first section is, however, impressive and suggests Maeterlinck's influence in the heightened significance with which it seeks to supercharge intensely felt natural details:

> HE: The birds are fearful in the twilight hour;
> They circle and flutter on the surcharged air,
> Then drop like plummets towards the water's lap,
> As if to explore the branches mirrored there,
> And frightened turn away again and scream, –
> As if Life's enigma peered out at them.
> But we are only filled with the world's pain,
> And hushed and deadened by the city's roar.
> Will they not cease? – they tear my timid heart.

As the poem progresses the dialogue seems to reveal the lake as an actual scene they are observing, but there is no firm distinction between vivid description:

> See, a fish
> Leaps from the water and then falls again.
> Perhaps he leapt into the warm air to feel
> The coldness fold on him.

and symbolic import.[95]

This presentational technique is paralleled by 'Evening', which combines close description with disquieting, sinister intimations:

> One rose petal
> Falls to the moss
> With the weight of dew, –
> Dusky red on darkening green.

A red rose trembles
In the twilight –
Glimmering silence
And sleeping things.

In the dun earth
Beneath the mosses,
A rosetree tightens
Its lace of roots;

And the earth quivers.
What is passing?
What is present? –
Dusky red on darkening green.[96]

The poem is top-heavy with portentousness, its slight body unable to bear the weight of significance which Flint intends. The prominent alliteration and use of colour-contrasts are reminiscent not only of 'Monody', but also of Symons's early poems, and indeed this 'impressionist' technique forms the crucial link between the 1890s and Imagism. One can, I think, discriminate between the effect of this poem and Flint's other 'Symbolist' work. The scene is undoubtedly intended to evoke a mood, but the unusually elaborate attention devoted to phenomenal minutiae, and the merely implicit imaginative engagement of lines 11–12, foreshadow H.D.'s objectivist techniques.

The natural world thus becomes important for its own sake rather than merely as an index of the poet's consciousness. The impression of indeterminate significance – related in my earlier definition to the objectivist poet's unwillingness to guide his reader's response but merely to vividly present the object as inherently interesting – is accentuated by the final line of the poem, in which Flint pointedly declines to offer an interpretation. Only rarely did his later work display such reticence.

Flint's poetry offers accordingly a compendium of the influences of the age. His mingling of Yeatsian with French Symbolism reveals him at a crossroads prior to breaking free from an imaginatively exhausted idiom. Nevertheless isolated poems already foreshadow his development towards the empathetic Symbolist techniques of Imagism, and these, together with his championship and fitful employment of free verse, earn his place i' th' story.

The importance of the 'forgotten school' lies therefore not in its actual achievement, but in the difficult task it undertook of initiating the process of poetic renewal. Hulme stands out as the leading figure: a dilettante poet but an extremely important catalyst. His significance lies in the poetic and aesthetic results of his critique of Idealism and subsequent espousal of a metaphysical, empathetic aesthetics.

The historically valuable stylistic iconoclasm which Hulme's relativism inspired preluded his occasional employment of an empathetic Symbolist technique. In this he was joined by Flint, whose poetry, under the influence of French Symbolism, began to break free from the exhausted idiom of the preceding generation.

Of greater significance for my study, however, is Hulme's Lippsian and Bergsonian empathetic aesthetic. This, I shall argue, represents the spirit of the age in post-Impressionist painting and poetry: the shared anti-materialist outlook which unifies Futurism, German Expressionism and Imagism/Vorticism.

# 4 The New 'Classicism'

In following the evolution of Imagism/Vorticism, my path now intersects with Edwardian politics. Chapter 3 analysed Hulme's literary theory; I shall now examine how he developed the new 'classical', 'religious' attitude which led him to switch his interest from literature to the visual arts, before considering in Chapter 5 the close relationship between literary and artistic movements in pre-war England which conditioned the Imagist/Vorticist aesthetic.

The so-called new 'Classicism' has for many years made an obligatory appearance in discussions of Hulme, Eliot and Lewis, mostly detached from its original context with, accordingly, often irrelevant critical speculation. But this puzzling aesthetic reorientation becomes much more comprehensible if viewed in its contemporary setting and this will therefore be my approach in this chapter.

'Romantic' and 'classic' are now for better or worse established critical terms, used either with a precise literary historical reference or else to denote a particular approach to literature, involving either subjectivity or objectivity, the use of a strict stylistic form or restrained diction. Yet in Edwardian England they were primarily gambits in ideological debate. Facile equations could be established at the individual's whim: for example, Bergsonism = Romanticism = Liberalism. I shall now try to recapture this forgotten atmosphere of political aesthetics, which provides the crucial context for Hulme's rejection of Bergsonism and hence of an empathetic theory of art in favour of abstraction. Two journalists who were colleagues of Hulme – J. M. Kennedy and Anthony Ludovici – are here of vital importance. Their crude cultural parallels, inspired by Nietzsche, distort aesthetics into ideological propaganda and equate artistic styles with desirable social structures. Whether under the influence of Kennedy or Ludovici or not, bizarre as it may now appear, Hulme and Storer's politically motivated change in aesthetic outlook was actually characteristic of the age. Ronald Schuchard's formulation of the widely held view that 'Hulme was the first twentieth-century Englishman to take an important critical stance against the protean forms of Romanticism and Liberalism',[1] will accordingly receive some major qualifications.

There was in Edwardian England a keen interest in theories concerning the organisation of the state. Writers were frequently more involved in political than in stylistic speculation. The prevailing tendency in politics was towards Liberalism, but this was countered by various élitist theories, and among the radical Right there was a common search for an aristocratic revival in art and in social and political life. Social Darwinism, which then enjoyed widespread currency, notably in Galton's eugenic theories, maintained that it was men's 'religious duty' to further the progress of evolution by fostering 'superior strains' of men and women and discouraging the reproduction of 'sickly breeds'. In 1908 a Eugenics Education Society was formed in England, and in 1909 the *Eugenics Review* founded.[2]

Such movements bore witness to a deep-seated sense of insecurity. Edwardian England was undergoing a transition from a social classification on the basis of birth, largely tied to an outmoded agrarian economy, to one based on wealth, reflecting the increasing pre-eminence of cosmopolitan financiers. Plutocracy was replacing aristocracy. At the same time the Tory Party, displaced from government and unable to win elections following the Liberal landslide of 1906, and faced with increased Labour representation in the Commons, was under direct attack through the Parliament Bill designed to curb the refractory House of Lords and its rebellious predominance of Tory peers. Battle-lines were drawn up between those who believed in egalitarian democracy and those who attempted to hold on desperately to hereditary privileges. The alternatives at the time appeared to be either the prospect of mass enfranchisement or else the maintenance of a rigidly stratified, hierarchical society. It was the latter which Hulme, Storer, Ludovici and, more equivocally, Kennedy preferred.

Their search for arguments to justify this 'classical', oligarchical form of polity led to Nietzsche, whose rise to popularity in England between 1909 and 1913[3] coincided strikingly with his pragmatic importance for the political ideology of the Edwardian radical Right. Ludovici and Kennedy were among the translators of the first complete English edition of Nietzsche between 1896 and 1913; the former used Nietzschean arguments to reinforce publicly his own instinctive hatred of the masses, Kennedy to supplement his home-grown Churchillian 'Tory democracy'. Storer and Hulme found their reading of his theories attractively confirmed in the literary criticism of the French Nietzschean and member of *L'Action française*, Pierre Lasserre. I must begin therefore by considering some aspects of Nietzsche's philosophy. I shall then explain his vital influence on Ludovici and Kennedy before, in the second section of the chapter, examining how his arguments were mediated for Hulme and Storer.


I   *'THROUGH A GLASS, DARKLY': NIETZSCHE AND THE NIETZSCHEANS*

The problematic nature (and correspondingly the fecundity) of Nietzsche's views arises from his uneasy attempt to integrate what in the abstract is an attractive ideal – optimum self-realisation – into a social context. There is an unresolved tension between a philosophy of existentialist self-overcoming and the place which such individuals could actually adopt in society. Capitalising on this, the English Tories appropriated the abstract framework of Nietzsche's anti-democratic élitism, to transform his advocacy of an oligarchic meritocracy into a defence of hereditary, aristocratic privilege.

The prime contention of Nietzsche's mature philosophy is that there are two conflicting moral systems – 'master morality' and 'slave morality' – which embody the characteristics of these opposed social castes. In the aristocratic code, compassion is scorned as a mark of weakness; rights exist only among equals; patronising 'sympathy' towards those lower in the social hierarchy is simply a means for the aristocrat to channel his superabundance of power. The expedient slave morality, by contrast, emphasises those qualities which alleviate practically the common burden of suffering: sympathy, compassion and humility. Innocuous emotions are designated 'good', while 'evil' denotes the terrifying, dangerous results of uncontrolled power (*WdB*, II, 730–3).

Nietzsche traces the struggle for supremacy between these two opposed ideologies to the Jewish 'slave-revolt in morality' (*WdB*, II, 653). Politically impotent within the Roman Empire, the world's strongest aristocratic hierarchy, the only way the Jews could assert their identity was by taking intellectual revenge, in a subversion of the aristocratic morality. Their priests disseminated the doctrine that the qualities denoted by the whole word-field of secular power and eminence were 'evil'. Their impotent yet implacable hatred – *ressentiment* – exalted the poor, lowly, suffering and sick as 'good'. A future life of heavenly blessings was promised in compensation for present torment, when the powerful aristocratic caste, now labelled 'godless', would be condemned to eternal damnation (*WdB*, II, 779–80).

Christianity, Nietzsche maintains, developed directly from this Jewish ethical revolution. The Christian religion of love is a sublimation of Jewish *ressentiment* in a rebellion of the earthly pariahs and failures against aristocratic breeding and success. Nietzsche supports this contention by analysing the imposition of Christianity on the Germanic race, who, having establish un-challenged supremacy over the indigenous slave races of Europe, fell victim to a civilising process of *taming*. The unpredictable, barbaric energy which had assured their national hegemony was then channelled against them by priests who labelled their natural instincts 'evil' and, through the creation of 'bad conscience', rendered their cruelty and will to power self-consumptive.[4]

Nietzsche's point is that, although the individual capacity for self-transcendence depends on innate vigour, the mass of men who lack this vital force fear the aristocrat's creative but potentially anarchic energy, which they attempt to curb through insidious social and moral pressure towards conformity.[5] This must be construed as a *political* as well as an ethical stratagem, a negation of 'the world' itself, the values and conditions of ascending life.

Nietzsche stresses the political character of this contest between master morality and slave morality in later history. He cites the Renaissance Neo-Classical revival of the cultivated man of *virtù*, which was thwarted by the English and German Reformation, a movement of vulgar *ressentiment*. Similarly the cultural aristocracy of seventeenth- and eighteenth-century France fell victim to the French Revolution, a plebeian movement of *ressentiment*, ironically just before Napoleon, the last great political aristocrat, made a mockery of their doctrine of universal equality.[6]

Nietzsche's indignation at this recurrent suppression of the intellectual aristocracy was exacerbated by his reading of Darwin. Despite human evolution, Nietzsche concluded, there was less of a difference between man and the higher primates than between these and the lower primates. History showed no progress in that gifted individuals appeared in all ages indiscriminately, while the average human being was scarcely distinguishable in his herd instinct from animals. The distinctively human qualities which alone would validate mankind could only be cultivated if this inadequate specimen were greatly surpassed by the redevelopment of an aristocratic élite of 'supermen': powerful, intellectually independent individuals.[7] Given that natural selection usually promoted the mediocre, rather than the isolated individual whose more complex constitution rendered him more vulnerable, this goal could only be achieved by creating a social structure in which the extraordinary would thrive.

This ideal would, however, conflict totally with most existing polities and the Christian humanitarianism of both socialism and liberalism, or what Nietzsche termed the 'herd animal morality' of contemporary Europe (*WdB*, II, 659–62). Such egalitarian sympathy with the diseased and unsuccessful was, Nietzsche argued, the will to self-destruction, the 'décadence-Moral'.[8] Enduring strength depended on the dynamic capacity to master either one's baser self or external adversity. Yet the social valetudinarianism of democracy abolished the challenging element of strife which was indispensable to the dialectic advance of the species. Its malignant consequence was the contemporary European disease, paralysis of the will.[9]

The remedy which Nietzsche prescribed was a hierarchical polity. For a strong social structure rested, he contended, on the 'pathos of distance', the will to distinguish oneself, between the naturally ranked castes (*WdB*, II, 1013–14, 1205–6). Only through the observance of marked stratification within society did the aristocratic desire for ever-higher inner cultivation arise. By contrast democratic legislature to promote the chimerical ideal of 'the common good' sought to control individual activity, resulting in a general levelling into mediocrity. A truly enlightened polity would therefore aim instead to establish an élite caste by sacrificing the mass of the people to incomplete personal development and physical drudgery in order to provide a secure foundation from which a single, stronger species could evolve.[10]

In early Edwardian England the possibility of establishing an aristocratic caste to remedy the shortcomings of the present democracy became a widespread topic of interest. David Thatcher has noted how 'The rise of imperialism, the spread of political corruption, the popular appeal of yellow journalism, new discoveries in the field of social psychology had combined to produce grave anxieties about the basis, value, and effect of mass enfranchisement.'[11]

The most important emotive stimulus behind the heated controversy in England about aristocracy and democracy was, however, the Parliament Act finally passed in August 1911. Asquith's Liberal government, elected on a landslide majority, found its attempts to pass reforming legislation (as in Lloyd George's 'People's Budget' of 1909) blocked by the refractory Conservative majority in the House of Lords, whose suspicion of the proposed Liberal reforms was exacerbated by the all-too-evident shift in social and political alignment represented by the election of fifty-six Labour MPs to the 1906 Parliament. The intransigent rebellion of the 'Diehard' Tory peers was intolerable and indeed reached the extremity where George V himself guaranteed that if necessary he would create 250 Liberal peers to ensure the passage of the Bill through the Lords. By Tories the constitutional crisis was viewed as an attempt by the party of commercial interests and the *nouveaux riches* to rescind the legitimate veto of the House of Lords, the representatives of the feudal, patrician spirit.

In the resulting war of propaganda, the association of the *New Age* with English Nietzscheanism was of crucial importance to the emergence of the new 'Classicism' (from May 1907 until the end of 1913 it included some eighty items relating to Nietzsche). A. R. Orage, its editor from 1907 to 1922, had devoted seven years' research to Nietzsche, which bore fruit in *Friedrich Nietzsche: The Dionysian Spirit of the Age* (1906) and *Nietzsche in Outline and Aphorism* (1907).[12] Hulme's involvement with the *New Age* would necessarily have exposed him to the ideas and theories of other contributors (notably Kennedy and Ludovici), which bear a close similarity to his own.[13]

Kennedy, a former *Daily Telegraph* reporter, wrote regularly from 1909 onwards on foreign affairs under the pseudonym of 'S. Verdad' and on literature and politics; Ludovici, the former secretary of Rodin, was the art-critic whose attack on Epstein, discussed in Chapter 5, provoked Hulme to enter the artistic arena. My present concern is with the political aesthetics which determined Ludovici's views as expressed in *Nietzsche and Art*, which distorts art into an illustration of Ludovici's political élitism in a more radical although essentially similar fashion to that in which Hulme was to attempt to use the new abstract art as evidence for the appearance of a new anti-humanist *Weltanschauung*.

Hulme's was a fashionable approach in an age which delighted in analogies between artistic and literary styles and the organisation of society. Both Kennedy and Ludovici attempted to apply to contemporary England Nietzsche's description in *Der Fall Wagner* of decadent style as an 'anarchy of atoms' in which the individual element, whether word, sentence or page, usurps an undue amount of attention at the expense of the aesthetic whole, a parallel to a decadent society in which, with the political theory of equal rights for all, the undisciplined masses arrogate to themselves undue individual importance.[14]

It is important to discriminate carefully what Nietzsche understands by individualism. The keystone of his philosophy is existentialist and most frequently he thinks of the individual in isolation. When his attention focuses on how such individuals can exist in society he is driven to the best compromise for absolute individualism – an oligarchy. Put crudely, for Nietzsche only a few men are worthy of being regarded as individuals. In the abstract he attacks democracies on principle as totalitarian states which repress the individual, fearing the consequences of original thought and intellectual development (*WdB*, I, 683–5). Instinctively Nietzsche defends intellectual freedom *per se* from all possible external restriction, yet at the same time argues that only the exceptional individual can benefit from this freedom for self-development. The mediocre masses can never develop sufficiently to warrant individual attention and so their claim to equal rights is an irrelevance which handicaps the potentially much greater self-cultivation of an innately superior élite. Thus, while Nietzsche deprecates *a priori* an authoritarian state, in practice his élitist oligarchy, by making the masses subservient to the promotion of the intellectual élite, would tend to adopt the rigid stratification which, Nietzsche argues, prevents the adequate functioning of a meritocracy. The problem is that Nietzsche's thought is essentially a-social, his attempts to integrate the individual into society often clumsy and confusing. His unequivocal commitment to individualistic élitism leads him to advocate an oligarchy, but he would, I feel, have rejected in practice state enforcement of rigid stratification (which Ludovici, Lasserre, Hulme and Storer championed) as precluding the social mobility essential to his ideas.

Ludovici's *Nietzsche and Art* presents the supposed contemporary anarchy in art (epitomised by the controversial exhibition of Manet and the Post-Impressionists, which was widely regarded as a wilful subversion of artistic tradition) as an obvious representative symptom of wider social disintegration into democracy. The problem, as he sees it, is that of exaggerated individualism: society is swamped by a strident mass, 'each of whom has a "free personality" which he insists upon expressing, and to whom severe law and order would be an insuperable barrier'.[15] The result is naïve praise of technical experimentation for its own sake, simply by virtue of its being the novel expression of a subjective consciousness, held *a priori* to be as significant as any other.[16]

He traces the ultimate causes of this decay back to Christianity with its fundamental doctrines of 'the equality of all souls, the insuperable depravity of human nature, and the insistence upon Truth'. The pernicious influence of these was temporarily lessened by the Catholic Church 'by its rigorous discipline and its firm establishment upon a hierarchical principle', before Martin Luther and the Reformation again championed importunate individualism and 'a general rebellion against authority'. This had the result of elevating the importance not only of the individual's soul, but also of his emotions.[17] Thus Ludovici takes over Nietzsche's historical analysis, which presented the Reformation as a movement of vulgar *ressentiment* and associated Christianity with democracy, but appends comments of his own on the importance of the Catholic Church as an institution for the maintenance of a strong social hierarchy, a viewpoint common to all the other English and French writers discussed in this chapter, but wholly alien to Nietzsche, who respected Christ but detested institutionalised religion in any form.

Ludovici argues, again evidencing the period's fascination with literary and sociological parallels, that Christianity has led to Realism in art by its 'devotion to a truth that could be general, which perforce has reduced us to vulgar reality'.[18] The link of Christianity and Realism is Ludovici's own and is in line with more recent research on the historical development of the English novel from seventeenth-century spiritual autobiographies. But the unwarranted and rather facile value-judgement which he appends to this is a stale echo of the late-nineteenth-century artistic debate between ivory-tower aestheticism and the Naturalist argument that no subject can be excluded from artistic treatment.[19] Ludovici's aestheticism, as with many French Symbolists, takes the form of philosophical Idealism. He equates Protestantism with empirical philosophy, on the lines that its thesis that everyman could interpret truth for himself necessarily restricted knowledge to what could be apprehended by all: unmediated sense experience.[20] This leads him to reiterate the aesthetic and Symbolist reaction against experimental science's destruction of the mythical in the natural world, and general impoverishment of imaginative beauty. Only the artist can counter this reductive tendency. His role is that of *interpreter* of our environment: his significance lies in what he can appropriate and transform imaginatively into his own spiritual possession.[21] Whether consciously or not, Ludovici is here raising again the central questions of German Romantic philosophy, but what had then been a debate of the utmost spiritual significance is cheapened in his hands and pressed into service as an argument in favour of a social system. Just as the artist imposes order and meaning on the flux of experience, so, Ludovici adds, in the ideal polity a strong authoritarian élite should impose discipline on the anarchic masses who recalcitrantly and misguidedly insist on their individual significance.

Ludovici derives further sanction for this outlook in what must be the first summary in English, hitherto unnoticed by literary and art-critics, of the arguments of Riegl and Worringer (Hulme did not read their work until over two years later). He is particularly attracted by Worringer's refutation of the prevailing view that primitive decoration resulted from an imitative instinct. It was instead 'the result of a genuine desire for order and simple and organized arrangement, and an attempt in a small way to overcome confusion. "It is man's only possible way of emancipating himself from the accidental and chaotic character of reality." '[22] He finds here an expression of the 'will to power' (most of his quotations from Nietzsche are from the textually unreliable *Will to Power*) and terms this imposition of an ordering will 'Ruler-art'. He instances the Romantic preference for the picturesque over the formal landscaped park, associating the former with democracy and expressing horror that 'the same man who honours government and an aristocratic ideal may often be found to-day dilating upon the charms of chaotic scenery'. The only way to overcome the contemporary decadence in art is, he insists, to change the social structure it reflects.[23]

One can readily imagine a scene in a late-eighteenth-century novel with a character revealing his moral recklessness, perhaps even Jacobinism, by expressing a taste for sublime, wild landscape. The parallel is instructive, for Ludovici is resurrecting an eighteenth-century debate which, no longer a live issue, sounds merely quaint and artificial in his bald statement. The originally disturbing taste for Romantic landscape has been absorbed into the general consciousness and its initial connotations forgotten. For Ludovici in 1910 to protest that a true-blue Tory should praise a Versailles (his own example) and unequivocally condemn un-cultivated landscape (and, presumably, an 'englischer Garten') is therefore not merely faintly risible but, more importantly, empha-sises his impractically cerebral desire to revive a sensibility which is no longer instinctive and with it the stable social structure which was its natural accompaniment. The supposed parallel with the Nietzschean 'will to power' (a phrase which referred primarily to existentialist self-overcoming and personal development, not the literal authoritarianism of Ludovici's and, more drastically, the Nazis' interpretation) is a spurious attempt to give a fashionable patina to an anachronism. Nietzsche's theory – an abstract concept and therefore dangerously susceptible to various realisations at odds with its genuine meaning – with its convenient catch-phrase is literalised into an image of external domination, which in Ludovici's elaboration becomes synonymous with the aggressive political repression within an oligarchy.

To prove that Ruler-art can only flourish if fostered by an élitist society, Ludovici contrasts the two 'Art-Wills' in Ancient Greece: 'A superior will aiming at a Ruler-art form' and 'an inferior will aiming at realism'. The former coincided, he argues, with the sixth-century zenith of Greek civilisation; the latter's ultimate triumph in the fifth century introduced a national decline.[24] As an example of Ruler-art he cites the Egyptian statue of King Khephrën, which apotheosises the aristocratic values of the Egyptian people at their apogee, in a convention consciously adopted as an alternative to the contemporary realistic statue of the Lady Nophret. He finds in it

> that autocratic mode of expression which brooks neither con-tradiction nor disobedience; the *Symmetry* which makes the spectator obtain a complete grasp of an idea; the *Sobriety* which reveals the restraint that a position of command presupposes; the *Simplicity* proving the power of a great mind that has overcome the chaos in itself and has reflected its order and harmony upon an object.[25]

Ludovici's trivial comments reveal his blinkered insensitivity to art as anything other than an illustration of his élitist political views.

The opening of this quotation demonstrates exactly how by skilful manipulation of tone Ludovici draws out the fundamental concept of Nietzsche's 'will to power' (indicated with reasonable accuracy in Ludovici's comments on 'Sobriety' and 'Simplicity') into an insidious justification of political authoritarianism. As I explained, Nietzsche himself is partially to blame for such treatment in that he failed to reflect sufficiently on the social implications of his philosophy of individual sublimation. Even in his own work there is occasionally a disquieting tendency for the vocabulary of increasing self-mastery to be applied equally to the imposition of a mastering will on others; with his journalistic facility Ludovici has little difficulty in making his and Nietzsche's ideas an apparently seamless whole. He concludes by giving Worringer's arguments a 'Nietzschean' admixture in the cause of political propagandism. Ruler-art, he maintains, can spring only from an aristocratic society which depends on

(1) Long tradition under the sway of noble and inviolable values, resulting in an accumulation of will power and a superabundance of good spirits; (2) leisure which allows of meditation, and therefore of that process of lowering pitchers into the wells of inner riches; (3) the disbelief in freedom for freedom's sake without a purpose or without an aim; and (4) an order of rank according to which each is given a place in keeping with his value, and authority and reverence are upheld. [26]

Ludovici's critical divagations with their eclectic mixture of Idealism, Nietzscheanism and social *hauteur* could be dismissed as no more than the opinionated pronouncements of a temperamental reactionary, were it not that they seem to reflect so accurately the mood in 1910–11 of the radical Right. Determined to construct an argument for the prolongation of the House of Lords as an emblem for (or, as some believed, a guarantee of) an outmoded aristocratic society, polemicists plundered disparate areas of experience for analogies, however remote, which might support their emotional attachment to established traditions of social organisation. Increased Labour representation in the Commons, Suffragette agitation, bewildering new artistic movements, Liberal legislation laying the foundation of the Welfare State, which, although it now seems a shabby palliative, appeared radical to Edwardian Tories, all combined to disconcert the privileged or the timid. As all aspects of the society they cherished stood in peril of change, they reacted by attempting to establish for the defence a theoretical connection of as many emotive subjects as possible, expanded at will by various hands, like the more incongruous outgrowths of medieval cathedrals. Although the results now appear absurd, at the time they were intended to imply that the removal of a single stone or buttress from their unified cultural structure would endanger the stability of the whole precariously balanced edifice.

The contemporary vogue of simplistically transferring arguments from aesthetics to politics also found favour with J. M. Kennedy. He states boldly in the Preface to his *Tory Democracy*, which collects articles published in the *New Age* between May and September 1911, that 'The distinction between classicism and romanticism in literature is no greater than the difference between Liberalism and Conservatism in politics – the distinction, indeed, arises from the same causes and leads to the same results.'[27] Like Ludovici, Kennedy traces the decay of the state back to the Reformation – 'The Roman Catholic theory tends to compactness and order in the nation. The Protestant theory tends to unrestrained individualism' – and he notes that the political struggles of the last two hundred years have been waged between those who extended the principle of theological individualism into philosophy and politics and those 'who believed in a social as well as in a theological hierarchy'.[28] For Kennedy, like Ludovici, religious and secular authoritarianism have the same interchangeable value, although he stresses the political potential of a Catholic revival for imposing a new secular order less than the writers of *L'Action française* who influenced Hulme and Storer.

Nietzsche's theories could, Kennedy believes, introduce fresh inspiration into English politics by their advocacy of a rigidly stratified social hierarchy, representative of permanent values, instead of the rather hazily defined Liberal goal of 'progress'. Kennedy is attempting to apply Nietzsche's arguments for an intellectual aristocracy which would in effect be a classless meritocracy of strong individuals to justify the totally different, purely class-based hierarchy which is the English aristocracy. In elaborating this idea Kennedy comes implicitly close to Hulme's 'religious' conception of man: the Liberal

looks upon the innate and inherited forces of man as being susceptible of change from day to day and year to year. He is not concerned with man in his fixed and permanent state, but with some idealistic human being who is in a constant condition of transition from a state of 'evil' into a state of 'good', the definition of what is good and what is evil naturally varying from generation to generation.[29]

But for Kennedy this excursion into political philosophy is determined by its contemporary relevance. In England, he claims, tradition manifests itself in respect for the 'hereditary principle' in connection with the Throne and the then threatened House of Lords, which unlike the Commons does not concern itself exclusively with transient issues.[30] At this stage Kennedy invites Randolph Churchill to step forward to help correlate the threads of pseudo-Nietzscheanism and religio-secular authoritarianism. He quotes from a speech delivered on 6 November 1885:

[Tory democracy] is a democracy which believes that a hereditary monarchy and hereditary House of Lords are the strongest fortifications which the wisdom of man, illuminated by the experience of centuries, can possibly devise for the protection, not of Whig privilege, but of democratic freedom. The Tory democracy is a democracy which adheres to and will defend the Established Church, because it believes that the Establishment is a guarantee of State morality, and that the connection between Church and State imparts to the ordinary functions of executive and law something of a divine sanction.[31]

The similarities and divergences between Kennedy and Nietzsche are encapsulated in the following quotation. In April 1912 Kennedy contrasted 'Liberalism, pseudo-Socialism, and Christianity' (a collocation which to Nietzsche represented the herd morality of democracy) not with Nietzsche's idiosyncratic oligarchy of supermen but instead with the religio-secular authoritarianism and hereditary aristocracy which differentiated the English and French right-wing radicals from Nietzsche. Kennedy's political ideal and that of his colleagues was

the spirit represented by the Catholic Church (which is not exactly a Christian church) and Toryism. The 'Church' and Christianity represent . . . very different principles and types of mind. The aristocratic, hierarchical spirit of the Church forms a distinct contrast to the levelling, revolutionary spirit of Christianity itself, this latter spirit being found . . . in Nonconformist and Low Church circles.[32]

Beyond the immediate reference to the traditional Nonconformist connections of Liberalism, epitomised at that time by Lloyd George, the framework of Kennedy's distinction is Nietzschean. In an earlier article he quoted from a 'romantic' speech delivered by the Principal of the Baptist movement, which asserted an optimistic faith in man's potential to evolve towards a millennial state. He balanced this by a 'classicist' citation from Thucydides to the effect that man's essential nature is constant. Unlike the Christian who attempts to escape from the real world into the clouds of idealism, the classicist (whose touchstone is his reaction to Nietzsche's doctrine of the Eternal Recurrence) 'can bear the burden of the world as he sees it. To use Nietzsche's expression, he says Yea to life.'[33] Kennedy could not resist the temptation to use as a political weapon this presumed Christian focus on a distant, idealistic future which ignores present reality and tends to assume that social ills will disappear of their own accord in the millennium. He selected as easy prey the book by the Liberal cabinet-minister C. F. G. Masterman, *The Condition of England*, an acute example of the shortcomings of Edwardian Liberalism in its sentimental sympathy for the poor, but shortage of practical remedies save staunch religious faith.[34]

Kennedy's criticism of the Baptist parallels Nietzsche's attack on Eduard von Hartmann's advocacy of passive abandonment to a necessary historical process culminating in the Last Judgement, in which present misery and iniquity is justified as a subtle element in God's teleological plan, designed to lessen man's attachment to the world, with the ultimate goal of world redemption. From his atheist position Nietzsche countered by insisting that man must break free from such damaging illusions to concentrate his energy instead on improving practically the human condition:

Indeed the time is long overdue for advancing with all the general levy of satirical malice against the aberrations of the historical sense, the extravagant delight in the historical process at the expense of present existence and life, and the unreflecting postponement of all future perspectives. (*WdB*, i, 272)[35]

The Nietzschean concept of the 'Eternal Recurrence' differs from

Kennedy's somewhat glib use. For Nietzsche the fact that God is dead was an undeniable axiom: the onus was therefore on the individual to create his own significance in a meaningless world. The most dispiriting thought which could afflict such an individual would be the sense that he was powerless to alter this state of affairs, that man could never evolve and the present absurdity never be overcome. There could be no more dramatic confirmation of this than if the present moment were to recur, with all the contingent misery and pettiness it now contains, as part of a cyclical alternation *ad infinitum*. This characteristically near-masochistic *hypothesis*, for it is no more, posited as the most extreme form of intellectual nihilism, is accordingly made the supreme test of Zarathustra's capacity for self-mastery. If he can come to terms with what would be unsurpassable evidence of cosmic irrationality and yet still will to continue living then he would be making the supreme affirmation of his own intellectual strength or, as Nietzsche elsewhere phrased it, his Dionysian spirit (*WdB*, ii, 166–7, 351, 464–7; iii, 853). The *actual* rather than *hypothetical* belief in necessary cyclical recurrence and human constancy would not have found favour with Nietzsche. He believed that man through a process of self-overcoming could in the future evolve into a 'superman' and that human nature was accordingly not necessarily constant, although like the English Augustans he recognised that history to date gave no evidence of progressive development (see *WdB*, i, 217). The use of this argument to thwart Romantic or Liberal eudemonistic faith in Progress (which Nietzsche would, however, have condemned as sapping the individual will on which alone the capacity for development rests, just as he condemned the Hegelian view of history) is therefore a mild distortion of Nietzsche's doctrine. Nevertheless Kennedy's stress on the need for active effort towards progress rather than the passive complacency of Liberals is completely in the spirit of Nietzsche's philosophy, unlike Hulme's 'classical' view of human constancy adopted from Flinders Petrie's cyclical view of history, which is in effect a literalisation of Nietzsche's 'Eternal Recurrence'.

While Hulme on a plane of largely abstract thought concerned himself with Original Sin, Kennedy's interests were more practically oriented. His opposition to Romanticism came instead from Burke and Disraeli. He associates the individualistic school (Paine, Bentham and Mill) with the party which has always promoted the interests of the entrepreneurial capitalist at the expense of the workman – the Liberals – and regards a state founded on an individualistic basis as one in which every one has individual freedom to exploit every one else. [36] The Tories' interests by contrast have always lain in the land rather than in industry,

> and it is the territorial influence of the landowners and 'lords of the manor' which has been effectual in preserving for so long the feudal spirit in England – that is to say, the hierarchical and anti-individualistic spirit which one is usually safe in associating with the spirit formed and developed by the Church of Rome. [37]

He concedes that the aristocracy neglected their responsibility towards the lower orders in the eighteenth century, but lays more blame overall for oppression on the greedy middle classes. Kennedy's political ideal is therefore similar to Yeats's (although Yeats's ideas were more realistically rooted in an Ireland which remained largely agrarian, and derived from other sources). His favoured social order is a benevolent aristocracy enjoying a traditional harmonious relationship with their tenants, rather than the capitalist exploitation of the masses by the bourgeois.

It is a paradox of the period that one of France's most 'right-wing' politicians, the syndicalist Georges Sorel, believed in the use of the general strike as a political weapon. This divergence from present-day political demarcations is confirmed by Kennedy's insistence that increased Labour Party representation in Parliament has had the effect of reducing or holding static workmen's wages since 1902 or 1903, while they even co-operated with the Liberals to get the 1911 strikes settled as quickly as possible although at the expense of the workmen. The radical Right and the radical Left were united in their detestation of capitalism and indecisive Liberal compromise. [38]

But, although Kennedy believes in an oligarchy, his goal, unlike Nietzsche's, is social justice. For Kennedy an aristocratic, hierarchical polity is simply the most efficient way to organise the state. His programme for social reform is based, somewhat oddly at first glance, in a form of neo-feudalist, hierarchical guild organisation (similar to that advocated by Orage and A. J. Penty) which would circumvent the present capitalist plutocracy by reviving traditional values of craftsmanship and, to a limited extent, prolonging established rural communities in their inherited social organisation by decentralising power to parish and manor-house. This neo-feudalist interest in professional guilds and decentralised power parallels that of *L'Action française* outlined below. Large manufacturing industries would be maintained to provide wealth for the state and working-conditions in these improved, while at the same time individual crafts would be maintained.[39] Like Storer, whose reactionary politics were conditioned by sentimental nostalgia, Kennedy's more practical revulsion from capitalism was partly aesthetic. Materialist values in society, as Ruskin and Morris had earlier proclaimed, necessarily created soulless ugliness in mass-produced industrial artifacts. Kennedy's programme foresees T. S. Eliot's *Notes towards the Definition of Culture*:

> The workman would be in a position of greater dignity and responsibility; and gilds [*sic*] would, as formerly, become responsible for the quality of their wares: they would not be merely industrial organisations, but social and religious organisations as well. Furthermore, the parish would once again take its place as an important governmental unit under the control of the local aristocracy instead of a soulless 'Board'.[40]

Kennedy's traditionalism reveals how the English Tories' élitism differed from that of Nietzsche. While they were motivated by nostalgia for a hereditary aristocracy now being supplanted by capitalist plutocracy, Nietzsche would have rejected their uncritical, parasitic attachment to the past (what he termed the 'antiquarian' view of history – *WdB*, I, 219–30) as being just as damaging to constructive future development as Liberal complacent faith in Progress. Although Kennedy's views with their specific proposals for social reform are more realistic than the reactionary intransigence of Ludovici, Storer and Hulme, they too would surely have fallen victim to Nietzsche's iconoclastic destruction of malignant illusions.

In his later book *English Literature 1880–1905*, Kennedy aligns these political views with the contrast between Romanticism and Classicism. His use of the terms shows more awareness of literary history than Hulme's (although 'Romantic' seems to merge into 'baroque') but, like Hulme's, is still primarily propagandist. Literary Romantics correspond to political Liberals:

> men who saw nothing in the influence of tradition in art or literature, who acted as if the world were re-created from day to

day and year to year, who chafed under . . . artistic discipline . . . who desired free play for 'individuality', who thought that every author was quite right in laying down his own artistic canons; the men who experimented with curious metric forms. . . . Their ideas were not expressed with the simplicity of diction that characterised the authors who followed classic models. In their works we find puny thoughts enveloped in mystic, florid, symbolic language.[41]

These equations of a classical style with a rigid social hierarchy linking secular and religious authoritarianism, at the same time contrasting the Liberal eudemonistic faith in Progress with Tory belief both in the permanent values held to be embodied in a hereditary aristocracy, and in the constancy of human nature, resemble strikingly Hulme's development of a reactionary philosophy and propagandist aesthetic, in which he was joined by Edward Storer, his fellow poet from the 'forgotten school of 1909'.

## II  *L'ACTION ANGLAISE: HULME AND STORER IN 1911*

While Hulme's relationship with the *New Age* Tories has received some limited critical discussion (see *supra*, n. 13), Storer's connection with the *Commentator*, to which Hulme also contributed, has gone totally unnoticed. During 1911 they both used its columns for political commentary, while Storer continued to write its art-criticism until May 1913. Their articles explain the background to Hulme's rejection of Bergson's philosophy and consequent movement away from an empathetic aesthetic.

The British Conservative Party was in a state of crisis, unable to win elections, following the Liberal landslide of 1906 and the two indecisive polls of 1910.[42] In Hulme and Storer's view this disorientation was abetted by the emotional appeal of the Fabian movement for the young intellectual, in the absence of a vigorous Conservative philosophy. Looking to France, they saw grounds for optimism in the success of *L'Action française* in converting young intellectuals from Socialism to Neo-Royalism, and attempted to transplant the ideas of Maurras and Lasserre into England.[43]

*L'Action française* was founded in 1899 by Charles Maurras and

Henri Vaugeois; Maurras's leading ideas were first fully expounded in *L'Enquête sur la monarchie* (1900). The movement's fortnightly *Revue de l'Action française* appeared from July 1899 until 1908, when it was succeeded by the daily newspaper *Action française*. Maurras, although France's leading Neo-Royalist, advocated a monarchy not from a belief in the divine right of kingship but on patriotic ('integral nationalist') grounds. His main doctrine was anti-democratic in its belief that all forms of government should be based on authority, order and hierarchy. The maintenance of a hereditary, privileged aristocracy was simply a practical means of preserving continuity and embodying in an ordered form the stratification already evidenced in unequal human abilities. Maurras's views on human inequality echo Nietzsche's, but his ideal polity, like that of the English radical Right, departs from Nietzsche in its pragmatic compromise equating a desirable élite caste with an existing and partly degenerate hereditary aristocracy.

The framework of Maurras's policies is essentially social, stressing that the group is more important than the individual. He criticises the atomistic nature of post-Revolutionary French society, with its political and economic individualism, which has introduced a legalistic, contractual polity. He maintains that the pre-Revolutionary occupational and administrative groups should be restored, reviving professional guilds, resurrecting the old provinces with their communal powers and privileges instead of a centralised bureaucracy working through artificial *départements* divorced from traditional local life. He would also reinstate the Catholic Church's influence on family and education, which, although himself an atheist, he valued as an authoritarian social institution opposed to Protestant religious individualism.[44] As with his English contemporaries who held similar views, Maurras could never acknowledge the incompatibility of his feudalistic nostalgia with the irreversible transition which had taken place from an agrarian economy with a social structure based on status to an industrial, capitalist society.

Maurras's anti-individualist politics derived from his aesthetic views; demand for social order was simply an extension of his belief in the prime importance of discipline in personal life and literary style. His early association with the literary *École romane* had involved him in a reaction against German Romanticism and the individualistic experiments of the Symbolists, in favour of the restrained Classicism of sixteenth- and seventeenth-century French

literature, a direct manifestation of its society's respect for traditional values. Yet, while Maurras had initiated the campaign
against Romanticism, its foremost exponent in literary criticism was
the Nietzschean Pierre Lasserre, who as editor of the *Revue de l'Action
française* developed in its literary columns the ideas of *Le Romantisme
français*. He was the literary critic of the newspaper *Action française*
until he left the movement in 1914, disillusioned with Maurras's
inflexible dogmatism in literary taste.

In March 1911 Hulme refers for the first time to *L'Action
française*.[45] From then on his attitude towards Bergson becomes
increasingly ambiguous. Indication of his divided personality is
provided by his skilful use of the pseudonym 'Thomas Gratton'
(derived from his birthplace, Gratton Hall), the disguise Hulme
employs to mask his incipient change in outlook. At the same time
that Hulme was enthusing in the *New Age* over Tancrède de Visan's
*L'Attitude du lyrisme contemporain*, which elucidates recent poetic
developments as an aesthetic reflection of Bergson's philosophy,
enraged by the Parliament Act controversy he was deep in
Lasserre's argument for a disciplined social hierarchy, which found
expression in *Commentator* articles. Then in November 1911 in the
*New Age* under the protection of his pseudonym the Bergsonian
'disciple' revealed a crisis in his allegiance to the master, while later
in the month (as 'T. E. Hulme') defending Bergson in the *New Age*'s
correspondence columns, continuing his 'Notes on Bergson', lecturing on Bergson and undertaking to translate Bergson's *Introduction to
Metaphysics*.[46]

As the Nietzschean *Le Romantisme français* is a key work for both
Storer and Hulme I shall outline Lasserre's argument. He criticises
chiefly the 'cowardly eudemonism' of Romanticism, which ignores
the fact that, whatever the potential of the human animal, it is
nevertheless a delicate creature which can flourish only in the most
ordered political societies. Hence the paradoxes of Romantic
terminology in which disorder becomes Liberty, confusion Genius,
instinct Reason and anarchy Energy. He tracks this confusion to
Rousseau, whose social malaise led him to seek isolation in an ideal
world where dreams could be fulfilled without prior need for
individual effort;[47] Lasserre is echoing directly Nietzsche's disgust
at the contemporary European disease, 'paralysis of the will', which
has accompanied the rise of democracies in the nineteenth century.
But Lasserre's own brand of élitism, following Maurras, is directly
authoritarian. Ironically Nietzsche's views have been turned into

advocacy of a State resembling the Hegelian model he detested so much in the contemporary Bismarckian *Reich* (see *WdB*, ɪ, 627). Lasserre stresses constantly the importance of discipline and social duty. Romanticism deifies the individual, which is ethically anti-social and emotionally mawkish.

The unexplained recrudescence of Original Sin in Hulme's work originates here. According to Michelet, until 1789 the dogma of Original Sin had corrupted the religious, political and social institutions of Europe by establishing them on an iniquitous foundation. Original Sin in religion necessitates Grace, in temporal affairs requires indulgence. Romanticism supersedes this dogma by inaugurating the Kingdom of God on earth: 'La Révolution n'est autre chose que la réaction tardive de la justice contre le gouvernement de la faveur et la religion de la grâce.'[48] Hulme accordingly adopted the dogma of Original Sin as an element in a political manifesto.

Like Kennedy, Lasserre echoes Nietzsche's frequent attacks on the widespread nineteenth-century faith in an optimistic, self-realising historical process, pointing out its Germanic origins. A logical outcome of Romanticism is, he argues, idealistic faith in Progress:

> Les uns l'attribuent à l'action immanente et mystérieuse d'une force universelle, sorte de Providence panthéistique, qui, par le développement même de sa nature, mène l'humanité, d'étape en étape, vers un suprême état d'épanouissement dans la perfection. Cette 'nuée' nous vient de la Germanie. Les autres . . . jugent que le Progrès dans une seule direction, dès lors qu'il y a des raisons certaines de croire que, dans cette direction, il ne s'arrêtera plus, entraîne nécessairement le progrès dans toutes les directions; en d'autres termes, que le progrès des sciences (dénommées significativement, mais sophistiquement 'la Science' premièrement, ne s'arrêtera qu'à l'omniscience, du moins au sens expérimental et positif, deuxièmement, porte avec lui le perfectionnement de l'homme et de la société dans tous les sens.[49]

Lasserre follows the idea that Future and Utopia are synonymous through its major French exponents: Condorcet, Mme de Staël, Victor Cousin, Hugo, Renan. He concludes that emotional Romanticism focuses the individual's aspirations on an illusory ideal of happiness, whilst ideological Romanticism claims as imminent a social order which by abolishing human egoism and the natural hardships of life would inaugurate universal contentment. This clearly parallels Nietzsche's views on the degenerate 'herd animal morality' of contemporary democracies and their social valetudinarianism. Such hollow daydreams merely indicate the decay of vital energy in those who cherish them. To foster these illusions the Romantics had to imagine forces capable of realising this earthly Paradise, intoxicating the individual and founding the State on justice and spontaneous goodness. These deities, Nature and Progress, were synthesised into Pantheism.[50] Lasserre's central themes are obvious. The exaltation of the individual, related to 'pure democracy', leads to social disaster. There must instead be strict social discipline imposed by an enlightened oligarchy. Human nature is not divine; belief in necessary progress is naïve. In the case of the English Tories Hulme and Storer, Lasserre was preaching to the converted.

In his articles Storer takes a less philosophical approach than Hulme; his prime concern is with contemporary politics. His analysis is, however, amateurish and emotive beside Kennedy's more incisive convictions. Storer's published references to the *Action française* writers predate Hulme's and he could have introduced Hulme to their views. But Storer's use of their work lacks Hulme's assurance, and in this, as in his literary output, he remains a minor figure.

His attack on Romanticism is inspired by Nietzsche. Lasserre had criticised the idealistic faith in necessary progress which had developed during the nineteenth century, gaining further strength from optimistic evolutionary thought. For Storer this has damaging repercussions in the beliefs it inspires both about human nature and political change. He can see, first, no evidence that man as a species is still developing and opposes Darwin's theory by De Vries's mutation theory, which maintains that 'changes in species are effected, not by infinitely subtle alterations, but by leaps, and once a species is fixed, it remains fixed'. Thus human nature is not a matter of necessary 'Progress'. Storer then applies this refutation of a gradually unfolding historical process to its socialist exponents. Their absurd teleological beliefs form the natural counterpart to their unrealistic democratic theories, in which Storer finds illustrated the Nietzschean definition of decadence as 'enlarging particulars at the expense of the whole': 'Socialism is a typical piece

of Romanticism in its conception of the whole State, as subordinated to the proletariat part of the State'. His fervour is
impressive but sophistical:

> The world's Social Democrats stand for the ruthless egotisms of
> Marx and Lassalle. The various peoples are gigantic units or
> individuals, bent on exploiting themselves, without regard to the
> nation as a whole.

> The proletariat is only a class, and because it is a class of millions
> it is not necessarily more important than an aristocracy of
> thousands. One has yet to learn that there is more virtue in
> quantity than quality.[51]

This is Nietzsche reduced almost beyond recognition. Storer, like
Kennedy, is talking in terms of social classes; his aristocracy is the
English peerage, not Nietzsche's élite caste whose members have
established their pre-eminence by virtue of individual tenacity and
force of character.

Storer's work is ultimately disappointing in its inner contradictions. Kennedy had maintained a cogently argued case against
Liberal economic individualism, but Storer, who also attacks
plutocracy, does so on purely emotive grounds, from an instinctive,
aesthetic disdain. His suspicion of Liberal reforms simply con-
ceptualises his sentimental revulsion at the incipient shift in the
criteria of social stratification from birth to wealth. In the
Edwardian age social pre-eminence was beginning to pass from
the landed gentry to parvenu factory-owners and financiers.[52] The
enormous influx of gold into Europe after 1890, following the
development of new South African mines, helped to fuel inflation
and to create a formidable, capitalist plutocracy[53] who spent their
money as ostentatiously as the Elizabethans had their New World
silver, and were even welcome members of the Edwardian court-
circle. In Storer's mind a hazily defined 'Socialism' in politics
paralleled this displacement of 'heredity' by 'Gold'.[54] Political
agitation for the abolition of the House of Lords formed an
associative parallel with 'the levelling power of money' which could
elevate a newly ennobled business man above the hereditary
aristocrat, who embodied traditional values and the feudal spirit of
continuity. He singled out as tangible proof of the irresistible rise of
plutocracy the unprecedented price of £100,000 paid for

Rembrandt's *Mill*, a transaction whose symbolic import was enhanced by the fact that it had belonged to the Marquis of Lansdowne, then leader of the Tory opposition in the House of Lords. The key political issue was therefore the maintenance of the House of Lords as an aristocratic bulwark against capitalism:

> Our unfortunate people are asked to vote down – in the House of Lords – one of the last remaining safeguards that stand between them and the monstrous rapacity of Cosmopolitan financiers, and half-educated, unscrupulous business men, under the lure of a war-cry and a banner bearing the very strange and cynical device, 'Democracy'.[55]

Yet Storer's insistence that 'It is not from any hatred or lack of love of the people that one renounces the democratic fallacy. . . . It is because democracy is merely the shield and disguise under which an unscrupulous plutocracy exploits its victims'[56] carries less conviction than Kennedy's desire for social reform. His remoteness from the realities of everyday life is revealed in 'The Chorus',[57] where he denies that the masses have 'aggravating and soul-destroying duties to perform'. Instead he contends that they are content with menial subordination, which is a matter of 'love' as much as 'fear'. Storer's problem is that his abstract aristocratic ideal, recalling the harmonious microcosm of such country-house poems as Jonson's 'To Penshurst' or Marvell's 'Upon Appleton House', is no longer realisable in contemporary industrial society. Not surprisingly he never descends to the detail of how such a structured hierarchy would work in practice and does not concede that his social ideal is a sentimental anachronism in a society in which large country estates and the social structure they engendered have disappeared with the change from an agrarian economy in marked decline since the 1870s.

A further emotive impulse in Storer's rather muddled articles was his delusion that the maintenance of the House of Lords as an influential legislative body would somehow ensure the preservation nationally of a strong aristocracy. This in its turn would, he thought, enable a revival of patronage to take place which would counter the second-rate art at present produced to comply with purely commercial considerations, and the uniformity of style and opinions dictated by the near-monopolist publishing-organisations.[58] Although Storer's inference that prolonging the anachronistic status of the

Upper Chamber would somehow guarantee an equally anachronistic country-house society was unwarranted, his realisation of the
malignant influence on literature of market-forces and the consequent need for patronage was an important issue, soon to become
a life-long concern of Pound, affecting the emergence of Vorticism,
his quarrel with Amy Lowell, and beyond that, for example, the 'Bel
Esprit' project, as I shall show in Chapter 7.[59]

In 1911 Hulme was likewise involved in political propagandism.
Early in the year he read Lasserre's work, which seemed incompatible with Bergson's philosophy. In April 1911 therefore Hulme
visited Lasserre for discussions.[60] Bergson's insistence in his first two
books on the complexity of subconscious experience and his notion
of 'real time' (the qualitative and indivisible flow of duration) were
being manipulated by Liberals and progressives as a political
weapon against reactionaries. The Conservative philosophy of
*L'Action française*, as expounded by Lasserre, was based on

> intellectual discipline. We think that the only road to sanity in
> these matters is to take as a guide for theory and practice the
> natural and necessary relations of things. We believe, then, in the
> existence of laws which express what we know of the necessary
> and permanent characteristics of any social and political order,
> which laws can be drawn by induction from the experiences of
> history or by deduction from the elementary knowledge that any
> man may have of human nature and the exigencies of life in
> society.

Bergson's philosophy, however, grounded in Darwinian evolutionism, stressed the mysterious unpredictability of phenomenal life.
Liberals used 'real time' to argue that, as each moment is a unique
configuration, historical parallels are impossible. Thus the arguments of *L'Action française* in favour of oligarchy were unfounded:
'If we point out that history does or does not show us any prosperous,
strong, and conquering nation, which was at the same time a
democracy, they retort, history would not be history if it were not
change itself and perpetual novelty.'

Hulme enthused over Bergson's later notion of *l'élan vital* (an
extension of the psychological notion of 'real time' to a universal,
underlying dynamism in the created world realised in constant
evolutionary development) in 'The Philosophy of Intensive
Manifolds', a lecture he gave in November 1911, but when pushed

by Lasserre finally abandoned it as untenable. Nevertheless he still believed in the validity of Bergson's description of subconscious experience and was therefore forced to equivocate and maintain that *la durée réelle* does exist, but only in the individual:

> M. Lasserre then endeavoured to prove to me that Bergsonism was nothing but the last disguise of romanticism. If I thought this was true, I should be compelled to change my views considerably. I can find a compromise for myself, however, which I roughly indicate by saying that I think time is real for the individual, but not for the race.[61]

One could summarise broadly Hulme's change in outlook as the growing conviction that Bergsonism was indeed 'the last disguise of romanticism', particularly in its relation to the Romantic faith in necessary or automatic evolution towards Utopia. In this he was soon to be echoed by T. S. Eliot, who criticised the association of Bergsonism and Progress in terms strikingly similar to Hulme's in his address to the Harvard Philosophical Society in 1913 or 1914, 'The Relationship between Politics and Metaphysics'.

During his stay in Paris in 1911 Eliot had attended Bergson's lectures at the Collège de France and in a paper written after May 1911 had drawn attention to terminological inconsistencies in Bergson's discussion of the distinction between quality and quantity. By 1913 or 1914 these reservations had become ideological rather than merely technical and found expression in the Harvard address. Eliot criticises Walter Lippman's attempted application to politics in *A Preface to Politics* (1913) of the ultimately biological Bergsonian view of life as continuous and unpredictable development. He regards this as a damaging procedure, for Bergsonism tends to reduce conscious effort in decision-making, and hence ethics, to a mere epiphenomenon which takes no account of the relevancy of contextual criteria. The political need to abstract from life in order to frame intentions is at odds with Bergsonian vitalism. For the theory of progress as a biological generalisation is confused with the teleological sense of the word, which leads to its hypostatisation as something independent of human need and meaning which takes its necessary course while man abdicates from intellectual responsibility. Eliot cannot accept Lippman's contention of the purely pragmatic relevance of political creeds and systems, intended to answer a momentary need with no pretence to finality. Beyond Lippman's position lies a Bergsonism of the extreme Left, which by its thesis that life is an irreversible process would deny the relevancy of the past and hence tradition.[62]

In his 'Notes on the Bologna Congress', following his recent discussions with Lasserre, Hulme voiced doubts about Progress and referred to 'the classical ideal of the fixed and constant nature of man' (*FS*, 26). The Parliamentary crisis provided the occasion to utilise Lasserre's arguments in favour of a strictly ordered society:

> The State or nation can only be in a healthy condition when it submits itself to a kind of discipline. There must be a hierarchy, a subordination of the parts, just as there must be in any other organisation. A pure democracy ends all this, for discipline can only be kept up when the centre of authority is to a certain extent independent of the people governed.

If the power of the Lords was circumscribed this would result in 'uncontrolled democracy'. Lasserre claimed that the individual needed the support of a strong social structure to curb his anti-social excesses; Hulme transposes this argument to the Parliament Bill: 'Here you have a proposal to do away with all the traditional restraints, the hierarchy, that makes social life possible and healthy'.[63] Like Storer, Hulme seizes on Lasserre's advocacy of an aristocratic order.

Hulme's development of this outlook differs from Storer's, however. He is more interested in the theoretical aspects of political philosophy. Bergson's psychological evolutionism rested on the notion of continual progression, while Progress in a more teleological sense was at the heart of Lasserre's critique of Romantic eudemonism. In Hulme's mind the two aspects merged, associating Bergson's philosophy with the sentimental complacency of the Liberal or the Fabian, which, as I have shown, Kennedy was to attack. Their idealistic faith in Progress explained why the Liberals could countenance the muzzling of the House of Lords. The 'democratic' standpoint is 'a belief in inevitable "Progress", the belief that the forces of things are themselves making for good, and that so good will come even when things are left to themselves'.[64] The Conservative, who does not believe in this kind of progress, attempts instead to strengthen the framework of society:

> He believes that man is constant, and that the number and types

of the possible forms of society are also constant. And, further, that history shows that the only types which are healthy and enduring are those in which there is an independent authority, in which the rulers are to a certain extent independent of the ruled, and that the only way in which to preserve a good social order is to take definite steps towards it by preserving the restraining framework inside which such order is alone possible. [65]

Hulme's 'classical' and 'religious' theory originates therefore in the political polemics of 1911.

He found a useful ally in his attack on constant progress in Flinders Petrie, to whose work Yeats later referred in preparing *A Vision*. In *Revolutions of Civilisation* Petrie outlined a cyclical conception of history: 'that civilisation is not a constantly increasing, but a recurrent phenomena [*sic*]'. I explained above how this differs from Nietzsche's 'Eternal Recurrence'. Petrie uses this cyclical alternation to justify oligarchic society:

> The necessary foundation, he asserts, of any new period of civilisation, so far as government is concerned, is strong personal rule. The next stage is an oligarchy in which the unity of the country is maintained by law instead of by autocracy. Then comes the transformation to a democracy, and with it the gradual end of things. 'When democracy has obtained full power the majority without capital necessarily eat up the capital of the minority, and the civilisation steadily decays until the inferior population is swept away to make room for a fitter people. . . .' [66]

Hulme adds the topical coda that this should persuade one to preserve the restraining influence of the House of Lords.

Storer perhaps acquainted Hulme with De Vries's mutation theory (although Bergson had referred to it in *L'Évolution créatrice*) and Hulme uses De Vries's contention that 'Variations of intellect follow just the same invariable law as variations in the length of limbs in the animal species' to prove that 'the percentage of capable and disinterested people in any society is always the same and is always small'. [67] Hence democracy must lead to social disaster. Beneath the superficial similarity with Nietzsche's élitism Hulme's outlook is more pessimistic. Nietzsche might be described as a realist who discarded life-perpetuating illusions with a compulsive self-laceration but nevertheless retained the humanist hope that a superman could evolve. Hulme by contrast, like Ludovici and Storer, is almost totally negative; reactionary, traditionalist intransigence replaces Nietzsche's courageous faith in the human capacity for self-transcendence. While Nietzsche is exuberantly Dionysian in the face of his tragic conception of life, the disciplinarian Hulme and Eliot's revival of Original Sin represents the approach of extirpating vital energy which Nietzsche so persistently decried. Thus for Hulme 'Romanticism' derives from Lasserre and denotes naïve faith in progress and belief in the importance of democracy. Its hollow evolutionism leads to the 'classical' reaction, whose creed Hulme conveniently summarised under four headings: 'Constancy', 'Order, Authority', 'Hierarchy' and 'Nationalism'.[68]

In 1911, therefore, literature merged with politics in a struggle against Romanticism and Liberalism by Tory, religio-secular authoritarianism. Traditional values in art were presented as the natural correlative of neo-feudalism or an aristocratic, agrarian society. If Hulme's reactionary ideas are now familiar by virtue of their similarity to Eliot's, an examination of their original context helps to illuminate Edwardian literary history, revealing to what extent aesthetic reorientation may be directly conditioned by sociological factors. Far from being detached philosophical or stylistic speculation, the new 'Classicism', which led Hulme from literature to painting, was firmly rooted in contemporary political debate.

# 5 Towards Abstraction

In Chapters 2 and 3 I analysed the re-emergence of empathetic and transcendentalist beliefs in English art-criticism of the 1890s and in the work of Lipps and Bergson. I hope now to demonstrate how this quasi-mystical aesthetics, most influentially epitomised by Bergsonism, saturated the visual arts of the pre-war years, rendering Futurism, German Expressionism and Vorticism essentially congruous movements, a fact which the predominantly formalistic approach of recent critics has obscured.

The abstract expressionist Symbolism established in *fin-de-siècle* poetry was now extended to the visual arts in the semi-abstract or abstract expressionism of the *Blaue Reiter*, the Futurist Balla and the Vorticists. At the same time the reaction against scientifically dispassionate, photographic Impressionism developed beyond the imaginative subjectivism of the 1890s into the empathetic animism of the Bergsonian Futurists, the Schopenhauerian Franz Marc, the Theosophist Kandinsky, and the Vorticists. The two tendencies are therefore not mutually exclusive: the same stylistic vocabulary might serve for different varieties of Symbolism. The crucial point is that Vorticism, far from evidencing a life-denying impulse as Hulme and later commentators have maintained, was in fact imbued with animism, expressing symbolically either an abstract state of consciousness or empathetic interaction with the external world. A chronological account, beginning in 1911, will place this in perspective.

The last chapter recounted the revolution in Hulme's socio-political views. This necessitated a new aesthetic, as Hulme explains:

> I came to believe first of all, for reasons quite unconnected with art, that the Renaissance attitude was coming to an end, and was then confirmed in that by the emergence of this art. (*Spec*, 79).

About the time that I arrived at this kind of conviction I saw

119

> Byzantine mosaics for the first time. . . . Finally I recognised this
> geometrical character re-emerging in modern art.   (*Spec*, 81)

Early in 1911 Hulme's ideological outlook was changed by Lasserre,
and when in April 1911 he saw Byzantine mosaics in Ravenna this
helped to mould his 'classical' convictions. Bergson's vitalism and
Hulme's hitherto empathetic theory of art were then seen as
evidencing the final extraordinary efflorescence of post-Renaissance
humanism before its imminent decay (cf. *FS*, 119–20).

Hulme's gradual rejection of Bergsonism invalidated not only his
empathetic aesthetics but also his 'impressionist' poetics. Hence
Bergsonian Futurism, which combined both, attracted Hulme's
scornful dismissal as 'the deification of the flux, the last efflorescence
of impressionism' (*Spec*, 94).

As far as literature is concerned, some aspects of Marinetti's
Futurist experiments recall the poetic technique Hulme had
suggested in his 'Lecture on Modern Poetry'. In his manifesto
'Destruction of Syntax – Wireless Imagination – Words at Liberty'
(May 1913; trs. in part in *Poetry and Drama*, Sep. 1913) Marinetti
argued that the accelerated pace of modern technological society
demanded from the writer a revolutionary literary medium to give
adequate expression to the new sensibility this had engendered. The
result is a form of telegraphic verse, liberated from syntactic
connections and strict punctuation, in which the writer will
breathlessly 'assault your nerves with visual, auditory, olfactory
sensations, just as they come to him'. Marinetti's reliance on
onomatopoeia    was    innocuous,    but    his    statement    that
'Images . . . are not flowers to be picked and chosen parsimo-
niously. They constitute the very life-blood of poetry. Poetry must
be an uninterrupted sequence of new images. Without this it is only
anaemic and chaotic' was too close for comfort to Hulme's earlier
ideas.[1] In literary technique, therefore, the Futurists were a
disquieting reminder of the past. Hulme's chief reason for attacking
the Futurists, however, was the artists' Bergsonian, empathetic
aesthetic.

It is only recently that the relations between Futurism and
Vorticism have received the attention of critics, previously satisfied
with only fleeting references. Hugh Kenner, for example, who
ignored Futurism in *The Poetry of Ezra Pound* (1951), in his
monumental *The Pound Era* writes simply, 'The Vorticists disowned
Futurism because it denied tradition.' Robert Ross cites comments

on the Futurists' praise of the machine; Hugh Witemeyer writes that 'the task of Marinetti's Futurism' was the recording of 'continuous images of the accelerated contemporary world', while Donald Davie's *Ezra Pound: Poet as Sculptor*, which with that title might have been expected to pay some attention to the relationship between Vorticism and Futurism, and his *Ezra Pound* pass over the movement altogether.[2]

Following Wees's exposition of Wyndham Lewis's propagandist manoeuvrings in relation to Marinetti which lay behind the emergence of *Blast*, the tendency is to treat Futurism in terms of what Lewis called 'Automobilism', Marinetti's rather puerile excitement at machinery and speed.[3] Ronald Bush, for example, who explicitly bases his treatment of Vorticism on Wees, commences his rather ill-informed account by a reference to 'a Futurist painting like *Nude Descending a Staircase*' and by commenting on Lewis's paintings that they 'made use of rhythmic lines, a Futurist idiom, but his theory explicitly rejected Futurist rationale. To Lewis, the moving-picture pretensions of Marinetti were absurdly "impressionist and scientific," and prevented the Futurists from attaining the true artist's deliberateness and control.'[4] The emphasis in this description of Futurism is clearly on dynamism as an external property of movement, which is indeed the analysis offered by most authoritative histories of modern painting.

Werner Haftmann, for example, writes, 'What the Futurists discovered in modern civilisation was dynamism, "vehement sensations of movement and speed, the exuberance of action"', and, later, 'The actual aims of Vorticism are hard to define. The word was meant to suggest suction, whirlpool, maelstrom, a state of exaltation, spiritual daring, aggressive intellectual action. All this of course was close to Futurism . . . .' George Heard Hamilton comments, 'They called for the immediate identification of artist and spectator with the particular character of modern life which for them was to be found in the city, in an environment of men and machines moving at a new and exhilarating tempo', and, although he does refer to the movement's debt to Bergsonism, he belittles the importance of this influence, reading 'universal dynamism' principally as 'dynamic sensation' and physical motion. In the standard work on the movement, Marianne Martin grasps neither the fundamental importance nor the essential nature of Bergson's influence on the Futurist painters, seizing on accidentals rather than the anti-positivist philosophy which underlies them. In her only specific reference linking Bergson with the Futurist painters, she suggests that Bergson's *Matter and Memory* and *Time and Free Will* are the inspiration behind Russolo's *Ricordi di una notte*, in which he attempted to 'paint the processes of memory itself, i.e. the flux of spiritual states', experimenting with 'the pictorial possibilities of simultaneous, interpenetrating imagery suggested by Bergson's evocative descriptions of psychic duration'.[5] The Futurists one encounters in text-books are accordingly intent on devising a technique to represent the experience of movement in a formalistic manner related to contemporary experiments in photography. There is little understanding of what they intended by their use of 'force-lines' other than just this representation of objects in various stages of motion.

Now intoxication with speed and activity is exactly the view one would form of Futurism from Marinetti's first manifesto and his travelling circus of noise-tuners and poetic happenings with their loud declamations of onomatopoeic verse. But if one reads a range of Futurist manifestos which explain clearly the aspirations behind their technical experiments it soon becomes apparent that Marinetti, who was a gifted publicist but not a creative artist, had little grasp of the aesthetic aims of the Futurist painters and sculptors. Their writings present an unmistakably unorthodox view of Futurism if one has been conditioned to see this chiefly as Marinettism. I wish therefore to challenge the prime relevance of the established view of Futurism and to suggest a common interest, not merely technical, between Futurism and Vorticism in terms of spiritual perception, the empathy which I have traced from its Romantic origins. My argument will accordingly prove somewhat disconcerting to those familiar with the existing critical consensus; my aim is to shake these preconceptions and to reveal the pervasive transcendentalism which present-day critics are reluctant to acknowledge.

In March 1912 the annotated catalogue to the *Exhibition of Works of the Italian Futurist Painters* at the Sackville Gallery (which had moved from the Bernheim-Jeune gallery in Paris the previous month) published 'Initial Manifesto of Futurism' (20 Feb 1909), 'Futurist Painting: Technical Manifesto' (11 Apr 1910) and 'Exhibitors to the Public' (5 Feb 1912). These texts provided a valuable summary of the Futurist aesthetic, most importantly that of Boccioni.

Their central tenet derived from Bergson's belief in an uninterrupted flux of experience evidenced in continuous and unpredictable development both in the *durée réelle* of the individual and in the *évolution créatrice* of the external world. Boccioni in particular argued that this revealed an underlying identity between an object or person and the environment: the aim of the painter was accordingly to penetrate by intuition to an object's '*dynamic sensation,* that is to say, the particular rhythm of each object, its inclination, its movement, or, more exactly, its interior force' and, by extending into structural decomposition the 'force-lines' of this characteristic dynamism (the object's 'absolute motion') to demonstrate the interpenetration and interaction of the object with its surroundings (its 'relative motion') and the surcharged atmosphere, a mystical aura, it produced (cf. Plate 5). This clearly resembles Pound's remarks on *virtù* in Cavalcanti, investigated in Chapters 6 and 8.[6]

The Futurists' catchword of 'dynamism' and their painterly adaptation of the recent photographic experiments of Muybridge, Marey and Anschütz aroused the understandable misconception perpetuated in their critical heritage. Their fascination with the representation of the indivisible flow of movement was, however, not primarily formalistic but mystical, provoked by their aspiration to retain an absolute fidelity to Bergson's transcendental account of experience. If one could capture the essence of *rhythm*, one was thereby representing the individual quintessence of an object, realised and therefore made perceptible in its force-lines (compare Symons's equally animistic use of this term). Kandinsky (whose views are discussed below), as if to emphasise the fundamental similarity between his mystical perception of the world and that of the Futurists, also spoke of the inner 'vibrations' which objects arouse.[7]

The importance of *Einfühlung* or intuition to the Futurists is revealed unequivocally in the exhibition catalogue. They maintain that, just as human beings are judged by their mood, so inanimate objects have a psychic aura revealed through their force-lines which vary 'according to the characteristic personality of the object and the emotions of the onlooker'. This perceptual relationship gives primacy therefore to emotional interaction with the environment, which then becomes the subject of the painting. Through a mysterious intuitive affinity – '*physical transcendentalism*' – one becomes aware of the atmospheric quality an object creates through the emanations of its force and 'We interpret nature by rendering these objects upon the canvas as the beginnings or the prolongations of the rhythms impressed upon our sensibility by these very objects.'[8]

The Futurists' dislike of Cubist painting reveals why Hulme, rejecting the Bergsonian aesthetic, moved towards abstraction. Boccioni, from a position of Bergsonian animism, attacks the Cubist 'objective knowledge of reality', whose 'concept of form is the result of dispassionate, scientific measurement, which kills . . . dynamic warmth'. Picasso's formal and intellectual analysis of an object offends Boccioni, just as Bergson was horrified by the dissection of the personality by associationist psychologists; Picasso, he claims, dispassionately removes the life from the object he depicts. There is a divergence in attitude between the emotional lyricism of the Futurists, for whom form was an expression of the object's spiritual essence through its force-lines, and the detached objectivity of Cubist painting. Boccioni stresses again that 'We live out the object in the motion of its inner forces; we do not depict its incidental appearance.' 'Inspiration' is 'the act in which the artist totally immerses himself in the object, living out its characteristic motion'.[9]

The pervasive influence of Bergson's empathetic aesthetics (and in this case his Romantic evolutionism also) was further evidenced in the magazine *Rhythm*, launched in June 1911 by John Middleton Murry. Its first issue opened with an article by Frederick Goodyear asserting that the ideal society, formerly distanced either historically, geographically or metaphysically, was now about to be realised.[10] Thanks to Bergson, Utopia had turned up on our very doorstep: 'Thelema, the soul's ideal home, has become a plain practical issue'; it lies simply in 'the ordinary human future':

> This vast access of hope that has come to the race has been conditioned by the growth of the evolutionary idea. Men have always sought for a permanent stable reality in this world of flux. At last they have found it in the principle of flux itself. Change, the old enemy, has become our greatest friend and ally. Because of this identification of the absolute and the relative we are able to look forward with confidence to the realization of our wildest aspirations. We have all become futurists, for it is impossible to miss the moral implicit in Hegel and Darwin.

One can imagine Hulme or Eliot grimacing at Goodyear's rather ill-executed attempt at dialectic sleight-of-hand. There could be no

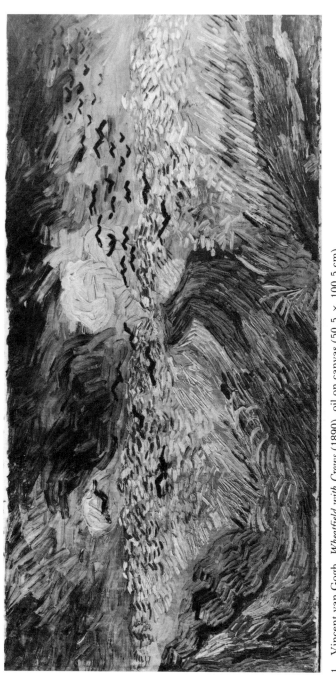

1 Vincent van Gogh, *Wheatfield with Crows* (1890), oil on canvas (50.5 × 100.5 cm)

2  James Abbott McNeill Whistler, *Nocturne in Black and Gold: The Fire Wheel* (1875), oil on canvas (54.3 × 76.2 cm)

3   James Abbott McNeill Whistler, *Nocturne in Blue and Gold: Old Battersea Bridge* (c. 1872–5), oil on canvas (67.9 × 50.8 cm)

4   Stanhope Forbes, *The Health of the Bride* (1889), oil on canvas (152 × 202 cm)

5  Umberto Boccioni, *Dynamism of a Soccer Player* (1913), oil on canvas
(193.2 × 201 cm)

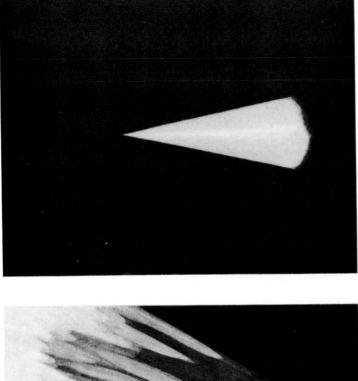

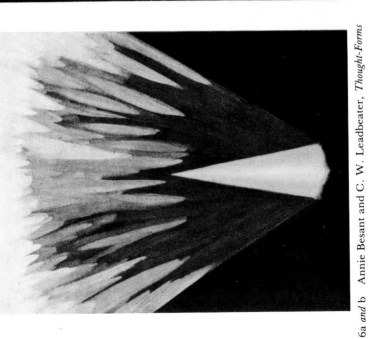

6a *and* b   Annie Besant and C. W. Leadbeater, *Thought-Forms*

The right-hand thought-form depicts the 'Upward Rush of Devotion', the left-hand the 'Response of the LOGOS to the appeal made to Him'. It is remarkable that the 'vibration' of divine energy in Plate 6a is represented graphically in a fashion similar to the dynamic force lines of Boccioni or Franz Marc. The shared concept of the radiation of psychic 'influence' or *virtù* is expressed in the same representational vocabulary.

7 Franz Marc, *Tierschicksale* (*Die Bäume zeigten ihre Ringe, die Tiere ihre Adern*) The Fate of the Animals (The Trees showed their Rings, the Animals their Veins) (1913), oil on canvas (195 × 263.5 cm)

8   Wyndham Lewis, *Planners: Happy Day* (c. 1912–13), pen, pencil and gouache
(31 × 38 cm)

clearer indication of the association of Bergsonism with Romantic eudemonism; that this was editorial policy was confirmed by Murry's verbiage. He enthuses over Art's eternal evolution which removes veils between man and 'the great divinity immanent in the world'. Bergson's importance, Murry proclaims, is his defence of the supremacy of the intuition and spiritual vision of the artist over scientific rationalism. He has overcome the crude opposition of subject and object by revealing an underlying spiritual unity: artistic modernism 'penetrates beneath the outward surface of the world, and disengages the *rhythms* that lie at the heart of things'.[11] Their common Bergsonian derivation explains the similarity of these views with those of the Futurists. (Further striking illustration of the contemporary animistic and anti-materialist usage of 'rhythm' in the arts is provided by Huntly Carter's effusively Bergsonian *The New Spirit in Drama and Art* (1912) and Laurence Binyon's account of the importance of cosmic 'Spiritual Rhythm' in Chinese art.[12])

The extraordinary currency of such sentiments is revealed by the vatic strains of the lecture Roger Fry delivered at the Grafton Gallery at the close of the exhibition 'Manet and the Post-Impressionists'.[13] Fry begins in the sober tones one would expect of the former buyer for the Metropolitan Museum in New York, who had been offered the directorship of the National Gallery. Yet his peroration recalls the fervent emotionalism of Bergson's lecture 'L'intuition philosophique', which Hulme heard in April 1911.[14]

Fry presents the Post-Impressionists as embryonic abstract expressionists whose work directly stimulates the imagination not through representational qualities but rather through arrangements of form and colour analogous to the musician's arrangements of sound.[15] In evidence he cites the decorative patterns on some of the pottery in the exhibition[16] which have mere hints at representation, yet still arouse emotion through the 'spiritual correspondences' of 'Particular rhythms of line and particular harmonies of colour'. His argument develops the English *fin-de-siècle* interest, engendered by *art nouveau* and Burne-Jones's paintings, in the expressive potential of line and abstract design (cf. MacColl on pp. 37–8 *supra*), correlating also, like Whistler, the symbolic, non-discursive qualities of abstract art with those of music. As an external equivalent for a mental state an abstract painting depends on an intuitively perceived relationship between its formal qualities and the spectator's emotions: what Fry terms 'spiritual correspondences'. But Fry is not content with this psychological explanation; instead he attempts to associate this subordination of mimetic representation to imaginative suggestivity, with the contemporary reaction against materialism.

Overstating his case somewhat as far as their paintings were concerned, Fry notes the transition in the Post-Impressionists 'from an entirely representative to a non-representative and expressive art' relying on 'significant and expressive form'.[17] This has released again the 'imaginative appeal' of painting which Fry (curiously recalling Yeats) regards as not an isolated phenomenon, but merely one indication of the general orientation away from the 'scientific or mechanical view of the universe'. His line of argument strikingly resembles Kandinsky's in *The Art of Spiritual Harmony*. The 'vast' and 'desirable' possibilities of scientific exploitation have 'tended to blind our eyes to other realities; the realities of our spiritual nature and the justice of our demand for its gratification. Art has suffered in this process, since art, like religion, appeals to the non-mechanical parts of our nature, to what in us is rhythmic and vital'. But now with the Post-Impressionist movement art has once again become 'conterminous [*sic*] with the whole range of human inspiration and desire'. Thus Fry's Bergsonian employment of 'rhythm' as a quasi-spiritual, 'non-mechanical' or noumenal quality (similar to *durée réelle*) and not merely a formal property of a canvas recalls Symons's equally ambivalent usage.

By February 1912, perhaps when he read the Futurists' Bernheim-Jeune catalogue, Hulme had assembled a nexus of ideologies associated by Bergsonism: Futurism, Fabianism and Romanticism shared a horror of 'constancy' and a faith in 'rhythm' and 'dynamism'. The correlation is expanded in 'A Tory Philosophy' from the lecture Hulme gave in February 1912 to the 'Heretics' on 'Anti-Romanticism and Original Sin'. There Hulme linked Rousseau and H. G. Wells (like Frederick Goodyear in their belief in an evolving ideal society), continuing,

Repeat the word 'Progress' often enough and it is easy to delude oneself into denying the truths of the doctrine of Original Sin amidst the mess of hypothetical Utopias, which ignore the principle of the constancy of Man. It never occurred to the Classicists to have any illusions about Progress; and here Mr Hulme launched forth on a diatribe against Lady Welby [a rival translator of Bergson], Goethe, Mr Lowes Dickinson, Mr

Alfred Benn, and all those who take the Spiral as the symbol of the Nature of man. . . .

To judge by the reviewer's colourful account Hulme was at his most obstreperous: '*Dynamic, Vibration, Rhythm* ("they even have a paper") were words which he abhorred and on this note of abhorence [*sic*] the paper came to a close. A long and lively discussion followed, in which Mr Hulme expended much energy in convincing the uninitiated that their questions were irrelevant.'[18] Politics and aesthetics again fused to determine Hulme's movement towards a fixed, hierarchical society with religious sanctioning, and ultimately an abstract art which isolated objects from the flux of experience to endow them with aesthetic permanence.

The question of how this anti-Romantic sensibility might find expression was, however, problematical. Storer, who had started from the same premises as Hulme, but lacked the theoretical standpoint which Worringer was to provide, was clearly disoriented. He applied Nietzsche's stylistic critique of Wagner to the neurasthenic decadence of the 1890s: 'Theirs was almost simply the art of sensation, the art of creating an "atmosphere," the art of attacking first and foremost the nerves of their public.' He detests this over-emphasis of the personality, and its ephemeral cultivation of the momentary artistic sensation, the method of Impressionist painting and poetry.[19]

Uncontrolled emotionality also characterised the Barbizon painters and their followers, the 'Hague school'. This Fontainebleau 'miasma' exerted, Storer felt, a malignant influence on contemporary art:

Beauty . . . in the hands of nine out of every ten painters to-day has become a formula . . . a dreamy-creamy thing, a *mélange* of subtle colours, an association of moonshine and mist, a languor, a yearning. It is nearly always wet, too. . . .

Storer defined this artistic technique as 'crepusculism'; its sentimental vagueness approximated to the diction of Nineties poetry against whose 'Crepuscular Spirit' Pound planned a 'Revolt'.[20] In reaction against this 'romantic' landscape therefore Storer welcomed 'the cold austerity of the modern classical school struggling into existence with the aid of the geometric and archaic formulae of modern French and German artists'.[21]

But, despite his intuitive feeling that a new direction was urgently required in painting, Storer lacked the critical vocabulary and the ideological overview which Worringer provided. Hence the new Classicism at the end of the rainbow seemed always to elude him. In principle he welcomed the Post-Impressionists, but his enthusiasm for them and later *avant-garde* movements fluctuated more than Hulme's. He praised Gauguin but regarded Cézanne's reputation as inflated, and on other occasions felt dubious about the experimental trappings of modern art. He appreciated Picasso's drawing, but criticised the intellectual vagaries of Cubist methods, which were for him a trivial mannerism. The new art would, Storer hoped, be refined from this rather crude ore. He accordingly located the richest lode of English art in the work of Gertler and Currie rather than in the semi-abstract paintings of Wyndham Lewis, who, Storer felt, had not found an appropriate technique.[22]

On purely literary questions Storer felt on safer ground. His later poetry comprises adaptations and translations from Greek which embody his hope for a Hellenistic revival in modern art and literature. He valued classical directness and austerity, its refusal to strive for passionate sensationalism; modern art sacrificed overall balance to accentuate the minor element.[23] Not surprisingly Storer's taste turned to eighteenth-century English poetry. His best piece of writing, the introduction to his selection of poems and letters by William Cowper, provides a sympathetic and historically grounded account, more impressive than Hulme's catch-all terms, of a viable, 'anti-Romantic' literature.[24]

Unlike Storer, Hulme never expressed his new aesthetic in poetry. The original title of 'Romanticism and Classicism' when first delivered in 1912 was 'The New Philosophy of Art as Illustrated in Poetry' but at this stage the new philosophy was still Bergsonism. The only additions to his earlier arguments are the rather trite distinction between imagination and fancy, and the propagandist framework of *L'Action française*. His 'German Chronicle' written for June 1913 shows him still preoccupied with language and the psychology of style, and it seems possible that he saw no direct application in literature for his discovery of Worringer's explanation of abstraction in art.[25]

For the focus of Hulme's interests had once again changed, moving from stylistics to ideologically conditioned criticism of the visual arts. Just as Ludovici had reduced art to an illustration of his political beliefs, so Hulme, although to a less extreme degree, was now to seize on the hitherto sporadic experiments in abstraction of artists such as Epstein, and to exert pressure on them to develop in this direction as a tangible realisation of the validity of his new anti-humanist theories. His earlier views on literary style had helped to influence Imagism by returning poetic language to visual, denotative concreteness, and the perceptual 'image' instead of the atmospheric vagueness and calculated imprecision of the English 'Symbolist' epigones. His empathetic Symbolist poetry likewise looked forward to Imagism proper. Now Hulme's defence of abstract art provided crucial public support for the Vorticist artists.

For it was in art rather than literature that Hulme found contemporary realisation of the tragic intensity of the 'religious attitude', at first in Epstein's sculpture. Epstein had produced an isolated experiment in primitive distortion in the 1910 *Sunflower*, but his major work in this technique only began with the carvings in 'flenite' (actually serpentine) of 1913. The instinctive adoption by contemporary artists of a form of geometrical abstraction akin to that in which the sensibility of earlier hierarchical societies had found expression seemed to Hulme implicit confirmation of his thesis of the break-up of post-Renaissance humanism and the modern progressive conception of life (as evidenced in the association of Bergson's *évolution créatrice* with Romantic eudemonism – *Spec*, 77–82, 91–4, 86, 9; *FS*, 105–6, 119–20). Accordingly his aesthetic interest focused on the visual arts, dismissing as misguided or irrelevant his earlier enthusiasm for literary neo-classicism (*FS*, 113). This ideological fervour provoked in December 1913 Hulme's rather ironic confrontation over Epstein with Ludovici, whose position was actually quite close to Hulme's own.[26]

In his *New Age* art-criticism Ludovici maintained the viewpoint expressed in *Nietzsche and Art*. The arts, he argued, reflect the prevailing social structure and interpret the external world in terms of its shared and accepted *Weltanschauung*. In the absence of a hierarchically ordered polity they had lapsed into the chaos of individualism and undisciplined technical experimentation: Epstein's art and Roberts's *Ulysses* were symptomatic of just such 'individualism à outrance'.[27] His reply to Hulme's intemperate defence of Epstein elaborated this viewpoint. In May 1913 Ludovici had already condemned the 'filthy anarchy of the Cubists, the Futurists and the Independents', which he now categorised as 'the Protestant doctrine of self-expression', the right to individual interpretation of reality without reference to any superior order, and characteristically equated with political anarchy. Their arbitrary expression of subjective states conflicted with the 'hierarchical principle' in accordance with which the enlightened aristocratic few established rigid canons of conventional acceptability.[28]

It seems paradoxical that Hulme's promotion of the new abstract art should derive from approximately the same ideological premisses as Ludovici's condemnation, but so events developed. He presented the new geometrical artists as a constructive development from Cézanne and analytical Cubism, who, having studied archaic forms as an aid to formal simplification, did not simply adopt them as a romantic, imitative decoration like Fry's Bloomsbury painters, but rather attempted to express in contemporary terms the intense sensibility to which their receptive sympathy had responded in the 'primitive' art (*FS*, 113–18). The new attitude was 'a desire for austerity and bareness, a striving towards structure'; it was realised in the hard, clean forms of Vorticist painting. Artists' attention had turned from the organic to the mechanical; they produced not the simple geometric forms of archaic art but instead more complicated structural relationships associated with the idea of machinery.

Hulme's rigorous anti-humanism (as dogmatic as Ludovici's 'Nietzscheanism') led therefore to the unwarranted assumption that the adoption by the future Vorticists of a painterly vocabulary of mechanical forms evidenced an anti-vitalist aesthetic, an attempt to extirpate the traditional empathetic delight in natural detail and the organically transient, rather than a desire (influenced by the technical experimentation of other *avant-garde* movements) to communicate emotions in a symbolic medium appealing directly to the contemporary imagination (*Spec*, 95–109).

*A priori* inflexibility leads Hulme, like Ludovici, to assume that a formal vehicle is absolutely indivisible from a particular sensibility or ideology:

> There are two kinds of art, geometrical or abstract, and vital and realistic art, which differ absolutely in kind from the other. They are not modifications of one and the same art, but pursue different aims and are created to satisfy a different desire of the mind.   (*FS*, 119)[29]

His assertion that abstract art is only possible if it coincides with a non-vital, anti-humanist impulse is untenable.

Thus while Hulme's explanations of the artists' techniques were almost uniquely enlightened for their time, the anti-humanist ideology he advanced to explain their supposed intentions was at odds with the artists' own aims. Compare William Roberts's remark that Hulme's 'philosophic ideas' 'certainly played no part in the rise of the English cubist movement in general. Hulme's role . . . vis-à-vis his cubist friends was that of an apologist, their Public Relations Officer as it were.'[30] While Hulme proclaimed that their 'geometrical' abstraction derived from a hieratic sensibility akin to that underlying Byzantine art, to the artists themselves at the time (Lewis's well-known theories resembling those of Hulme, as expounded most notably by Geoffrey Wagner,[31] are a later development not corroborated by his articles in the Vorticist period) it was merely a new technical vehicle for empathetic or, less frequently, abstract expressionist Symbolism.[32]

Hulme therefore, although an indispensable voice in public support, whose strong personality indubitably encouraged the artists to pursue their new experiments, stood in theoretical isolation from the empathetic art of the Futurists, Expressionists, Neo-Realists and Vorticists which was the predominant aesthetic of the period.

Wadsworth, more representative than Hulme of the attitude of the Vorticist artists, stated, 'logically this axiom must be accepted: that the artist can employ any forms (natural, abstracted or abstract) to express himself, if his feelings demand it'.[33] Hulme by contrast took explicit issue with an article by Charles Ginner, whose master was van Gogh, which advocated a representational form of expressionism.[34] Ginner was attempting to found a 'Neo-Realist' movement in opposition to 'Naturalism' which he termed 'the photography of Nature'. Adopting the interpretation of Post-Impressionism popularised by Roger Fry, whose exhibition has been described as 'In a way . . . an explicitly anti-Impressionist manifesto', Ginner contrasted the 'scientific' realism of the Impressionists and Neo-Impressionists with the 'self-expression' of the Post-Impressionists.[35] In this Ginner was simply voicing the profoundly felt general aspirations of artists who wished to reject the sort of objective detachment from a world they perceived as full of vital, spiritual significance, which Hulme was now advocating. Indeed, as I shall show in detail, there had been an almost universal adoption of empathetic theories in the visual arts in reaction against 'scientific', 'materialist' Impressionism. Hulme's dispassionate attitude towards the external world was exactly what the age was rejecting. While he attempted to redirect attention away from what he regarded as the organically transient by making it artificial and therefore in a sense dead (the accepted view of Lewis's 'Vorticist' aesthetic, by virtue of his later reformulations), those around him still held to the Romantic, anti-materialist animism Hulme had now disavowed.

This antithesis had been the focus of interest in English art ever since Desmond MacCarthy's preface, written from Fry's notes, to the exhibition catalogue *Manet and the Post-Impressionists* in November 1910.[36] MacCarthy explained the technical innovations of the Impressionists as designed to capture 'hitherto unrecognised aspects of objects', grouping them with no distinction with the scientific theories of the Neo-Impressionists (a term he did not employ), Seurat, Cross and Signac. This detached concern with external appearance was regarded by the Post-Impressionists as insufficient. Not content merely with 'recording impressions of colour or light', they utilised the Impressionists' discoveries 'to express emotions which the objects themselves evoked'. The Impressionists had elevated the reproduction of appearances to a dogma which had lost sight of the individual's interaction with what he perceived. Their desire to create an illusionistic record of the perception of light-effects, in the face of conventional representational prejudices, led them to forget that what they were depicting was not simply a superficial husk but had an individual haecceity. In the vocabulary of German Romantic philosophy, they never penetrated beneath representations to things-in-themselves. In MacCarthy's words, their

> receptive, passive attitude towards the appearances of things often hindered them from rendering their real *significance*. Impressionism encouraged an artist to paint a tree as it appeared to him at the moment under particular circumstances. It insisted so much upon the importance of his rendering this exact impression that his work often completely failed to express a tree at all; as transferred to canvas it was just so much shimmer and colour. The 'treeness' of the tree was not rendered at all; all the emotion and associations such as trees may be made to convey in poetry were omitted.

Their successors had come to realise again that 'the most important subject matter of art' was 'exploring and expressing that emotional *significance* which lies in things'. Their attempt to recapture this lost lyricism led them to subordinate pure imitation of appearances to formal simplification. As MacCarthy proclaimed, with all the force of a new revelation, 'Primitive art, like the art of children, consists not so much in an attempt to represent what the eye perceives, as to put a line around a mental conception of the object . . . . there comes a point when the accumulations of an increasing skill in mere representation begin to destroy the expressiveness of the design.'[37] This stress on imagination and the inner 'significance' of objects is, as I shall show, the keystone of Lewis's Vorticist theory. The important element in art, it was gradually becoming clear, was empathetic interaction with the environment.

The 'Neo-Realist', according to Ginner (accentuating the empathy implicit in Furse's remarks, discussed *supra*, pp. 39–40), would not just portray the 'superficial' aspects of what he perceived but rather interpret it through his personal vision and record this intense perceptual interaction with nature by accurately depicting the scene as an expressive embodiment of the emotional state it had engendered:

> Neo-Realism must be a deliberate and objective transposition of the object . . . under observation, which has for certain specific reasons appealed to the artist's ideal or mood, for self-expression. When the artist is carried away by an intense desire to interpret an object or an agglomeration of objects, the only sure means at his disposal to find and express that unknown quantity in the object which raised his desire, mood, or ideal, and which united his inner self with the aforesaid unknown quantity, is a deliberate research, concise study and transposition. It is only this intimate relation between the artist and the object which can produce original and great work.

The indispensable element was the empathetic perceptual relationship – 'A pictorial work of Art must be a complete expression of the artist in relation to Nature.'[38]

An almost identical reaction against Impressionism was taking place simultaneously in Germany, where the impact of the Post-Impressionists had been just as belated as in England.[39] The emerging Expressionists, who were the predominant influence on Pound and Wadsworth at the time of Vorticism (and probably on Lewis, although he characteristically never acknowledged this, just as he found it convenient to drop Marinetti and to deny any influence from Cubist technique on Vorticist art) had an unmistakably empathetic aesthetic.

In Munich, where Kandinsky arrived in 1906, there was a movement towards expressive simplification of reality (as in the earlier, wholly representational Dresden group, *Die Brücke*) and, ultimately, the communication of emotion exclusively through the formal elements of a painting. Under the influence first of the Post-Impressionists, then of early Matisse, Kandinsky's paintings evidenced increasing simplification of form and intensification of colour, which he began gradually to liberate from direct attachment to objects, allowing it to assume an independent function as the main expressive element. In 1910 he produced his first partially non-objective works; after 1913 objective paintings were rare.[40]

Far from being purely technical experimentation, however, Kandinsky's development was inspired by an anti-materialist spiritualism. In his view the two major influences on modern art were:

1. The breaking up of the soulless-material life of the nineteenth century; that is, the falling down of the material supports which were thought to be the only firm ones, the decay and dissolution of the individual parts.
2. The building up of the psychic-spiritual life of the twentieth century which we are experiencing and which manifests and embodies itself even now in strong, expressive, and definite forms.[41]

His first point alluded to the metaphysical impact the splitting of the atom had made on his scientific studies, robbing him of any faith in the permanence and stability of the material world, but delighting him on reflection by its suggestion of the 'imminent' 'dissolution of matter'.[42] This experimental revelation of phenomenal transience merely confirmed Kandinsky's determination, like that of his fellow Theosophist Piet Mondrian, to further through abstract (and hence unmaterial) art what he regarded chiliastically as 'The Epoch of the Great Spiritual'.[43]

Thus the introductory section of *The Art of Spiritual Harmony*, paralleling Fry's lecture discussed above, is a sustained attack on the insufficiency of scientific method, and advocacy of a new spiritual art of the 'soul', now beginning to awake from the 'nightmare of materialism' (in other words exactly the same Romantic animism which had first drawn Hulme to Bergson, and which he now rejected). Like Yeats in the 1880s and 1890s, Kandinsky found confirmation of this spiritual reorientation in Mme Blavatsky, Indian mysticism and Maeterlinck's plays, adding further evidence in the paintings of Cézanne which raised still-life to the point of ceasing to be inanimate through his intense awareness of the 'inner life' of objects, and those of Matisse in which he endeavoured to 'reproduce the divine'.[44]

This emphasis on the noumenal quality of art rendered the artist's choice of formal vehicle of secondary importance, provided that it was an authentic expression of his 'inner necessity' – that is, dictated by the promptings of his creative personality. Form was the realisation under emotional pressure of the artist's 'inner resonance', a phrase which denoted a mystical and not simply an aesthetic quality: 'the fact that we are beginning to feel the spirit, the *inner resonance*, in everything'.[45] In Kandinsky's view this 'inner resonance' was beginning to find expression in two distinctive forms of painting: 'the great realism' and 'the great abstraction'. The former was achieved when the artist neglected the superficial 'practical–purposeful' aspects of the object he was depicting, in favour of an intuitive response to the object's essential nature as a thing-in-itself (the parallel with Schopenhauer and Bergson will be obvious).[46] Kandinsky saw evidence of this quality in the naïve, unclouded perception of children's drawings and in the paintings of the French primitive Henri Rousseau, which

> endeavor to drive the outwardly artistic out of the picture and to embody the content of the work by simple ('inartistic') reproduction of the simple solid object.
> The outer shell of the object, which is understood and fixed in the picture in this way, and the simultaneous striking out of the usual obtrusive beauty, expose most surely *the inner resonance of the thing*. Especially through this shell and by this reducing of the 'artistic' to the minimum, the *soul* of the object stands out most strongly, since the outer palatable beauty can no longer divert.[47]

Naïvety, like the formal simplification of the Post-Impressionists, restored primacy to the empathetic perception of the artist.

Kandinsky's personal search for the most immediate communication of the spirituality he saw beneath the phenomena of the external world – '*The world resounds. It is a cosmos of spiritually acting beings. So dead matter is living spirit*' – led him from the great realism to the great abstraction. In so doing he hoped to avoid the distracting appearances of external representation, to

> eliminate, apparently fully, the objective (the real), and . . . embody the content of the work in 'unmaterial' forms. The abstract life of the objective forms is reduced to the minimum, and consequently, the striking predominance of the abstract units expose the inner resonance of the picture most certainly.[48]

This fascination with 'inner resonance' was elucidated and justified in *The Art of Spiritual Harmony* (1912). Long has noted Kandinsky's initial insecurity about the communicative adequacy of abstract form and colour and consequent use of hidden religious iconography to reinforce the expressiveness of his paintings (see n. 40). His fears were allayed, as Ringbom has demonstrated, by a Theosophical text, Annie Besant and C. W. Leadbeater's *Thought-Forms*, which maintained that mental phenomena generated supersensible 'vibrations', manifested in distinctive (thought-) forms and colours, which were in effect symbolic equivalents for complex moods (cf. Plates 6a and 6b).[49] The 'vibrations' of their characteristic aura provoked, as if on a Chladni sound-plate, an identical resonance in the perceiver, who intuitively translated this rhythmic pattern back into the unique affective state which it expressed. In moving towards a non-objective art, therefore, Kandinsky could maintain with some assurance that colours have a '*psychic effect*', producing 'a corresponding spiritual vibration' in the perceiver.[50] I shall argue in Chapter 6 that Pound drew from this fashionable interest in spiritual vibrations or 'rhythm' the notion, crucial to his poetics, of art as the symbolic transmission of psychic energy.

A close friend of Kandinsky, who shared his transcendentalist outlook and provides a further accurate pointer to trends in the period which will help to elucidate similar views in England, was the painter Franz Marc. Before breaking away to form the *Blaue Reiter* group in December 1911, the two had been members of the *Neue Künstlervereinigung* (NKV) in Munich. The circular issued to mark this group's foundation stated, 'Our starting-point is the belief that the artist is constantly engaged in collecting experiences in an inner world, in addition to the impressions he receives from the external world, from nature.'[51] It is interesting to note that the

NKV, which later rejected Kandinsky's work as too extreme, chose as its common basis the desire to evoke in painting an expressionist interaction with the external world. The aim of the Munich *avant-garde*, like Ginner's Neo-Realists, was to progress beyond the techniques developed by the Impressionists for the direct recording of their objective perception of momentarily fluctuating appearances, by fusing these with a more creative, self-projective element. The artist was to be not merely a detached recording machine of unprecedented accuracy, but someone who was engaged empathetically with what he perceived.

Fry and MacCarthy's strictures on Impressionism resembled the views of Franz Marc, in his comments on the second exhibition of the NKV in September 1910:

All the pictures include a plus-factor, which robs the public of its pleasure, but which is in every case the principal merit of the work: the completely spiritualized, de-materialized inwardness of perception which our fathers, the artists of the nineteenth century, never even tried to achieve in their 'pictures'. This bold undertaking, to take the *matière* which Impressionism sank its teeth into, and spiritualize it, is a necessary reaction, which began with Gauguin in Pont-Aven

and, later:

Today we search behind the veil of appearances for the hidden things in nature which seem to us more important than the discoveries of the Impressionists. . . . We seek and we paint the inner, spiritual side of nature, and we do this not out of whim and caprice for the novel, but because we *see* this other side, as in former times they saw suddenly purple shadows and objects veiled in ether.[52]

Kandinsky's delight in the haecceity of all things, their 'inner resonance', was echoed by Marc's pantheistic reverence for all created life, particularly animals, in which he intuited a 'virginal sense of life'.[53] A letter of December 1908 stated, 'I try to intensify my sensitivity for the organic *rhythm* of all things; I seek pantheist empathy with the *vibration* and flow of the blood of nature – in the trees, in the animals, in the air' (cf. Plate 7).[54] Encouraged by the emotionally intense colour in the paintings of Kandinsky and his friend August Macke, Marc began to use colour in an unnaturalistic manner, exclusively as an indication of his emotional mood, developing a system of associative symbolism.

His aim was to create an alternative mode of representation from that which reproduced the visual image on the retina. Marc wished to penetrate beneath appearance to essence and realise this haecceity from within the object rather than by approaching it externally. His ideal was to avoid reducing an animal to an element of a humanly perceived landscape and hence a conveniently labelled entity, but instead to force the spectator to take account of its mysterious otherness by a painterly technique which deliberately flouted unreflecting preconceptions. Unnaturalistic use of colour was Marc's programmatic indication that he was symbolically representing the soul of an animal as it affected him emotionally, not merely its phenomenal exterior. Like Kandinsky, he seemed to echo Schopenhauer and Bergson:

> Everything has appearance and essence, shell and kernel, mask and truth. What does it say against the inward determination of things that we finger the shell without reaching the kernel, that we live with appearance instead of perceiving the essence, that the mask of things so blinds us that we cannot find the truth?[55]

A technique of descriptive reproduction, such as Impressionism, had the effect, in Marc's view, of imposing the subjective dominance of human rationality on landscape and creatures alike. This was denying the mysterious individuality of anything outside the perceiving self by reducing the perceived to a common, un-differentiated state (the attitude Schopenhauer had labelled '*theoretical egoism*'):

> Art is metaphysical . . . it will free itself from man's purposes and desires. We will no longer paint the forest or the horse as they please us or appear to us, but as they really are, as the forest or the horse feel themselves – their absolute being – which lives behind the appearance which we see.[56]

Marc's viewpoint was ethical; his pantheism and intense, em-pathetic sensibility assured him that all created things had a soul, a spiritual truth implicitly ignored by the reductive objectivity of all traditional art. His almost unrealisable dream was to move away from anthropocentric perception to create works which revealed the multiplicity of subjective awarenesses, animal as well as human, which comprised the spiritual world.

The technical innovations and spirituality of German Expressionism provoked a lively debate in England. In 1912 Michael Sadler, an assistant editor of *Rhythm* and the first English translator of *Über das Geistige in der Kunst*, introduced Kandinsky's theories to England.[57] He summarised the main contentions of the book as, first, the belief that man and the external world are linked by an underlying spiritual identity which the artist reveals to his fellow men. Secondly, that this art concerned with 'expressing the *inner* soul of persons and things will inevitably stray from the *outer* conventions of form and colour; that is to say, it will be definitely unnaturalistic, anti-materialist'. While praising expressionistic licence in departing from absolute fidelity to external detail, Sadler recorded Kandinsky's early doubts that such anti-naturalism could degenerate into pattern-making or merely symbolic use of form and colour, adding the personal coda that 'reality is as essential as naturalism is deplorable'. In August 1913 Roger Fry enthusiastically praised some of Kandinsky's early abstract masterpieces on view at the 1913 Allied Artists' Association salon, giving them his seal of approval: 'They are pure visual music, but I cannot any longer doubt the possibility of emotional expression by such abstract visual signs.'[58]

Controversy in England centred on the extent to which an expressionist art should proceed towards abstraction. Ramiro de Maeztu, despite being a regular attender at Frith Street and heavily influenced ideologically by Hulme, retained a belief, like Ginner, in empathy, which he conveyed in Schopenhauerian terms remarkably reminiscent of Franz Marc:

Painting is the art which shows and proves that the things of Nature and man, as a thing of Nature, have a soul. But the soul is not the individual ego of every being; just the contrary. The soul of each creature is much more than that which he has in common with every other creature in the world. In that sense, painting is always religious. Everyday life shows us only the independence of things, their mutual indifference, and the tragic and hateful impassibility of Nature in face of our pain. . . . Painting, on the contrary, gives us back the unity of things with ourselves and of ourselves with things.

Like Ginner, de Maeztu rejected 'the naturalist and impressionist prejudices' in favour of an art which depicted an object's '*soul*' not merely its 'appearance'. The problem he found with abstract expressionism was that in such a painting as Lewis's *Kermesse*, which presumably represented the spirit of the Kermesse, the viewer was unable to recognise the object whose essence the artist had elicited.[59] In the spring of 1914 there was accordingly one element common to most groups: an abandonment of what was regarded as Impressionist photographic transcription for an 'anti-materialist' art which penetrated beneath superficial aspects to the 'soul' of objects. Opinion was divided, however, on how this empathetic perception should be conveyed. Among English critics Hulme stood alone, on grounds of ideological dogmatism, as the intransigent opponent of empathy.

C. R. W. Nevinson, who had developed from a member of Lewis's Cubist group into the only English Futurist painter of note, stressed what he regarded as the fundamental identity in aesthetic aim beneath the modern movements.[60] All had broken away from 'the superficial and highly accomplished colour-photography into which the Impressionist School degenerated', abandoning 'representation of concrete forms or colours for interpretation by means of abstract forms and colours'. A picture, he insisted, 'must be a plastic abstraction of an emotion, remembered, seen, smelt or heard, not visually but mentally felt'. The principal influence on Nevinson's theories was Kandinsky; revealingly, his argument closely resembles the Vorticist Wadsworth's comments in 'Inner Necessity'. Nevinson pointed out that music is not criticised for being not an imitation or representation of natural sounds, but instead an abstract genre employing formal contrasts: 'So in painting, by means of contrasts, of abstract colour, form, lines, planes and dimensions that don't in the least imitate or represent natural forms, it is possible to create emotions infinitely more stimulating than those created by contemplating nature.' The Futurists developed this doctrine, according to Nevinson's popularising account (prepared in conjunction with Marinetti as a lecture), by attempting to evoke their subjective interpretation of the intensity of modern life, whose distinctive feature is speed, through the dynamic representation of movement, involving simultaneity of viewpoint and displacement of objects.

Far from revealing a common aim among the English artists, however, Nevinson provided a pretext for Lewis to establish his own secessionist movement. I must now turn briefly to the political manoeuvrings which lay behind the formation of the Vorticist group to demonstrate why Lewis's and Pound's pragmatic dissociation of themselves from Futurism and, in Lewis's case, Kandinsky and Cubism, cannot be taken at face-value. Then I shall illustrate the fundamental similarities between the Vorticist aesthetic and the varieties of empathetic Symbolism discussed above.

Nevinson had committed the *faux pas* of appending to his and Marinetti's manifesto 'Vital English Art', published in the *Observer* on 7 June, the signatures of the Rebel Art Centre artists. Precipitated into a coherent group by their common indignation at Nevinson's presumption, they temporarily forgot the petty dissension and divisive bickering which hastened the closure of the Rebel Art Centre (although Bomberg remained as ever a staunch individualist). Now calling themselves 'Vorticists', they responded by a public repudiation printed in several national newspapers and by heckling a performance at the Doré by Marinetti, Nevinson, and Russolo's *intonarumori*.[61]

The English artists had earlier welcomed the Futurists enthusiastically, as propagandist allies in their campaign to awaken Edwardian England from its torpid insularity and give it a cosmopolitan awareness of experimental techniques in literature and the visual arts. As Pound recalled, 'It was definitely our job, London 1908 to '14 in the workings of one intellectual blood circuit to eliminate our ignorance of ten years' continental plastic and forty years' continental writing.'[62] The time-lag was, if anything, more pronounced in the visual arts than in literature. Only with the Post-Impressionist exhibition of 1910 was a determined large-scale attempt made to familiarise the English public with innovations from the France of twenty years earlier (although from 1907 Sickert's Fitzroy Street group showed the influence of Gauguin). Into an ambience in which the Impressionists, apart from Degas and Manet, were generally regarded unsympathetically as a passing craze who could be conveniently ignored, rushed suddenly in the few remaining pre-war years the bewildering cross-currents of Post-Impressionism, Futurism, Cubism and German Expressionism.

Marinetti had lectured in London in 1910 and 1912, on the latter visit accompanied by the first international Futurist exhibition with its English catalogue, whose contents, studied earlier in this chapter, raised as much controversy as the paintings themselves. In 1913 they returned again, Severini mounting an extremely successful one-man show in April, while in November Marinetti performed at the Cabaret Club, the Poets' Club, the Poetry Bookshop, Clifford's Inn Hall, the Doré Gallery and at a private dinner arranged in his honour by a committee of the rebel English painters, comprising Lewis, Nevinson, Etchells, Hamilton and Wadsworth. [63]

Public interest in Futurism was mounting. The principal space in Harold Monro's *Poetry and Drama*, September 1913, was devoted to the manifesto 'Wireless Imagination and Words at Liberty' and translations of poems by Marinetti, Buzzi and Palazzeschi. In the next issue, however, Monro qualified the Futurists' condemnation of *passéisme* as too violently extreme for the English as opposed to the Italian situation; he was similarly disillusioned by Marinetti's poetic style, which he regarded as merely 'an advanced form of verbal photography' – a criticism which the Vorticists were to extend to Futurist painting, which they dismissed, following Hulme, as simply accelerated impressionism. [64]

The Futurists' vituperative onslaught against *passéiste* complacency, 'the infamy of publishing monopolies and the venality of the critics', was more congenial to Pound, who was concerned not simply with England but also with the more reactionary provincialism of America. [65] In spring 1914, when Marinetti again lectured, Pound and Lewis's sympathy with his views led to a performance at the Rebel Art Centre in May, which also sponsored a lecture at the Doré Gallery, the setting in May and June for a major exhibition of seventy-nine works by Futurist painters and sculptors. Skilful management of press coverage ensured that overwhelming public interest was generated by Marinetti's outrageous propagandist activities. He and Russolo completed a week-long engagement with the *intonarumori* at the Coliseum music-hall; enterprising salesmen cashed in on the fashionable fad by attaching the arbitrary label 'futurist' to all manner of consumer products. Futurism, by now established as a generic term for all innovative art, threatened to eclipse totally Pound and Lewis's own movement. They needed consequently to create a distinct identity which would dissociate them in the public mind from Marinetti, of whose public pre-eminence Lewis was probably jealous. Lewis selected as an easy target the accidental aspect of the propagandist Marinetti's rather puerile 'Automobilism', which he rightly regarded as immature excitement at mechanical inventions *per se*. [66]

This political manoeuvring diverted attention from the fact that the two groups of painters, despite their disparate techniques, shared the same empathetic premisses. An advertisement for *Blast* as late as 15 April had promised merely 'Discussion of Cubism, Futurism, Imagisme and all Vital Forms of Modern Art', as though to confirm the underlying unity beneath these groupings.[67] In his *Blast* articles, however, Lewis, eager to maintain that his own movement had no external ancestry but had sprung fully formed from his own head, dismissed Cubism and Kandinsky as well as Futurism. Pound by contrast, understandably out of step with Lewis's abrupt changes in policy, in his 'Vortex' explicitly refers to 'Picasso, Kandinski [*sic*], father and mother, classicism and romanticism of the movement'. This makes clear that for propagandist purposes Lewis was prepared to disavow vociferously movements and critics whose aesthetic and technique he at the same time echoed without acknowledgement. Although at the time he attacked Kandinsky, forty years later, no longer directly threatened by competing movements, he recalled that his aims had been close to the Russian's.[68] He similarly admitted having begun his career by wholeheartedly espousing Bergsonism;[69] something as *prima facie* implausible as what I argue was his actual Vorticist aesthetic if, following the critical consensus, one superimposes his later, more familiar views on the Lewis of the pre-war years.

I shall now examine Lewis's Vorticist writings to show what his views, as expressed at the time, actually were. Their main burden is the by-now familiar thesis of the primacy over Impressionist, photographic realism of the imagination's emotional realisation of the essential significance and potentialities of an object:

> It is always the POSSIBILITIES in the object, the IMAGINATION, as we say, in the spectator, that matters. Nature itself is of no importance.
> The sense of objects, even, is a sense of the SIGNIFICANCE of the object, and not its avoirdupois and scientifically ascertainable shapes and perspectives.[70]

He elaborately contrasted Leonardo's 'electric', 'delicate' creatures with Rubens's crude, fleshy figures, a viewpoint which Pound reiterated in distinguishing between the ethereal figures of early Renaissance painting and their more carnal successors about 1527: 'The people are corpus, corpuscular, but not in the strict sense "animate", it is no longer the body of air clothed in the body of fire. . . .'[71] They concurred in placing the value of art in this capacity to respond creatively to the essential qualities of an object and charge its external representation with spiritual significance. Lewis disparaged the 'scientific registration' of a scene by the 'Naturalist' painter (by whom he implied Ginner and the Camden Town group) with the Vorticist's capture of its 'essential truth', instancing Wadsworth's 'Blackpool'. Wadsworth, it appears, would have corroborated this interpretation. He commented enthusiastically on Kandinsky's views, 'European artists of the past have treated art almost entirely from a too obviously and externally human outlook. Europe to-day, which is laying the solid foundations of the Western art of to-morrow, approaches this task from the deeper and more spiritual standpoint of the soul.'[72]

Lewis's abstract canvases were accordingly symbolic vehicles for an emotional state (either autonomous or more frequently derived from empathetic engagement with the external world), the common aesthetic basis of Vorticism, as Pound repeatedly insisted. (Cf., for example, *Composition*, 1913; *Planners: Happy Day*, c. 1912–13 (Plate 8); and *The Crowd*, 1914–15.) Since about 1909 he had been searching for new forms of expression in a desire to create a new art emancipated from outmoded representational conventions which would interpret the spirit of the emerging new age in terms of its characteristic mechanical environment. He sought to establish in Vorticism an independent alternative to the European *avant-garde* which would capture the energy of Futurism in a medium which suggested at the same time the controlled austerity and stasis of Cubism. The adoption of a vocabulary of mechanical forms was intended to represent man heroically and hence energetically in a medium of direct contemporary relevance. He was trying to utilise the vigorous attributes of machinery, whose 'lines and masses imply force and action' held in potential beneath an impassive, rigid exterior, to express an idealised analogy for man's powerful inner life.[73]

Pure abstraction was rarely employed by Lewis and in this he paralleled Gaudier's and Epstein's sculptural compromise between description and geometrical simplification. His paintings of the Vorticist period merely selected the language of machinery with its ready-made abstract forms, usually combined with distorted or simplified representational elements, as an appropriate metaphor for his empathetic interaction with his surroundings. Characteristically his work maintains a recognisable relation with or close derivation from descriptive appearances; he was loath to eliminate entirely the starting-point in external reality. This semi-abstraction was the hallmark of Vorticism, seen also in Wadsworth's abstract woodcuts and gouaches. These are based on machinery motifs but create an independently referential world which invites interpretation in terms of industrial landscapes or aerial perspectives, while not excluding a more purely formalistic reading.[74]

In 1915 Lewis gave a pithy summary which explains unequivocally what, at the time of the movement, he understood by the term 'Vorticism':

> By Vorticism we mean (a) *Activity* as opposed to the tasteful *Passivity* of Picasso; (b) SIGNIFICANCE as opposed to the dull or anecdotal character to which the Naturalist is condemned; (c) ESSENTIAL MOVEMENT and ACTIVITY (such as the energy of a mind) as opposed to the imitative cinematography, the fuss and hysterics of the Futurists.

The Cubists (an unacknowledged echo here of Boccioni) were disparaged for their heavy, lugubrious still-lifes, which were manually contrived, not organised and invented by the imagination.[75] Lewis's glosses on his second and third points, utilising a vocabulary with by-now familiar resonances (cf. particularly the Futurists' arguments on pp. 122–4; MacCarthy's on 132–3; Kandinsky's on 135–6 *supra*), are of more direct concern to the relationship between Vorticism of the visual arts and Pound's literary variety:

> (b) The impression received on a hot afternoon on the quays of some port, made up of the smell of tar and fish, the heat of the sun, the history of the place, cannot be conveyed by any imitation of a corner of it. The influences weld themselves into a hallucination or dream (which all the highest art has always been) with a mathematic of its own. [Cf. Pound's usage of 'equations' in Chs 6 and 8.] The significance of an object in nature (that is its spiritual weight) cannot be given by stating its avoirdupois. What a thing spiritually means to you can never be rendered in the terms of practical vision, or scientific imitation.
>
> (c) Moods, ideas and visions have movements, associating themselves with objects or an object. An object also has an ESSENTIAL movement, an essential environment, however intimate

and peculiar an object it may be – even a telephone receiver or an Alpine flower.[76]

The Vorticists' interest in abstraction seems in historical perspective no more than a brief, exaggerated interlude, encouraged enthusiastically by Hulme for primarily ideological reasons, but never espoused unequivocally by the artists themselves. Epstein, Hulme's prime theoretical exhibit, recalled that 'with artists [Hulme] was humble and always willing to learn'; he regarded Pound by contrast as rather pretentious, with little grasp of the new developments. On a visit to Epstein's studio in 1913 to view the *Rock Drill*, 'Pound started expatiating on the work. Gaudier turned on him and snapped, "Shut up, you understand nothing!"'[77] Championed by Hulme, the only critic who defended him publicly, Epstein's work for a short period relied increasingly on abstraction. The two men complemented one another. Epstein was the practitioner chosen to illustrate Hulme's speculations; he planned an essay on Epstein for *Blast* and the manuscript of a book on the sculptor's work perished with Hulme at Nieuport in 1917.

Lewis, always characterised by a suspicious insecurity verging on paranoia, seems to have been jealous of Epstein's occupation of what Lewis regarded as his rightful position.[78] In *Blasting and Bombardiering*, Lewis's recollections over twenty years later, the Vorticist period is subjected to a theatrical heightening. Characters assume melodramatic roles in Lewis's impressionistic staging of a world of intrigues and counter-putsches. Fully in keeping with this attitude is the following statement about Hulme, which contrives to put him in his place with barbed dismissiveness, yet bears witness at the same time to Lewis's chagrin at his unjust personal neglect at Hulme's hands, which he attempts to disguise by retrospectively rewriting the scenario:

[Hulme] was a journalist with a flair for philosophy and art, not a philosopher. Of both these subjects he was profoundly ignorant, according to technician-standards. . . . It was mainly as a theorist in the criticism of the fine arts that Hulme would have distinguished himself, had he lived. And I should undoubtedly have played Turner to his Ruskin.

All the best things Hulme said about the theory of art were said about my art. . . . We happened . . . to be made for each other, as critic and 'creator'. What he said should be done, I *did*. Or it would be more exact to say that I did it, and he said it.

Neither Gaudier nor Epstein would, he maintained, have been 'abstract' enough to satisfy Hulme.[79]

Social considerations prevented close co-operation between Lewis and Hulme. They had come to blows in early summer 1914 over Kate Lechmere, who transferred her affections from the former to the latter, and this animosity provoked the exclusion from *Blast* of the Epstein essay, to which Hulme reacted by labelling the Rebel Art Centre painters as 'derivative' (*FS*, 135). He had always paid more attention to Epstein than to Lewis and, following this personal row, ignored Lewis totally to praise instead the more radically innovative experiments in abstraction of David Bomberg. This must have exacerbated Lewis, for at the very moment when he most needed publicity and critical praise – at the launching of *Blast* – he had alienated this outspoken apologist for the *avant-garde*, just as he had earlier a major establishment critic, Roger Fry, over the Omega Workshops feud.

It seems clear, however, that the Vorticists and Epstein drew on Hulme for confirmation of their experiments, perhaps even to the extent of allowing themselves to be deflected from their natural idiom. Bomberg recalled that Hulme was the only contemporary critic who had any idea of what they were doing. His articles made him 'the spokesman for the innovators in the first exhibition of the London Group'. But Bomberg added that 'there is no evidence whatever of [Hulme's] having had any influence on visual art or artists. He helped innovators by trying to explain the deeper significance of visual form but his explanations were in terms of speech and therefore had no influence on the artists.' This, I feel, misses the point. Hulme could naturally offer no technical guidance – but he undoubtedly contributed much enthusiastic support and, through his domineering personality, exerted emotional pressure, however unconsciously, on artists less resolutely independent than Bomberg. Richard Cork suggests that Gaudier's *Red Stone Dancer* may well have been constructed according to Hulme's geometrical theory of art; Gaudier's projected essay for *Blast* II, 'The Need of Organic Forms in Sculpture', perhaps indicates his more instinctive attitude.[80] Certainly both Epstein, whose sculpture, like Gaudier's, was chiefly inspired by a tender response to organic forms, and Lewis later had little interest in abstraction.

Epstein was in retrospect patronising towards the 'experimental pre-war days of 1913' and his 'ardour for machinery (short-lived)'. The discipline of 'simplification of forms, unity of design, and co-ordination of masses' he then learnt had influenced his later figurative work, 'But to think of abstraction as an end in itself is undoubtedly letting oneself be led into a cul-de-sac and can only lead to exhaustion and impotence.' He told Samuel Hynes he was 'always uneasy about' his abstract work, while Kate Lechmere and Lewis both thought Hulme pushed Epstein into doing abstraction, when he was naturally inclined to model.[81] Hulme seems to have had a similar, though less acute effect on Lewis. Geoffrey Wagner in his excellent monograph corroborates this interpretation. He writes, 'To some extent, the phenomenon of total abstraction in Lewis' work may be attributable to two sources, first, as complete a reaction as possible to English academicism, and second, infatuation with the teaching of T. E. Hulme'; 'Lewis has admitted that he saw Hulme as his mentor in art.' While I agree with Wagner's view that the direction of influence was from Hulme to Lewis and not *vice versa* as Lewis later maintained, I must dissent, however, from his claim that already in 1914–15 Lewis had adopted Hulme's anti-humanist artistic theory.[82] As I have argued, this directly contradicts the articles Lewis wrote at the time.

Lewis insisted that '*vorticism* was purely a painters affair (as *imagism* was a purely literary movement, having no relation whatever to *vorticism*, nor anything in common with it)'. He had come to this conclusion when attempting to find for *Blast* a literary counterpart to the artistic experimentation: 'nothing was being written just then that seemed within a million leagues of the stark radicalism of the *visuals*. It was with regret I included the poems of my friend Ezra Pound.' The Imagists were '*pompier*', Pound 'compromisingly passéiste'. He attempted to devise a suitably extreme literary equivalent in his own play 'The Enemy of the Stars', but when he tried to extend an innovative, abstract style to the writing of his novel *Tarr* found the aspiration futile. He hoped to eliminate any parts of speech less essential than nouns or verbs but soon realised that 'words and syntax were not susceptible of transformation into abstract terms, to which process the visual arts lent themselves quite readily'. The result was no more disconcerting than the stylistic reforms of the Imagists – the elimination of 'clichés', 'sentimental archaisms' and 'Rhetoric'. He could merely prune diction and syntax of redundancy in the same way he had reduced visual representation to its simplified essentials. To delineate character 'there was no way of reducing your text to anything more skeletal than that produced by an otherwise normal statement, even if abnormally abrupt and harsh'. The composition of *Tarr* with its human interest, coupled with his stylistic disillusion and the even greater shock of the war, drove Lewis away from geometrical abstraction, which now seemed 'bleak and empty'. He continued to regard structural organisation as fundamental to painting but his own work gravitated towards figurative representation.[83]

As earlier with his speculations on poetic diction and the 'image', Hulme had given influential expression to ideas generally 'in the air', even though the ideology which accompanied his defence of abstraction was at variance with the empathetic aesthetic of the Vorticist artists. It was his powerful personality which strengthened the temporary feeling (inspired initially by Cubism and Futurism) that abstraction was the only suitable vehicle for artistic expression, leading Pound and Lewis to attempt to reproduce this in literature. Lewis conceded defeat; Pound reformulated the Symbolist aesthetic but could devise no new style. Symbolism itself had experimented with a paratactic assemblage of images which subordinated syntactic to emotional connection. There was little opportunity for innovation save in respect of length and it was to this problem that Pound turned his attention in September 1915 in starting to compose 'Three Cantos'.

# 6  Ezra Pound: the Pre-Imagist Phase

Pound's early poetry is, by critical consensus, pervaded by transcendentalism. There is, however, disagreement about the intermediate position between this early verse and the acknowledged visionary *Cantos* occupied by Imagism/Vorticism. That movement is generally explained as a formalistic preparation for the major epic and its place in Pound's continuum of thought ignored. As with the contemporary movements in the visual arts discussed in the previous chapter, I feel that such an approach neglects a crucial aesthetic dimension. This chapter provides accordingly a prolegomenon to Chapter 8 by analysing the transcendentalism which remained central to Imagism/Vorticism.

My investigation focuses on the dialogue between Yeats and Pound. Earlier criticism of this topic has discussed Pound's possible influence on Yeats's middle period and Pound's stylistic indebtedness to early Yeats.[1] I argue instead for a wider *ideological* influence which determined the course of Pound's early development, helped to make Symbolist theory more significant than it would otherwise have been and created the linguistic assumptions on which the *Cantos* depend. Yeats appears in two guises: first, as instigator, where a direct influence on Pound is demonstrable; secondly, where conclusive proof of such influence is lacking, as a striking counterpart to Pound, casting valuable illumination on his aspirations. There are, of course, evident differences in tone and nuance between the formulations of the two poets. While granting this, I hope to demonstrate that despite the apparent divergences their views are nevertheless in important respects essentially congruent.

In section I of this chapter I consider Pound's quest for a contemporary Renaissance, which implied for him a spiritual revival, Unity of Culture, and a nationalist resurgence accompanied by propaganda machinery. The practical aspects of this theme are discussed in Chapter 7; here I trace the aesthetic. Yeats's account of the Irish Renaissance provides the point of departure. This inspired Pound with apparent evidence of a country which had maintained its Unity of Culture and pantheistic beliefs despite contemporary materialism. Its anachronistic situation was further reflected in the continuing currency of its mythology, which provided an ideal symbolic vehicle for the guarded expression of private religious experience. Yeats's Celtic nature mysticism thus stimulated Pound's earliest attempts to create a poetic mythology in which to express his anti-materialist cosmology.

In 1910–11 this Celticism was discarded in favour of a renewed classical mythology expressed in metamorphosis, and, more frequently, the use of a female figure drawn from the Stilnovist poets, medieval dream vision, and Rossetti's recreation of this genre, as the conventional symbol for a mediating principle producing spiritual enlightenment through ecstasy. This stylistic transition accompanied Pound's discovery of a Renaissance more congenial than the Irish and of lasting importance: the twelfth-century Provençal vortex.

## I  TOWARDS A RENAISSANCE

Pound's ambition was to emulate in an American literary renaissance Yeats's leading function in the Irish. In a footnote to 'Redondillas' (1911) he characterised Yeats as 'specialist in renaissances'; he had described his own aims in 1909 as 'a strife for a renaissance in America of all the lost or temporarily mislaid beauty, truth, valour, glory of Greece, Italy, England and all the rest of it'. In 'From Chebar' and 'Epilogue' Pound dons the mantle of a prophet in exile, gathering the sacred books and the critical standards to redirect his own nation.[2] For both Yeats and Pound this projected Renaissance was spurred by spiritual and aesthetic revulsion from contemporary materialism. Only later was this translated into the desideratum of a polity restoring to the arts their former social importance. This religious aspect therefore demands attention first, leading directly into Yeats's developing vision of 'Ireland'.

Yeats's lifelong quest for a spiritual rather than a materialist cosmology was first significantly expressed in Celtic mythology. But his first conception of fairyland was topographical rather than metaphorical; it was a fantasy world or imaginary locale of wish-fulfilment (comparable with his earlier Arcadian and Indian poetry) into which one journeyed from the utilitarian drabness of the late Victorian era, fulfilling his temperamental requirement of 'a universe where all is large and intense enough to almost satisfy the emotions of man', which would 'make our world of tea-tables seem but a shabby penumbra'. His earliest poetry was 'almost all a flight into fairyland from the real world', while 'The Island of Statues' (like the paintings of Watts, Burne-Jones, Moreau or Puvis) was conceived as 'a region into which one should wander from the cares of life'. [3]

Pound's first poems reveal a similar inability to accept at its apparent value drab, modern civilisation and consequent trans-mogrification of the mundane into the mythical or transcendental. Under Yeats's influence 'Domina', 'The Wind' and 'Rendez-vous' depict Hilda Doolittle as lured away from her lover by the Sidhe. [4] Further inspiration came from medievalism, both authentic and Victorian, particularly Morris's romances. In 'The Arches' the simple 'crow's nest' in Hilda's garden which was the couple's regular meeting-place becomes in Pound's imagination

> That wind-swept castle hight [*sic*] with thee alone
> Above the dust and rumble of the earth

referred to later in the poem as 'this our keep'. Hence the castle from the Tristram and Iseult legend in 'Li Bel Chasteus' is simply their tree-house, in which 'Is-hilda' (or 'Ysolt') meets Ezra. [5] Hilda appears as Pound's muse in 'Praise of Ysolt', uniting her themati-cally with Rossetti's 'Hand and Soul', just as 'Donzella Beata' contrasts her with the 'blessed damozel', and 'Era Venuta', when published as 'Comraderie', equates her with Beatrice. [6] '*Sancta Patrona Domina Caelae*', 'Ver Novum', and the Pre-Raphaelite 'For Ysolt. The Triad of Dawn' also figure the beloved as a mediator for the divine. [7] Pound's prevailing mood in these early years is encapsulated in 'To the Dawn: Defiance', and the line from *A Lume Spento* retained as the epigraph to *Personae*: 'Make-strong old dreams lest this our world lose heart'. [8]

In the case of both poets, however, this apparently facile escapism heralded more profound theories of mythology as the symbolic expression of mystical experience.

'The mystical life' was, Yeats stressed, of central importance for all his aspirations, for 'I have always considered myself a voice of what I believe to be a greater renaissance – the revolt of the soul against the intellect – now beginning in the world'. [9] This rejection of the associations of 'intellect' (encompassing self-analysis, complexity, reason, materialism, Naturalism) in favour of naïvety and, above all, the imagination, dictated the course of Yeats's development.

From whatever source, he had clearly absorbed the German Romantics' historicist accounts of the ever-increasing complexity and ideality of civilisation, culminating in self-conscious modernity. [10] But to Yeats, unlike Symons, modernity was antipathetic. He abhorred its evidence both in religious scepticism and in the psychological analysis of contemporary literature; Tito in *Romola*, for example, was 'as interesting as a cat on the vivisection table'. [11] Great literature by contrast was 'synthetic, homeric', the latter an epithet Yeats repeatedly applied to the epic poetry of Sir Samuel Ferguson. The heroic 'simplicity' of such modern Irish poets, who returned to legendary material and epic or ballad forms, whose heroes were men of action and whose style appealed to man's whole undivided nature (that 'Unity of Being' [12] or undissociated sensibility whose loss was Yeats's version of the Symbolist myth of an aesthetic Fall), persuaded Yeats that the largely untapped resources of Celtic mythology could provide the basis for an imaginative revival which would not merely energise Ireland but would spearhead a wider revolt against materialism. [13]

As the important historicist lecture 'Nationality and Literature' (1893) explains, Yeats saw Ireland's situation as what he might later have termed 'out of phase'. [14] Unlike nations such as England which had attained a more complex stage of civilisation and lost their common culture, Ireland, by virtue both of being still in the ballad or epic phase of literary evolution and the survival among the peasantry of an imaginative mythology, remained an anachronistic bastion of heroic wholeness in a world of materialism and self-analytical decadence. [15]

Yeats accordingly saw the opportunity for an Irish literary efflorescence, utilising Celtic mythology as a symbolical vehicle to articulate the poet's subjective states. By virtue of the widespread currency of this folklore, sophisticated poetry which employed it could nevertheless not fail to command a popular audience. Of course, this was largely wish-fulfilment: as Denis Donoghue wittily remarks, Yeats 'invented a country, calling it Ireland'. [16] Only much later did Yeats concede that the Unity of Culture of which he dreamed was no longer possible in the modern world, Byzantium supplanting his earlier vision of Ireland.[17] The peasantry undoubtedly believed in the existence of the Sidhe, as Yeats's scrupulous gathering of folklore material, analysed increasingly in the sophisticated light of comparative mythology, confirmed.[18] But this faith in a supernatural otherworld cognate with that of Christianity was not the same thing as Yeats's poetic recourse to legends effectively familiar only to scholars and thus largely a cerebral re-creation. Equally Yeats's advocacy of myth as primarily a stylistic vehicle for the embodiment of emotions did not do justice to his understanding of its complexity and was a makeshift position conditioned partly by Celtic propagandism.[19]

One must accordingly distinguish two aspects, a public and a private, in Yeats's understanding of mythology; as I shall discuss below, his account of symbolism is similarly dualistic. It was not merely a stylistic vehicle for subjective emotions, as he often maintained in nationalist articles avowing the literary potential of Irish mythology, but was more profoundly a symbolic embodiment of the poet's intuitions of noumenal reality. To the initiate such as Yeats the contemporary fascination with folklore was principally evidence of an impending widespread affirmation of 'the ancient supremacy of imagination. Imagination is God in the world of art' in opposition to 'the atheists who would make us naught but "realists," "naturalists," or the like'.[20] Folklore was of spiritual significance, for, as Yeats explained, 'fairies' were emanations from the world soul which manifested themselves temporarily in forms borrowed from the visionary's own subconsciousness. The sceptic might dismiss them, or their accidental shape might be susceptible to psychological or rational explanation, but to the adept this did not disguise their transcendental origin:

> The fairies are the lesser spiritual moods of that universal mind, wherein every mood is a soul and every thought a body. Their world is very different from ours, and they can but appear in forms borrowed from our limited consciousness, but nevertheless, every form they take and every action they go through, has its significance and can be read by the mind trained in the correspondence of sensuous form and supersensuous meaning.[21]

The visionary or mystic perceived accordingly images which by their analogical or correspondential function (the premiss of Yeats's Rosicrucian religion) assured him in a desacralised world of the interrelatedness and essential spirituality of all creation.[22] Mythology or symbolism provided a conventional and appropriately guarded expression of this esoteric experience. It was not surprising that, under the influence of that 'strong enchanter' Yeats, Pound should also be drawn to mythology to express his instinctive Idealism; it offered the perfect stylistic vehicle for the poetry of an animistic Renaissance. Pound accordingly began by reproducing the pattern of Yeats's 1890s interests; the congruity of his later position with Yeats's post-1903 views is discussed in section II.

The conception of literature as implicit but indirect revelation of esoteric experience is central to both Yeats's and Pound's views on mythology. As Yeats explained, 'Emotions which seem vague or extravagant when expressed under the influence of modern literature, cease to be vague and extravagant when associated with ancient legend and mythology, for legend and mythology were born out of man's longing for the mysterious and the infinite.'[23] Myth provided a means of expressing private religious sentiments which by its conventional nature would deflect the jeers of atheists, as the poet could maintain that he was merely echoing an accepted poetic tradition.

As early as 'The Dublin Hermetic Society' Yeats had regarded poetry as an oblique expression of chiliastic or esoteric beliefs, in which 'the old revelations' were uttered 'under the mask of phantasy'.[24] This approach served likewise as the poetic basis for Pound's use of classical mythology and the expression of his Provençal mystery religion.

As most critics of Pound's early poetry have indicated, a predominant theme is the insecure, fragile existence of the artist, the bearer of privileged imaginative insights, in a society which misunderstands and undervalues him.[25] He dramatised this feeling in 'Purveyors General', while 'The Decadence' and 'Prometheus' articulated it through readily available myths.[26] Pound's response to his sense of the alienation imposed on the artist by his finely tuned but delicate sensibility assumed two forms: first, reliance on the Romantic belief in the outcast artist's compensating power to subject an indifferent world to his imaginative transformation; secondly, the adoption of symbolic masks or *personae* – in this sense metamorphic myths and later the veiled obliquity of Stilnovist mysticism – to protect his spiritual epiphanies from direct exposure to a hostile society.[27] In 'Salve O Pontifex', which presents Swinburne as a high priest of Eleusinian mysteries, Pound was absorbed less by Swinburne's factitious paganism, than by the concept of the poet as interpreter of esoteric wisdom which 'men may not/Over readily understand'. The persecution such misunderstandings might entail was expressed in 'For the Triumph of the Arts' (revised to allude specifically to the Albigensians), which dramatises artists as the suppressed oracles of mysterious 'Truths' rejected by a materialist world.[28] One recalls Pound's familiar argument that Greek myth 'arose when someone having passed through delightful psychic experience tried to communicate it to others and found it necessary to screen himself from persecution'.[29]

Pound's first speculation on the origin of metamorphic myth arose from his High Romantic belief (expressed in 'Cino', 'In Durance' and 'Plotinus'[30]) that the artist's social exile is relieved by epiphanic surges of inspiration, which enable him to repossess imaginatively an alien and uncongenial world. In a fragmentary essay, after an introductory section apparently indebted to Shelley, Pound wrote,

> Of the dawn's reflexion . . . feeling the flowing of the essences of beauty . . . until they gradually grouped themselves into form. Of such perceptions rise the ancient myths of the origin of demigods. Even as the ancient myths of metamorphosis rise out of *flashes of cosmic consciousness.*
> *vid.* The Tree. (an attempt to express a sensation or perception which revealed to me the inner matter of the Daphne story). . . . Certainly the beauty of the morning of which I write took unto itself a personality.[31]

A later article confirms that this interpretation of the origin of myth as a symbol for an otherwise inexpressible epiphany underlay such early poems as 'La Fraisne' and 'The Tree':

> perceiving that no one could understand what he meant when he said that he 'turned into a tree' [early man] made a myth – a work of art that is – an impersonal or objective story woven out of his own emotion, as the nearest *equation* that he was capable of putting into words.[32]

The potential of myth to express circumspectly spiritual experience was undoubtedly a major factor in its adoption by Yeats and Pound. Of equal importance was its communication in a popular form of post-Romantic nature mysticism, reviving in a new guise the poetic habit of transferring religious veneration from an increasingly remote deity to the natural world itself. In Yeats's words,

> An obsession more constant than anything but my love itself was the need of mystical rites – a ritual system of evocation and meditation – to reunite the perception of the spirit, of the divine, with natural beauty. . . . Commerce and manufacture had made the world ugly; the death of pagan nature-worship had robbed visible beauty of its inviolable sanctity. I was convinced that all lonely and lovely places were crowded with invisible beings and that it would be possible to communicate with them.[33]

Mythology, Yeats asserted, restored to man a sense of communion with a desacralised natural world, as the poet unlike the materialists around him was imaginatively aware of the essential spirituality of what he perceived and could embody in a congenial form this animistic faith:

> All these stories are such as to unite man more closely to the woods and hills and waters about him, and to the birds and animals that live in them, and to give him types and symbols for those feelings and passions which find no adequate expression in common life.[34]

This pantheistic mysticism was temporarily combined with Yeats's nationalism in a vision of Ireland which foreshadows strikingly Pound's conception of Provençal culture.

Yeats's plan was for an Order of Celtic Mysteries, a project unrealisable owing to the conflicting expectations of its conceivers, but nevertheless in active consideration from 1894 to 1902.[35] Yeats and AE saw the designated site for the Order, Castle Rock on Lough Key, as a shrine for Celtic tradition. AE's letters to Yeats demonstrate his overriding faith in a Druidic religion, whose gods had returned to Ireland.[36] Yeats was more eclectic and probably envisaged the venture as an attempt to fuse Celtic nationalism with Rosicrucianism. His Rosicrucian creed taught the immanence of

God in the universe (hence his interest in Celtic pantheism). Equally he had learnt in the ritual for the $5=6$ grade in the Golden Dawn (into which he was initiated in June 1893) that the 'Mysteries of the Rose and the Cross' had been practised at Eleusis and Samothrace.[37] This belief in an animistic mystery religion persisting through the centuries (to be echoed by Pound in 1911) led to the hope that Castle Rock might become a temple for 'mysteries like those of Eleusis or Samothrace'.[38] Yeats's and AE's plan was therefore for an idealist renaissance similar to New England Transcendentalism, in which art would be the natural complement to a distinctively Celtic mysticism, with an accompanying bid for political autonomy.[39] It was Yeats's accounts of this movement, providing evidence of a natural world peopled with 'gods', reflected also in his poetry of this period and *The Celtic Twilight*, which captured Pound's imagination.

Yeats's comments on the sanctity of Ireland and the survival of pagan religion in the supernatural beliefs of the peasantry form a direct model for Pound's later assertions of the continuing Mediterranean belief in Eleusinian mysteries. Similarly, his repeated injunctions to make every modern country (although particularly Ireland, of course) a 'Holy Land' of the imagination with a living pantheistic faith, together with his plans for Eleusinian mysteries at Castle Rock, prefigure Pound's desire to 'replace the statue of Venus on the cliffs of Terracina . . . [and] erect a temple to Artemis in Park Lane' as evidence of the persistence of 'a light from Eleusis'.[40] What Kenner terms the 'Sacred Places' of the *Cantos* were foreshadowed in Yeats's aspiration in his thought as in his writing 'to bring again in[to] imaginative life the old sacred places – Slievenamon, Knocknarea – all that old reverence that hung . . . about conspicuous hills'.[41]

On at least three occasions Yeats emphasised the peasant belief in the 'ancient gods', drawing explicit parallels with the significance Greek mythology once enjoyed, before summarising his views on the 'Holy Land' of Ireland in an article for the *North American Review* which Pound may perhaps have read. In any case Pound could scarcely have avoided encountering some of Yeats's numerous other references to this theme.[42] As Yeats explained, in the modern world the traditional sanctity of the landscape had been forgotten, the stories of its deities relegated to what utilitarians and materialists regarded as the triviality of fairy-tales. Yet the persistence of the old beliefs among the Irish peasantry, coupled with his own vatic mysticism, persuaded Yeats of Ireland's key role in a potential spiritual renaissance:

> [If Ireland] can make us believe that the beautiful things that move us to awe, white lilies among dim shadows, windy twilights over grey sands, dewy and silent places among hazel trees by still waters, are in truth, and not in phantasy alone, the symbols, or the dwellings, of immortal presences, she will have begun a change that . . . will some day make all lands holy lands again.

He returned to the theme in two sections of *Discoveries* (1906), 'Religious Belief Necessary to Religious Art' and 'The Holy Places'. Here his views on popular art are less optimistic than in the 1890s. He reiterates that symbolic art can avoid insubstantiality only if grounded in a coherent mythology expressing a popular religious faith. Three years earlier he was convinced this existed in Ireland; now his disillusionment with the Abbey Theatre spilled over into melancholia at the limited potential of modern art: 'All symbolic art should arise out of a real belief, and that it cannot do so in this age proves that this age is a road and not a resting-place for the imaginative arts.'[43]

Yeats eventually overcame this dilemma by creating two alternative mythologies, valid, however, only within the corpus of his own work: the mystical system of *A Vision* (intended to be as irrefragable as a medieval or classical cosmology) and his idealised Protestant ascendancy, which elevated his own friends to mythological status. But it was Yeats's earliest mythological model from the 1890s which Pound adopted as the appropriate stance for the modern poet, utilising first the metamorphic convention then an idealised re-creation or 'Holy Land' of Provence cognate with Yeats's original hopes for Ireland. I shall examine first Pound's adaptation to his own requirements of Yeats's account of Celtic mythology.

In a letter in 1907, quoting Blake, Coleridge and Swedenborg on poetry as mystical experience, Pound wrote with a characteristic hint of pomposity, 'I am interested in art and ecstasy, ecstasy which I would define as the sensation of the soul in ascent, art as the expression and sole means of transmuting, of passing on that ecstasy to others.'[44] 'Ecstasy' was in the late nineteenth century a critical concept as vague as the equally popular 'beauty'. For Pound it usually denoted a momentary transcendental experience revealed in mystical perception, in sudden insight into character, or in psychological peripeteia (compare his familiar comments to Carlos Williams on the 'dramatic lyric'[45]). I shall consider later other aspects of this term, restricting my attention for the present to the close parallel between Pound's expression of this ecstatic mystical perception (the 'flashes of cosmic consciousness', referred to *supra*, p. 156) in metamorphic myth, and Yeats's remarks in 'The Celtic Element in Literature' on 'ecstasy' in the contemplation of nature. There Yeats reiterated his interpretation of mythology as a symbolic vehicle for primitive man's awareness of divine immanence in the world, manifested in constant metamorphosis. That 'natural magic' which Arnold had perceived in the style of Celtic mythology was but 'the ancient religion of the world, the ancient worship of Nature and that troubled ecstasy before her, that certainty of all beautiful places being haunted, which it brought into men's minds'. 'Ecstasy' was the mark of people who regarded nature not merely in the modern 'poetical' fashion, but with the eye of 'the ancient religion'.[46]

Pound had originally adopted at second hand this mythology made accessible by the Celtic revival to express his own intuition of a spiritual principle in nature. In an early note to 'La Fraisne' he drew an explicit analogy between *The Celtic Twilight* and the epiphanic awareness of identity with the natural world expressed in that poem.[47] Yet in an American poet this Irish mythology – unlike classical mythology never a generally adopted convention – could never be more than an artificial mannerism, demanding that Pound devise an alternative symbolism for his religious sentiments. He sought this first in classical mythology, then in Stilnovist poetry, approaches which both derived from his trip to northern Italy in 1910.

Pound's subjection to Yeats's diffuse stylistic influences had reached a point of crisis in *Exultations* (1909). In that volume Yeats dominates even those poems ostensibly striving towards a different cultural inspiration: 'Sestina for Ysolt' and 'Portrait' owe their rationale to 'He remembers Forgotten Beauty'; 'Nils Lykke' and 'Planh' despite their titles adopt an incongruous stage-Irish; while the extremity of pastiche is attained in 'Laudantes Decem Pulchritudinis Johannae Templi', which hesitates between a conceptual debt to Rossetti and a seemingly ineluctable reliance on Yeats's idiom.[48] Pound stood at a crossroads in his development; the new direction was indicated early in 1910.

In 1907 Pound had written a weak eulogy 'To the Raphaelite Latinists', praising their attempt to preserve the significance of the old classical mythology in a world which no longer gave it credence, and sympathetically aligning himself with their endeavour. He had commented earlier on the poetry of Capilupus,

> The old gods and tutelar deities are no mere machinery for the decoration of poetry, but the very spirits of the trees and meres . . . .
>
> Capilupus has seized what the neoplatonist had sought for, what the devout among the humanists had been striving to prove: It is not pagan to worship beauty; the old gods are not really dead, nor pagan . . . .

In 1908 he argued that the vital significance of Celtic myth in the contemporary world corresponded to that of classical myth for the Renaissance Latinists, implying that he regarded them as stylistic equivalents.[49] The viability of classical mythology as a poetic symbolism was apparently brought home to Pound in 1910 at Sirmione, the setting for the poetry of Flaminius.

During his stay there Pound revised the proofs of *The Spirit of Romance*, in which he reiterated that in Flaminius's poetry 'myths and allusions are not a furniture or a conventional decoration, but an *interpretation* of nature'. The Renaissance classical revival had reintroduced 'a certain kind of nature-feeling which had been long absent', evidenced in Flaminius's poetry in 'signs of the scholar's sensitiveness to nature, both to the natural things themselves and to *those spiritual presences therein, which age after age finds it most fitting to write of in the symbolism of the old Greek mythology.*'[50] (Compare Yeats's comment on pantheistic myth on p. 157 *supra*.) The description of Sirmione itself in the draft first Canto affirms directly Pound's emotional desideratum of 1908: 'For Metastasio was quite right when he sang that the Golden Age is not a dead thing, but still living in the hearts of the innocent.' The lines

> '*Non è fuggito.*'
>
>                  'It is not gone.' Metastasio
> Is right – we have that world about us

introduce an extended visionary passage, handled admittedly with less assurance than those in the *Cantos* themselves.[51]

But, while Pound's adoption of classical mythology signalled the first stage in his independence and provided a major stylistic vehicle for all his later poetry, his emancipation was only completed by another development also inspired by that Italian journey of 1910. His exploration of the Provençal cultural Renaissance and its Italian legacy led to the other principal *Leitmotiv* of the *Cantos*: the female figure bringing wisdom, inspired by *trobar clus* and the Eleusinian mysteries.

At this point in 1910–11 the vision of Renaissances which directed Pound's ambition in the pre-war years came to dominate his thinking, as artistic and patriotic aspirations mingled as they had for Yeats in the 1890s. Yeats's apparently incompatible nationalist, literary and mystical ambitions were paralleled by Pound's vacillation between commitment to his American roots and an affinity for the culture of medieval Europe. Yeats's first attempt to hammer his thoughts into unity created the Order of Celtic Mysteries; Pound sought to reconcile his conflicting aspirations by transplanting into America a Renaissance modelled on successful European precedents.[52] His inspiration was to continue the animistic revival Yeats had initiated in Celtic mythology as the foundation for an Irish national resurgence, by resurrecting the spirit of the Latin Renaissance and twelfth-century mysticism. The recurrent manifestations in the *Cantos* of an ideal *forma* of Unity of Culture derive ultimately from Pound's excitement in 1910–11 at the Provencal cultural vortex.

Pound's plans are illuminated by his comments at this time on Tagore's poetry, which displayed the same characteristics as the pantheistic poetry of the Celtic revival and the Renaissance Latinists: 'The Bengali brings to us the pledge of a calm which we need overmuch in an age of steel and mechanics. It brings a quiet proclamation of the fellowship between man and the gods; between man and nature.' A direct mental association between this poetry and Pound's own experiences at Sirmione is suggested by his description of Tagore's work as 'sunny, *Apricus*, "fed with sun," "delighting in sunlight."' In draft Canto I he recalled Sirmione as a place where 'The air is solid sunlight, *apricus*, / Sun-fed'.[53]

Tagore shared the same instigatory importance in the Bengali cultural revival that Yeats did in the Irish; Pound envisaged this in terms which suggest a correlation in his mind between Bengal and Ireland as 'out of phase' nations similar to Yeats's earlier account of Ireland. He remarked significantly that beneath Bengal's 'phonographs and railways', 'there would seem to subsist a culture not wholly unlike that of twelfth-century Provençe [*sic*]'.[54] If Unity of Culture either persisted or could be revived in these countries, why could this *forma* not also be realised in America?

Pound paralleled the impact of Tagore's mystical poetry in the modern world with that in 'Europe in the days before the Renaissance' of 'the sense of balance', 'The "mens sana in corpore sano", the ethic of the Odyssey'.[55] To explain this he referred to his essay 'Psychology and Troubadours' on the introduction of humanism at the time of the Renaissance: 'Man is concerned with man and forgets the whole and flowing.' Receptivity to 'the whole and flowing', we learn there, implied for Pound both an animistic cosmology (mythopoeic *'interpretation'* of 'the vital universe' 'of fluid force') and the sexual mystery discussed in section II *infra*. Tagore served therefore to support Pound's own programmatic aims: 'And this sort of humanism, having pretty well run its course, it seems to me we have the balance and corrective presented to us in this writing from Bengal'.[56]

To tie these diverse strands together: Pound was searching for an alternative to 'this sort of humanism', a concept which implied for him contemporary materialistic trends, but also that loss of mystical perception (examined below) which he traced back to various dates, 1527 being the most common.[57] He began to prepare for this mystical and patriotic Renaissance in his early London years, reproducing the pattern of Yeats's 1890s interests. Mythology was an important factor in his thinking as the veiled, symbolic expression of a reality more profound than the external world of phenomena susceptible of scientific analysis.[58] At the same time Pound's developing mystical interests and fascination with the twelfth-century Renaissance led to his discovery of another variety of poetic mask of even greater obliquity in which to express guardedly his religious sentiments. I must therefore turn my attention to his interpretation of Stilnovist poetry.

## II  *POET AS ALCHEMIST*

Most of summer and part of autumn 1910 Pound spent translating Cavalcanti, intrigued by the realisation that the acute emotional psychology of his poetry frequently dwelt on the mystical state of

ecstasy 'when the feeling by its intensity surpasses our powers of
bearing and we seem to stand aside and watch it surging across
some thing or being with whom we are no longer identified'.
By September 1911 he was planning an essay on paganism in
troubadour poetry.[59]

The essay, 'Psychology and Troubadours', presents *trobar clus* in
the same light as that of Flaminius as 'interpretative': 'it manifests
something which the artist perceives at greater intensity, and more
intimately, than his public'. This 'something', Pound argues, is
mystical communion with a spiritual principle. Pound had earlier
translated the *Pervigilium Veneris*, a poem portraying the eve of the
three-day Sicilian festival in honour of Venus, marked by the
epiphany of the goddess. Without distinguishing these May Day
celebrations sacred to Aphrodite from the autumn rites of Eleusis,
Pound maintained that the spirit of the Hellenic mysteries, in which
the act of coition itself was a sacrament or spiritual initiation,
survived in Provence.[60] Pound hinted that this rather than
Manichæism might have been the real reason for the massacre of
the Albigensians (an interpretation he had read in 1906); in any
event he felt justified in his hypothesis that Mariolatry had imposed
an intellectual patina on an alternative religion of sensual illumin-
ism, in which spiritual 'ecstasy' was interfused with preternaturally
intense awareness of physical beauty ('a glow arising from the exact
nature of the perception').[61]

Peter Makin has examined thoroughly the intellectual background to Pound's interpretation of *trobar clus* and the relationship between sensual love and mystical illumination. He
discriminates three successive phases of courtly-love lyric: first, in
which the lover feels that 'to approach near his beloved would be to
rise to a higher level of existence'; second, in Arnaut Daniel, where
the element of worship in courtly love made it a potential rival to
Christianity, absorbing Christianity within itself, or regarding
Christianity as merely an extension of itself; third, in Guinizelli,
Cavalcanti and the Stilnovisti, in which the lady is regarded as the
source of wisdom for her lover.[62] The medieval habit of figural
reading enabled the lady to be regarded simultaneously as a
physical presence and an incarnation of spiritual illumination. A
further source for Pound's love poetry was the medieval psychological distinction between the 'active' and 'possible' intellect. All
men shared the 'possible' intellect enabling them to penetrate
beneath superficial appearances to essential qualities, but this

required stimulation by the 'active' intellect, which was the gift of divine grace. Poets by the third phase summarised above, and, Pound argued, Arnaut Daniel also, constantly figured the active intellect as their lady, the source of light-as-wisdom. This equation with human sexuality was already present in medieval philosophers, many of whom held that activating wisdom was a divine irradiating force which was female and that its relation to activatable wisdom was that of lady to lover. Thus 'suprasensible knowledge' arose through 'the *copulatio* of the possible and the active intellect'.⁶³

In adopting this 'chivalric' poetry, therefore, Pound was utilising an inherited mystical philosophy and its conventional stylistic vehicle as a veiled symbolic expression for his private spiritual experience. Its hermetic style (parallel to Pound's conception of the origin of myth) was an instinctive defence-mechanism which permitted only the initiate to decipher its essential significance. It formed therefore a counterpart to the metamorphosis as a literary genre which embodied a pantheistic experience bringing spiritual illumination in the same oblique fashion as Cavalcanti and Daniel communicated their variety of mystical experience.

There were, Pound suggested, two alternative paths to transcendental illumination. The ascetic path proceeded through 'contemplation', which Pound employed in the sense of Richard of St Victor's categorisation of three modes of thought: (1) cogitation, 'the aimless flitting of the mind'; (2) meditation, 'the systematic circling of the attention around the object'; (3) contemplation, 'the identification of the consciousness WITH the object'.⁶⁴ This forms the counterpart to Pound's pantheistic beliefs and is obviously related to empathy. The alternative path lay through the 'ecstasy' of sex in which the sensual and intellectual were fused, so that the 'chivalric love' of Provence assumed mediumistic properties; the physical oblivion and loss of the self in orgasm being sublimated into an intellectual sense of union with the absolute or 'life-force', which found expression in a literary convention which used the physical Lady as a symbol for mystical illumination. The Stilnovist and the metamorphic conventions provided, therefore, two symbolic vehicles which offered protection for fragile, esoteric experience similar to that devised by the early artists or myth-makers: 'I assert that a great treasure of verity exists for mankind in Ovid and in the subject matter of Ovid's long poem, and that only in this form could it be registered.'⁶⁵

Having traced Pound's development of two major symbolic masks I now wish to examine a fundamental aspect of his early work, hitherto ignored by critics. The stylistic influence of French Symbolism on his early poetry is relatively slight. Nevertheless he had evolved, as will now emerge, a Symbolist poetics derived from Neoplatonic and hermetic theories.

Repeatedly he describes poetry as 'equations', a concept which, although expressed in mathematical terms, characteristically owes less to science than to mysticism. The doctrine which the mathematical phraseology obscures is revealed in an otherwise tedious poem, 'Guillaume de Lorris Belated', where Pound describes his visionary experience in correspondential terms:

> And dulled some while from dream, and then become
> That lower thing, deductive intellect, I saw
> How all things are but *symbols* of all things,
> And each of many, do we know
> But the *equation* governing.[66]

Pound, whose early poetry dwells on the neglect or persecution of the artist by a materialist society, was doubtless attracted by a theory which gave the poet unwonted importance. As seer he interpreted and controlled the analogical structure of the universe: the 'equations' or forms which generate its phenomena.

In *The Spirit of Romance* (1910) Pound maintained a tongue-in-cheek distance from this early Yeatsian belief:

> Poetry is a sort of inspired mathematics, which gives us equations, not for abstract figures, triangles, spheres, and the like, but equations for the human emotions. If one have a mind which inclines to magic rather than to science, one will prefer to speak of these equations as spells or incantations; it sounds more arcane, mysterious, recondite.[67]

But, I shall argue, his deeper understanding of Stilnovist poetry later in 1910–12 and his interest in scientifically influenced mysticism tempered this equivocation, which itself was no more than an exaggerated version of Yeats's own post-1903 uncertainties. For, as I hope to demonstrate, beneath the characteristic wryness Pound's conception of poetry as the symbolic generation of archetypal states of consciousness was essentially congruous with

Yeats's post-1903 position. Let me begin by recalling briefly Yeats's early Symbolist beliefs, then examining Pound's discovery of similar hermeticism in Stilnovist poetry.

The first major phase of Yeats's work culminated in *Ideas of Good and Evil* (1903). In 'Magic' (1901) and several other essays collected there he explained that the symbols of poetry (a form of verbal enchantment) had the power, like the magical symbols Yeats employed in mystical experiments, to evoke from the Great Memory shared by all mankind archetypal states of consciousness.[68]

As Harper has indicated, 'Magic' is essentially a public exposition of Yeats's beliefs; its esoteric counterpart is the document 'Is the Order of R. R. & A. C. to remain a Magical Order?'[69] There Yeats makes clear that the importance of symbols (and the talismanic structure of the Golden Dawn itself as a microcosmic reflection of the supersensuous world) lies in their power to evoke correspondentially the forces and *energy* of that hidden world, the 'personality' of the super-conscious Being of their Order.[70] Yeats came nearest to giving this doctrine public expression in his remarks apropos Blake and AE on the inspired artistic imagination as symbolic 'revelation' of the world of eternity. In this transcendental interpretation a symbol was 'the only possible expression of some invisible essence, a transparent lamp about a spiritual flame', not because the artist merely summoned into being a virgin linguistic creation but rather because the hermetic literary symbol, by virtue of vertical correspondences, actually instantiated at a remove divine truths.[71] Hence,

> All art that is not mere story-telling, or mere portraiture, is symbolic, and has the purpose of those symbolic talismans [Yeats's word for the microcosmic organisation of the Order of the Golden Dawn] which mediaeval magicians made with complex colours and forms, and bade their patients ponder over daily, and guard with holy secrecy; for it entangles, in complex colours and forms, a part of the Divine Essence.[72]

After 1903, as I discuss below, Yeats had discarded the unequivocally religious aspects of this doctrine. The result was a largely psychological, agnostic theory of poetry as the linguistic evocation of archetypal states of mind, a view shared by Pound, after he had found Yeats's early hermeticism paralleled in Stilnovist poetry.

Pound approached *trobar clus* in 1910–12 with the same hiero-phantic outlook as the Yeats of a decade earlier. He introduces his account in 'Psychology and Troubadours' (1912) with portentous intimations of its character as an incantation practised by and directed towards adepti:

> [*Trobar clus*] must be conceived and approached as ritual. It has its purpose and its effect. These are different from those of simple song. They are perhaps subtler. They make their revelations to those who are already expert.[73]

Earlier critics' reluctance to pursue Pound's tantalising opacity has led to partial misinterpretation of familiar statements about this period. Consider that notorious conversation with Hulme:

> When the late T. E. Hulme was . . . fussing about . . . Bergson . . . I spoke to him one day of the difference between Guido's precise *interpretive* metaphor, and the Petrarchan fustian and ornament, pointing out that Guido thought in accurate terms; that the phrases *correspond* to definite sensations undergone

Frank Kermode, for example, comments that Hulme 'went into the metaphysics of such distinctions, whereas to Pound this was merely taking the argument where it was of no use to anybody'.[74] On the contrary, metaphysics, although of a different variety from Hulme's academic philosophising, was very much Pound's concern.

Pound's emphasis on the precision of Cavalcanti's language is subordinate to the assertion that Cavalcanti's metaphor was vivid because it was a fusion of intellectual and sensual experience; for Cavalcanti, unlike the later Petrarch, the metaphors had a charged mystical significance and were consequently vivid *equations*, like the metamorphic myths (cf. quotation on p. 156 *supra*), for an otherwise inexpressible experience. Cavalcanti, Pound argued in terms reminiscent of Yeats's esoteric theory of symbols as talismans, used language for its 'connotations alchemical, astrological, meta-physical, which Swedenborg would have called the correspon-dences'. Pound's point is not that precise language *per se* is the strength of Cavalcanti's poetry, but that such fidelity to intense perceptual experience actually re-creates, at a necessary defensive remove, a symbol or instantiation of the godhead: 'In Guido the *"figure"*, the strong *metamorphic* or "picturesque" expression is there with purpose to convey or to *interpret* a definite meaning'[75] (cf. Pound's usage of 'interpretation' on pp. 161 and 163 *supra*).

Petrarch's ornament and fustian arose, therefore, from the loss of clear mystical perception which, Pound held, was indivisible from precise discrimination in thought and expression: 'We appear to have lost the radiant world where one thought cuts through another with clean edge, a world of moving energies . . . .'[76] Compare the assertion that in a Guinizelli sonnet 'the preciseness of the description denotes . . . a clarity of imaginative vision. . . . The Tuscan poetry is . . . of a time when the seeing of visions was considered respectable, and the poet takes delight in definite portrayal of his vision.' A later article makes the import of the Hulme conversation indisputable:

[In medieval Provence] men, concentrated on certain validities, attaining an exact and diversified terminology . . . displayed considerable penetration; . . . this was carried into early Italian poetry; and faded from it when metaphors became decorative instead of *interpretative*; . . . the age of Aquinas would not have tolerated sloppy expression of psychology concurrent with the exact expression of 'mysticism'.

He remarks in conclusion that there is also 'wisdom' of this sort in Ovid's *Metamorphoses*.[77]

This conception of poetry as talismanic symbol is central to Pound's view of *trobar clus*. The lady in such poetry, he suggests, fulfilled a function similar to Richard of St Victor's belief that by naming over all the most beautiful things one knows one might evoke a vestigial glimpse of paradise; her various excellences became a *mantram* (defined elsewhere as 'a word for conjuring').[78] This transmogrifying effect was achieved by the talismanic poem redirecting the energy of the lady's ethereal radiation, her *virtù*.[79] In Pound's words,

In [Ballata v] Guido speaks of seeing issue from his lady's lips a subtle body, from that a subtler body, from that a star, from that a voice, proclaiming the ascent of the virtu [*sic*]. For effect upon the air, upon the soul, etc., the 'lady' in Tuscan poetry has assumed all the properties of the Alchemist's stone.[80]

Pound also employed 'virtue' in the sense of quiddity, to denote the inimitable stylistic quality of an author. This Paterian acceptation, as in Pound's article 'On Virtue', is tangential to my investigation and will therefore not be pursued.[81] I am concerned rather with its mystical implications, glossed appositely by Yeats's employment of the word 'virtue' to describe the energy or power channelled by a symbolic 'talisman'.[82]

I have now shown Pound's familiarity with hermetic conceptions of poetry as the symbolic evocation of psychic energy. But, it might be objected, what evidence is there of his belief in their contemporary relevance, particularly to his own poetics? The answer lies, as I shall now explain, in Pound's fusion (wholly characteristic of the age) of science and transcendentalism. While Yeats after 1909 anxiously resorted to spiritualism in search of reassuring confirmation of his emotionally indispensable, but now undermined, mystical beliefs, Pound turned to a scientific mysticism.

Consider this statement by Pound from November 1910:

> The *equations* of alchemy were apt to be written as women's names and the women so named endowed with the magical powers of the compounds. *La virtù* is the potency, the efficient property of a substance or person. Thus modern science shows us radium with a noble virtue of energy. Each thing or person was held to send forth magnetisms of certain effect . . . .
>
> It is a spiritual chemistry, and modern science and modern mysticism are both set to confirm it.[83]

Far from being eccentric, Pound's approach was fully representative of contemporary anti-materialism. His definition of *virtù* (despite his later strictures, prompted by Lewis, on Futurist art) provides a perfect gloss on the Futurists' attempt, discussed in Chapter 5, to represent the 'force-lines' of the individual's aura.[84] The new scientific terminology is being employed to describe a Neoplatonic universe of vital energy or fluid force, cognate with noumenal 'rhythm' as employed by Symons, Murry and Fry, and Kandinsky's inner 'vibrations'.

Pound's obvious fascination with what he terms 'spiritual

chemistry' is explained, I believe, by the fashionable interest (cf. *supra*, p. 136) in mystical circles in psychic photography and in the 'thought-forms' produced by the radiating vibrations of the individual's aura. It is possible, as Pound dabbled at this period in occult and mystical texts, that he read Besant and Leadbeater's *Thought-Forms*; it is inconceivable in view of his proximity to Yeats and the Theosophist G. R. S. Mead that he failed to hear of the considerable excitement aroused by the experiments it describes.[85] It provides therefore useful evidence of ideas 'in the air'.

The attraction for Pound in such inquiries was the speciously scientific patina they gave to mysticism; in 1910, for example, he maintained that astrology, if taken in hand systematically by 'modern science' would provide definite discoveries.[86] Temperamentally he was reluctant to commit himself unreservedly to mystical beliefs, while nevertheless desiring to grant them more than merely hypothetical validity. The apparently imminent confirmation by modern physicists of psychic radiation enabled Pound by utilising a scientific idiom to reconcile his transcendentalist bias with a respectably *avant-garde* stance. I suggest therefore that Pound's metaphor (discussed *infra*, pp. 214–15), which epitomises the Vorticist aesthetic, of the artist's 'order-giving vibrations' transmuting phenomenal contingency into a patterned form (or rather Neoplatonic *forma*) analogous to that produced by a magnet beneath a plate of iron-filings, derives from the Theosophist notion of thought-forms.[87] The metaphor's scientific aspect is obvious; what I wish to emphasise is its latent mysticism.

The recent discovery of radium, and the research of Röntgen, had captured the public's imagination. This physical proof of the existence of radiation encouraged Besant and Leadbeater to maintain that it was only a matter of time before psychic radiation also was verified.[88] Their arguments depend on the traditional occult belief, familiar to Pound and Yeats, that man is surrounded by an 'etheric' envelope which

responds very readily to the influence of human thought, and every impulse sent out, either from the mental body or from the astral body of man, immediately clothes itself in a temporary vehicle of this vitalised matter. Such a thought or impulse becomes for the time a kind of living creature, the thought-force being the soul, and the vivified matter the body.[89]

They term this a 'thought-form', but it is close to Yeats's post-1903 conception of what he had earlier called a 'mood'.

During the 1890s in Yeats's Paterian formulations the term 'mood' had acquired a liturgical resonance which appropriately indicated Yeats's reverential faith in this doctrine of the interpenetration of the temporal and the transcendental.[90] The publication of *Ideas of Good and Evil* (1903) marked in this respect the end of an era. In a well-known letter to AE of May 1903 Yeats wrote,

> I am no longer much in sympathy with an essay like 'The Autumn of the Body,' not that I think that essay untrue. But I think I mistook for a permanent phase of the world what was only a preparation. The close of the last century was full of a strange desire to get out of form, to get to some kind of disembodied beauty, and it now seems to me the contrary impulse has come. I feel about me and in me an impulse to create form . . . .[91]

A complex of factors were involved here, including Yeats's recent discovery of Nietzsche and disillusionment at Maud Gonne's marriage, but it seems right to emphasise the transition from his disappointed expectations of the later 1890s in an imminent millennial 'revelation', which were indivisible from his belief in a new anti-materialist phase in literature. The non-realisation of his prophecies cast into doubt the validity of spiritual doctrines earlier accepted without question. The emphasis of Yeats's formulations altered accordingly. No longer absolutely convinced of the supernatural origin of the 'moods', which he had frequently used as a synonym for something approximating to angels or supernal *visitations*, Yeats laid more stress on the projective rather than the receptive aspect of the imagination. This is evidenced in a change of idiom: the term 'moods' disappears, leaving undecided the issue of whether in visionary moments, including poetic creation, one imagines transcendental beings temporarily clothed in forms borrowed from his subconsciousness, or simply archetypal states of mind.

This reorientation brought Yeats towards a position more congenial to Pound, as expressed in 'Religio' (1918) and 'Axiomata' (1921). Here Pound explained that a 'god' was an 'eternal state of mind', manifest 'When the states of mind take form'. He took as axiomatic that 'The intimate essence of the universe is *not* of the same nature as our own consciousness' and that this might conveniently be termed *theos*. Its ontological status was, however, uncertain and it was open to question whether a particularly remarkable sensation was 'a mirage of the senses, or an affect from the theos'. As he wrote in Pisa,

> Le Paradis n'est pas artificiel
> States of mind are inexplicable to us.[92]

The notion of 'thought-forms' would have provided the ideal compromise solution to this ontological dilemma. It offered a psychological and apparently scientifically respectable explanation of imagination as the unconscious projection of states of consciousness through form-giving psychic 'vibrations'. Pound's familiarity with this view is, I suggest, indicated by his unexplained adoption (apparently in 1912)[93] of the scientific metaphor of the artist's 'order-giving vibrations' creating form (curiously in April 1912 he defined the poet as someone 'on the watch for . . . new *vibrations* sensible to faculties as yet ill understood').[94]

To explain the phenomenon of psychic radiation Besant and Leadbeater employ an analogy with Chladni figures. A Chladni's sound-plate is made of brass or plate-glass on which sand is scattered. The plate is set in vibration by stroking its edge with a violin bow (or by feeding an electromagnet held near it with alternating current); the agitated sand then forms a pattern whose configuration depends on the frequency of the initial vibrations. Substitute for these physical vibrations those 'set up in the mental or astral body, and we have clearly . . . the *modus operandi* of the building of forms by vibrations'.[95] The crucial analogy therefore is that between the 'vibrations' of physical and of psychical energy, both of which call (thought-) forms into being. In itself this theory of imagination was insufficiently dynamic for Pound. He required a complementary account of how the artist's original 'vibrations' may be reactivated from their latency in the poem. He found it in the Symbolist thesis of the generative energy of language.

In 1912 Pound drew a comparison between poet and abstract mathematician. Mathematical equations governed the abstract laws which generated individual geometrical figures; Pound envisaged them as analogous with Platonic forms. Behind all possible circles was 'the circle *absolute*, its law; the circle free in all space, unbounded, loosed from the accidents of time and place'. This symbolic language, when manipulated by the technical adept, had the power to create new physical entities:

> Is the formula nothing, or is it cabala and the sign of unintelligible magic? The engineer, understanding and translating to the many, builds for the uninitiated bridges and devices. He speaks their language. For the initiated the signs are a door into eternity and into the boundless ether.

Similarly poets, more percipient than ordinary men, had the power through verbal incantations (their variety of 'equations') to bring into being hitherto unperceived 'states of consciousness'.[96]

The register of this extract, with its allusions to 'cabala', 'magic', 'the initiated', clearly owes a conceptual debt to the traditional hermetic account of poetry, reformulated influentially by Yeats. Its fusion of science with animism is paralleled in another contemporaneous article which likewise draws an analogy between scientist and poet. Just as the scientific researcher directed the 'latent energy' of the physical world, so the donative artist channelled the energy or *virtù* of the spiritual: 'he draws [from the air about him] latent forces, or things present but unnoticed, or things perhaps taken for granted but never examined'.[97] Pound was refurbishing for a scientific age the traditional doctrine of the poet as hermetical mage, making explicit the analogy between physical and psychical radiation.

This idiosyncratic combination of science (although 'alchemy' might be more accurate) with a Neoplatonic animistic cosmology became the cornerstone of Pound's poetics. The first quality to emphasise is the latent energy Pound insists is concentrated in the 'equation' or *forma* of a poem or scientific formula. A *forma* to Pound is a Platonic archetype, but the aspect he emphasises is its potential to *generate* new developments. In keeping with the Symbolists he holds as axiomatic that this power is inherent in language itself. In the '*absolute* rhythm' of a poem we are offered a fundamental matrix or pattern of consciousness. He transposed this for the visual arts (a topic treated in detail in Chapter 8) by describing Vorticist paintings as 'equations of eternity' and later Brancusi's sculptures as 'master-keys to the world of form – not 'his' world of form, but as much as he has found of 'the' world of form. They contain or imply, or should, the triangle and the circle'. (Compare Pound's subsequent analogy between Brancusi's 'pure form' and 'the form of the analytic geometers'.[98]) Pound's mental association here with mathematical equations is revealed by his fascinated accounts elsewhere (as on p. 173) of the equation for the 'circle *absolute*'.[99]

In his Vorticist writings *passim* Pound developed the notion of painting as an '*arrangement*'; 'form', which to the Vorticist artists implied 'design', implied for Pound *forma*. Here as so often Pound was echoing Yeats (although the term 'arrangement' presumably derives ultimately from Whistler). Compare Yeats's suggestive comment:

> Because an emotion does not exist, or does not become perceptible and active among us, till it has found its expression, in colour or in sound or in form, or in all of these, and because no two modulations or *arrangements* of these evoke the same emotion, poets and painters and musicians . . . are continually making and unmaking mankind.[100]

Yeats treats first the problem of finding an external equivalent for an emotional state: the ontological concern of aesthetics since Kant wondered if there was a common basis for aesthetic judgement and therefore how artistic emotions could be said to be embodied in art. Yeats's implicit answer is that an emotional response (probably not identical, but recognisably similar in most cases) is stimulated by an evocative symbol or what Pound would term an 'equation' (Eliot resorted likewise to a scientific vocabulary for his definition of a symbolic structure or objective correlative as the 'formula' of 'that *particular* emotion'.[101])

But Yeats's thought is more far-reaching and this aspect also is repeated by Pound. Consider the phrase 'continually making and unmaking mankind'. The assertion is that an artistic symbol is a formulaic equivalent for an archetypal state of consciousness and that as such the language of the poem, like a hermetic incantation or philosopher's stone, could be said to command a latent psychic energy which actually created that emotion, unavoidably necessitated its realisation.[102] Similarly for Mallarmé verbal interaction within the poem conjured up an imaginative vision of an otherwise unrealisable ideal world. The linguistic structure approximated towards the instantiation of an *idée*, serving merely to release it and render it communicable. I hope now to demonstrate Pound's ideological indebtedness to this Symbolist faith, represented by Yeats and Mallarmé, in the alchemy of language.

During his metaphysical crisis in 1866–9 Mallarmé's deepening atheism and intense experience of 'le Néant' was replaced by the recurrent but unsustainable hope of an underlying intelligible structure in the universe, derived idiosyncratically from two disparate cosmologies – Neoplatonic hermeticism and a clouded form of Hegelianism.[103] Inspired by this idealist vision he began the quest for an all-inclusive 'Grand Œuvre' or 'Livre' which would provide the 'explication orphique de la Terre'.[104]

As a poet 'chargé de voir divinement', persuaded of 'la corrélation intime de la Poésie avec l'Univers', Mallarmé aspired to express his new conception of cosmic order in poetry purified from its usual vitiating contingency.[105] The project, which was visualised in correspondential, hermetic terms,[106] required the purification of language into a medium sufficiently refined for this task, restoring in poetry the lost power of the word as *Logos*, its creative, virtual energy.[107] In Mallarmé's terminology 'le Verbe' (or *Logos*) corresponded to the Hegelian Absolute which objectified itself in 'le Langage' to form speech ('la Parole') and writing ('l'Écriture'). The poet could foster the recovery of the primordial unity of 'le Verbe' by disengaging from 'le hasard' the latent analogical patterns in the 'gestes de l'Idée se manifestant par la parole', preserving them and indicating their interrelationship. This entailed recapturing the former 'sens virtuel' of words, and the original absolute significance of the letters of the alphabet as mysterious analogical creations.[108] Hence Mallarmé created sound-patterns more faithful to the moods they were intended to evoke, resurrected lost etymological meanings, and resorted to indirection and obliquity, utilising extra-linguistic resources[109] and reinvoking the talismanic properties of language itself.

Mallarmé's frequent references to his projected 'Grand Œuvre' in terms of alchemy reflected his belief, like Yeats's, that poetry was cognate with magic.[110] The resemblance between the incantations practised by mage and poet lay in the power of language to create both through evocative analogies and the hermetic virtual energy of words themselves ('la force virtuelle des caractères divins') a hitherto non-existent entity, whether imaginary or physically present:

Évoquer, dans une ombre exprès, l'objet tu, par des mots allusifs, jamais directs, se réduisant à du silence égal, comporte tentative proche de créer: vraisemblable dans la limite de l'idée uniquement mise en jeu par l'enchanteur de lettres jusqu'à ce que, certes, scintille, quelque illusion égale au regard.[111]

Only the alchemy of language assured Mallarmé that his desired ideal world was accessible; poetry offered a validation of his imaginative faith poignant in its ephemerality. 'Un coup de dés' movingly depicts man's attempt to achieve a lasting realisation of universal rationality, imaged by the intelligibility implicit in 'Le Nombre', the elusive dice-throw of double-six symbolic of the conquest of phenomenal chaos ('le hasard'), and intimated by the emerging pattern of the constellation.[112] More frequently Mallarmé symbolised his Neoplatonic vision of a permanent realm of Beauty in the subtle but serene mirage of ideal flowers, precariously elicited by the poet's ritual incantations through which alone they achieve imaginative substantiality.[113] As in the 'lotos' rising out of the sunlight and the 'unimaginable/Zero summer' of Eliot's *Four Quartets*, perceptual ambiguities introduce a poetics of absence. Arresting analogies, militating against discursive thought, transmogrify objects into the transient illusion of a desired but probably unattainable ideal, reinforced by the evocative qualities of the poem's verbal music and its intimation through the white intervals in its typographic disposition of a mental space pregnant with virtuality.[114] A brief digression will serve to indicate the lasting significance for Pound of this belief in the generative power of poetry, reflected not in the local stylistic detail of the *Cantos* but in what I believe are their Symbolist premises.

Although Pound was of a mystical inclination and the *Cantos* could be termed a religious work, from his Imagist period onwards he was not interested in finding experimental confirmation of his faith. On several occasions he emphasised his scepticism towards Yeats's psychical research, probably surfeited by three winters as his secretary at Coleman's Hatch during Yeats's most intense period of spiritualist investigation.[115] He was equally uninterested in Yeats's attempts to establish in technical detail the nature of life after death and undoubtedly found the desire to dogmatize or schematise on such points antipathetic. Nevertheless, Pound's own conception in 'Religio' of 'states of mind' taking form resembles his paraphrase of Yeats's view 'that the world of spirits is fluid and drifts about seeking shape'.[116] His explication of the ghost in *Awoi no Uye* reveals his grasp of Yeats's notion that psychic energy, derived from passionate or emotional experience in life, enables a ghost to materialise using the vehicle of the Anima Mundi and re-enact part of a past life (in the necessary 'Dreaming Back' or 'Return' process prior to becoming a 'timeless Daimon'[117]). Thus from their various orthodox and unorthodox Neoplatonic sources the two shared a belief in a permanent world of psychic energy able to be realised through the individual imagination. At this point Yeats's 'Great Memory' elides into Pound's more orthodox Neoplatonism derived from Cavalcanti, just as the invocation which opens the *Cantos* draws Pound close to Yeats.

In his 1930 Diary Yeats wrote on the phenomenon of 'Dreaming Back':

> It was the opinion of those Cabbalist friends that the actions of life remained so pictured but that the intensity of the light depended upon the intensity of the passion that had gone to their creation. This is to assume, perhaps correctly, that the greater the passion the more clear the perception, for the light is perception.

The parallel with Pound's developing Neoplatonic light philosophy becomes clear if one quotes briefly from his translation of Cavalcanti's 'Donna mi prega':

> In memory's locus taketh he [Love] his state
> Formed there in manner as a mist of light

and from the *Pisan Cantos*:

> nothing matters but the quality
> of the affection –
> in the end – that has carved the trace in the mind
> dove sta memoria

The congruity of their views on memory is revealed in Yeats's poem of that title which puns on the word 'form' to present the 'mountain hare', Maud Gonne, as an indelible *forma* or Idea in Yeats's memory.[118]

Despite Pound's disparagement of Yeats's psychical research, it is remarkable that he chose to open the *Cantos* with the *nekuia* from the *Odyssey*. It seems possible that Yeats inspired Pound to adopt this technical device (emphasised by the phrase 'Lie quiet Divus', as though dismissing a spirit[119]) which helped resolve the structural indecision evident in the early versions of the *Cantos*. In 'The Grey Rock' (awarded the 1913 prize by *Poetry*, of which Pound was foreign editor) Yeats experimented for the first time in combining 'ghosts' of friends or historical personages, elevated to mythological status as the tragic generation, with more conventional mythological figures, the Celtic gods at Slievenamon. This combination of historical and mythological material, although not wholly distinct in conception, foreshadows the method of the *Cantos* but had admittedly been adumbrated by Pound without success as early as 'Redondillas' (1911). 'The Grey Rock' relies implicitly on a seance or invocation structure (a genre employed slightly later in 'In Memory of Major Robert Gregory' and 'All Souls' Night'), utilising the experience of Yeats's spiritualist experiments, which Pound had observed, to make explicit the relationship expounded in 'Magic' between the poet's images and moods from the Great Memory, the memories of disembodied souls.[120] The *Cantos* would accordingly be a visionary exploration of the wisdom held in the memories of ghosts, invoked by an initial blood libation, like the psychical 'phantasmagoria' of 'shadows [who] have drunk from the pool of blood' which Yeats described in the 1914 essay 'Swedenborg, Mediums, and the Desolate Places'.[121] The *nekuia* provided for Pound both a rationale for and an arresting way of introducing his Neoplatonic philosophy, conjuring with the force of the imagination, and thus with talismanic power, the *formae* held in the memory of earlier periods of Unity of Culture.

Yeats's interest in this phenomenon was confined chiefly to its implications for the individual personality: the psychic energy seeking form of the beholder's or ghost's permanent self or daimon.[122] But Pound stressed the phylogenetic as well as ontogenetic aspects of this belief: the *forma* of a civilisation was preserved in the memory like the record of passionate personal experience. Each attracted a psychic energy which ensured, perhaps even necessitated, its potential future realisation.

For Pound believed that an ideal *paideuma*, whether city or civilisation (such as Wagadu, which existed 'in the mind indestructible') or period of Unity of Culture (such as the Provencal Renaissance or *quattrocento* Italy) having once been realised remained a perpetual possibility as a matrix or *forma*.[123] In the memory of the race it embodied a latent energy able to inspire a new realisation of its imagined pattern.[124] The poet's humanist task was therefore to channel this energy through the power of language, to reveal to man his own creative potential as memorialised in such ideal paradigms, just as in his symbolic 'equations' he made men aware of their imaginative capacity by revealing hitherto un-perceived states of consciousness. But the exhilarating faith that the alchemy of language might inspire the permanent realisation of this utopian dream faded after the outbreak of the Second World War into the acknowledgement that language was not after all *Logos*; its creative power had dwindled to the impotent isolation of a disillusioned 'ego scriptor'.[125] This digression has emphasised the continuing importance of Pound's hermetic theory; I must now return in conclusion to its origins.

By the end of 1911 Pound had assembled the essential elements of his poetics and was confident of an imminent artistic Renaissance. *Canzoni* (1911), his most programmatic and radically disparate volume to date, reflects this poised assurance (a point hitherto neglected by critics, who have failed to grasp Pound's intentions in this volume). Significantly a new satirical thrust accompanies the mystical theme of the lady's aura or *virtù*.[126] Representative of both these perspectives is the ambitious 'Und Drang', which aspires to being a turbulent preparation, like the German movement to which its title alludes, for a major literary revival.[127] To adapt Nietzsche (his obvious inspiration, especially in the first five poems of the sequence) Pound here poeticises with the hammer, testing new ideas, directing irony against his own poetic modes and those of his idols, but balancing iconoclasm with affirmation. Above all, therefore, like 'Mauberley' nine years later, 'Und Drang' is a transitional poem.

The sequence opens with a tongue-in-cheek proclamation of Pound's self-imposed task as poetic 'over-man', overburdened but gathering strength for the transvaluation of received poetic values. (Pound's parabolical account of the trials of the leader-figure resembles those of another period of poetic revaluation, the early 1930s, such as Auden's 'The Orators' and Eliot's 'Coriolan II'.) His irony turns in sections III and IV against the Celtic school and the tenuous, fragile rhythms of his own early work, particularly 'La Fraisne'. The burlesque impressionist creed of the second half of 'Elegia' heralds the parody of Symons in section V, with VI as a corollary imitating the sort of Paterian epiphany Symons mem-orialised, only to reject it in favour of his own transcendental manifesto in sections VII and VIII, which correlate Rossetti, Pre-Raphaelite iconography, Provence, Cavalcanti and Sirmione.[128]

Pound's affirmation here of his faith in numinous experience, whether via pantheism or the Provencal love mystery, is not undercut by the sequence's concluding satire of Pound's own metropolitan existence and then the otherworldly interpretations of love in Yeats's 'The Cap and Bells', just as the quotidian banalities of 'Redondillas' leave its resolutely visionary claims unimpaired.[129] The confessional element in these poems of revaluation (more apparent in the latter's desultory, Whitmanesque pastiche) necessitates the portrayal of all aspects of Pound's interests, and there is no apparent reason to regard some as less sincere than others. Both satire and transcendentalism were essential elements in Pound's Imagist/Vorticist Renaissance; fittingly both are present in his programmatic 'Redondillas', where 'I sing of risorgimenti'.[130]

To recapitulate: in his early London years Pound was preparing for an artistic Renaissance able to be transplanted into America. Chapter 7 will examine its practical aspects; here I have discussed its spiritual dimension, evidenced in Pound's development of an anti-materialist, animistic cosmology. This found expression in a poetic symbolism drawn from metamorphic mythology and Stilnovist mysticism, and a Symbolist poetics cognate with Yeatsian hermeticism and the empathetic, animistic aesthetics discussed in Chapters 2, 3 and 5. The final chapter will demonstrate the central importance of this approach to Imagist/Vorticist aesthetics.

# 7 The London Vortex: Pound's Renaissance *Forma*

In the previous chapter I examined the aesthetic and spiritual dimensions of Pound's desired Renaissance. In considering the practical aspects of this, his first attempt to realise an ideal *forma* of civilisation, I now wish to offer a new interpretation of the external history of Vorticism.

A predominant theme in discussions within the Imagist/Vorticist circle was undoubtedly financial difficulties. The most attractive remedy for this pressing impecunity was to search for a patron (on Italian *quattrocento* models) first in Kate Lechmere, then in Amy Lowell. In this Pound occupied the centre of the stage; for two reasons. First, he was the only figure of sufficient vision to conceive the multidisciplinary project of the Rebel Art Centre or London 'vortex'. Secondly, his indefatigable propagandist activities on behalf of the other artists and writers assured his position of aesthetic director, an isolated leadership which in time provoked his downfall. For, although the other Imagists acquiesced in Pound's manifestos and accepted his flamboyant control for as long as he was their only publishing-outlet and source of income, Aldington became more restive once he obtained the assistant editorship of the *Egoist* in January 1914, and his, H.D.'s and Flint's long pent-up resentment and jealousy erupted into open rebellion once Amy Lowell provided a secure publishing alternative in the series *Some Imagist Poets*.[1] The result was the artistically negligible 'Amygism', the final pre-war secession group. A brief chronological survey will sketch in the background to these backstair intrigues and shifts in aesthetic alignment.

My exposition in Chapter 6 left Pound on the verge of Imagism, having published the programmatic *Canzoni*. The story resumes early in 1912. That February he published an essay, 'Prolegomena', probably written in December 1911, which contains the 'Credo' adumbrating the Imagist position.[2] Soon afterwards Pound's independent, innovatory movement began to take shape when Richard Aldington and Hilda Doolittle took rooms opposite Pound's in Church Walk, Kensington. Pound began to comment on and criticise their poetry; at the foot of the manuscript of 'Hermes of the Ways' he scrawled excitedly 'H. D. Imagiste'.[3] Probably in April 1912 the three reached a compromise formula, curbing the Hellenism of the younger two, of three fundamental principles of poetic composition which could serve as a manifesto:

1. Direct treatment of the 'thing' whether subjective or objective.
2. To use absolutely no word that does not contribute to the presentation.
3. As regarding rhythm: to compose in the sequence of the musical phrase, not in sequence of a metronome.[4]

With an eye to publicity Pound soon christened the group 'Les Imagistes', a title which first appeared in print in October 1912 in the appendix to his *Ripostes*.

On 18 August 1912 Pound agreed to collaborate in Harriet Monroe's new magazine, *Poetry*, sending a poem on Whistler, together with 'Middle-Aged', which he described as 'an over-elaborate post-Browning "Imagiste" affair', the beginning of his propagandist mystification.[5] A month later he became the magazine's foreign correspondent. *Poetry*, despite Pound's discomfort at Harriet Monroe's editorial censorship, her belief that poetry should be written for a mass audience, and her uncritical predilection for mediocre Mid-West poets, proved a useful platform for the new movement until they managed to commandeer the literary section of the ailing feminist periodical the *Freewoman*, which was renamed the *New Freewoman* in June 1913, to appear as the *Egoist* from 1 January 1914 until December 1919. The second issue of *Poetry*, in November 1912, included three poems by Aldington, described as 'a young English poet, one of the "imagistes", a group of ardent Hellenists who are pursuing interesting experiments in *vers libre*; trying to attain in English certain subtleties of cadence of the kind which Mallarmé and his followers have studied in French', while the January 1913 issue contained further intimations of their aims and a group of poems signed 'H. D.

Imagiste', a label which both Aldington and its bearer regarded as somewhat ridiculous, but complied with Pound's propaganda as he was their only contact for publication.[6] Pound had introduced Aldington to Orage, who published several of his poems in the *New Age* in November 1912 and January 1913.

The March 1913 issue of *Poetry* saw the appearance of 'Imagisme', in which Flint introduced Pound's 'A Few Don'ts by an Imagiste', the Imagist manifesto, which had originally been intended to accompany rejection slips to would-be contributors to *Poetry*.[7] Pound's chief concern was publicity. In a letter of 20 January 1913 he asked Flint to hurry up with the 'Imagist Interview' as he'd just written an 'Ars Poetica' and wanted the interview to appear first. New York had already been writing to Chicago to find out 'what is Imagism?' and Pound was hoping to take over two columns once a week in a London daily for 'serious criticism'.[8]

That summer the first catches rose to Pound's bait. Amy Lowell, intrigued by what she had read in *Poetry* about Imagism and armed with a letter of introduction to Pound from Harriet Monroe, established base camp at the Berkeley Hotel in Piccadilly. She and Pound took to one another and he arranged for 'In a Garden' (probably her first attempt at *vers libre*, which had appeared in *Poetry* for July 1913) to appear in the *New Freewoman*. Together with Aldington, H.D. and Flint, Pound subjected her poetry to stringent criticism in an attempt to remould her insipid style.[9] By September Pound had begun to assemble an anthology of Imagist poets to boost the work of Aldington and H.D. before each had enough material for a volume, as he was to assemble the *Catholic Anthology* in 1915 to launch T. S. Eliot. That month Aldington wrote of 'Ezra's Anthologie'; already in June Robert Frost had asked Flint to explain 'what all this talk of a post-Georgean [*sic*] anthology means'.[10] This makes clear that the Imagist anthology was intended as a direct reply to Marsh's Georgian anthology, which itself had broken new poetic ground, implying ('post-Georgean') that they regarded it as already obsolete. By early November the editors of the *Glebe*, Alfred Kreymborg's New York periodical, had accepted the anthology for publication as soon as possible.

There were, however, already hints of impending discord. John Gould Fletcher, who had left America in 1908, had since autumn 1912 devoted all his time to studying French literature. He believed that poetry was an idealistic, non-commercial activity (as with a

private income he could well afford to) and in 1913 himself financed
the printing of five volumes of his own poetry. In May 1913 he met
Pound in Paris, where, Fletcher claims in his autobiography, Pound
asked him to support a literary review under his editorship. Fletcher
readily agreed to this project, having bid unsuccessfully in 1911 for
the *English Review* when it passed out of Ford's hands. Now a
published but unsuccessful author, he believed his income could
best be employed in providing a publishing-outlet for struggling
young writers. But while supplying funds monthly to pay contributors to the *New Freewoman*, Fletcher stipulated that he would not
himself submit material to this journal nor allow his name to be
mentioned in its columns, being unwilling to continue being
published only by virtue of his own subsidy. In late autumn 1913,
however, he changed his mind on this issue.[11] This attractively
retouched picture of Fletcher as Maecenas glosses over his bitterness
at the time, as I shall soon explain.

In June 1913 Lowell and Fletcher met in London. He showed her
his poems, 'Irradiations', and outlined his conception of free verse.
Both the poetry and the theories greatly impressed Lowell, who
adopted his technique in her own work. Pound's attitude to Fletcher
at this time was divided but generous. His poetry conflicted with
Pound's own canons but nevertheless moved him and he insisted
that Harriet Monroe must publish it in *Poetry*. Although Fletcher
sometimes employed rhetoric and used abstractions, Pound ap-
proved of his attempt to write colloquial poetry dealing with the
'real' and the 'contemporary' and applauded his acquaintance with
modern French innovations.[12]

On 7 September 1913 Fletcher wrote to Lowell explaining that
Pound had attempted to undertake in the *New Freewoman* what
Fletcher regarded as log-rolling activities on his behalf and he had
withdrawn his financial support from this literary clique. Fletcher
was undoubtedly hypersensitive in his reactions, but Pound's
enthusiastic proselytising on behalf of authors whose talents he
believed unjustly neglected, such as Williams, Joyce and Eliot,
could be curiously ill-judged. For example, he disinterestedly
promoted the work of Robert Frost at a time when Frost could find
no publishers, but this association was terminated when Pound sent
Frost's poem 'Death of the Farm Hand' to *Smart Set* without
requesting prior permission.[13] Fletcher had, he wrote, refused on
several occasions to contribute to the proposed anthology and, out
of respect for Lowell's work, which he rated more highly than that of

Pound or Aldington, advised her strongly to withdraw. The real editor of the anthology was, he claimed, that 'silly cub' Aldington, who was married to H.D., 'another "arriviste" '. The volume was intended simply to boom them and Pound in America, using the other contributors as mere satellites whose weakest work would be chosen as a foil to the main three. Fletcher's mildly paranoiac distortion of the facts was all the more damaging for being partly grounded in truth: the anthology was indeed intended to boost H.D. and Aldington, but the rest of Fletcher's insinuation is sheer malice, to which Pound had recklessly exposed himself by virtue of the puzzlingly ill-assorted gaggle of poets he had paraded for the occasion, who defied all objective attempts to establish a rationale which would explain their appearance together. Lowell should insist on being given more space, Fletcher counselled, or back out, in which case he was willing to put up equal shares and issue another anthology in England on the basis that he could select or reject anything he wanted and that she would have the same privilege.

Lowell read sufficient between the lines of Fletcher's outburst to make her uneasy. She wrote to Pound stating that if his was to be an Imagist anthology she did not think she belonged in it; she received no reply. [14] As Pound was able to include Joyce's 'I Hear an Army' in the anthology in January 1914, following Yeats's recommendation in December 1913, it is difficult to believe that he could not have altered Lowell's contribution had he so wished. It thus seems likely that her poem 'In a Garden' was included in *Des Imagistes* mainly because of the financial resources with which she could supply the movement. [15]

*Des Imagistes* appeared as the February 1914 number of the *Glebe* and was issued in New York as a book in March, and in London, using the same sheets, by Harold Monro's Poetry Bookshop in April. At the time both Aldington and H.D. objected to the inclusion of Lowell. They regarded her only published volume, *A Dome of Many-Coloured Glass* (1912), as 'the fluid, fruity, facile stuff we most wanted to avoid'. They were suspicious of her recent conversion to *vers libre* and sudden transmogrification to a more austere style with a wave of Pound's blue pencil. [16]

Early in 1914 further problems began to emerge in Pound's correspondence with Amy Lowell. He seems never to have regarded her as an artistic contributor, but rather as a wealthy potential supporter of the struggling artists, himself included, whose interests he ceaselessly furthered. He had hoped that Harriet Monroe's magazine, *Poetry*, would signal the prelude to an American Renaissance by introducing international standards of artistic excellence. In this, for the reasons indicated above, he had been disappointed. His influence in the magazine was less than he desired and it was only after January 1917 in the *Little Review* that he found a reliable and sympathetic publisher for his work and that of Eliot, Joyce and Lewis. In a row over the contents of *Poetry* in November 1913 Pound resigned from the magazine in favour of Ford, who resigned in his turn in Pound's favour. By early December he was reinstated, but still querulous.[17] His attention in 1913–14 was accordingly focused on the establishment of a subsidised periodical in which he would play a major editorial role; he believed that Amy Lowell could supply the finance for this. At the same time in London Lewis's girlfriend Kate Lechmere, soon to become Hulme's mistress, was providing the capital to establish the Rebel Art Centre, which was to act as the 'vortex' for the group of *avant-garde* artists Pound and Lewis were assembling. Let me place these Renaissance aspirations in context.

Despite spending most of his life abroad, Pound's prime concern was always America. Driven to Europe in an attempt to escape provincialism in critical standards, he mounted an unceasing campaign to obviate the need for other Americans to do so. Apart from the 25 per cent tariff on the import of foreign books, Pound saw the main barriers against the success of American writers as 'the dead-hand of the past generation composed of clerks and parasites and . . . our appalling *decentralization*, i.e. lack of metropoles and centers, having full publishing facilities and communication with the outer world . . . also our scarcity of people who know'.[18] Following Henry James and Whistler, Pound's method of overcoming the provincial standards and decentralisation of America had been to move to 'the double city of London and Paris'.[19] He termed such a metropolitan civilisation a 'vortex', which had for him the primary meaning of a concentration of intellectual energy, usually in a group of exceptional minds. America, 'a province without a centre', was a stark contrast to London, which 'is like Rome of the decadence, so far, at least, as letters are concerned. She is a main and vortex drawing strength from the peripheries'.[20] The interchange of ideas among the leading intellectuals whom such a capital necessarily attracted made the outmoded or inferior indefensible.[21] In the course of time Pound's ideas on the optimum size and feasibility of such a unit began to change. The metropolis was too large; what was required was instead a publishing-organ which would maintain the highest (and therefore uncommercial) standards, or alternatively an academy which would create a stimulating intellectual atmosphere to foster individual creation and a fruitful interchange between the various art forms.

He began his series of articles on America, 'Patria Mia', with the statement that America is not really a nation as it lacks an 'Urbs' or city to which all roads lead. On a visit to New York in 1910–11 he had seen in architecture the first signs of a new modernity; his enthusiasm for what, following Whistler, he saw as a revival of the *campanile* form was perhaps the first inkling of his hope for an American *Risorgimento* or *Risvagliamento* along Italian Renaissance lines.[22] The Italian *quattrocento*, the age of Sigismundo Malatesta, had seen a localised fostering of the arts under aristocratic patronage in a union of 'the vortices of social power' with the 'vortices of creative intelligence'. A revival of this sort of patronage was, Pound believed, the only possible solution to the contemporary financial crisis in the arts. The economics of publication meant that the only way to avoid mediocrity was to assemble a self-sufficient group of artists in emulation of the Renaissance system.[23] The Italian Renaissance had begun when Valla grasped the significance of

> the great Roman vortex . . . the value of a capital, the value of centralization, in matters of knowledge and art, and of the interaction and stimulus of genius foregathered. . . . That . . . reawakening to the sense of the capital, resulted . . . in the numerous vortices of the Italian cities, striving against each other not only in commerce but in the arts as well.

The American Renaissance must, Pound argued, similarly proceed through the conscious use of riches to create an art capital or vortex as the Ptolemies had in Alexandria or the Medici in Florence.[24]

Consistently Pound reiterated the feasibility of and urgent need for localised patronage. He believed that some of the money devoted to sterile, 'German', academic research could be channelled into an academy of the creative arts: 'Any city which cares for its future can perfectly well start its vortex. It can found something between a graduate seminar and the usual 'Arts Club' made up of business men and of a few "rather more than middle-aged artists who can afford to belong".'[25] In October 1912 he published the

proposal that government resources or a millionaire's 'centraliz-
ation of power' could subsidise a group of one hundred artists in a
*'college of the arts'* in New York, San Francisco or Chicago. He
repeated the proposal in May 1913 and in the final version of *Patria
Mia*, completed probably in June 1913, stressing that it was within
the financial capability of a millionaire. He suggested that 'a sane
form of bequest would be an endowment of 1,000 dollars per year,
settled on any artist whose work was recognized as being of value to
the community, or as being likely to prove of value to the
community provided it were left to develop unhampered by the
commercial demand'.[26] This was more than a passing whim of
Pound's; he was to argue in August 1915 in similar terms to the
Secretary of the Royal Literary Fund on behalf of a grant for James
Joyce, and in 1922 to try to arrange through the 'Bel Esprit' project
a guaranteed income which would free T. S. Eliot from physically
wearing work in Lloyd's Bank and enable him to devote all his time
to writing.[27]

The situation in America was acute, but in England also Pound
saw evidence of what he interpreted as a conspiracy on the part of
society, the *status quo*, or simply an undefined malignant force, to
destroy or handicap artistic innovation and to suppress knowledge
in order to maintain an inequitable system. The later label 'usury'
was a convenient rationalisation and specious explanation of this
instinctive suspicion.[28] Pound remarked later, 'Whatever economic
passions I now have, began *ab initio* from having crimes against
living art thrust under my perceptions.'[29]

Pound's first suspicions of public obstructionism arose when Ford
Madox Ford* lost control of the *English Review*, which had been
founded to provide somewhere to publish Hardy's 'A Sunday
Morning Tragedy', a poem rejected as indelicate by the commercial magazines.[30] Ford maintained a consistently high standard
from December 1908 to February 1910, publishing Lewis, D. H.
Lawrence and Pound as well as the leading established writers such
as Galsworthy, Conrad, James, Yeats and Wells. Crippling financial losses and his lack of business acumen forced Ford to sell out to
the financier Sir Alfred Mond. This left an indelible impression on
Pound's mind that (as Storer and the Futurists also believed) the
economics of magazine-publishing and the reactionary editors of
the establishment formed an effective block on artistic innovation

---

* I follow the conventional critical practice of standardising all references to
Ford Madox Ford, even for the years before his surname was changed from Hueffer.

and imposed mediocre standards.[31] The only alternative seemed to be an independent organ whose unavoidable commercial losses could be borne by patrons who believed in the welfare of the arts, or by financial subsidy of deserving but indigent artists.[32] He was soon able to add further names to his pantheon of suppressed genius. By the year of *Des Imagistes* he was convinced of a necessary conflict between artistic excellence and public finance.

In 1913 and 1914 Robert Frost, surely the authentic voice of New England, could not find an American publisher; in autumn 1913 Pound was full of enthusiasm for Allen Upward, whose *The New Word* (1907) had, like his other important books, been published at his own expense and whose challenging speculations were, it seemed to Pound, ignored to avoid public disquiet, as Pound pointed out in articles published in November 1913 and April 1914.[33] Epstein's Strand statues and sculpture on Oscar Wilde's tomb had suffered public vilification, his work was refused by the Tate Gallery, yet Pound had vivid first-hand proof of his outstanding ability in the *Rock Drill*, which he had seen beginning to take shape in December 1913. Gaudier, with whom Pound had struck up a close friendship following the Allied Artists' Association exhibition in July 1913 and regarded as '*the* coming sculptor', was at starvation level while engaged from January or February until May 1914 on *The Hieratic Head of Ezra Pound*.[34] Dublin had rejected Sir Hugh Lane's bequest of pictures and Ireland had rejected Synge and driven Joyce abroad. These matters would have been live issues to Pound in the winter of 1913–14 as he worked as Yeats's secretary at Coleman's Hatch. In December 1913 Yeats brought Joyce's plight to the attention of Pound. He included in the Cuala Press edition of *Responsibilities: Poems and a Play*, which he was then preparing, a long note emphasising his anger at the Lane controversy and the reception of Synge's *The Playboy of the Western World*, having in December 1913 written from Coleman's Hatch two letters to *The Times* protesting at the withdrawal of *The Playboy* from the matinee programme of Liverpool Repertory Theatre after performances had been disrupted.[35] Yeats's 1909 Journal records Ricketts's explanation of the broken lives of contemporary men of genius as lack of patronage.[36]

Action had, it seemed, become imperative if the leading artistic innovators were not to be stilled by the financial system (compare Pound's 'The Rest', first published in November 1913). Pound accordingly sought patrons to realise his dream of a magazine voice for the cultural élite and a neo-Renaissance academy of artistic excellence. Discussions with Yeats, whose poem 'To a Wealthy Man who promised a Second Subscription to the Dublin Municipal Gallery if it were proved the People wanted Pictures', written in December 1912 and reprinted in *Responsibilities: Poems and a Play*, eulogises the patronage of the arts by the *quattrocento* Dukes of Ferrara and Urbino, and Cosimo de Medici's support of the architect and sculptor Michelozzo, were doubtless for Pound an encouraging confirmation of the plans he formulated at Coleman's Hatch.[37]

Pound's dream of a College of the Arts seemed to be about to be realised when in the early spring of 1914 he and Lewis, who had had little apparent contact since a disastrous first encounter in the Vienna Café in 1909, became involved in the planning of the Rebel Art Centre in opposition to the Bloomsbury-financed Omega workshops. Lewis had similar grandiose plans for more than a simple productive *atelier*. Lecture-programmes, plays, dances, exhibitions and Saturday artistic salons would follow the opening on 26 April of an art-school of the *avant-garde* under Professor Wyndham Lewis.[38] Imagism would become merely the literary element in 'Vorticism', a new movement uniting all the art forms, which Pound christened sometime between April and June.[39] Pound's aspirations at this time are revealed in the later prospectus, printed in November 1914, for the College of Arts, a 'centre of intelligent and intellectual activity', in which he proclaimed that 'We aim at an intellectual status no lower than that attained by the courts of the Italian Renaissance.' The 'Professors' included Gaudier for Sculpture, Lewis for Painting, Alvin Langdon Coburn for Photography (arguably the leading photographer of the Edwardian period, he had first taken Pound's portrait in October 1913 and later devised 'vortographs'), Edward Wadsworth for Design, Dolmetsch for Ancient Music, and Pound for Comparative Poetry.[40]

In a letter to Flint, apparently from 25 March 1914 and therefore immediately prior to the opening of the Rebel Art Centre, Pound, eager to push his scheme for the College of the Arts, asked Flint if he would be prepared to 'cram' pupils at a guinea per hour in Modern French Poetry if this could be arranged, and also to read out his *Poetry and Drama* articles at £5 per hour to audiences of between three and forty. On the one hand Pound wanted to offer Flint what he regarded as easy money; on the other he needed for his College a name which carried some authority on the subject. As a 'favour' could Pound put Flint's name on a 'prospectus'? – he could withdraw later if he wished:

> Ecco – some musicians are going to America to grab the german [*sic*] trade in pupils. There's no reason why pupils shouldn't study litterature [*sic*] as well as music.
> Lastly it will be a good *adv.* and may lead to a market in American magazines.[41]

Flint refused to play ball (his relations with Pound were somewhat strained, and maintained only by his dependence on Pound as publishing-agent[42]) but Pound pressed on undaunted by this minor setback unfortunately all too premonitory of larger failures to come.

The Rebel Art Centre in practice failed to correspond to Pound's and Lewis's aspirations. Its downfall in June was brought about by Lewis's lack of business acumen and organisational ability, abetted by his suspicious nature, which refused to allow other artists to become members, fearing that Hulme and Epstein wanted to usurp his leadership of what as usual he effectively reduced to a movement of one; the artists in their turn refused to contribute to the rent, offering the unsatisfactory alternative of a commission on largely non-existent sales. Pound had little say in the management of the Centre, as its capital was provided by Lewis's mistress Kate Lechmere, but in early spring at least he was optimistic about the success of this vortex. His attention was therefore transferred from what seemed a relatively secure College of the Arts to establishing with the help of Renaissance-style patronage a periodical under his editorship which would maintain uncompromisingly the highest standards and foster commercially unviable, neglected genius.

Since 1912 the irrepressible Pound had been badgering Harold Monro to turn over the *Poetry Review* and later *Poetry and Drama* to the Imagist group and their associates. Monro 'had a struggle to prevent the review from falling overmuch under the influence of Pound – whose judgement he respected even while disapproving of his occasional violent outbursts – and becoming the organ of a limited group of poets however brilliant.' He had also hoped, as I indicated, to edit the *New Freewoman*, financed by Fletcher. In the winter of 1913–14 Pound thought he had more positive hopes elsewhere. On 4 January 1914 he wrote to Joyce, explaining that the *Egoist* could not pay for articles but was a useful alternative for material too personal or too outspoken to send to the usual magazines. One comment reveals both Pound's vision of the ideal magazine and his bitterness at the commercial publishing-system: 'We want it to be a place where a man can speak out. It is not a device for getting a man who ought to be paid, to work for nothing, which is more than I can say for some arty magazines'. He told Joyce that *Poetry* paid two shillings per line but was sluggish and unreliable in its judgement, a dissatisfaction reiterated to Louis Untermeyer four days later: ' "Poetry" isn't entirely glorious. I've resigned once as a protest against the rot they put in, & I've gone back in the vain hope of keeping it from getting worse. Still I think their intention is moderately good.' He added, 'I should have some hopes of a new paper here, The Egoist, if I had sufficient financial backing.'[43] In this respect Amy Lowell's financial independence and interest in contemporary literature appeared to fit the bill exactly.

She apparently was looking for her own literary periodical and in February 1914 Pound wrote offering Lowell the editorship of the *Egoist* in return for financial backing. He seems to have hoped that she would send the cash from Boston and preside *in absentia*, leaving him a relatively free editorial hand in London. The plan foundered when the *Egoist* obtained finance elsewhere, but Pound did not give up his desire to have a hold on a periodical and a salary, suggesting that Lowell run a quarterly from Boston. While she did not accept either of these proposals she nevertheless sent Pound money to distribute as he thought fit.[44] Pound's determination is revealed by the fact that only two days after he had written to Lowell informing her that the *Egoist* deal had fallen through he wrote again proposing 'that she finance an international quarterly modeled on [the *Mercure de France*]'.[45]

During the first half of 1914 Pound's outbursts against the public became more outspoken and vituperative. Wees, adopting George Dangerfield's tendentious historical analysis of the pre-war years in *The Strange Death of Liberal England* (1936), has seen this as an artistic mirror of the increasing reluctance in public affairs to accept the traditional machinery of compromise and instead to resort to intransigence and even violence.[46] This is undoubtedly an element in Vorticism's verbal onslaught, but I suggest that it is more illuminating to regard Pound's increasingly extreme diction as the logical culmination of his accumulating feelings of frustration, which had reached a head in the winter of 1913–14 and could be contained no longer. His desperate conviction that economic forces

and the establishment were united against the artist led him from
the time of opening epistolary negotiations with Amy Lowell in
February 1914 to praise anything remotely satirical.

His article printed that month on 'The New Sculpture' displays
little aesthetic appreciation; it is instead a dogmatic statement of the
value of Epstein and Gaudier as rebellious innovators in the 'war
without truce' that 'the aristocracy of the arts' is mounting against
social and commercial repression. The rather tedious self-
dramatisation of the artist as violent antagonist becomes at least
more understandable if one recalls his contemporary projects and
hopes. In an article on Lewis, published in June, he voiced his
contempt for the 'man in the street' and claimed that 'The rabble
and the bureaucracy have built a god in their own image and that
god is Mediocrity.' He avoids detailed artistic discussion of Lewis's
*Timon* drawings (produced almost two years earlier in summer
1912) but interprets them instead for his own purposes as an
expression of 'the sullen fury of intelligence baffled, shut in by the
entrenched forces of stupidity'.[47] Read in sequence, his articles in
the first half of 1914 form an implicit manifesto for the new artistic
élite. In his obituary of Remy de Gourmont Pound recalled his visit
to Paris in April 1913 when he witnessed a 'vortex' of French
intellectuals plotting, as the *Blast* 'vortex' were to do, a gigantic
'blague' or 'satire upon stupidity, . . . the weapon of intelligence at
bay'.[48] Pound had commenced a phase in which a form of tunnel
vision would permit him to see only satire in any new work of art.
Lewis's *Tarr* and Joyce's *Ulysses* were read primarily as mopping-up
operations undertaken against the establishment. Just as Pound was
to succeed briefly in forcing Eliot into the mould of satirist, so in
1914 Yeats's poetry was read by Pound as largely satirical. In
reviewing different editions of *Responsibilities* Pound singled out 'A
Coat' for praise as the voice of 'the wild wolf-dog that will not praise
his fleas'.[49] The reference is to the last line of Yeats's 'To a Poet, who
would have me Praise certain Bad Poets, Imitators of His and
Mine', which in versions published before 1916 read 'But where's
the wild dog that has praised his fleas?' The addition of the 'wolf'
element is Pound's; his comment forms a gloss on the backs-to-the-
wall rebellion against 'Cowardly editors' which inspired his own
poem with its title drawn from Villon, 'Et Faim Sallir les Loups des
Boys', published in *Blast*, ii (July 1915). It is interesting that Pound
maintained that his debt to Yeats was 'Considerable encourage-
ment to tell people to go to hell, and to maintain absolute

intransigeance [*sic*]', and it is possible that Yeats's indignation at middle-class philistinism expressed in 'September 1913' and 'Paudeen' may have influenced Pound's attitude in the winter of 1913–14.[50] (Pound included 'Paudeen' and 'A Coat' in the group of poems by Yeats he sent for publication in the May 1914 issue of *Poetry*.)

*Blast*, the voice of the 'Great English Vortex', appeared on 2 July 1914, opening with Lewis's exultant 'Long live the great art vortex sprung up in the centre of this town!'[51] It was a defiant attempt to produce a periodical incorporating revolutionary art of the highest quality and hence uncommercial, whose impact would be accentuated by outspoken and uncompromising expression of the impoverished artist's disgust at the establishment which conspired against him. Just as Pound harboured grudges, so Lewis, most of whose pre-*Blast* work had a satirical bias, was eager to voice stridently his dissatisfaction with the Royal Academy, the hide-bound traditionalism of the Slade and the limited innovations of Sickert's London group, the old *avant-garde*. His recent quarrel with Roger Fry at the Omega Workshops over the commission for the Ideal Home Exhibition had only served to sharpen his personal jealousy of Fry, at that time regarded universally as the leading exponent and populariser of continental innovations, and his antagonism towards the Bloomsbury artists as a group who refused to venture beyond Cézanne or the curvilinear, simplified forms of Matisse to explore the more revolutionary possibilities of abstraction. Like Marinetti the Vorticists felt that the only way to disturb public apathy to art was to resort to shock tactics, in a deliberately provocative form of intellectual terrorism. This analogy with revolutionary politics – another form of taking to the streets – derives from Lewis's later consideration of the implications of their mood at the time.[52]

The arrogantly dismissive attitude of the manifesto reflected their cynosural sense of importance. The label 'vortex' in its commonly accepted primary sense was an insolent assertion that they were England's intellectual centre and that, like a whirlpool, it was around their energy that all the activity was taking place. Lewis's statements at the time, as recollected by Goldring, support this view. He explained, ' "You think at once of a whirlpool. . . . At the heart of the whirlpool is a great silent place where all the energy is concentrated. And there, at the point of concentration, is the Vorticist." ' This version of Pound's sense of 'vortex' as a concentration of intellectual energy underlay both their art and their art-politics. It provided a rationale for attacking the supposed passivity of Impressionism and an explanation for their stress on imaginative creativity, while Expressionism in a more narrowly activist sense obviously inspired the explosive outburst of *Blast*. I think it a mistake, however, to regard Pound's and Lewis's *Publikumsbeschimpfung* as an end in itself and to assert, with Wees, that '*Blast* set about establishing a new, virile civilization based on hardness, violence, and the worship of energy.'[53]

Wees had earlier voiced this exaggerated claim in stressing the supposed *violence* in Vorticist art and their admiration for 'harshness' and 'extremes', qualities which a more disinterested observer might feel were being read into the woodcuts of Wadsworth and the abstract canvases of the other members of the group. He saw a parallel in Pound's supposed aesthetic change from Imagism to Vorticism: Pound

> began to break the cool, decorous serenity of the Image and its 'hard light, clear edges', by developing a new, more violent mode of expression.

> The dry, hard, Imagist decorum is gone; a totally new tone, sometimes angry and moralizing, sometimes satirical, but certainly more declamatory, more 'rhetorical' than Imagist doctrine allowed, has taken over.

Lipke and Rozran corrected this view by indicating that some of the most extreme *Blast* poems had appeared in April 1913, the month after the Imagist manifesto, and could therefore not be evidence for a 'new', 'harsher' Vorticist aesthetic. Pound's polemical declamations were therefore one aspect of his early poems.[54]

The truth lies somewhere between the two positions, I feel. Wees is right to stress the contemptuous, outspoken attitude of Pound's articles in the first half of 1914, for which I have suggested reasons above. His error, I think, lies in trying to maintain that this destructive attitude – sterile in the long term as Pound's experiences in the 1930s and 1940s show only too clearly – was intended as an injection of violent energy into ailing Imagist poetics. Pound as a genuinely innovative writer would naturally develop his poetic experiments and resist stagnation in any particular technique, but he never discarded the fundamental Imagist tenets or abandoned wholly the 'dry, hard, Imagist decorum'. He could never espouse exclusively a 'Vorticist' poetics which offered such limited scope for the creative imagination. Aldington saw Pound's satirical contributions to *Blast* with their 'enormous arrogance and petulance and fierceness' as a 'wearisome pose', a comment which fittingly suggests their merely accidental importance.[55]

*Blast* was, I feel, an iconoclastic tract for the times of partly transient relevance, designed to shatter public complacency by a gigantic 'blague' and stimulate discussion. The squib-like facetiousness of the lists of Blasts and Blesses reflects their informal, random assemblage; they were drawn up at a party at South Lodge with all guests chipping in with suggestions.[56] Its lively satirical jabs and light-hearted, intellectual sparring were an attractively provocative accompaniment to the more serious aesthetic ideas of Lewis, Gaudier, Pound and Wadsworth. Lewis conveyed accurately this balance between aesthetic theory and incisive wit in a contemporary letter to Lord Carlow: 'Such things as *Blast* have to be undertaken for the artist to exist at all. When you have removed all that is *necessarily* strident, much sound art-doctrine is to be found in this puce monster.'[57] While the 'Blast' mentality belongs to contemporary artistic politics, however, the aesthetic theory, as I argued in Chapter 5, is firmly in the empathetic tradition. One must accordingly distinguish between the superficial, brash polemics and the more essential artistic concerns which they helped to bring to public attention. Pound was then primarily engaged artistically with the Fenollosa manuscripts, which produced the *Noh* translations and *Cathay*, works scarcely compatible with a hypothetical new aesthetic of violent abuse. His Imagist poetics remained essentially unchanged. He had, however, entered on a new path of urgent social *engagement* which was to accompany throughout his later poetry his more instinctive lyrical gift.

But amid the excitement at *Blast*'s publication, economic difficulties moderated some of its contributors' delight. By the time the magazine appeared the 'Vortex's' headquarters had closed. Pound resumed urgent negotiations with Lowell, now in London to attend the Vorticist celebration dinner on 15 July. Prejudiced by Fletcher against the new 'vorticist' Pound as soon as she arrived in England, Lowell was in no mood to bargain. Pound had refused to join any Imagist anthology not edited by him. Aware that he depended on her finance, Lowell was confident he would back down, but nevertheless prior to the Vorticist dinner took the precaution of enlisting against Pound the support of Aldington, H. D. and Flint, effectively ensuring that a conflict must take place.[58]

Her 'Imagist dinner' two days later assembled most of the contributors to *Des Imagistes* with Fletcher and Gaudier. Pound had again broached with Lowell the subject of the international review discussed in their correspondence. He suggested that he should become the salaried editor of the *Mercure de France*, to which Lowell would of course be free to contribute any number of poems, in addition to the $5000 annually which they both agreed was the minimum outlay for such a venture. Not unreasonably she insisted that her income was insufficient, to which Pound retorted by upbraiding her with an unwillingness to donate to the arts. She settled instead on the more modest idea of helping a few writers by republishing the Imagist anthology with the same contributors each year for three years in the hope of making the same public impact as the Georgians. Her pride had been wounded by the inclusion in *Des Imagistes* of only one of her poems and she determined to make the new anthologies more democratic, with no capricious exclusions and inclusions. Each poet would be allotted equal space, their names would appear alphabetically and they would publish as a group of friends with similar tendencies rather than dogmatic principles. The Aldingtons and others were enthusiastic, but Pound saw his leadership being usurped. Tactlessly he demanded that unless Lowell provided $200 annually for an indigent poet, an approach which she regarded as 'blackmail', he would not join. He tried to force the Aldingtons to choose between him and Lowell and even to join in an anthology which would exclude her. Though torn in their loyalties they believed Lowell's plan to be more equitable (as did Flint, Lawrence and Ford), resentful at Pound's desire to maintain control over them at all costs.[59] Lowell and Pound remained on amicable terms but he was now isolated from the movement he had begun. By August 1914 the new group had started to formulate the preface to their first independent anthology.[60]

It is difficult to estimate how much Pound's concern was with his own precarious financial position – he had just got married in April 1914 and needed freedom from financial worry to concentrate on his own poetry – and how much with the fact that as controlling editor he would have a wholly dependable means of giving direct practical help to his many *protégés*, especially as financial problems had forced the closure of the Rebel Art Centre. Notoriously clumsy in handling human relationships and with an aggressive seriousness in artistic matters, Pound simply managed Lowell badly. Before his pathetic withdrawal into silence in the 1960s Pound was never modest in his self-estimation and it never occurred to him to doubt that it was Lowell's responsibility as someone who believed in the arts to help to support him as a leading practitioner. He simply miscalculated the extent of her resources. Having written the script for a grandiose scenario which Lowell was unable to afford, Pound was left dumbfounded at her apparent recalcitrance to fit into his scheme for her – 'why can't she conceive of herself as a Renaissance figure instead of a spiritual chief, which she ain't'.[61]

Pound's initial hopes for a Renaissance had thus been frustrated. His bitter reaction is recorded in the 'Hell' Cantos and before long he was to abandon the unsympathetic London establishment for the headier *milieux* of Parisian literati and Mussolini's Italy. Pound's attachment, as I argued in Chapter 6, was to an ideal *forma* of civilisation (a Neoplatonic, utopian vision which like Yeats's was 'A something incompatible with life'[62]) which he persistently tried to impose on a stubbornly resistant world of fact. The result, like Auden's similar pursuit of 'the Good Place', was ultimately chimerical; but the attempt, I would assert, deserves respect for the courage with which Pound, like Mallarmé, held to his unrealisable Neoplatonic ideal despite a series of crushing disillusionments.

# 8 Imagism

Chapter 6 examined the Symbolist beliefs which pervade Pound's pre-Imagist poetry. My aim in this chapter is to emphasise the essential continuity of these throughout Pound's Imagist/Vorticist period, despite superficial changes in the vocabulary in which they were expressed. I shall conclude by considering the relationship between Pound's poetry and that of the other Imagists and adumbrate the future development of Imagism into Objectivist poetry.

## I  IMAGIST/VORTICIST AESTHETICS

Pound's first significant development was from the stilted archaisms and macaronic diction of his early volumes, universally lamented by reviewers.[1] His gradual movement towards a more prosaic, conversational idiom was principally inspired by Hulme's relativist critique[2] and, improbably, by a Symbolist aesthetic.

The latter derived from his Provençal reading. Consider his revealing comment from November 1910 in the Introduction to his Cavalcanti translations:

> I believe in an ultimate and absolute rhythm as I believe in an absolute symbol or metaphor. The perception of the intellect is given in the word, that of the emotions in the cadence. It is only, then, in perfect rhythm joined to the perfect word that the two-fold vision can be recorded. I would liken Guido's cadence to nothing less powerful than line in Blake's drawing. . . . The line is unbounded, it marks the passage of a force, it continues beyond the frame.[3]

The important stress is on the epithet 'absolute'. Pound asserts that a poem is the equation or symbolic equivalent of a fundamental matrix of consciousness. The poem conveys this by combining the affective resources of rhythm with the connotative qualities of the words themselves: the result is what Pound termed in 1913 an 'intellectual and emotional complex' – an 'absolute symbol' or *image*.[4]

His comparison between Guido's symbolic cadence and Blake's symbolic line is suggestive. In the following paragraph Pound explains their ability to act as the external equivalent for an emotional state by paraphrasing a Lippsian *Einfühlungsästhetik* which must derive from Hulme. The perceiver, Pound argues, responds by reproducing subliminally the psychic 'rhythm' of the work of art. In his view, therefore, both Guido's cadence and Blake's line embody an *absolute* state of consciousness, transmitting its psychic *energy* (*virtù*) or 'force' (compare the Futurist use of 'force lines'). Emphasising the Symbolist, non-discursive cast of this belief, later in the Introduction and in a letter in January 1911 Pound defined 'absolute rhythm' as 'an exact *correspondence* between the cadence-form of the line & some highly specialized or particular emotion'.[5] The choice of the hermetic term is, I believe, not coincidental.

This sensitivity to the expressive potential of metrical variation and verbal music was confirmed by Pound's reading of Arnaut Daniel, who, he felt (unlike Swinburne or the Nineties poets), wrote poetry with no stylistic redundancy, in which each word contributed to either sound or sense, frequently both; precise in observation and reference, Daniel epitomised *melos*, 'the union of words, rhythm and music'.[6] Pound came accordingly to the realisation that the supposedly 'poetic' qualities of poetry could be conveyed by the verse-movement and verbal music alone, without the need for redundant verbal embellishment. This found expression in 'En Breu Brisaral Temps Braus', probably written late in 1911:

> we must have a simplicity and directness of utterance, which is different from the simplicity and directness of daily speech, which is more 'curial', more dignified. This difference, this dignity, cannot be conferred by florid adjectives or elaborate hyperbole; it must be conveyed by art, and by the art of the verse structure, by something which exalts the reader.[7]

It was characteristically a refurbishing of familiar ideas rather than a radical redirection of attitude: Pound's early concept of poetry as 'ecstasy' is reformulated as verse 'exalting' the reader. Pound eloquently re-emphasised this approach as late as November 1913. [8]

Pound's other important early Imagist statement, his 'Credo', was written in December 1911. There he reiterates his belief in *interpretative* absolute rhythm, again lays stress on free verse and, significantly, introduces the new 'presentational' technique. [9] This section, 'Symbols', is readily demystified if one compares the similarly tripartite Imagist manifesto formulated with Aldington and H.D., which I quoted on p. 183 *supra*, and Pound's 1913 statement that 'the natural object is always the *adequate* symbol'. [10]

English 'Symbolist' poetry characteristically consisted of the abstract portentousness and vague immensities evident in some of Flint's and Pound's early poetry (cf. Ch. 3). A stylistic counterblast naturally assumed the form of an attack (as outlined by Hulme) on vague conceptualisation in diction with corresponding emphasis on the prime need for authentic perceptual experience. The deficiency of English 'Symbolism' was that frequently there had been no credible correlative – imaginary or actual – for the emotional experience it was desired to communicate: it was a symbolism without the symbol. The Imagist, empathetic Symbolist reaction therefore laid weight, as Flint had done in his essay 'Of the thing called "Symbolism"' on the indispensability of a phenomenal articulation of the mental state, without which the poem lost all imaginative value and lapsed into purely abstract assertion.

Having provisionally placed Pound's Imagism in an empathetic Symbolist ambience, I shall now develop this argument by examining his dissatisfaction with Ford's impressionist aesthetic (expressed in terms which echo the contemporary polemic against Impressionist painting) and Pound's Symbolist and Neoplatonic response to Vorticism in the visual arts.

I disagree with those critics who have seen Pound's Vorticism as a fundamental reorientation. Schneidau, for example, presents Pound's Imagist years as a dramatic vacillation between 'esoteric Yeatsism' and Ford's 'modernism'. Mysticism, which had initially remained separate from Imagism, was discarded after the arrival of the Fenollosa manuscripts, by which time 'Pound had realized that he could never subscribe to the mystical conception of the universe required by Yeats's Symbolism'. Pound accordingly turned over the Noh-play material 'with its heavy suggestiveness and supernatural machinery' to Yeats, retaining instead the Chinese lyric poetry as close to 'his own aesthetic of clarity, economy and precise synecdochic implication'. Schneidau's error lies, I feel, in conflating under the heading 'mysticism' Yeats' *spiritualist* experiments (which Pound deprecated, as I explained in Chapter 6) with Yeats's Neoplatonic cosmology, and implying that in rejecting the spiritualism Pound necessarily rejected the 'mysticism' also. Nothing could be further from the truth than Schneidau's assertion that at the time of Vorticism Pound was consciously trying to 'jettison Symbolism and concentrate on a concrete, visible, "realistic" universe'.[11] As Schneidau himself admits, a mystical element is important in the *Cantos*. Why, then, should one assume that this was temporarily rejected during Vorticism, particularly given the extremely close relation between Pound's Noh translations and the planning and composition of 'Three Cantos' between September 1915 and April 1916?[12]

By way of introduction consider Pound's comment from 1912 on Ford's poetry:

> His flaw is the flaw of impressionism, impressionism, that is, carried out of its due medium. Impressionism belongs in paint, it is of the eye. The cinematograph records, for instance, the 'impression' of any given action or place, far more exactly than the finest writing. . . . A ball of gold and a gilded ball give the same 'impression' to the painter. Poetry is in some odd way concerned with the specific gravity of things, with their nature.
>
> Their nature *and* show, if you like; with the relation between them, but not with show alone.
>
> The *conception* of poetry is a process more intense than the *reception* of an impression. And no impression, however carefully articulated, can, recorded, convey that feeling of sudden light which the works of art should and must convey.[13]

The theme of the article was Ford's lack of 'intensity', which included the by-now familiar touchstone that Ford had forgotten that poetic diction must be more 'dignified' than colloquial speech. A further reason for Pound's dissatisfaction was the diffuseness of Ford's poetry, which conflicted with Pound's early assumption that poetry implied the 'ecstasy' of the lyric and rendered Ford's work for Pound a disappointing combination of 'conversational passages' (in context a euphemism for 'padding') and others 'more intense'. Yet Pound's attitude was not only shaped by this Poe-like and Yeatsian

stress on lyric intensity; it was, I believe, conditioned equally by
contemporary art-criticism, a point hitherto unnoticed by critics.[14]

Pound's divergence from Ford was a matter of perceptual
attitude. Ford is castigated for the detached concern with externality and the mere recording of sense-data which since the 1890s
had been regarded as the hallmark of artistic Impressionism. Just as
Lewis was later to refer to the 'spiritual weight' of objects (cf. *supra*,
p. 145), so here Pound refers to their 'specific gravity' or essential
nature as things-in-themselves. Eleven years later, in acknowledging
his debt to Ford's ideas on poetic diction, Pound repeated this
reservation about Ford's impressionism:

> I think Hueffer goes wrong because he bases his criticism on the
> eye, and almost solely on the eye. Nearly everything he says
> applies to things *seen*. It is the exact rendering of the visible image,
> the cabbage field *seen*, France *seen* from the cliffs.

By aligning his own position in contrast with the 'intensity' of Yeats
and by an emphasis on the 'musical properties of verse', which he
had always regarded as the necessary emotional complement to
prosaic diction, Pound implied a correlation between the jejune
quality of Ford's poetic language and his detached perceptual
attitude.[15] Pound's concluding remark in the first quotation on
Ford – that no impression can convey 'that feeling of sudden light' –
contrasts dispassionate perception of superficial appearances with
an epiphanic experience. Poetry, Pound was stating, is a matter not
of objective detachment, but rather of the moments of ecstatic,
empathetic contemplation so central to his pre-Imagist work.

In Ford's definition, any piece of Impressionism was

> the record of the impression of a moment; it is not a sort of
> rounded, annotated record of a set of circumstances – it is the
> record of the recollection in your mind of a set of circumstances
> that happened ten years ago – or ten minutes.

The subjectivity which the impression reflected should, he believed,
be excluded from its literary recreation. The work was an expression
of personality by virtue of its subjective viewpoint and the writer's
selection of material, but the actual intrusion of his personality into
the style itself should be avoided by 'presentation', namely
Flaubertian objectivity. In Ford's ideal, authorial self-effacement

allowed the events to achieve the same impact on the reader as they had earlier on the narrator, triggering, it was hoped, the same emotional experience from this stimulating complex of phenomena. The effect would be lost if the author attempted by elaborating his own reaction to guide or predetermine the reader's response.[16] As an abstract statement of a presentational method this resembles the empathetic Symbolist style Pound favoured at the time of Imagism. The difference between this and Ford's poetic style was that in Ford's poems his emotions and the external world were two disjunct topics. The reader is told directly of Ford's feelings, just as he is presented directly with a recording through sense-data of the external location of these emotions (as in Symons's more extreme sensationalist experiments). There is no interaction between the poet and the world around him: subjective consciousness and landscape remain discrete entities. In December 1913 Aldington equated Marinetti's poetry with 'impressionism', which he defined in his case as catalogues of sense-data, combined with 'utterly unrestrained rhetoric', 'abstractions' and 'vagueness'.[17] Such a style was no more than an extreme development of Ford's dualistic technique.

The Preface to Ford's *Collected Poems* provides a striking example. There he recalls his strong feelings on emerging from the Shepherd's Bush Exhibition into 'a great square of white buildings all outlined with lights'. The unusual intensity of light impressed him and the 'crowds and crowds of people – or no, there was, spread out beneath the lights, an infinite moving mass of black, with white faces turned up to the light, moving slowly, quickly, not moving at all, being obscured, reappearing'. The stark particularity of these details with their powerful chiaroscuro already suggests emotions to the reader, inarticulable perhaps, but for that very reason aesthetically interesting. Not satisfied with this, Ford proceeds to try to explain the effect, expatiating in paragraphs of sentimental reflections largely disconnected with the original experience, which in their turn stimulate further mawkish pages. I have singled out this instance of Ford's record of the 'impression of a moment' because of its resemblance to Pound's experience at La Concorde which was the basis of the empathetic Symbolist 'In a Station of the Metro'. The divergence in the two responses highlights the ultimate incompatibility of their attitudes.[18]

Pound's early interest in a poetry of 'ecstasy' survived in his definition of the image as an intellectual and emotional complex presented 'instantaneously' to produce 'that sense of sudden liberation; that sense of freedom from time limits and space limits; that sense of sudden growth, which we experience in the presence of the greatest works of art'. The phraseology here recalls the conclusion of Pound's Pre-Raphaelite/Stilnovist epiphany, 'The House of Splendour':

> there are powers in this
> Which, played on by the virtues of her soul,
> *Break down the four-square walls of standing time.* [19]

Pound's 1912 criticism of Ford (cf. *supra*, p. 203) had likewise alluded to a 'feeling of sudden light' which works of art must convey. As he sought greater linguistic compression in the Imagist reform of diction, he came to see the *hokku* as another suitable matrix for such epiphanies. He spoke later of 'the sense of the "special moment" which makes the hokku', a clear difference from Ford's 'impression of a moment'. In the empathetic Symbolist 'In a Station of the Metro' Pound stated that he was 'trying to record the precise instant when a thing outward and objective transforms itself, or darts into a thing inward and subjective'; he added, 'This particular sort of consciousness has not been identified with impressionist art.' [20]

An embarrassed footnote in *Poetry* in June 1914 proclaimed, 'Mr Hueffer is not an *imagiste*, but an impressionist. Confusion has arisen because of my inclusion of one of his poems in the *Anthologie des Imagistes*.' [21] Ford himself confirmed Pound's remarks. Although only about ten years older than 'Les Jeunes', as he insisted on calling them, he adopted the jocular persona of the doyen of the movement, coaching from the ringside now that his advanced age rendered him too old for aesthetic rough-and-tumble. His attempts to create a poignant vignette of the craftsman of a venerable tradition facing an artistic generation-gap, despite the sentimentalism and conscious whimsicality, are probably quite close to the truth. [22] His contemporary articles reveal him as neither an Imagist nor Vorticist, and as understandably out of touch with the frenetic redesignation of groups that took place in 1914. Ford's puzzling appearance in *Blast*, despite Pound's enthusiasm for 'On Heaven', was probably in acknowledgement of his earlier literary influence on Pound and publication in the *English Review* of both Pound and Lewis.

In spring 1914 the Vorticist group, at that stage still the English

'Cubists', were undergoing the influence of the German Expressionists as they had earlier those of the Cubists and Futurists.
Wadsworth was translating the selections from Kandinsky which
appeared in *Blast*. Ford obviously caught their discussions, which
formed the basis of his muddled account of the distinction between
his aesthetic and theirs. He first claimed that the arts in France
which reflect 'advanced thought' were 'religious' and 'otherworldly' and in 'reaction from materialism' and 'deniers of
mystery'. He referred specifically to Marinetti and the Cubists,
whose portraits he saw as attempts to represent not the sitter but
instead their emotional response to the sitter, his 'soul'.[23] A week
later, probably following hysterical scenes with Lewis, Ford
discerned two divergent trends in 'Futurism', which (perhaps
deliberately to annoy Lewis, for Ford delighted in his pose of
avuncular detachment) he persisted in employing as a generic term
for all modern art. Literary Futurism was representational, but
all its 'plastic–aesthetic products' were becoming increasingly 'geometric, mystic, non-material'.[24] The earlier Futurist painters
(i.e. the Italian Futurists) were, he claimed, working along the same
lines as Flaubert and Maupassant: 'They gave you not so much the
reconstitution of a crystallised scene in which all the figures were
arrested . . . as fragments of impressions gathered during a period
of time, during a period of emotion, or during a period of travel.'[25]
He contrasted this rendering of accumulated sense-data with the
'Cubists' (Lewis's name from November 1913 for his own group),
who were 'emotionalists' and 'anti-materialists'.[26]

This 'emotionalism' or expressionism is explained in a comment
by Pound which must refer to Monet: 'The organization of forms is a
much more energetic and creative action than the copying or
imitating of light on a haystack.'[27] It is indicative of Pound's limited
acquaintance with art, but fascination with it as an illustrative
parallel to his own theories, that the example he unfortunately chose
should be one of Monet's late works, painted when he was
beginning to move away from pure Impressionism to an embryonic
form of abstract expressionism. Nevertheless Pound's dissatisfaction
with the dispassionate externality of Impressionism is clear.

In 'Vorticism' Pound repeated the distinction from his 1912 Ford
article between 'cinematographical' impressionism and what he
now termed Vorticism, reiterating the conception/reception contrast outlined there, as if to underline its centrality to his ideas. He
added an amplificatory gloss:

In the 'eighties there were symbolists opposed to impressionists, now you have vorticism, which is, roughly speaking, expression- ism, neo-cubism, and imagism gathered together in one camp and futurism in the other. Futurism is descended from im- pressionism. It is, in so far as it is an art movement, a kind of accelerated impressionism. It is a spreading, or surface art, as opposed to vorticism, which is intensive.[28]

Pound's politically motivated disparagement of Futurism, which he connects in the following paragraph with Marinetti, is peripheral. More important is his implicit analogy between the lack of 'intensity', which he criticised in literary impressionism, with that of artistic Impressionism. They are both 'surface' art with a perceptual superficiality to be distinguished from the intense contemplation of Vorticism. By linking Vorticism with Expressionism and Symbolism ('neo-cubism' refers to the movement's formalistic debts, which Lewis himself would not acknowledge) Pound makes clear that for him, as for Lewis, the movement was primarily empathetic Symbolist, laying principal weight on the artist's imaginative interaction with the external world.

The ground is now prepared for an examination of Pound's Vorticist aesthetic. The first point to make is that there is no difference between Imagism and Vorticism. In his 'Vortex' Pound stated that the 'primary pigment' of Vorticist poetry is the 'IMAGE', and gave as an example of a Vorticist poem H.D.'s 'Oread', which, doubtless to his chagrin, was to be printed in *Some Imagist Poets* (1915). The 'Vorticism' article was originally entitled 'Imagisme', while Pound explained that the term 'Vorticist' was devised to provide 'a designation that would be equally applicable to a certain basis for all the arts. Obviously you cannot have "cubist" poetry or "imagist" painting.'[29] This 'basis' which in Pound's view unified the various Vorticist media was not a matter of formalistic emulation (as critics hitherto have assumed) but instead lay in the common search for symbolic equivalents, necessarily differing in technique, for states of consciousness or what Pound termed Neoplatonic 'forms'.

In February 1914 Pound explained that he had found Hulme's lecture 'Modern Art and its Philosophy' unintelligible and admit- ted that the 'jargon' of the sculptors was beyond him. His next article on the subject substantiates his acknowledgement that he found the painting less easy to discuss than the sculpture: the best comment he could manage was that Cubism was 'an art of patterns', more specifically 'a pattern of solids'. The staleness of Pound's exposition is revealed by Yeats's comment of 1898, itself by no means innovative, that 'Subject pictures no longer interest us, while pictures with patterns and rhythms of colour, like Mr. Whistler's, and drawings with patterns and rhythms of line, like Mr. Beardsley's in his middle period, interest us extremely.'[30] Compared with Hulme's articulate accounts, Pound's appreciation of the new abstract or semi-abstract medium was extremely uncertain. In private he had already conceded that *Blast* was 'mostly a painters magazine with me to do the poems'.[31]

Pound's Vorticist writings will accordingly disappoint those seeking illumination on the technical procedures of the artists. Their value lies in the independent nature of Pound's response to the artists' empathetic and abstract expressionist Symbolism; his alignment of the Vorticists with his own symbolist aesthetic and instinctive Neoplatonism demonstrates the unbroken continuity of his beliefs from the pre-Imagist phase to the *Cantos*.

I believe therefore that literary critics (encouraged by the predominantly formalistic bias in art criticism and understandably eager to demonstrate that Pound was moving away from the limited scope of his Imagist experiments) are misguided in attempting to uncover traces of a structural influence on Pound from his close acquaintance with painters and sculptors. At the time of Vorticism Pound clearly desired to write a long poem. He greatly admired Ford's 'On Heaven', while the fact that Pound began writing the *Cantos* in September 1915 and published 'Near Perigord' in December 1915 reveals his concern with finding a principle of structural organisation which would serve for longer poems. It appears, however, that in this connection in 1914–15 his interest was more in Browning's *Sordello* than in the visual arts. Thus I am unconvinced by Wees's attempt, following Kenner and Davie, to imply a direct formative influence on the structure of the *Cantos* from Lewis's painting or Gaudier's sculpture:

The innumerable disparate elements that make up the *Cantos* can be thought of as 'planes in relation', as 'diverse planes' that, like fragments of Japanese armor, 'overlie in a certain manner', and are united visually, or spatially, in the same manner as a Lewis painting or a Gaudier carving. To the extent that Vorticism was responsible for this concept of form in Pound's work, it had a profound impact on all his later poetry.[32]

The reader's cognitive experience of the *Cantos*, as of Eliot's *The Waste Land*, is undoubtedly similar to that of early abstract art. Faced by a Cubist, Futurist, or Vorticist canvas one attempts to find a perceptual *Gestalt* which will introduce order into the initially chaotic confusion of line, form and disembodied colour areas. The attempt is likely to be inadequate, if not actively thwarted, and on subsequent viewings of the same painting one will probably trace different perceptual structures. The result is an unresolved interplay of alternative structuring operations, which the perceiver holds in a satisfying imaginative tension.

Despite the mythological structures beneath the *Cantos* and *The Waste Land* which offer a minimal rationale for these formally dislocated works, the reader's experience of these poems is, I would argue, similar to that of abstract painting. Hesitant efforts to establish an all-embracing interpretation are frustrated, leaving a work which stubbornly resists any straightforward naturalisation. Reading becomes an exploratory process of various half-formed, figurative meanings rather than a progression towards any un-equivocal semantic resolution. The poem's import lies accordingly in the tentative construction of a complex of overlapping but divergent hypotheses which it provokes: the characteristic poly-semousness of Symbolist poetry.

Yet there appears to be no evidence that these ambitious poetic structures, despite their similarity in effect, were evolved under the conscious influence of contemporary painting. They are instead, I would suggest, a natural development from Symbolism. For the structural employment of discontinuous ideograms or 'luminous details' is essentially similar to that of the paratactic, emotionally congruous images of Symbolist poetry, although entailing more of an intellectual, discursive effort of relationship. If Pound was helped in this direction by his daily exposure to Vorticist painting, the realisation must have been retrospective, for his writings during the Vorticist period itself display a naïve and idiosyncratic understand-ing of the painting – not in formalistic, but in Neoplatonic terms.

Thus on several occasions (including a passage just after that which Wees quotes and which refutes Wees's argument) Pound went out of his way to emphasise that he was 'only moderately

interested in form', stressing that form assumed overriding importance only for the painter or sculptor, not the poet, whose 'primary
pigment' was the 'image'.[33] The influence of Vorticism had, he
maintained, been on his perception of the external world, sharpen-
ing his response to form in the environment.[34] It is, I believe, a
mistake to see any direct influence in the structure of Pound's
poetry, as opposed to a heightened visual precision in his imagery, of
this new formal sense. Instead the fundamental unity of the
Vorticist media lay in the aspiration which united Pound's Imagist
with his pre-Imagist poetry – in Pound's words,

> This is the common ground of the arts, this combat of arrange-
> ment or 'harmony'. . . . we are indissolubly united . . . by our
> sense of this fundamental community, this unending adventure
> towards 'arrangement', this search for the equations of eternity.

'Arrangement' had for Pound no *formal* implications for poetry; in
his usage it was merely a synonym for 'equation' or 'symbol', as
Pound's otherwise puzzling correlation, as representatives of this
approach, of 'The musician, the writer, the sculptor, the *higher
mathematician*' demonstrates.[35] (Cf. *supra*, pp. 173–5, on 'equations'.)

The unifying tenet of Vorticism was that 'one is interested in the
creative faculty as opposed to the mimetic'.[36] The problem was
accordingly to find a symbolic equivalent for one's mental state, or
in Pound's term one's psychic or emotional *energy*. Pound's views
from 1910–11 on 'absolute rhythm' are merely translated into the
vocabulary of the visual arts and, under Whistler's and Kandinsky's
influence, given a new conceptual dress as 'arrangements' rather
than 'equations'. Thus in keeping with his belief in poetry as a
symbolic equation for archetypal states of consciousness he described Lewis's *Timon* as 'a type emotion . . . delivered . . . in lines
and masses and planes'.[37]

Apropos Vorticist art he explained that 'An organisation of forms
expresses a confluence of forces. These forces may be the "love of
God," the "life-force," emotions, passions, what you will.' His new
discovery was that painting, sculpture or design could employ what
he called 'form-motifs' as symbolic embodiments of a mental state in
a fashion analogous to musical harmonies or the words, images and
rhythms of poetry. (Compare his argument in 'As for Imagisme'
(1915) that the 'force' or 'energy' of 'intense emotion' caused

'pattern-units, or units of design', or, alternatively, 'rhythm form' or 'the Image' to arise in the mind.[38])

In Chapter 6 I noted Pound's conception in 1911–12 of the artist as channeller of psychic energy or *virtù*; this emphasis on poetry as the transfer of force was reiterated in November 1913 in 'The Serious Artist'.[39] It seems likely that by this stage Pound's reading of the Fenollosa papers, which presented language as activity or the transference of force, had confirmed his Stilnovist hermeticism.[40] The metaphor of energy therefore developed Pound's interest in the alchemy of language and the generative power of symbolic equations, and also provided a vivid means of distinguishing the imaginative activity of Vorticist expressionism from the passivity of Impressionism.[41]

The clearest way to demonstrate the continuity of Pound's Symbolist aesthetic is to trace his argument through 'Vorticism'. The first important section is his account of Imagism. He begins by reiterating his belief in 'absolute rhythm': 'I believe that every emotion and every phase of emotion has some toneless phrase, some rhythm-phrase to express it'. The corollary to this is that 'a like belief in a sort of permanent metaphor is . . . "symbolism" in its profounder sense. It is not necessarily a belief in a permanent world, but it is a belief in that direction'. Here Pound is, I suggest, attempting to defend Symbolism as the expression of archetypal states of consciousness (or Platonic 'forms'), as he had in his pre-Imagist phase, while dissociating himself in public from the mystical or transcendentalist implications this might seem to entail. Significantly, in a letter to his father in 1927 (when obviously no public mask was required), Pound described the metamorphoses of the *Cantos* as 'bust thru from quotidien into "divine or *permanent* world"'.[42]

The reasons for his following statement that 'Imagisme is not symbolism' then become apparent. The crucial point is that Pound restricts 'symbolism' to the practice of its English epigones. Hence 'symbolism has usually been associated with mushy technique': flaccid synaesthesia and the 'crepuscular spirit' Pound had attacked in 1909. His phrase 'They degraded the symbol to the status of a word' has proved problematical.[43] Pound's point is that the indefinitely suggestive (Yeatsian 'emotional') symbol was reduced to an 'intellectual' symbol with a fixed value and in some cases to allegory. (His reference here and two pages later to 'crowns, and crosses' recollects Yeats's instance of 'such obvious intellectual symbols as a cross or a crown of thorns'.[44]) Pound is surely referring to the sham sublimity, euphuism and decorative conceits which characterised, for example, some of his own and Flint's early poetry. A possible further overtone is that the English 'Symbolists' sacrificed its alchemical, talismanic properties, leaving it a mere 'word' rather than an evocative 'equation'. This interpretation is supported by Pound's concluding antithesis between Symbolism as arithmetic and the 'variable significance', or polysemous character, of the Imagist's generative algebra (I return to this question below).

Pound's argument is rendered unnecessarily obscurantist by his polemical requirements: to present the expressionist basis of Imagism/Vorticism as radically innovative and to distinguish this forcibly from public association with effete 'Symbolism'. Consider his comments that 'The Return' 'is an objective reality and has a complicated sort of significance' and that 'Heather' 'represents a state of consciousness, or "implies," or "implicates" it'. 'The Return' is a perfect example of 'absolute rhythm', just as 'Heather' is an empathetic Symbolist poem; to assert that they are not 'symbolism' but rather 'impersonal' 'absolute metaphor' is merely casuistical.[45] Their designation as 'Imagisme' renders this term synonymous with the symbolic articulation of states of consciousness.

Pound's strategy rests therefore on establishing an analogy between the (semi-) abstract expressionism of Kandinsky and Whistler and his own 'Imagisme' (Yeats's emotional symbolism) in contradistinction from 'literary values' or allegory in art, 'programme music', and discursive qualities or allegory in poetry.[46] The predominant theme is that Imagist poetry is a matter of autonomous emotional symbolism and may successfully be just as self-referential as music or abstract expressionism in painting.

Predictably Pound fell back on his earlier mathematical analogy to explain this. He reiterated his argument from 'The Wisdom of Poetry' (cf. *supra*, pp. 173–4) that the artist's equations resembled those of the analytical geometer in their generative capacity, differing only in subject-matter from this more abstract variety of Platonic archetypes.[47] Pound's mental correlation of Yeats's, Whistler's and Kandinsky's 'arrangements', Platonic archetypes and poetic symbols is then made explicit as the keystone of Vorticism:

The statements of 'analytics' are 'lords' over fact. They are the thrones and dominations that rule over form and recurrence. And in like manner are great works of art lords over fact, over race-long recurrent moods, and over to-morrow.

Great works of art contain this . . . sort of equation. They cause form to come into being. By the 'image' I mean such an equation; not an equation of mathematics . . . having something to do with form, but about *sea, cliffs, night*, having something to do with mood.[48]

The continuity is obvious with Pound's pre-Imagist views on the *virtù* of symbolic talismans to channel psychic energy and on the alchemy of language evoking hitherto unperceived states of consciousness. Despite his disavowal of 'symbolism' he is clearly employing 'moods' in the Yeatsian post-1903 sense, of archetypal states of mind. Thus, when he asserts that great works of art 'cause form to come into being', one is prepared to interpret this as Neoplatonic *forma* or what Pound elsewhere termed 'equations of eternity'.

At the time of Vorticism, therefore, Pound's interest in 'form' was not structural, as critics have supposed, but Neoplatonic. His idiosyncratic response to abstract expressionism was to remark that a work of art was the medium by which man was

carried out of the realm of annoyance into the calm realm of truth, into the world unchanging, the world of fine animal life, the world of pure form. And John Heydon, long before our present day theorists, had written of the joys of pure form . . . inorganic, *geometrical* form, in his 'Holy Guide'.

There is an implicit association of form or *forma* with Pound's mathematical equations. Thus, while the artists concerned themselves with exploring formal relationships, he read into their terminology a mystical and profoundly traditional significance. The probable association in Pound's mind was that Impressionist painting was concerned with transient effects of light – an art of visual appearances – whereas the Vorticists' interest in 'form' and 'structure' devoted attention to the essential and unchanging.[49] On a technical level a bad poem was one in which insincerity had produced a work which was not an organic expression of the artist's emotion. A perfect work of art – a matter of 'pure form' – was, however, something transcendental. It differed from Impres-

sionism, which was passive receptivity to sense-data, because ecstatic emotion produced a charged, almost ineffable symbol: in
the poet's imagination 'order-giving vibrations' found verbal
expression in the 'image', which fused with *melos* to 'organise form'
by creative transmutation of his perception.[50] Pound's suggestive
analogy was that of a magnet applied beneath a plate of iron-filings;
its force created in the otherwise 'ugly' metal an expression of order
and vitality and hence beauty. To Pound this imperceptible
imaginative energy held the promise that the artist, faced with the
contingent phenomena of the external world, could create from this
disorder an image of a world of more permanent value, the world of
'pure form'. Poetry was accordingly an essentially transcendental
activity which evoked 'The *forma*, the immortal *concetto*'.[51] One
might compare Eliot's

> Only by the form, the pattern,
> Can words or music reach
> The stillness[52]

Pound never abandoned this search in art for the realisation of
Platonic archetypes – whether states of consciousness or ideal
*paideumas*. As a final illustration of the origins in Symbolist theory of
this approach I shall cite his essay from 1921 on Brancusi:

> Dante believed in the 'melody which most in-centres the soul';
> . . . I have tried to express the idea of an absolute rhythm, or the
> possibility of it. Perhaps every artist at one time or another
> believes in a sort of elixir or philosopher's stone produced by the
> sheer perfection of his art; by the alchemical sublimation of the
> medium; the elimination of accidentals and imperfections.

Pound's phraseology still retains vestigial traces of Stilnovist and
Yeatsian hermeticism; his position is, I believe, conditioned by a
faith in the correspondential nature of symbols, accompanied by the
generative energy or *virtù* of a verbal 'philosopher's stone' or
talisman. It is accordingly not surprising that he should speak in
mystical terms of Brancusi's 'exploration toward getting all the
forms into one form' as 'as long as any Buddhist's contemplation of
the universe or as any mediaeval saint's contemplation of the divine
love'; nor that the result should be an ovoid, a 'mundane egg'.[53] For
Pound's belief that 'An organisation of forms expresses a confluence

of forces', expressed in poetry in 'absolute metaphor' or 'absolute rhythm', is essentially similar to the animistic aesthetics whose progress I have charted from the 1890s with its stress on art as the symbolic channel for 'rhythms' cosmic and noumenal.

## II  *POUND'S IMAGIST POETRY*

In the previous section I demonstrated Pound's maintenance throughout the Imagist/Vorticist period of a Symbolist aesthetic. I shall now argue that his Imagist poetry remains almost exclusively within a Symbolist ambience in attempting to construct a suggestive linguistic equivalent for a mental state before moving tentatively towards an objectivist poetics, similar to that developed by H.D. and, fitfully, Flint.

Scattered evidence survives of Pound's familiarity prior to Imagism with the stylistic aims of Symbolism (in its late nineteenth-century sense). 1908 saw him advocating a diluted form of 'suggestion':

> Beauty should never be presented explained. It is Marvel and Wonder, and in art we should find first these doors – Marvel and Wonder – and, coming through them, a slow understanding (slow even though it be a succession of lightning understandings and perceptions) as of a figure in mist.[54]

He achieved this limited aim in 'Nel Biancheggiar' (whose original title was 'Blue grey and white'), which in a Symons-like fashion fuses the sensuous play of sounds and rhythms with visual suggestivity to evoke his mood on hearing Katherine Heyman's musical performance.[55]

Pound's chief source for what constituted Symbolism was, however, Yeats. This is evidenced in his prose[56] and particularly in the poetry of *Exultations* (1909). I noted in Chapter 6 Pound's extensive debt here to Yeats; the chief distinction is Pound's greater reliance on verbal mellifluence, emphasised in 'Sestina for Ysolt', for example, by the tight formal structure necessitating an incantatory pattern of refrains.[57] At this stage Pound adopted chiefly the accidentals of a 'Symbolist' style (largely the *topoi* of the 1890s), while his interest in *melos* derived from Provence rather than Verlaine.[58] Only in 1912 did he consciously develop the techniques of empathetic and abstract expressionist Symbolism.

In February 1912 Pound published two poems in a new style. 'Δώρια' and 'Sub Mare' were love poems, inspired by Dorothy Shakespear, but they differed from Pound's earlier ventures in this genre.[59] The images in 'Δώρια' were Yeatsian – 'the eternal moods/ of the bleak wind', 'the strong loneliness/of sunless cliffs/ And of grey waters' – but had a starkness of definition absent from Pound's earlier work and a functional prominence rather than decorative obtrusiveness. The poem resembles Pound's earlier work in fixing on a lyrical moment, adding a dramatic element with its closing implication of a narrative. Its innovation lies in attempting to establish an equation for an emotional attitude through a series of congruous images, drawing also on the affective resources of patterns of long, languid vowels, whose hypnotic quality is accentuated by the prominent enjambement. Pound is now willing to let the images and evocative cadences assume the full life of the poem. One elides the narrative coda, but the suggestive natural details remain fixed in one's mind.

'Sub Mare' reveals a similar concern with finding an imagistic equivalent for powerful emotions of love, in this case the initial sense of bewilderment created by a deepening relationship with an attractive but still unfamiliar stranger. Pound begins the poem with a deliberate statement about his state of mind, confident only in the limited scope of its assertion, before articulating his emotions in images which reflect his pleasantly confused disorientation. In the third line the setting dissolves into an imaginary insubstantiality which suggests metaphorically his mingled emotions (an ill-defined sense of well-being, tempered perhaps in 'autumn' with a hint of melancholy), while the fourth line captures the unlocated inconsequentiality characteristic of perceptions in a state of intoxication or mental disequilibrium. The second stanza completes this evocation, in the metaphor which gives the poem its title, the bizarre mental landscape complemented by the disconcerting metrical lurches of the enjambements. As in 'Δώρια' Pound again conveys the principal import of the poem imagistically, but his final rather pretentious comment with its discursive reinforcement indicates an insecurity about the communicative adequacy of this Symbolist convention.

Two important remarks must be made at this stage about
Pound's new experimentation with stylistic procedures resembling
French Symbolist poetry. The first is that this new technique did not
displace his earlier metamorphic and Stilnovist symbolism. Instead
these were integrated with the new variety of Symbolism: principally by their characteristically elaborate conceits undergoing
stylistic compression into one or two evocative images and being
expressed in more denotative, conversational diction. Secondly, the
examples so far cited ('Δώρια' and 'Sub Mare') approximate to
Pound's 'belief in a sort of permanent metaphor' and 'absolute
symbol or metaphor' (cf. *supra*, pp. 200–1 and 212). An instance
from the same period of his new Symbolist experimentation with the
complementary 'absolute rhythm' is provided by 'The Return'
(published June 1912).

Pound had always been a master of poetic rhythm. 'La Fraisne'
(written in late 1906 or early 1907), for example, is a compendium
of rhythmic experimentation which counterpoints the vigorous,
businesslike utterances of the councillor with the formally freer,
more delicate cadences which reveal the spiritual change he has
undergone. Similarly Pound's typescript revisions of 'An Idyl for
Glaucus' reveal how much he worked at perfecting the rhythmic
modulations of the speaker's voice as an expression of her diffident
vulnerability. It is a dramatic monologue Browning could not have
written, relying more on lyrical poignancy. It is hardly an
overstatement to say that it is the *metre* of the poem which embodies
its meaning; the hesitant delivery carries as much of the psychological burden as the explicit connotation of the individual words
themselves. The distinction between these and 'The Return' is that
in the latter Pound dispenses with the narrative context, leaving an
unlocalised vision which realises his belief in a symbolic 'absolute
rhythm'.[60]

Simultaneously with the satire which predominated in the poems
Pound published in *Poetry* in April and November 1913 and under
the title 'Zenia' (*sic*) in *Smart Set* in December 1913[61] exists an
alternative, more lyrical and mystical strain in a more directly
Imagist style. In common with Aldington and H.D., Pound wrote
many poems at this period on Greek themes, whether the
Persephone myth or Bacchic rites (see, for example, 'Surgit Fama',
'April', 'The Faun', 'Coitus'[62]). These mythological and metamorphic poems evidence his new direct diction as much as the
satirical poems, but complement this with a concentrated and

intense use of imagery. The climactic moment of 'April' is encapsulated in the single line 'Pale carnage beneath bright mist', which simply 'presents' a single detailed image, leaving it to engender an independent emotional effect. 'Gentildonna' is an Imagist reworking of 'Ballatetta' which discards the associative apparatus of Pound's earlier Stilnovist symbolism, reducing the style to its stark essentials. The elaborate simile of the aether from 'Canzone: Of Angels', stanza iv, which had been more briefly employed in 'Apparuit' and 'A Virginal', is now merely an objectively denoted perception – 'the air she severed'. The fanciful conceit which closed 'Ballatetta' now becomes 'Fanning the grass she walked on then'. Pound is content to rely on the registration of natural, observable detail to embody the poem's emotional meaning. The most striking instance of the new technique is, however, the final line of the poem. As in 'April', Pound crams everything into an imagistic summary: 'Grey olive leaves beneath a rain-cold sky'. The image, unlike those in the early pastiche Nineties 'Symbolist' poetry of *A Lume Spento*, may be read both figuratively and literally. It is an evocation of the setting, but also a metaphor for the poet's epiphany; the two interpretations complement one another. When the poem first appeared, in November 1913, Pound was deep in the work of Allen Upward, who in *The New Word*, as Pound reminds us, associated olive-leaves with the adjective *glaukos*, which in section vi of *Hugh Selwyn Mauberley* Pound linked to the eyes of the archetypal Pre-Raphaelite lady, Elizabeth Siddal. Pound's association elsewhere of 'Glaukopos' with visions of spiritual presences is revealed by its use in the draft First Canto to describe the 'gods' at Sirmione.[63] These overtones would obviously not have been available to the contemporary reader, but they suggest the connections in Pound's mind. The grey olive leaves are thus a visual, associative shorthand for the eyes of this lady, who might be either goddess or idealised lover. Yet even if one is ignorant of these allusions one's enjoyment is undiminished. The line, now indefinite in its implication, still remains emotionally suggestive, creating effects which vary with the individual reader and his mood. The two levels exist simultaneously; the knowing reader responds to both.

Two poems published in December 1913, 'Alba' and 'The Encounter', still retain the simile framework beside the new imagistic style, but most of the poems Pound published in February 1914 in the anthology *Des Imagistes* rely exclusively on objective presentation of natural objects as embodiments of an emotional state ('Δώρια', 'The Return', 'Liu Ch'e', 'Fan-Piece, for Her Imperial Lord'[64]). From this it was but a short step to a technique which presented a natural object as inherently significant, but Pound's early work (with the idiosyncratic exception of 'Ts'ai Chi'h'[65]) does not proceed as far as the Objectivists, whose poetry delights in the contingent *Dinglichkeit* of objects themselves. The natural objects in his Imagist poetry are employed to externalise the emotion which remains the prime subject of the poem. External particulars are presented in more acute detail than in the 'Idealist' poetry of the English 'Symbolist' epigones, but they are still subservient to the poet's *état d'âme*.[66]

Donald Davie's attempted distinction between Imagism and Symbolism – 'Imagism as Pound promulgated it, or as he later elaborated it into "Vorticism", is not a variant upon Symbolism but an alternative to it' – therefore overstates the case. At the time of Imagism and Vorticism Pound still employed what Davie regards as the Symbolist technique of using the external world as a metaphorical correlative for the poet's emotional state; he had not yet moved on to the more directly objectivist technique of the *Cantos*. Similarly Davie's contention that Pound 'seemingly had no interest' in 'the *idea* of music, the idea of a poetic art that should be non-referential or self-referential like the art of music', while attractive in the light of his later technique, is completely untrue if applied to the Vorticist period.[67]

The same fallacy, in his case implicit, undermines Tony Tanner's chapter 'Transcendentalism and Imagism' in his brilliant *The Reign of Wonder*. Tanner's 'Imagism' is exclusively that of Williams and could not be applied to Pound's earlier version – whether Williams himself can be termed an Imagist is another question. Tanner describes suggestively the perceptual viewpoint of Williams's poems, an attitude of 'reverent concentration' beside the natural world, which Tanner sees as symptomatic of alienated Modernist man substituting 'momentary awe for systematic theology', seeking refuge instead in 'examining only the palpable fragment'. I believe, however, that his account of Williams's poetry, in which 'The scattered objects of the world no longer form God's palimpsest, but are available for anchoring and delineating the poet's mood', forces onto Williams a rather Imagist position, at odds with his own Objectivist technique and that of the later Pound. Both of them viewed the objects of the phenomenal world as interesting on their own terms, by virtue of their very otherness, as unpredictable life independent from that of the poet and not an analogical equivalent for his mood. [68]

On this question Wallace Martin offers a formulation which characterises accurately the Objectivist reorientation but, like Davie, suggests a premature date for its accomplishment: 'The early writings of Hulme and Pound show that they were seeking not objects to correlate with their emotional states, but a means of presenting objects that in some sense embodied emotion.' [69] I would quibble only with Martin's choice of 'embodied', which is, I feel, insufficiently differentiated from Symbolist practice. For, as I argued in Chapter 2, Objectivism, to which Martin rightly sees Pound heading, no longer treats the poem as a metaphorical vehicle or embodiment of the poet's own state of consciousness. The Objectivist does not attempt to articulate his emotions with even the limited predetermination of the reader's response which the indirect methods of Symbolism entail. Instead the poem's artificiality extends only to the minimal framework it introduces to establish the aesthetic distance required to ensure the reader's contemplative attention. Its distinction from perceptual experience is reduced to the initial act of contextual transposition, reinforced conservatively by the connotative resources inherent in the conventions of poetry, most notably those of rhythm.

Owing to the procedures of naturalisation established by Romanticism and Symbolism, the reader instinctively assumes that the Objectivist's presentational technique is intended as an oblique index to his state of mind. The expectation is misguided, if understandable in that the presentational technique preceded the reorientation in perceptual attitude which was its natural accompaniment. Instead the Objectivist is concerned not to communicate *his own* emotions (although of course the poem implicitly records his imaginative engagement), but rather to allow the direct presentation of the object itself to inspire in the reader an unprepossessed, spontaneous response, whose conjectural resemblance to the poet's own is irrelevant.

My account of Objectivism intentionally exaggerates its aesthetic tendencies for clarity of exposition. For, despite the notoriety of Williams's 'Red Wheelbarrow', poems of this unadulterated degree of Objectivism are comparatively infrequent; further examples are the less familiar 'View of a Lake', 'Autumn', 'The Swaggering Gait', and 'Between Walls':

**Between Walls**

the black wings
of the

hospital where
nothing

will grow lie
cinders

in which shine
the broken

pieces of a green
bottle[70]

This may be taken as the purest form of Objectivism, comprising simply the unprepossessed presentation of phenomena (more usually Williams adds the winning reflections which give his poems their characteristic speaking-voice). It might be compared with Zukofsky's 'The Guests', unfortunately too long to quote, which evidences the technique at its best, utilising a skilfully shifting viewpoint and short end-stopped lines which generate syntactic ambiguities, to force the reader constantly to readjust his perceptual image of the scene and endow the mundane with an aura of unfamiliarity.[71]

For my present purposes, by virtue of their resemblance to the aims of H.D., I am most concerned with those poems by Williams which with varying degrees of obliquity record his empathetic engagement with the environment, such as 'Trees', 'Spring Strains' and 'Spring and All'.[72] Consider 'Young Sycamore':

I must tell you
this young tree
whose round and firm trunk
between the wet

pavement and the gutter
(where water

is trickling) rises
bodily

into the air with
one undulant
thrust half its height –
and then

dividing and waning
sending out
young branches on
all sides –

hung with cocoons
it thins
till nothing is left of it
but two

eccentric knotted
twigs
bending forward
hornlike at the top[73]

While H.D. uses an ambiguous vocabulary (discussed below) to imply her imaginative engagement, Williams relies almost exclusively on rhythm to transform the denotative diction. After the initial importunity of 'I must tell you', whose breathless launch *in medias res* captures the reader's attention and establishes an expectant rapport, Williams's voice is then effaced beside the compulsively unfolding cadences. An almost total absence of punctuation leaves syntactic relationships purposefully suspended, with the result that the reader hesitates at each line, momentarily uncertain of its direction. The constantly changing rhythm accordingly assumes a mimetic role, providing an organically indeterminate image of the tree's physical extension, whose arbitrary (because unpunctuated) conclusion reproduces the tree's energetically unresolved development. The point I wish to emphasise is the poet's self-effacement beside the detailed rendering of the object, whose phenomenal configuration is regarded as an indivisible extension of its inner life as thing-in-itself.

An analysis of representative examples of Pound's Imagist poetry

will illuminate their distinction from Objectivism. I shall begin at
the subjective extreme of the spectrum with 'Heather', which, as
Pound explained, 'represents a state of consciousness, or "implies",
or "implicates" it'. A letter to his father provides an additional gloss:

> Re/'Heather.' The title is put on it to show that the poem is a
> simple statement of facts occurring to the speaker, but that these
> facts do not occur on the same plane with his feet, which are
> solidly planted in a climate producing Heather and not leopards,
> etc.[74]

As in empathetic Symbolism, the *méprises* of 'Heather' signal to the
reader that this is an imaginary rather than an actual landscape,
whose ontologically uncertain status indicates the empathetic fusion
of the poet's consciousness with what becomes an equivocally
external scene. The witty interplay between matter-of-fact statement and disconcertingly supernatural occurrences suggests the
heightened sensibility which is the poem's theme.

This metaphorical correlative differs only in the degree of its
obliquity from 'Fan-Piece, for Her Imperial Lord' and 'Alba',
which both employ overt similes to articulate a mental state.[75] The
slight interest of 'Alba' lies in Pound's reliance on the precise visual
image to embody the poem's meaning, a strategy paralleled by
'Fan-Piece', which compresses a poem translated in Giles's *History of
Chinese Literature*.[76] The fan symbolises what the writer, for reasons
of decorum, will not otherwise express. But, unable to assume his
reader's familiarity with the conventions on which the Chinese
poem depends, Pound is forced to add the simile in the final line to
make the meaning clear. The original ten-line poem comprises the
courtesan's address to the fan and relies on the reader's deduction of
the analogy with her own situation. Pound's adaptive procedure is
to add the comment of line 3 to an abbreviated version of lines 1 and
2 of Giles's translation, thus concentrating the meaning of the poem
in the metaphorical implications of 'white', 'silk', and 'frost',
accentuated by this new isolation.

'Liu Ch'e', which also derives from Giles, moves a step closer to
Objectivism by virtue of the elaboration it gives to the external
scene for its own sake, the emphasis on its concrete actuality.[77]
Pound's presentational method leaves largely implicit its function as
an index to the poet's emotions, but nevertheless the naturalising
conventions which the post-Romantic reader instinctively employs

ensure its intended communication of the poet's state of mind.

Pound's transformation of his source-material provides an insight into his gradual movement towards an objectivist technique similar to H.D.'s. He abandons the original's stylised couplets for mimetically protracted constatations which insist on weighty pauses at the commas and, despite the enjambement, at the line-endings also. This makes the poem enact the poet's perception, dwelling inordinately on observations which accordingly assume an unwonted significance. The objectivity with which this is recorded relies on the reader's assumption that the wholly credible reality of the scene is simultaneously a sympathetic metaphor, a naturalisation to which line 5 gives retrospective confirmation. Pound's presentational reticence is completed by his conversion of the original's concluding summary of the poet's emotions into a new imagistic coda: 'A wet leaf that clings to the threshold'. This dismal image harmonises with those earlier in the poem, suggesting transience, desolation and decay, but the slight visual detail is dwelt on with such disproportionate attention that it imperceptibly assumes an added dimension as a symbol for the dead courtesan herself. To characterise this poem, therefore, one would still employ Pound's Imagist dictum that 'The natural object is always the *adequate* symbol', but the techniques it displays, in particular the rhythmic disposition, already foreshadow Objectivism.

The progression towards Objectivism is completed by the idiosyncratic experiment 'Ts'ai Chi'h', which is uncharacteristic of Pound's Imagist poetry in having no specific emotional correlative.[78] It concentrates on a single *aperçu*, a moment of contrasting colours and textures:

> The petals fall in the fountain,
> the orange-coloured rose-leaves,
> Their ochre clings to the stone.

Here there is no implied observer; instead one is presented with what could be interpreted as an image for the fragile ephemerality of beauty and life itself, or enjoyed simply as a clear, precisely articulated perception of a natural detail. One is invited to regard the scene as inherently interesting: a beautiful tableau, whose emotional import remains purposefully indeterminate.

The impact of Vorticism on Pound's poetic technique was surprisingly limited. Apart from inspiring his dismal attempt to reproduce the effect of a Vorticist canvas in 'Dogmatic Statement Concerning the Game of Chess', its chief effect was temporarily to redirect Pound's attention towards the abstract expressionist variety of Symbolist poetry, as in 'Phanopoeia'.[79]

Only in 1915 did Pound begin to move with assurance towards his more recognisable *Cantos* style: structurally in 'Near Perigord' and at a verbal level in 'Provincia Deserta', the opening of which foreshadows impressively the *Cantos*, as does the evocative section beginning

> I have walked
>         into Perigord

in which the pronounced rhythmic discontinuity enforces the reader's attention to linger on individual phenomenal details of this literal landscape, transforming the lean, denotative diction in a manner characteristic of the early work of H.D.[80] It is arguable that the descriptive requirements of narrative poetry stimulated this change: one finds similar elaboration of natural detail in the backgrounds of many poems in *Cathay*. The fact remains that only after his Vorticist period did Pound significantly depart from a Symbolist approach which regarded the world of the poem as primarily a metaphorical articulation of the poet's consciousness.

## III   *DES IMAGISTES*

I noted in Chapter 7 that most poets in *Des Imagistes* displayed little awareness of Pound's Imagist principles. The exceptions were H.D. and, to a lesser extent, Aldington and Williams. As it is likely that the first Imagist poem to be written was 'Hermes of the Ways', which Pound corrected and then emulated technically, it is appropriate to begin a reading of Imagist poetry with this.[81]

The title implies a Classical allusion, just as Pound's early dramatic lyrics had a narrative coda, or the nature paintings of the early Romantics had titles which indicated a specious literary content, but the real subject of H.D.'s poem is her presentation of the landscape as an inherently significant thing-in-itself. The visual perspective in the first part oscillates between desolate panoramas of sand-dunes (11.4–9) and microscopic investigation of phenomenal plenitude, like Goethe's Werther marvelling at the insect-life on the grass blade:

> The hard sand breaks,
> And the grains of it
> Are clear as wine.

The meticulous observation, then the sensual responsiveness arrest one; this is a world explored tentatively with naïve unprepossession, in which contingent detail can still evoke a sense of wonder. It is also a world of harsh energy whose inhuman objectivity is transfigured only by lyrical vision. H.D.'s is an unsentimental eye which feels estranged in an alien natural world:

> Wind rushes
> Over the dunes,
> And the coarse, salt-crusted grass
> Answers.

Humans here, one feels, are intruders; yet, fascinated by the visual beauty of 'salt-crusted', one forgets momentarily the elemental violence to which it bears witness. What the poem gives one is a new *physical* awareness of nature. Nature for H.D. is not primarily a visual spectacle; instead it is a curious three-dimensional phenomenon explored with tactile and aural hypersensitivity. The disjunction between poet and external world is not an agonising matter of subjectivist isolation but rather cause for exultation in its mysterious otherness. For H.D., unlike the Imagist Pound, is an objectivist.

The second part of the poem reads,

> Small is
> This white stream,
> Flowing below ground
> From the poplar-shaded hill,
> But the water is sweet.
>
> Apples on the small trees
> Are hard,
> Too small,
> Too late ripened
> By a desperate sun
> That struggles through sea-mist.

> The boughs of the trees
> Are twisted
> By many bafflings;
> Twisted are
> The small-leafed boughs.
> But the shadow of them
> Is not the shadow of the mast head
> Nor of the torn sails.
>
> Hermes, Hermes,
> The great sea foamed,
> Gnashed its teeth about me;
> But you have waited,
> Where sea-grass tangles with
> Shore-grass.

By virtue of its relative brevity the narrative pretext for the poem, hinted at in the final stanza, assumes negligible importance. H.D.'s attention is wholly for the vividly realised natural scene. With the exception of 'desperate' in line 10 of the quotation, which suggests a human analogy, evocation is limited to constatations of physical properties. Like Franz Marc, H.D. is intent not to subordinate the natural world to a presiding human consciousness: it exists on its own terms as life independent from the perceiving human, for which the appropriate attitude is respect. Yet, although the presentation of the scene is objective, the sympathetic, observing consciousness of the poet is not far concealed. The typographic disposition and rhythmic discontinuity of the poem, enforcing a gradual unfolding of the scene in time, implies the progressive acquaintance with this scene which it records. The brief but nevertheless weighty lines of the first stanza suggest an eye lingering on individual details, absorbing their configuration as components in a larger panorama. The second stanza marks a transition from purely visual acquaintance to a tactile examination of the fruit, in which any hint of dispassionate, scientific observation is forestalled by the emotional connotations of 'desperate' and 'struggles', which fuse a suggestive visual image with the poet's own sympathetic interpretation. This tone assures a natural transition into the third stanza, in which 'twisted', twice repeated, is both an accurate visual description and at the same time implies an empathetic engagement by the poet with the trees. This dual reference to verifiable, perceptual detail and the poet's imaginative response recurs throughout the poem in the frequently repeated 'small', and in 'bafflings' (l. 14) and 'tangles' (l. 24). By means of this subtle use of vocabulary which primarily records objective detail, yet also invites a subjectivist reading, H.D. succeeds in making the poem a wholly credible record of a landscape perceived as thing-in-itself, yet at the same time indicates her own imaginative response. The two registers complement one another, fused by a sensibility which experiences objects physically rather than conceptually.

Most of her other poems in *Des Imagistes* are disappointing classical reworkings. 'Hermonax' is inspired by the Glaucus myth, 'Epigram' and 'Sitalkas' are lyrically attractive but wholly derivative, while the last stanza of 'Priapus', revealing the same ability as in 'Acon' to assemble mellifluently evocative groupings of natural products, is its only interesting point save for the line 'Thou hast flayed us with thy blossoms' in which H.D.'s disturbingly individual sensibility finds expression in the energetic verb out of all apparent proportion to the event it describes, reflecting her strongly sensual, almost erotic, experience of the natural world. [82]

At its best H.D.'s poetry provides a radically original perception of familiar phenomena, justifying the Romantic ideal of the innocent, childlike consciousness, as in the exhilarating sense of discovery captured in 'The Pool'. But more frequently her emotions are the aspect of the child's experience of the external world largely ignored by Romantic nostalgia: that of bewilderment or even terror in a strange, potentially hostile environment. Her poems printed in *Some Imagist Poets 1916*, in attempting to extend their length, reveal the extent to which she was becoming merely thematically repetitive: 'Sea Gods' expresses perfunctorily a ritual invocation of the gods and longing for their return. But amidst the verbosity of 'The Shrine' are characteristic flashes of preternaturally intense sense-impressions which impinge directly and almost painfully on her psyche:

> You are not forgot,
> O plunder of lilies –
> Honey is not more sweet
> Than the salt stretch of your beach.

'Temple – The Cliff' proclaims a Sylvia Plath-like sense of acute mental torture; the environment is perceived as a vital presence, alive but simultaneously threatening.[83] The same unevenness occurs in her diffuse contributions to *Some Imagist Poets 1917*. When she attempts to move beyond short intense lyrics or away from classical themes she generally fails, and indeed her slight output in the Imagist period indicates limited inspiration; but on her own restricted ground she is exquisite. Her feeling for the minutiae of landscape and plant life is striking and inimitable, bordering on the pathological in her reliance on violent, energetic verbs – to her vision all is movement, tension, frenetic life. Compare 'Storm', which, like 'Hermes of the Ways', employs a vocabulary which need only denote observable detail but at the same time is charged with an implicit empathetic interaction with what she perceives.[84]

A group of poems in *Some Imagist Poets: An Anthology*, 'Sea Lily', 'Sea Iris' and 'Sea Rose', in part make explicit the implicit imaginative identification with the scene in 'Hermes of the Ways' and to that extent are less subtle, but they evidence impressively the curiosity of the objectivist poet for the particularity of the perceived object, whose external appearance assumes a heightened significance as the sensuous extension of its inner life.[85] Unlike Pound's Imagist poetry, in H.D.'s poetry of this period the objects of the external world are not primarily correlatives for the poet's emotional state: instead they are independent beings with which the poet may identify, revealing implicitly his empathetic attitude, but seen as valuable for their own sake. Emotional engagement does not invalidate H.D.'s sensuous and imaginative responsiveness to the flowers as things-in-themselves:

> Myrtle-bark
> is flecked from you,
> scales are dashed
> from your stem,
> sand cuts your petal,
> furrows it with hard edge,
> like flint
> on a bright stone.

('Sea Lily', ll. 8–15)

> sea-iris, brittle flower,
> one petal like a shell
> is broken,

and you print a shadow
like a thin twig.

('Sea Iris', ll. 3–7)

The unusually brief lines insist on extraordinary attention being given to what would instinctively be dismissed quickly: in itself this forces us radically to alter our customary perceptual attitude. The typographical disposition as in 'Hermes of the Ways' mirrors the progress of the eye's detailed investigation of these flowers, the degree of attention paid being an index of the respect with which they are contemplated. H.D.'s emotional attitude is again skilfully embodied in her ambivalent vocabulary. The important stylistic and perceptual innovation is that the objects of the phenomenal world are regarded as inherently significant. The poet's gazing consciousness interacts with them to elicit their essential haecceity; and this, rather than the poet's emotional engagement itself (as in empathetic Symbolism) provides the theme of the poem.

Comparison with the other Imagists makes clear H.D.'s totally different technique and perceptual attitude. The majority of Aldington's contributions to *Des Imagistes* are pseudo-classical elegies in which the natural world appears as an occasional backcloth to the subjective emotions which are their theme. 'Choricos', like Pound's 'The Return', portrays the uncertain survival of the ancient gods, relying like Pound's poem primarily on rhythms for its evocative effect, rather than perceptual precision. Metrically it is impressive, but it is in a totally different genre from H.D.'s poems, looking back instead to the English 'Symbolists'. Aldington writes of death in lines which would blend inconspicuously into poems written twenty years earlier:

Thou art the dusk and the fragrance;
Thou art the lips of love mournfully smiling;
Thou art the pale peace of one
Satiate with old desires

The tone of his elegies is indistinguishable from the languor of the *fin de siècle*.[86] While H.D.'s verse is strongly sensuous, it is a sensuousness rooted directly in perceptual experience; Aldington's by contrast is a matter of synaesthesia. The lines quoted form a catalogue of emotional associations, disembodied fragments of the external world assembled as consciously beautiful. Aldington's images are in an artificial framework; one is in no doubt that these are elements of a purely mental landscape. This is not to condemn Aldington, for his poem is competent if derivative, but merely to emphasise that in these classical poems, such as 'Lesbia', 'To a Greek Marble', 'To Atthis' and 'Argyria', Aldington is working with conventions which resemble H.D.'s 'Epigram' and 'Sitalkas' rather than her more distinctive, objectivist style. [87]

A consideration of Aldington's response to this original perceptual attitude will help to clarify H.D.'s divergence from her associates and from the Symbolist, subjectivist tradition.

> I have sat here happy in the gardens,
> Watching the still pool and the reeds
> And the dark clouds
> Which the wind of the upper air
> Tore like the green leafy boughs
> Of the divers-hued trees of late summer;
> But though I greatly delight
> In these and the water lilies,
> That which sets me nighest to weeping
> Is the rose and white colour of the smooth flag-stones,
> And the pale yellow grasses
> Among them. [88]

Here, in 'Au Vieux Jardin', Aldington is at his closest to H.D.'s technique, but the distance between them is more noticeable than any similarities. Most importantly, we are given a landscape through Aldington's mediation: at regular intervals the personal pronoun 'I' recurs, emphasising that his consciousness is the determining filter for what we see. Unlike H.D.'s self-effacement beside the objects she presents, whose appearance is explored as a revelation of their 'character' (in the sense of Schopenhauerian Ideas) or as an eloquent record of natural process, Aldington's rational consciousness is impressed on the poem, shaping the scene rhetorically to illustrate his emotional state. The transitional point at line 7 is marked by 'But though I', followed two lines later by 'That which'; he has imposed an artificial order on the scene. Rather than tracing the natural contours of the garden, Aldington has selected some of its elements and placed them in an aesthetic framework, inviting us to view them in these terms. He responds to nature not as a mysterious world of independent life, but instead almost as an artifact, and, significantly, what affects him most, as he spells out explicitly at the end of the poem, is a painterly contrast of colours and textures.[89] We are left in no doubt that the subject of the poem is Aldington; the old garden of the title is merely the context for his emotions. There is no indication that he is profoundly engaged imaginatively with what he perceives or that he regards it with more than superficial attention. The essential difference is that Aldington's garden refers out from itself towards the poet; the natural world of H.D.'s objectivist poetry by contrast draws us profoundly into itself, revealing to our curiosity previously unimagined depths. In Aldington's considered definition, the task of modern poetry was 'rendering the moods, the emotions, the impressions of a single, sensitized personality confronted by the phenomena of modern life, and . . . expressing these moods accurately, in concrete, precise, racy language' and the primacy of his presiding consciousness is maintained throughout his contributions to the *Some Imagist Poets* series and his *Images (1910–1915)*.[90]

Flint's Imagist poetry, with occasional efforts at stylistic compression, mostly extends the intensely subjective themes of his earlier poetry discussed in Chapter 3. There is his familiar sense of disillusionment and despair in an urban environment and need for imaginative escape, accompanied by confessional works which embarrassingly dissect his feelings in public, untransmuted into art.[91] If such poems appeal it is largely for extraneous reasons; one sympathises with his all-too-apparent emotional distress, but this is hardly an aesthetic experience. His customary technique, like Ford's, combines sentimental commentary with impressionist gathering of sense-data which occasionally is heightened into an imaginative interpretation of the London scene, as in the following passage of unusual intensity, in which Flint foreshadows Eliot's Dantesque vision of the metropolitan crowd in 'The Burial of the Dead':

> Tired faces,
> eyes that have never seen the world,
> bodies that have never lived in air,
> lips that have never minted speech,
> they are the clipped and garbled,
> blocking the highway.
> They swarm and eddy

> between the banks of glowing shops
> towards the red meat,
> the potherbs,
> the cheapjacks,
> or surge in
> before the swift rush
> of the clanging trams, –
> pitiful, ugly, mean,
> encumbering.[92]

With rare objectivity Flint has here fused the observable motion and behaviour of the people with horrified but compulsive imaginative involvement in their plight. His interpretation of their limbo-like condition, expressed in the incantatory lines 2–5 of the extract, is rooted in the perceptual detail of the second part, with which it forms accordingly an organic whole. He responds to the London scene in the same fashion that H.D. did to the landscape of 'Hermes of the Ways', with a leisurely curiosity at odds with the frenetic bustle he beholds. What makes the passage so remarkable (and almost unparalleled in Flint's work) is the way in which empathetic perception does not preclude detailed visual rendering. His own viewpoint is established clearly, but Flint is concerned not to interpose this between the reader and his vivid realisation of the independent life of the crowd, achieved through simple presentation which retains the air of being wholly uncontrived, although the scenes he chooses and occasional words such as 'red' (l. 9) are tense with his instinctive revulsion.

'Houses' is another objectivist poem in which the various sounds and sights of the evening cityscape are simply recorded, with an accompanying implicit emotional attitude established in the first line, which states a verifiable fact but also indicates a mood:

> Evening and quiet:
> a bird trills in the poplar trees
> behind the house with the dark green door
> across the road.
>
> Into the sky,
> the red earthenware and the galvanised iron chimneys
> thrust their cowls.
> The hoot of the steamers on the Thames is plain.

No wind;
the trees merge, green with green;
a car whirs by;
footsteps and voices take their pitch
in the key of dusk,
far-off and near, subdued.

Solid and square to the world
the houses stand,
their windows blocked with venetian blinds.

Nothing will move them.[93]

The presiding mood subsumes poet and environment into a harmonious whole: the tranquillity is, one feels, as much an inherent quality of the objects themselves as of the poet, something they exude as an aura or communicate as attributes, rather than an importation by an alien consciousness. Flint's perceptual attitude is not empathetic, for this would imply a more intense engagement than the poem reveals, but nevertheless his sympathetic responsiveness acknowledges in these disparate objects a weighted, independent existence, conveyed through the carefully measured cadences of the poem, which makes of them more than a simple catalogue. One senses this effect clearly in line 3, for example, where 'dark green door' with its long, discrete monosyllables and bass notes implies a more than superficially apparent depth. In the history of twentieth-century poetry in English such experiments in allowing the world of external phenomena to assume aesthetic significance by virtue of its contingent particularity alone are of momentous importance.

Flint's objectivism is established by comparison with Eliot's 'Preludes' I and II, which evoke the inextricable involvement, both physical and imaginative, of their personae with the contingent life of the city, with the ambivalent emotions of compassion and desperation which this engenders.[94] Their divergence from Flint's 'Houses' lies in Eliot's combination of Flint-like, objectivist presentation in which his empathetic engagement remains implicit, with metaphorical, Symbolist techniques reminiscent of the contemporaneous 'Rhapsody on a Windy Night' and 'The Love Song of J. Alfred Prufrock'.

As evocations of moods, 'Preludes' fuse imaginatively cityscape and emotion in an ontologically ambiguous middle ground. In section I this is signalled by the animistic hints of line 1, which atmospherically suggest an anthropomorphisation of the scene, bringing by analogy the external world closer to human experience. This implicit engagement is further conveyed by the persona's vivid sense perceptions in lines 2 and 12 (the latter suggesting a sympathetic identity between him and the horse), his unwilled envelopment by the withered leaves and discarded newspapers (a syntactic parallel with the rain beating on the chimney-pots, which suggests a semantic equivalence between his experience and that of what become by implication animate objects), and the interpolated metaphor in line 4, which blurs the distinction between internal and external reality.

In section II likewise the opening five lines, by animising the morning and the street, persuade the reader of the essential identity of city-dwellers and cityscape. The disembodied 'feet' of line 4, 'muddy' to reinforce their osmosis with the setting, are presented as an indivisible metaphorical extension of the street itself, while their 'press[ing]' towards the coffee-stands assumes the air of an automatic, surging force independent of human volition and thus merely an aspect of the morning's consciousness.

This necessarily selective exposition permits an assessment of the significance of Imagism/Vorticism. It appears that, while H.D.'s objectivism heralded a major poetic reorientation, Pound by contrast maintained a Janus-faced attachment to both old and new. Thus his conception of life as *energy* was primarily mystical and Neoplatonic, but a ready transition was possible to accommodating this in a scientifically respectable vocabulary as *radiation* and, under Upward's influence,[95] beneath a spurious technical patina as the spiralling forces and interlocking gyres of the vortex. This compromise position renders Pound the more typical Modernist poet, in a period which hesitated uneasily on the threshold of the twentieth century and, unwilling to abandon its old gods, fused the reassuringly mystical with the programmatically *avant-garde*.

## IV  RETROSPECTIVE

Throughout this study I have argued that the pre-war carpet contains a frequently overlooked but crucially important figure.

This coherent pattern of transcendentalist aesthetics will now receive a final synthesis.

The reaction in the 1890s against materialistic determinism and Naturalism re-established the varieties of subjectivist aesthetics which dominated *avant-garde* movements in art and literature prior to the First World War. The growing importance attached by Moore and Sickert to subjective interpretation rather than dispassionate objectivity led in art from Impressionism to the empathetic, post-Impressionist aesthetic adumbrated by MacColl and Furse. The major alternative to this empathetic Symbolism was the abstract expressionist Symbolism variously exemplified by the second-generation Pre-Raphaelites, Watts and Image, and in poetry by Yeats. Symons's work develops from empathetic and abstract expressionist Symbolist poetry towards an empathetic, animistic aesthetic.

In the early twentieth century this legacy was re-evaluated. The reaction of Hulme and Flint against the English 'Symbolist' epigones redirected attention away from Idealism. Hulme's critique of the vapid *clichés* of conventional poetic diction, and his empathetic aesthetics re-emphasised the importance of perceptual experience, while their empathetic Symbolist technique foreshadowed Pound's belief that 'the natural object is always the *adequate* symbol'.

In the visual arts the Bergsonian and Schopenhauerian empathetic aesthetics which had emerged in the 1890s was firmly established in Futurism, Vorticism and in the work of Franz Marc, while Kandinsky's move towards abstraction reflected his attempt to create an appropriately non-materialistic art-form in which to convey his Theosophist millennialism. The fact that all these movements and the totally distinct Cubism share a similar vocabulary demonstrates the misleading insufficiency of the customary formalistic interpretation of their aims. By examining their professed underlying intentions, their neglected but essentially congruous transcendentalism is revealed: the aspect of Vorticism which, significantly, was stressed by Pound. His syncretic assimilation of the Vorticist artists' experiments in form to his own Neoplatonic interest in *forma*, accompanied by his association of their 'arrangements' with his 'equations of eternity', and his rejection of an Impressionist aesthetic, emphasises the predominant importance in his work throughout the Vorticist period of the Symbolist theory coloured by Neoplatonism and hermeticism which he had developed in his pre-Imagist phase.

This is paralleled in Pound's Imagist poetry by the almost exclusive use of an empathetic Symbolist technique of establishing metaphorical equivalents for states of consciousness. It was H.D. rather than Pound who completed the logical development of this impersonal, 'presentational' method with the shift in perceptual attitude which was its natural accompaniment. Her work thus depicts a literal rather than a metaphorical world, presented as significant for its own sake as thing-in-itself rather than as a symbolic vehicle for the mood which it has inspired in the poet. The elaborate attention she devoted to phenomenal detail implied that the contingent particularity of objects was itself a sufficient basis for aesthetic consideration. Her reticence and merely implicit engagement was soon replaced in Dada and in Objectivism by the refusal to condition the spectator's or reader's response save by the initial act of selectivity itself, a path which culminates in the ever-increasing sterility of aleatory Post-Modernism and minimal art.

Despite changes in vocabulary therefore, the *avant-garde* literature and painting of the pre-war years displays an uninterrupted development from the 1890s, retaining and frequently accentuating the transcendentalism of the *fin de siècle*. It is a fascinating period of transition in which continuity is more striking than change. For, although to their bewildered contemporaries the bold technical experimentation of the Modernist writers and artists provided their most salient characteristic, with the benefit of chronological objectivity we can now arrive at a more just appreciation of their hesitant, equivocal position, in which self-conscious innovation was balanced by emotional and spiritual nostalgia.

# Notes

NOTES TO CHAPTER 1: THE PERCEIVING IMAGINATION

1. Henry James, *The Art of the Novel*, ed. R. P. Blackmur (New York, 1934) 5.
2. Cf. *WWR*, II, 291. Vol. II, ch. 30 ('On the Pure Subject of Knowing', 367–75) is also vital to this argument.
3. I use 'post-Impressionist' to denote any movement chronologically later than Impressionism; 'Post-Impressionist' is restricted to its conventional acceptation in the history of French painting.
4. W. A. M. Peters, *Gerard Manley Hopkins: A Critical Essay towards the Understanding of his Poetry* (Oxford, 1948) 23, 2.
5. In his schematic account of the growing ideality of the various art forms Hegel makes similar comments on music; see particularly *Aesthetics: Lectures on Fine Art* (1835–8), trs. T. M. Knox, 2 vols (Oxford, 1975) II, 888–909. He stresses sound's abstract nature in comparison with the visual media and also the non-representational aspect of music: 'what alone is fitted for expression in music is the object-free inner life, abstract subjectivity as such. . . . Consequently the chief task of music consists in making resound, not the objective world itself, but, on the contrary, the manner in which the inmost self is moved to the depths of its personality and conscious soul' (ibid., 891).
6. Ibid., I, 12–13, 31–2.
7. Ibid., 46–7.
8. Cf. ibid., II, 972 on the exclusion of natural objects from the subject-matter of art.
9. Ibid., I, 518. See also 79–81, 517–29.
10. Stéphane Mallarmé *Œuvres complètes*, ed. Henri Mondor and G. Jean-Aubry (Paris, [1951]) 366.
11. See, for example, Yeats, *Essays and Introductions*, 193–4.

NOTES TO CHAPTER 2: SYMBOLISM, IMPRESSIONISM AND 'EXTERIORITY'

1. For a pioneer exploration of this topic, see Douglas Cooper, Introduction to *The Courtauld Collection: A Catalogue and Introduction* (1954) 29–45.
2. See A. G. Lehmann, *The Symbolist Aesthetic in France 1885–1895*, 2nd edn (Oxford, 1968) 37–50.
3. See Tom Gibbons, *Rooms in the Darwin Hotel* (Nedlands, Western Australia, 1973) 1–20. R. C. K. Ensor in *England 1870–1914* (Oxford, 1936) 140–1, 307, gives a more sceptical account of the Anglo-Catholic movement.

4. Samuel Hynes, *The Edwardian Turn of Mind* (1968) 138–45, 148, 164.

5. Yeats, *Uncollected Prose*, I, 322–3 (emphasis added). See also Yeats's comments on 'externality' from 1900 and 1898 in *Essays and Introductions*, 155, 169, 189–92.

6. See Yeats: *Autobiographies*, 81–3, 114–17, 123, 124–5, 133, 168–70, 173, 279; *Uncollected Prose*, I, 322–5, 344–6. For a thorough and stimulating account of the development of Yeats's artistic pantheon see the excellent article by D. J. Gordon and Ian Fletcher, 'Symbolic Art and Visionary Landscape', in their *W. B. Yeats: Images of a Poet* (Manchester, 1961) 91–107; and Ian Fletcher, 'Poet and Designer: W. B. Yeats and Althea Gyles', in *Yeats Studies No. 1*, ed. Robert O'Driscoll and Lorna Reynolds (Shannon, 1971) 42–79.

7. See Yeats: *Autobiographies*, 115–6, 90, 155–9; and *Letters*, 150, 154, 170. In the *Art Review* for 1890 Symons published an article in similarly programmatic vein, 'A French Blake: Odilon Redon', contrasting this 'visionary' with the tepid Naturalism of Bouguereau (the Bastien-Lepage of the previous generation – see *infra*, n. 67).

8. For an examination of some aspects of this English tradition, see John Dixon Hunt, *The Pre-Raphaelite Imagination 1848–1900* (1968).

9. Ian Fletcher has drawn attention to Image's articles in the two essays cited in n. 6.

10. G. F. Watts, 'The Present Conditions of Art', *Nineteenth Century*, VII (Feb 1880) 235–55; Symons, 'Watts', *Fortnightly Review*, n.s., LXVIII (Aug 1900) 193.

11. Richard Ellmann, *Yeats: The Man and the Masks* (1961) 12

12. Yeats's good friend Katherine Tynan also contributed to the 1888 volume of this periodical.

13. Yeats: 'William Blake and his Illustrations to "The Divine Comedy": I. His Opinions upon Art', *Savoy*, 3 (July 1896) 41; *Uncollected Prose*, II, 342–5.

14. Watts, 'The Present Conditions of Art', *Nineteenth Century*, VII, 235–40.

15. Ibid., 240–4.

16. Ibid., 251–2.

17. G. F. Watts, 'The Aims of Art', *Magazine of Art*, XI (June 1888) 253–4. Cf. Yeats: 'William Blake and the Imagination' (1896), repr. in *Essays and Introductions*, 111–15; and 'Mr Rhys' Welsh Ballads' (1898), repr. in *Uncollected Prose*, II, 91–2.

18. G. F. Watts, 'More Thoughts on our Art of To-Day', *Magazine of Art*, XII (June 1889) 253–6.

19. His friends York Powell, Katherine Tynan and Lionel Johnson all contributed to the *Century Guild Hobby Horse*, which carried much congenial material on Blake, Calvert and the Pre-Raphaelites. Cf. Yeats, *Letters*, 65, 67, 115, on Yeats's friendship with the magazine's editor, Herbert Horne, and perusal of back-numbers.

20. Yeats, *Autobiographies*, 168–9.

21. Selwyn Image, 'A Lecture on Art', *Century Guild Hobby Horse*, pt I (Apr 1884) 37–8, 41, 45–7.

22. Ibid., 48.

23. Selwyn Image, 'On the Theory that Art should represent the surrounding life', and 'On Art and Nature', *Century Guild Hobby Horse*, I (1886) 16, 18.

24. Francis Bate, 'The Naturalistic School of Painting', *Artist and Journal of Home Culture*, VIII (1886) 67–9, 99–101, 131–3, 163–5, 211–12, 243–4, 275–7, 307–10. Gordon and Fletcher, *Yeats: Images of a Poet*, 95, indicate the likely importance to Yeats of Image's attack on Bate; see also Fletcher's *Yeats Studies No. 1*, 49.

25. Bate, 'The Naturalistic School', *Artist and Journal of Home Culture*, VIII, 67.

26. Ibid., 131–2.

27. Ibid., 163; cf. conclusion on 310.

28. Ibid., 275, 244.

29. See Ch. 1, n. 3.

30. *Artist and Journal of Home Culture*, VIII, 307, 308.

31. Selwyn Image, 'A Note on a Pamphlet Entitled, "The Naturalistic School of Painting", by Francis Bate', *Century Guild Hobby Horse*, III (1888) 119–20.

32. Yeats, *Variorum Poems*, 162–3, 169–70.

33. Ibid., 155–6.

34. On this see Allen R. Grossman, *Poetic Knowledge in the Early Yeats* (Charlottesville, Va, 1969).

35. Yeats, *Variorum Poems*, 154.

36. Ibid., 161; James Joyce, *Chamber Music* (1907; repr. 1971) 40.

37. Yeats, *Variorum Poems*, 172. My interpretation is supported by the poem's original publication in the *Savoy* as a pendant to what was then termed 'The Shadowy Horses', that other poem of sexual experience analysed above, which was similarly written for Olivia Shakespear.

38. Yeats, *Variorum Poems*, 77–8.

39. Ibid., 79–81; see particularly lines 13–20. 'The Sad Shepherd' (ibid., 67–9) further displays Yeats's awareness of the Romantics' anxious relationship with, in this case, an unsympathetic natural world.

40. In retrospect Monet's development appears signalled as early as the Belle-Île and Étretat paintings of 1886, becoming unequivocal in the series of *Haystacks* (1889–91) and *Poplars on the Epte* (1890–1). See Alan Bowness, *Modern European Art* (1972) 27, 30; and Robert Goldwater, *Symbolism* (1979) 2–4.

41. D. S. MacColl, 'The New English Art Club', *Spectator*, LXVI (18 Apr 1891) 544.

42. James Abbott McNeill Whistler, *The Gentle Art of Making Enemies*, 2nd, enlarged edn (1892; repr. New York, 1967) 8.

43. Ibid., 127. This argument was repeated by Charles Furse of the NEAC in 'Impressionism – What It Means', *Albemarle*, II, 2 (Aug 1892) 50–1.

44. See 'Mr P. Wilson Steer on Impressionism in Art', repr. in D. S. MacColl, *Life, Work and Setting of Philip Wilson Steer* (1945) 177; D. S. MacColl, 'The Old Water-Colour Society', *Spectator*, LXVII (12 Dec 1891) 846.

45. Cf., for example, Joshua Reynolds, *Discourses on Art*, ed. Robert R. Wark (New York, 1966) 45–6, 47–8, with 202–3, 212–14, and particularly 228.

46. Ibid., 205, 211 (emphasis added).

47. Ibid., 50–1, 56–7, 169–72, 174, 176, 177, 179.

48. Ibid., 208–9 (emphasis added).

49. Ibid., 236, 239.

50. Whistler, *The Gentle Art*, 144.

51. Walter Sickert, 'Preface', repr. in MacColl, *Life, Work and Setting of Steer*, 176.

Cf. 'The New English Art Club Exhibition', *Scotsman*, 24 Apr 1889, 8; 'The Whirlwind Diploma Gallery. II and III', *Whirlwind*, I (19, 26 July 1890) 51, 67.

52. Steer, in MacColl, *Life, Work and Setting of Steer*, 177.
53. Walter Sickert, 'Art' and 'Literature', *Whirlwind*, I (28 June 1890) 6, 13.
54. See Walter Sickert, 'Modern Realism in Painting', in *Jules Bastien-Lepage and his Art. A Memoir by André Theuriet* (1892) 133–43. Bastien-Lepage's selection as scapegoat was logical if somewhat unfair, dictated by the strategic requirement of an instantaneously familiar example of the tendency under attack; a further arbitrary factor was doubtless the infighting in the NEAC between Sickert's London Impressionists and the followers of Bastien-Lepage: Clausen and the 'Newlyn School'. Bastien-Lepage was, ironically in view of Sickert's polemic, influenced by Millet, with whom his work shares an undeniable pathos, erring if anything on the side of mawkishness rather than lack of sentiment, although some paintings do display a rather irritatingly strenuous effort towards naturalistic exactitude.
55. Ibid., 135–6, 141, 135.
56. Furse, 'Impressionism – What It Means', *Albemarle*, II. 2, 49.
57. Joseph Hone, *The Life of George Moore* (1936) 179; *Men and Memories: Recollections of William Rothenstein 1872–1900* (1934) 171; MacColl, *Life, Work and Settting of Steer*, 66.
58. Walter Sickert, 'Mr George Moore on Painting', *Academy*, 1 (19 Dec 1896) 555; Douglas Cooper, 'George Moore and Modern Art', *Horizon*, XI (1945) 124.
59. Rothenstein, *Men and Memories*, 240–3; D. S. MacColl, 'Modern Painting', *Spectator*, LXXI (18 Nov 1893) 720–1.
60. For the background to Moore's rejection of Naturalism, see Hone, *Life of Moore*, 130–4, 142–4; and the account of Moore in Ruth Z. Temple, *The Critic's Alchemy: A Study of the Introduction of French Symbolism into England* (New York, 1953).
61. See Douglas Cooper, 'George Moore and Modern Art', *Horizon*, XI (1945) 113–29.
62. Wendy Baron, *Sickert* (1973) 18, 24–5, and *Sickert: Paintings, drawings and prints of Walter Richard Sickert 1860–1942* (1977) 8–9. See also Ronald Pickvance, 'The Magic of the Halls and Sickert', *Apollo*, LXXVI (April 1962) 107.
63. Its devotees included Symons, Moore, Dowson, Davidson, Gray, Le Gallienne, Image, Horne, Johnson, Headlam, Beerbohm, Wilde, Lord Alfred Douglas, Havelock Ellis and Gordon Craig.
64. Arthur Waugh, 'Reticence in Literature', *Yellow Book*, I (Apr 1894) 203–5, 209, 212–17 (emphasis added). Cf. Hubert Crackanthorpe's carefully argued 'Reticence in Literature: Some Roundabout Remarks', *Yellow Book*, II (July 1894) 260–1. Moore's famous 'Degas' essay – *Impressions and Opinions* (1891) 298–323 – valuable in defending work much maligned on moral grounds, as the later controversy over *L'Absinthe* demonstrated, is thus largely a literary appreciation of Degas's ability to rise above sordid treatment of *risqué* subjects. On the Degas controversy, see *The New Fiction (A Protest Against Sex-Mania) and Other Papers by The Philistine* [J. A. Spender] (1895).
65. Moore, 'The New Pictures in the National Gallery', *Impressions and Opinions*, 324–46.

66. Ibid., 328–32.
67. Quoted by Cooper, *The Courtauld Collection*, 34. Moore's indebtedness to Degas's dismissal of Bastien-Lepage is revealed in his quotation in 'The Grosvenor Gallery', *Hawk*, 13 May 1890, 553, of 'C'est le Bougureau [*sic*] du mouvement moderne'. Cf. his *Reminiscences of the Impressionist Painters* (Dublin, 1906) 32.
68. Cf. Moore: 'The Grosvenor Gallery', *Hawk*, 13 May 1890, 553; 'The Royal Academy', *Fortnightly Review*, n.s., LI (June 1892) 831–2 (quotation from 832); 'A Book about Bastien-Lepage', *Speaker*, V (20 Feb 1892) 227; 'The Glasgow School', *Speaker*, VI (10 Dec 1892) 707–8; *Modern Painting* (1893) 207–8; and 'The New Gallery', *Speaker*, IX (12 May 1894) 526.
69. Moore, 'Meissonier', *Speaker*, VII (22 Apr 1893) 452–3 (emphasis added). See also his 'Exteriority', *Speaker*, XI (22 June 1895) 684–6; 'A Diary of Moods', *Speaker*, VIII (9 Dec 1893) 641; 'Mr Steer's Exhibition', *Speaker*, IX (3 Mar 1894) 249; and 'The New Gallery', *Hawk*, 20 May 1890, 583. He had earlier made similar remarks on literature in *Impressions and Opinions*, 68, 140.
70. Moore, 'Values', *Speaker*, VI (27 Aug 1892) 258–9; 'An Orchid by Mr James', *Speaker*, VII (17 June 1893) 687; and 'The Royal Academy', *Speaker*, IX (5 May 1894) 500.
71. Moore, 'The New Gallery', *Speaker*, VI (8 Oct 1892) 436–7; *Modern Painting*, 116–17; 'The Royal Academy', *Fortnightly Review*, n.s., LI 835–6.
72. Moore, 'Two Landscape Painters', *Speaker*, IV (26 Dec 1891) 776. Cf. his forceful criticism of Monet's 'exteriority' in 'Claude Monet', *Speaker*, XI (15 June 1895) 658; and 'The New English Art Club', *Speaker*, VII (15 Apr 1893) 423.
73. Moore, 'Decadence', *Speaker*, VI (3 Sep 1892) 285–6 (quotations from 285).
74. D. S. MacColl: 'The Royal Academy [Second Notice]', *Spectator*, LXVI (9 May 1891) 660–1; and 'The Royal Academy. – II', *Spectator*, LXVIII (14 May 1892) 677. See also his 'Three Exhibitions', *Spectator*, LXVII (21 Nov 1891) 728.
75. D. S. MacColl, 'The New English Art Club', *Spectator*, LXVII (5 Dec 1891) 809. MacColl adopts a more balanced perspective on Monet in *Nineteenth Century Art* (Glasgow, 1902) 162–6.
76. D. S. MacColl, 'Painting and Imitation', *Spectator*, LXVIII (18 June 1892) 846. Cf. his 'Notes on a Recent Controversy', *Spectator*, LXX (1 Apr 1893) 421; and Image's remarks on design as self-sufficient pictorial arrangement in 'On Design', *Century Guild Hobby Horse*, II (1887) 117–18.
77. D. S. MacColl, 'The New English Art Club', *Spectator*, LXIX (26 Nov 1892) 769; see also his 'Handling: A Reply', *Spectator*, LXIX (24 Dec 1892) 925.
78. D. S. MacColl, 'Notes on a Recent Controversy', *Spectator*, LXX (1 Apr 1893) 421.
79. See *Illustrated Memoir of Charles Wellington Furse, A. R. A.*, [ed. D. S. MacColl] (1908) 55–6; emphasis added.
80. C. J. Holmes, 'Nature and Landscape', *Dome*, n.s., II (Feb 1899) 140.
81. Walter Pater, *The Renaissance: Studies in Art and Poetry* (1873), 5th edn (1910) 205–7, 210–13, 218–24 (quotations from 211).
82. Symons, 'George Meredith's Poetry', *Westminster Review*, 128 (Sep 1887) 696. See W. S. Peterson, 'Arthur Symons as a Browningite', *RES*, XIX (1968) 148–57, and Karl Beckson and John M. Munro, 'Symons, Browning, and the

Development of the Modern Aesthetic', *Studies in English Literature 1500–1900*, x (1970) 687–99.

83. Symons, *An Introduction to the Study of Browning* (1886) 6–7, 9, 11, 53, 72 (emphasis added). See also his 'Browning's Last Poems', *Academy*, xxxvii (11 Jan 1890) 19.

84. For details of Symons's new French contacts, see Temple, *The Critic's Alchemy*, 123; and Roger Lhombreaud, *Arthur Symons: A Critical Biography* (1963) 61, 66, 68.

85. Symons: 'Browning's Last Poems', *Academy*, xxxvii (11 Jan 1890) 19; review of Verlaine's *Bonheur*, *Academy*, xxxix (18 Apr 1891) 362–3.

86. Lhombreaud, *Arthur Symons*, 77.

87. Cf. his enthusiastic comments on Moore's *Modern Painting* in 'The Painting of the Nineteenth Century', *Fortnightly Review*, n.s., lxxiii (Mar 1903) 522.

88. Review in *Academy*, xxxix (21 Mar 1891) 274.

89. See Lhombreaud, *Arthur Symons*, 92.

90. Symons, 'Mr Henley's Poetry', *Fortnightly Review*, n.s., lii (Aug 1892) 190.

91. Ibid., 184; cf. his 'The Decadent Movement in Literature', *Harper's Monthly Magazine*, 522 (Nov 1893) 867.

92. W. E. Henley, *Poems* (1921) 135–6. Robert L. Peters, 'Whistler and the English Poets of the 1890s', *Modern Language Quarterly*, xviii (1957) 260, indicates the parallel with Whistler.

93. Henley, *Poems*, 192–8 (quotations from 196–8).

94. Symons, 'Paul Verlaine', *Black and White*, i (20 June 1891) 649; and 'Paul Verlaine', *National Review*, xix (June 1892) 501, 503. Cf. Symons's comments on *Romances sans paroles* in 'The Decadent Movement in Literature', *Harper's Monthly Magazine*, 522, p. 861.

95. Ibid., 858–9.

96. Ibid., 862, 859, 860, 866–7, 859.

97. Ibid., 864.

98. See Symons, 'At the "Chat Noir"', *Black and White*, iv (24 Dec 1892) 736–7; and 'Paul Verlaine', *National Review*, xix, 503. Edward Baugh in his unpublished PhD thesis, 'A Critical Study of the Writings of Arthur Symons with Particular Reference to his Poetry and Literary Criticism' (Manchester University, 1964) 156, also indicates this parallel.

99. Symons, 'The Decadent Movement in Literature', *Harper's Monthly Magazine*, 522, pp. 864–5. See also his 'An Apology for Puppets', *Saturday Review*, lxxxiv (17 July 1897) 55–6; and 'Pantomime and Poetic Drama', *Dome*, n.s., i (Oct 1898) 67–9. The subjective, 'suggestive' element in 'impressionism is emphasised in Symons's distinction between 'impressionism' and simple observation or description in 'Richard Jefferies', *Studies in Two Literatures* (1897) 225–6.

100. Symons, *Silhouettes*, 1st edn (1892) 81.

101. Paul Verlaine, *Œuvres poétiques*, ed. Jacques Robichez (Paris, 1976) 154, 156.

102. Symons: *Silhouettes*, 2nd edn (1896) 15; *Silhouettes*, 1st edn, 29; *London Nights* (1895) 16. See also his 'Pastel', *Silhouettes*, 1st edn, 13; 'At the Cavour', *Silhouettes*, 2nd edn, 27; the first two lines of 'Renée' and the first stanza of 'On the Stage', *London Nights*, 6, 15.

103. Symons, *Silhouettes*, 1st edn, 8–9; rev. version, *Silhouettes*, 2nd edn, 7.

104. Symons, 'For a Picture by Walter Sickert (Hôtel Royal, Dieppe)', *Academy*,

XLIV (23 Sep 1893) 252; rev. version in *London Nights*, 32.

105. Symons's 'In Autumn', *Silhouettes*, 1st edn, 89, also employs the year's decline as a sympathetic metaphor for the poet's emotional desolation.
106. Ibid., 4–5.
107. Verlaine, *Œuvres poétiques*, 36–40, 158.
108. Letter from Dowson to Arthur Moore, c. 1891, quoted in Desmond Flowers, Introduction to his edn of *The Poetical Works of Dowson* (1934) xxii.
109. Symons, *Silhouettes*, 1st edn, 86. See also his 'Veneta Marina', *London Nights*, 53; the feeble pastiche Verlaine of 'Absinthe. (Souvenir de Dieppe)', *Senate*, II (Oct 1895) 384; and 'For a Picture of Watteau', *Silhouettes*, 1st edn, 94–5. Cf. Verlaine, *Œuvres poétiques*, 92, 83, 147–8, 149.
110. Symons, *Silhouettes*, 1st edn, 56.
111. Ibid., p. 7. Cf. Symons's 'Twilight', *Amoris Victima* (1897) 26.
112. For details of the personal factors involved, see John M. Munro, 'Arthur Symons and W. B. Yeats: the Quest for Compromise', *Dalhousie Review*, XLV (1965) 140–2, and his *Arthur Symons* (New York, 1969) 40, 54–5, 61–3; Lhombreaud, *Arthur Symons*, 171–2.
113. See William M. Murphy, *Prodigal Father: The Life of John Butler Yeats (1839–1922)* (Ithaca, NY, and London, 1978) 581.
114. Symons, 'Maeterlinck as a Mystic', *Contemporary Review*, n.s., LXXII (Sep 1897) 351.
115. Symons first restricted 'decadence' to this stylistic acceptation in 'A Note on George Meredith', *Fortnightly Review*, n.s., LXII (Nov 1897) 677. Prudence, following Wilde's conviction and the collapse of the *Savoy*, doubtless counselled Symons's revision of the original title as advertised in the *Savoy*, 8 (Dec 1896) 93. For detailed and balanced evaluation of the volume, see Temple, *The Critic's Alchemy*, 153–65; Frank Kermode, *Romantic Image* (1971) 122–32; John M. Munro, *Arthur Symons*, 64–70.
116. Symons, *The Symbolist Movement in Literature* (1899) 10.
117. Symons, *Silhouettes*, 1st edn, 41–2; dated 'Paris October 1, 1889' in a manuscript at Harvard (Lhombreaud, *Arthur Symons*, 311).
118. Symons, *London Nights*, 24. Symons's later 'The Dance of the Daughters of Herodias' employs dance as a metaphor for the sexually destructive power of all women; see his *Images of Good and Evil* (1899) 42–8.
119. Symons, *London Nights*, 5; cf. the gestural description of 'Renée', ibid., 6.
120. Symons, *London Nights*, 7–8.
121. Ibid., 22.
122. See Kermode's masterly *Romantic Image*, 81–7; and 'Poet and Dancer Before Diaghilev', *Partisan Review*, XXVIII (1961) 48–75, particularly 55–73. Jan B. Gordon's 'The Danse Macabre of Arthur Symons' *London Nights*', *Victorian Poetry*, IX (1971) 429–43, deals stimulatingly with the topic, as does Ian Fletcher, 'Explorations and Recoveries – II: Symons, Yeats and the Demonic Dance', *London Magazine*, VII (June 1960) 46–60. See also Baugh, 'A Critical Study of the Writings of Arthur Symons', 101–23. For Mallarmé's account of the symbolic quality of dance, see *Œuvres complètes*, ed. Henri Mondor and G. Jean-Aubry (Paris, [1951]), 295–7, 303–7, and on Loïe Fuller in particular 307–9, 311–12.
123. See Symons: 'A New Art of the Stage', *Monthly Review*, VII. 3 (June 1902) 157–62; and 'The Price of Realism', *Academy*, LXIII (23 Aug 1902) 199–200. Cf.

Yeats, *Uncollected Prose*, II, 250–1, 292–3, 391–4, 401.

124. Cf. nn. 98 and 99; Symons, *The Symbolist Movement*, 153–4, 158–9; and his 'Eleonora Duse', *Contemporary Review*, LXXVIII (Aug 1900) 199–202.

125. See Symons: 'Ballet, Pantomime and Poetic Drama: Theories of Art', *Dome*, n.s., I (Oct 1898) 65–71; and 'Bayreuth: Notes on Wagner', *Dome*, n.s., IV (Sep 1899) 146–9.

126. Symons, 'The World as Ballet', *Dome*, n.s., I (Oct 1898) 67 (emphasis added).

127. Symons, *London Nights*, 7.

128. Yeats, *Uncollected Prose*, II, 285. For Yeats's interest in the stylization of Todhunter's poetic dramas and the hieratic acting style of Florence Farr, see *Letters to the New Island*, 112–14, 115–17, 134, 217–18.

129. Comments from 1902 and 1903, repr. in Yeats, *Explorations*, 87, 109 (emphasis added). See also ibid., 110.

130. See Symons: 'Mr Yeats as a Lyric Poet', *Saturday Review*, LXXXVII (6 May 1899) 553; and 'Mr Yeats' New Play', *Saturday Review*, XC (29 Dec 1900) 825.

131. Symons, 'The Lesson of Parsifal', *Dome*, n.s., I (Oct 1898) 71, 69.

132. Ibid., 69–70; cf. Symons's 'The Price of Realism', *Academy*, LXIII (23 Aug 1902) 200. Yeats describes the conception of the 'stage picture' in *Uncollected Prose*, II, 250; and *Explorations*, 178–9.

133. Symons, 'Bayreuth', *Dome*, n.s., IV, 149.

134. Ibid., 147–8; cf. the remarks on 'elemental music' on 149. By 1904 at least Symons was familiar with Schopenhauer's aesthetic, but probably read much earlier Haldane and Kemp's translation of *The World as Will and Idea* (1883–6), a favourite text of the *fin de siècle*; cf. Symons's *Studies in Seven Arts* (1907) 193–7. In March 1899 William Ashton Ellis had published an article in the *Fortnightly Review* (to which Symons regularly contributed) on Wagner's use of Schopenhauer's ideas, placing both in an anti-materialist context; see David S. Thatcher, *Nietzsche in England 1890–1914* (Toronto, 1970) 183.

135. Symons, 'Rodin', *Fortnightly Review*, n.s., LXXI (June 1902) 957 (emphasis added).

136. Yeats, *Essays and Introductions*, 268–9; this section was originally entitled 'A Banjo Player'.

137. Symons, 'Rodin', *Fortnightly Review*, n.s., LXXI, 957–8, 960, 967. He reiterated this animistic argument forcefully apropos Rodin and Carrière in *Studies in Seven Arts*, 46–8.

138. D. S. MacColl, *Nineteenth Century Art*, 67, 68; similar remarks are made on Corot on 79–80. Cf. Arthur Symons, 'The Painting of the Nineteenth Century', *Fortnightly Review*, n.s., LXXIII (March 1903) 524–6.

NOTES TO CHAPTER 3: THE MOVEMENT TOWARDS IMAGISM

1. Pound's term for them in 1912; see his *Shorter Poems*, 269.

2. See Wallace Martin, 'The Sources of the Imagist Aesthetic', *PMLA*, 85 (1970) 198.

3. Ibid., 196, 201–2.

4. MSS in Keele University Library; sheets corresponding to *FS*, 90, 80–1.

5. Théodule Ribot, *L'Évolution des idées générales* (Paris, 1897) 15.

6. Ibid., 127–8.

7. Ibid., 147, 253.

8. Ibid., 151–4 (quotations from 153); quoted also by Martin, 'Sources of the Imagist Aesthetic', *PMLA*, 85, p. 200.

9. Cf. *FS*, 15–20, 22–3. Martin (*PMLA*, 85, p. 201) indicates, but gives no account of, Hulme's interest in Gaultier.

10. Jules de Gaultier, *Le Bovarysme* (1892; 2nd edn, Paris, 1902) 60–2.

11. See, for example, ibid., 195–8, 210–12, 245–6.

12. Ibid., 272–3, 281–2, 294–8.

13. Cf. *Spec*, 223 §2, 229§2–4, 230 §2. Hulme's use of 'solid bank', 'pier', derives from Gaultier's 'digue' in *Le Bovarysme*, 282. Compare Hulme's attack on Haldane's Idealism in *FS*, 8–9, 12–13.

14. Cf. *FS*, 13–14; and Hulme, 'The New Philosophy', *New Age*, v (1 July 1909) 198. A major source, as yet unnoticed, for Hulme's argument on the crucial importance of authentic perceptual experience in creating a vivid, original style appears to be Schopenhauer. There are astonishingly close verbal parallels between Hulme's phraseology and that in *WWR*, ii, 71–3. The whole of Chapter 7, 'On the Relation of Knowledge of Perception to Abstract Knowledge' (ii, 71–90) is relevant.

15. Cf. *FS*, 46–55. Hulme's quotations from Laplace and Huxley derive from Bergson's *L'Évolution créatrice* (1907), repr. in *Œuvres* (Paris, 1959) 526–7.

16. I disagree therefore with Stanley K. Coffman's emphasis in *Imagism: A Chapter for the History of Modern Poetry* (1951; repr. New York, 1972) 58, 81–4.

17. See, for example, Michael Roberts, *T. E. Hulme* (1938); and Alun R. Jones, *The Life and Opinions of T. E. Hulme* (1960). The best critical accounts of Hulme are those by Wallace Martin in *The 'New Age' under Orage: Chapters in English Cultural History* (Manchester, 1967), and 'Sources of the Imagist Aesthetic', *PMLA*, 85, pp. 196–204. See also J. B. Harmer, *Victory in Limbo: Imagism 1908–1917* (1975); and Coffman, *Imagism*.

18. Martin, *The 'New Age' under Orage*, 172.

19. Both claim that Hulme was not wholeheartedly impressed by Bergson's ideas (Roberts, *Hulme*, 86; Jones, *Life and Opinions of Hulme*, 62, 65). Jones adds preposterously that 'Bergson's philosophy, properly interpreted in terms of literature, leads, inevitably, to the kind of novels written by Proust' (ibid., 43).

20. See *FS*, 72 (quoted *infra*, pp. 76–7).

21. Hulme never severed the connection completely, however; he, Flint and Pound contributed to *The Book of the Poets' Club* at Christmas 1909.

22. My discussion is confined to Hulme and Flint. The work of the others does not repay investigation; for an account see Harmer, *Victory in Limbo*.

23. On the question of indebtedness and who influenced whom (or Hulme?) see Martin's wise comments in *The 'New Age' under Orage*, 149–50, and *A Catalogue of the Imagist Poets*, ed. J. H. Woolmer (New York, 1966) 11; Christopher Middleton's cogent 'Documents on Imagism from the Papers of F. S. Flint', *Review*, xv (Apr 1965) 33–51; and the rather sterile discussion in Cyrena Pondrom's 'Hulme's "A Lecture on Modern Poetry" and The Birth of Imagism', *Papers on Language and Literature*, v (1969) 465–70.

24. Alun Jones, 'Imagism: a Unity of Gesture', *Stratford-upon-Avon Studies: 7. American Poetry* (1965) 120. Hulme paraphrases Cézanne's remark, recorded by Denis: 'something solid and durable, like the art of the museums'.

25. *Spec*, 125. Hulme could admittedly have first read Denis's article on Cézanne in

*L'Occident*, Sep. 1907, or, more accessibly, in Roger Fry's translation in the *Burlington Magazine*, xvi (Jan, Feb 1910) 207–19, 275–80. There is, however, no evidence in Hulme's writings prior to 1912 to suggest an awareness of developments in contemporary European art.

26. Albert Gleizes and Jean Metzinger, *Du Cubisme* (Paris, 1912); English trs., *Cubism* (1913), referred to in *Spec*, 103.

27. Jones: 'Imagism', *Stratford-upon-Avon Studies: 7*, 126; and *Life and Opinions of Hulme*, 93.

28. Jones, 'Imagism', *Stratford-upon-Avon Studies: 7*, 127.

29. See Richard Cork, *Vorticism and Abstract Art in the First Machine Age*, 2 vols (London, Berkeley Calif., and Los Angeles, 1976) 165ff., 172–6, 454–82.

30. Jones, *Life and Opinions of Hulme*, 104.

31. See William C. Wees, 'England's *Avant-Garde*: The Futurist–Vorticist Phase', *Western Humanities Review*, xxi (1967) 121; and Cork, *Vorticism and Abstract Art*, 139. Cf. Wilhelm Worringer, *Abstraktion und Einfühlung* (1908), 3rd edn (Munich, 1910), trs. Michael Bullock as *Abstraction and Empathy* (1953).

32. Cf. TLS from Hulme to Flint, postmarked 21 Feb 1913, HRC, Texas. Against D. L. Murray's chronologically dubious recollection (quoted in Jones, *Life and Opinions of Hulme*, 92) that as early as autumn 1911 Hulme was inspired by the 'non-humanistic' *plastique* of the Diaghilev Ballet should be set the contemporary evidence of Hulme's 'Bergson's Theory of Art' (Nov–Dec 1911), where he cites approvingly Berenson's empathetic aesthetics, which is completely congruent with the views of Bergson and Lipps. Cf. *Spec*, 168, with Bernhard Berenson, *The Florentine Painters* (1896), repr. in *The Italian Painters of the Renaissance* (1960) 55–6, and Theodor Lipps, *Ästhetik: Psychologie des Schönen und der Kunst*, 2 vols (Hamburg and Leipzig, 1903–6) i, 140.

33. Cf., for example, Bergson, *Œuvres* , 74–80, 755–60, 1377–92, 1410–16.

34. Ibid., 36–9.

35. Ibid., 80–92, 495–578, 747–807.

36. Ibid., 319–21, 460, 630–2.

37. Ibid., 86–7. Nietzsche had commented incisively on language's ineluctable glossing over of individual qualities in the interests of generally intelligible communication, and on the blurring of perceptual clarity in linguistic abstraction and conceptualisation in 'Über Wahrheit und Lüge im aussermoralischen Sinn' (1873), *WdB*, iii, 309–22. See particularly 313ff.

38. Bergson, *Œuvres*, 103–14, 277.

39. Ibid., 85.

40. Cf. *WWR*, i, 176–8; ii, 283–92. Schopenhauer's explanation of this state of affairs is, however, given a more élitist and sociological cast.

41. Bergson, *Œuvres*, 458–62. 1370–3.

42. Ibid., 1373.

43. Ibid., 1360–5.

44. Ibid., 1394, 1395. Cf. 645 and 784–5, where 'intuition' is again defined as 'sympathie'.

45. Lipps, *Ästhetik*, i, 91–4. (All translations mine.)

46. Ibid., 106–7.

47. Ibid., 140; ii, 28–32.

48. Ibid., 25.

49. Ibid., i, 120; cf. i 192.

50. Ibid., II, 88; cf. I, 122–5, 173.

51. His potted history of French developments derives often *verbatim* from André Beaunier, *La Poésie nouvelle*, 2nd edn (Paris, 1902) 10–11, 31–2, 44. For his debt to Gustave Kahn, see Wallace Martin, *The 'New Age' under Orage*, 157–8.

52. *FS*, 68, 70–2; quotations from 68, 72, 71. Tom Gibbons, *Rooms in the Darwin Hotel* (Nedlands, Western Australia, 1973) 74–6, 96–7, also remarks on the similarity with Symons.

53. *FS*, 70, 71–2. For Symons's suspicion of *vers libre* see his review of Verlaine's *Bonheur*, *Academy*, XXXIX (18 Apr 1891) 362; and 'Mr Henley's Poetry', *Fortnightly Review*, n.s., LII (Aug 1892) 192.

54. Martin, 'Sources of the Imagist Aesthetic', *PMLA*, 85, pp. 199, 200–1, has noted Hulme's reading of Ribot's *Essai sur l'imagination créatrice* but argues for an extended influence only in Pound's case. Hulme's indebtedness is, I believe, much clearer and more important.

55. Théodule Ribot, *Essai sur l'imagination créatrice* (1900), 6th edn (Paris, 1921) 169.

56. Ibid., 164.

57. Ibid., 153–4.

58. Bergson, *Œuvres*, 1401–2.

59. Ibid., 15–16.

60. Ibid., 14 (emphasis added).

61. Yeats, *Essays and Introductions*, 159, 163.

62. Alan Robinson, 'New Sources for Imagism', *Notes and Queries*, n.s., XXVII (1980) 238–40. For further instances of Hulme's application of the 'counter' approach, see *FS*, 77–9, 81, 9–11; *Spec*, 134–5, 151–2, 165–6.

63. For discussion of this point see Robinson, 'New Sources for Imagism', *Notes and Queries*, n.s., XXVII, 238–40.

64. On the dustjacket of Pound's *Ripostes* (Oct 1912), in which Hulme's 'Complete Poetical Works' were reprinted from the *New Age*, 25 Jan 1912, Hulme is termed a 'metaphysician'.

65. Cf. *Spec*, 154, with Bergson, *Œuvres*, 461.

66. Cf. his remarks on the 'classical style' (*Spec*, 120) and on 'modern' style (*FS*, 73). Another possible influence on Hulme's tone is the Japanese *haikai*, light or humorous linked-verse, discussed by the 'forgotten school' (cf. n. 81).

67. See Jones, *Life and Opinions of Hulme*, 177, 178.

68. MS loose sheet in Keele University Library.

69. See Jones, *Life and Opinions of Hulme*, 176; *Spec*, 267; *FS*, 217.

70. *FS*, 216, 214; cf. *Some Imagist Poets: An Anthology* (Boston, Mass., and New York, 1915) 28.

71. *FS*, 217; Jones, *Life and Opinions of Hulme*, 179, corrected by MS reading at Keele; *FS*, 218.

72. TS with A additions in HRC, Texas. Dated by references to two poems, 'To the Winds' (9 Apr 1907) and 'Limitations' (12 Apr 1907), there implied to be recently composed.

73. The passage beginning 'La contemplation des objets', ending with 'déchiffre-ments', in Stéphane Mallarmé, *Œuvres complètes*, ed. Henri Mondor and G. Jean-Aubry (Paris, [1951]) 869. Flint selects another passage from Mallarmé's interview with Huret as the epigraph to 'Recent Verse', *New Age*, III (15 Aug 1908) 312–13; cf. Mallarmé, *Œuvres complètes*, 867.

74. Pound, 'A Few Don'ts' (1913), repr. in *Literary Essays* 5.

75. F. S. Flint, 'Recent Verse', *New Age*, III (29 Aug 1908) 352–3.
76. Flint alludes to Yeats's 'Magic', repr. in *Essays and Introductions*, 48, and cites 'The Symbolism of Poetry', repr. ibid., 155, and *The Countess Cathleen*, ll. 946–8, *Variorum Plays*, 169. He had castigated 'concrete' symbolism earlier in 'Of the thing called "symbolism" ', [3] and [4].
77. Flint, 'Recent Verse', *New Age*, III, 352–3. On his distrust of hermetic symbolism, see 'Verse', *New Age*, V (30 Sep 1909) 412.
78. Flint, 'Recent Verse', *New Age*, III, 352. Flint is alluding also to Shelley's 'Defence of Poetry'; see *English Critical Essays: Nineteenth Century*, ed. Edmund D. Jones (1971) 110.
79. Flint, 'Recent Verse', *New Age*, III, 353.
80. Cf. for example his remarks on H. B. Binn's *The Good Companions*, Rhys's *The Masque of the Grail*, and a Miss Skovgaard-Pedersen's *Sea-Dreams, and Others*, in 'Recent Verse', *New Age*, III (15, 29 Aug 1908) 313, 353, and IV (24 Dec 1908) 186. For Flint's defence *contra* Ford of escapism see his 'Verse', *New Age*, VI (6 Jan 1910) 234.
81. This was apparently the forgotten school's principal area of activity. Experiments in *vers libre* accompanied those in the Japanese *tanka* and *haikai* forms, 'poems in a sacred Hebrew form, of which "This is the House that Jack Built" is a perfect model' and 'rhymeless poems like Hulme's "Autumn" '; see F. S. Flint, 'The History of Imagism', *Egoist*, II (1 May 1915) 71.
82. F. S. Flint, 'Recent Verse', *New Age*, III (11 July 1908) 212–13.
83. Flint, 'Recent Verse', *New Age*, III, 312. Cf. his 'Recent Verse', *New Age*, IV (26 Nov. 1908) 95; 'Verse', *New Age*, V (30 Sep 1909) 412, and VI, 234. His survey of French poets – 'Contemporary French Poetry', *Poetry Review*, I (1912) 355–414 – is essentially a study of how they use *vers libre*.
84. F. S. Flint, *In the Net of the Stars* (1909) 61–2.
85. Ibid., 14–15. For other examples of the theme of escapist vision, see 'As I Paced the Streets', 'Sunday in London' and 'The Heart's Hunger': ibid., 11–12, 13, 15–16.
86. See 'Foreword', ibid., 43.
87. Ibid., 30–1; cf. Pound, 'Apparuit', in *Early Poems*, 182–3.
88. Flint, *In the Net*, 43–56; cf. Pound, *Early Poems*, 117–20. The derivativeness is exacerbated by an obvious debt in the diction of the more sensual poems to the Song of Solomon, although this is tempered by the chaster imagery of Symbolist art.
89. See Flint, *In the Net*, 46–7, 45–6.
90. See, for example, Verlaine's 'Promenade sentimentale' in his *Œuvres poétiques*, ed. Jacques Robichez (Paris, 1976) 37.
91. Flint, *In the Net*, 17.
92. See, for example, Pound's 'Grace Before Song' and 'Anima Sola' in *Early Poems*, 7, 19–21; cf. Flint, *In the Net*, 24.
93. Ibid., 29–30. Compare the use of hair in 'The Forest of Vision' (67–8) as the locus of a world of imaginative release and emotional security – although here the conception, rather than the idiom, may also be coloured by recollections of the similar functions of Baudelairian 'chevelure'.
94. Ibid., 30.
95. Ibid., 35–8.
96. Ibid., 66.

NOTES TO CHAPTER 4: THE NEW 'CLASSICISM'

1. Ronald Schuchard, 'Eliot and Hulme in 1916: Toward a Revaluation of Eliot's Critical and Spiritual Development', *PMLA*, 88 (Oct 1973) 1085.
2. On Edwardian fears of degeneration and physical deterioration, see Tom Gibbons, *Rooms in the Darwin Hotel* (Nedlands, Western Australia, 1973) 25–6, 34–5; Samuel Hynes, *The Edwardian Turn of Mind* (1968) 19–33.
3. David S. Thatcher, *Nietzsche in England 1890–1914* (Toronto, 1970) 42.
4. *WdB*, ii, 776–7, 786–9, 825–6, 833–4, 881–3, 899–900, 979–82.
5. See Nietzsche's important illustrative parables of the coal and the diamond, and the bird of prey and the lamb: *WdB*, ii, 460, requoted 1033; 789–93.
6. *WdB*, ii, 780–1, 795–7, 936–7, 981–2, 1189.
7. *WdB*, i, 270; ii, 279, 340, 351, 465.
8. *WdB*, ii, 622–4, 817, 863, 1111, 1125–6, 1159, 1165–8.
9. *WdB*, i, 1130–1; ii, 284–5, 605–7, 671, 689–90, 728–9, 735–7, 1014–5.
10. *WdB*, ii, 728, 819, 1127–8; i, 676 §462.
11. Thatcher, *Nietzsche in England 1890–1914*, 205.
12. Ibid., 235. On Orage's faith in an evolutionary élite see Gibbons, *Rooms in the Darwin Hotel*, 108–10.
13. For some comments on the *New Age* writers, see ibid., 27–8, 32, 33; and Wallace Martin, *The 'New Age' under Orage: Chapters in English Cultural History* (Manchester, 1967) 213, 214, 219–34, who also discusses the later impact of Hulme's views.
14. See Gibbons, *Rooms in the Darwin Hotel*, 27–33, who quotes the Nietzsche passage (*WdB*, ii, 917) on 31.
15. Anthony Ludovici, *Nietzsche and Art* (1911) 8.
16. Ibid., 99–100.
17. Ibid., 43, 45–8. On the Romantic artist's lack of self-control, echoing Nietzsche's strictures on contemporary 'paralysis of the will', cf. J. M. Kennedy, *English Literature 1880–1905* (1912) 22–4.
18. Ludovici, *Nietzsche and Art*, 53.
19. Nietzsche had derided Naturalism in passing; see, for example, *WdB*, ii, 212, 994–5.
20. Ludovici, *Nietzsche and Art*, 55–6, vii.
21. Ibid., 63–97.
22. Ibid., 103–11 (quotation from 107).
23. Ibid., 125, 122–3, 162, 168–70.
24. Ibid., 210–11. In 'The Italian Futurists and their Traditionalism', *Oxford and Cambridge Review*, no. 21 (July 1912) 94–122, Ludovici termed these the 'masterly' and 'slavish' visions in art. See 107–9 for the definition, and 109–22 for its crass application.
25. Ludovici, *Nietzsche and Art*, 217; see also 224–6. Wilhelm Worringer had taken similar examples from Egypt; cf. his *Abstraction and Empathy* (1953) 11–12.
26. Ludovici, *Nietzsche and Art*, vii–viii.
27. J. M. Kennedy, *Tory Democracy* (1911) 7.
28. *New Age*, ix (10 Aug 1911) 341, repr. in *Tory Democracy*, 24. See also Kennedy, *English Literature*, 247–8.
29. *New Age*, ix (29 June 1911) 197. The version in *Tory Democracy*, 58–9, differs slightly.

30. *New Age*, IX, 197; *Tory Democracy*, 61–2. This recalls Charles Maurras's view of the King's role as anti-parliamentary 'superior arbiter'. On this see Eugen Weber, *Action française* (Stanford, Calif., 1962) 28–9.

31. Kennedy, *Tory Democracy*, 117.

32. J. M. Kennedy, 'Eupeptic Politicians. V: Protestantism', *New Age*, X (11 Apr 1912) 569.

33. J. M. Kennedy, 'Eupeptic Politicians. I: The Distinction', *New Age*, X (7 Mar 1912) 445.

34. J. M. Kennedy, 'Eupeptic Politicians. II: Mr Masterman's Diagnosis', *New Age*, X (14 Mar 1912) 466. Samuel Hynes in *The Edwardian Turn of Mind*, ch. 3, 54–86, discusses Masterman's evangelical attitude.

35. My translation. The whole section *WdB*, I, 265–76, is relevant; see also I, 217, 319.

36. Kennedy, *English Literature*, 247.

37. Kennedy, *Tory Democracy*, 27; 'lords of the manor' replaces the less grandiose 'the county families', which Kennedy had written in *New Age*, IX (10 Aug 1911) 341. See also *Tory Democracy*, 158.

38. Ibid., 123–33. On 90–1 he attacks Liberal legislation and the 'People's Budget' of 1909. Kennedy had written in 1910, 'Speaking as one who is, on the whole, a Conservative, I have no hesitation in saying that we Tories feel we have much more in common with the Socialists than with the Liberals' – ' "New Age" Policy' (letter), *New Age*, VII (14 July 1910) 261.

39. Kennedy, *Tory Democracy*, 186–95.

40. Ibid., 170.

41. Kennedy, *English Literature*, 8–9 (pp. 7–27 are all relevant).

42. See G. R. Searle, 'Critics of Edwardian Society: The Case of the Radical Right', in Alan O'Day (ed.), *The Edwardian Age: Conflict and Stability 1900–1914* (1979) 79–96.

43. Storer: 'The Conservative Ideal. A Coming Movement', *Commentator*, II (11 Jan 1911) 139; 'Sword and Shield', *Commentator*, IV (6 Mar 1912) 228. Hulme ('Thomas Gratton'): 'A Note on the Art of Political Conversion', *Commentator*, II (1 Mar 1911) 250; 'The Art of Political Conversion', *Commentator*, II (19 April 1911) 357–8; 'Theory and Practice', *Commentator*, III (8 Nov 1911) 388.

44. See Edward R. Tannenbaum, *The Action Française* (New York, 1962) 65–87; Weber, *Action Française*, 22.

45. Hulme, 'Note on the Art of Political Conversion', *Commentator*, II, 250.

46. Hulme: review of *L'Attitude du lyrisme contemporain*, *New Age*, IX (24 Aug 1911) 400–1; 'On Progress and Democracy', *Commentator*, III (2, 9 Aug 1911) 165–6, 179–80; 'Bergson Lecturing' [signed 'Thomas Gratton'], *New Age*, X (2 Nov 1911) 15–16.

47. Pierre Lasserre, *Le Romantisme français*, 3rd edn (Paris, 1907) 311, 17–18, 340, 71–4.

48. Quoted ibid., 325.

49. Ibid., 418.

50. Ibid., 536–7.

51. Storer, 'The Romantic Conception of History', *Commentator*, II (25 Jan 1911) 170–1.

52. See Douglas Goldring, *South Lodge* (1943) 71.

53. George Dangerfield, *The Strange Death of Liberal England* (1935; repr. 1966) 181–2.

54. Storer, 'On Revolution and Revolutionaries', *Commentator*, ii (8 Feb 1911) 203.

55. Storer, 'Some Reflections on Rembrandt's "Mill"', *Commentator*, ii (22 Mar 1911) 298. See also *Commentator*, iii (1911) 38, 140.

56. Storer, 'The Evil of Democracy. A Word to all Patriots', *Commentator*, ii (29 Mar 1911) 307.

57. Storer, 'The Chorus', *Commentator*, ii (3 May 1911) 390–1.

58. Storer, 'Democracy and Letters', *Commentator*, ii (12 Apr 1911) 342–3; 'Our Saviours', *Commentator*, iii (19 July 1911) 140; 'Art', *Commentator*, iii (4 Oct 1911) 315.

59. Storer's comment (*Commentator*, iii, 315) that 'The artists of the eighteenth century had few illusions about democracy and the sovereignty of the people. They knew that art would find short shrift at the hands of the populace. They knew that art is an aristocratic thing, the flower of leisure and repose' recalls Yeats's 'Upon a House shaken by the Land Agitation', written in August 1909, his first impassioned claim that flourishing culture depends on aristocratic values which are incompatible with the compromises of the everyday, commercial world. See Yeats: *Variorum Poems*, 264; *Memoirs*, 225–6.

60. All succeeding references in this paragraph to Hulme, 'Mr Balfour, Bergson and Politics', *New Age*, x (9 Nov 1911) 39–40.

61. Ibid., 40.

62. AMS notes on lectures of Henri Bergson (Paris 1910–11); AMS paper on Bergson (Paris 1910–11); AMS [Relation between Politics and Metaphysics], all held in the Houghton Library, Harvard University. In his article 'Eliot and Hulme in 1916', Ronald Schuchard makes a persuasive case for the influence on Eliot of Hulme's ideas, supplemented by their French sources, from as early as 1916, although Schuchard's assertion that Hulme and Eliot met is, Mrs Valerie Eliot assures me authoritatively, unfounded (TLS, 10 Nov 1981). The lecture I have summarised, however, suggests that Eliot was already moving independently towards a form of absolutism in ethics before he could have read Hulme's articles and that Hulme was accordingly not so momentous a catalyst as Schuchard believes.

63. Hulme, 'On Progress and Democracy', *Commentator*, iii (2 Aug 1911) 165–6. Cf. his 'A Tory Philosophy', *Commentator*, iv (3 Apr 1912) 295, repr. in Alun R. Jones, *The Life and Opinions of T. E. Hulme* (1960) 189–90, for the addition of the more familiar, 'religious' element to this attitude.

64. Hulme, 'On Progress and Democracy', *Commentator*, iii (9 Aug 1911) 179. Also see particularly, 'A Tory Philosophy', *Commentator*, iv (10 Apr 1912) 310, repr. in Jones, *Life and Opinions of Hulme* 192–3; *Spec*, 116.

65. *Commentator*, iii, 179, repeated in *Commentator*, iv, 295, repr. in Jones, *Life and Opinions of Hulme*, 189–91. Cf. also Hulme's distinction between intellectual 'capacity' and 'content' in *Commentator*, iv, 380, 388, repr. in Jones, *Life and Opinions of Hulme*, 196–8.

66. Paraphrased and quoted by Hulme in *Commentator*, iii, 180.

67. Hulme, 'Theory and Practice', *Commentator*, iii (15 Nov 1911) 404–5. Cf. *Spec*, 116–17; and *Commentator*, iv, 388, repr. in Jones, *Life and Opinions of Hulme*, 198. See Henri Bergson, *Œuvres* (Paris, 1959) 548–9.

68. *Commentator*, iv, 362, repr. in Jones, *Life and Opinions of Hulme*, 194–5.

NOTES TO CHAPTER 5: TOWARDS ABSTRACTION

1. *Futurist Manifestos*, ed. Umbro Apollonio (1973) 98; 'New Futurist Manifesto', trs. Arundel del Re, *Poetry and Drama*, I (1913) 323. Cf. *FS*, 73.

2. Hugh Kenner, *The Pound Era*, paperback edn (Berkeley, Calif., and Los Angeles, 1973) 238; Robert H. Ross, *The Georgian Revolt: Rise and Fall of a Poetic Ideal 1910–22* (1967) 61; Hugh Witemeyer, *The Poetry of Ezra Pound: Forms and Renewal, 1908–1920* (Berkeley, Calif., and Los Angeles, 1969) 183. Geoffrey Wagner gives a similar account of Futurism: see his *Wyndham Lewis: A Portrait of the Artist as the Enemy* (1957) 127–36.

3. See William C. Wees, 'England's *Avant-Garde*: The Futurist-Vorticist Phase', *Western Humanities Review*, XXI (1967) 117–28, and his *Vorticism and the English Avant-Garde* (Manchester, 1972); and William Lipke, 'Futurism and the Development of Vorticism', *Studio International*, 173 (Apr 1967) 173–9. Richard Cork also tacitly adopts this view of Futurism; see his *Vorticism and Abstract Art in the First Machine Age* (London, Berkeley, Calif., and Los Angeles, 1976).

4. Ronald Bush, *The Genesis of Ezra Pound's Cantos* (Princeton, NJ, 1976) 30, 31.

5. Werner Haftmann, *Painting in the Twentieth Century*, trs. Ralph Manheim, 2nd English edn (1965) I, 107, 153; G. H. Hamilton, *Painting and Sculpture in Europe 1880–1940*, paperback edn (Harmondsworth, 1972) 280, 284; Marianne W. Martin, *Futurist Art and Theory 1909–1915* (Oxford, 1968) 90. Jane Rye in the most recent account of the movement maintains this approach; see *Futurism*, 1972, pp. 11, 149. Alone among critics Joshua C. Taylor has seen a similarity in aim between Futurism and German Expressionism. His account in *Futurism* (New York, 1961) 11–13, touches on some of the points I raise, but his brief allusions to Bergsonism beg more questions than they answer. He tends, I feel, to interpret Bergson's continuous *évolution créatrice* in terms of motion and activity (revealingly he connects these ideas to 'a new kind of spiritual transport' Marinetti experienced through the speed of motoring) rather than Romantic animism. Our basic difference in viewpoint might perhaps be indicated by his distinction between the Futurists and Franz Marc on the lines that they sought mystical identity (whose nature in Futurist thought Taylor does not explain) 'not through contemplation but through action'.

6. Marinetti, *Futurist Manifestos*, 47, 30 §7, 92–3, 150–1, 179–80; Pound, *Translations*, 18–19.

7. See Bragaglia's Bergsonian arguments, and Boccioni's views from the same source, in *Futurist Manifestos*, 39, 40, 42–5, 88–9, 110; Wassily Kandinsky, *The Art of Spiritual Harmony*, trs. with an Introduction by M. T. H. Sadler (1914) 49, 52, 62–3, 91–2.

8. *Futurist Manifestos*, 48. Cf. 50, 52; 61 on Medardo Rosso; 63, 65, 90.

9. Ibid., 172–3, 177.

10. Frederick Goodyear, 'The New Thelema', *Rhythm*, I (Summer 1911) 1–3.

11. J. M. Murry, 'Art and Philosophy', *Rhythm*, I (Summer 1911) 9–12 (emphasis added). The 'veil' image, significantly without Murry's pantheistic implications, was used by Bergson in *Le Rire*; see *Œuvres*, 459. Murry may be conflating this passage with Shelley's 'Defence of Poetry'; see *English Critical Essays; Nineteenth Century*, ed. Edmund D. Jones (1971) 112. For Murry's enthusiasm for Bergson, and the origins of the title *Rhythm*, see his *Between Two*

*Worlds: An Autobiography* (1935) 126–8, 135, 155–7, 185; and F. A. Lea, *The Life of John Middleton Murry* (1959) 20–5, 27–9. See also Murry and Katherine Mansfield's 'The Meaning of Rhythm', *Rhythm*, ii (June 1912) 18–20, which when it occasionally departs from unreflecting jargon seems to fuse Bergsonian intuition with Nietzschean ideas similar to Ludovici's 'Ruler-art'.

12. See Huntly Carter, *The New Spirit in Drama and Art* (1912) 4–5, 46–7, 210, 215–16; Laurence Binyon, *The Flight of the Dragon* (1911) 12, 13, 15, 17–18.
13. Roger Fry, 'Post Impressionism', *Fortnightly Review*, n.s., lxxxix (May 1911) 856–67.
14. Bergson, *Œuvres*, 1363–5.
15. Fry, 'Post Impressionism', *Fortnightly Review*, n.s., lxxxix, 862, 857.
16. This was principally by the Fauves; see the list in Samuel Hynes, *The Edwardian Turn of Mind* (1968) 413.
17. This and succeeding references to Fry, 'Post Impressionism', *Fortnightly Review*, n.s., lxxxix, 867.
18. *Cambridge Magazine*, i (9 Mar 1912) 201. Cf. Hulme, 'A Tory Philosophy', *Commentator*, iv (15 May 1912) 388–9, repr. in Jones, *Life and Opinions of Hulme*, 199–201.
19. Storer, 'The Renaissance of the Nineties', *Commentator*, iii (5 July 1911) 108; cf. 'Art Notes', *Commentator*, ii (26 Apr 1911) 375. Cf. Nietzsche, 'Der Fall Wagner', *WdB*, ii, 912–20.
20. Storer, 'Art', *Commentator*, v (13, 20 Nov and 30 Oct 1912) 396, 415, 363. Cf. Hulme's use of 'damp', *Spec*, 127. Pound, *Early Poems*, 96–7.
21. Storer, 'Art', *Commentator*, v (26 June 1912) 78.
22. Storer, 'Art', *Commentator*, iii (18 Oct 1911) 348; iv (20 Dec 1911; 3 Apr; 1 May 1912) 76, 299, 364; v (23 Oct 1912) 347; vi (4, 11 Dec 1912) 27, 43.
23. Storer, 'On Hellenism', *Commentator*, v (4 Sep 1912) 237; 'Rodin and the Classical Ideal', *Commentator*, vi (26 Feb 1913) 203; 'Classicism and Modern Modes', *Academy*, lxxxv (6 Sep 1913) 293–4.
24. Storer, *William Cowper* [1912].
25. See note in *Poetry and Drama*, i (1913) 216; and Hulme, 'German Chronicle', *Poetry and Drama*, ii (June 1914) 221–8.
26. Hulme, 'Mr Epstein and the Critics', *New Age*, xiv (25 Dec 1913) 251–3, repr. in *FS*, 103–12.
27. Anthony Ludovici, 'Art', *New Age*, xiv (4, 18 Dec 1913) 152–3, 213–15.
28. Anthony Ludovici, 'Art', *New Age*, xiii (22 May 1913) 95, and, xiv (1 Jan 1914) 278–81. See also *New Age*, xiv (15 Jan 1914) 345–6.
29. Cf. Anthony Ludovici, 'The Italian Futurists and their Traditionalism', *Oxford and Cambridge Review*, no. 21 (July 1912) 109.
30. William Roberts, 'A Reply to my Biographer Sir John Rothenstein', 9, repr. in *The Vortex Pamphlets 1956–1958* (1958).
31. See Geoffrey Wagner: 'Wyndham Lewis and the Vorticist Aesthetic', *Journal of Aesthetics and Art Criticism*, xiii (1954–5) 1–17; and *Lewis: Portrait of the Artist*, 105–58.
32. On Gaudier's enthusiasm for Bergson compare letters quoted in H. S. Ede, *Savage Messiah* (1931) 40, 164, 169–70.
33. Edward Wadsworth, 'Inner Necessity', *Blast*, i (20 June 1914) 122.
34. Charles Ginner, 'Neo-Realism', *New Age*, xiv (1 Jan 1914) 271–2; *FS*, 120–8.
35. Alan Bowness, Introduction to *Post-Impressionism: Cross-Currents in European*

*Painting* (1979) 9. See Desmond MacCarthy, 'The Post-Impressionists', in *Manet and the Post-Impressionists* (1910) 7–8; and Roger Fry, 'Art', *Nation*, VIII (1910–11) 331–2. In the article Fry spoke of the 'photographic vision' of the nineteenth century and the 'science' of its art.

36. Desmond MacCarthy, 'The Art-Quake of 1910', *Listener*, XXXIII (1945) 124; Douglas Cooper, Introduction to *The Courtauld Collection: A Catalogue and Introduction*, (1954) 50.

37. MacCarthy, 'The Post-Impressionists', in *Manet and the Post-Impressionists*, 8, 8–9, 9, 11–12 (emphasis added).

38. Ginner, 'Neo-Realism', *New Age*, XIV, 272.

39. My chronological outline of German Expressionist painting derives from Peter Selz, *German Expressionist Painting*, paperback edn (Berkeley, Calif., Los Angeles and London, 1974); Hamilton, *Painting and Sculpture in Europe 1880–1940*; Wolf-Dieter Dube, *The Expressionists*, trs. Mary Whittall (1972).

40. Rose-Carol Washton Long has, however, demonstrated convincingly that even as late as 1914 Kandinsky still retained hidden eschatological iconography in what were accordingly not wholly abstract canvases. See her *Kandinsky: The Development of an Abstract Style* (Oxford, 1980) *passim*.

41. Wassily Kandinsky, 'Über die Formfrage', trs. in *Theories of Modern Art*, ed. Herschel B. Chipp (Berkeley, Calif., Los Angeles and London, 1968) 155–70; quotation from 170.

42. Kandinsky, *Art of Spiritual Harmony*, 92, 29–30. See also Selz, *German Expressionist Painting*, 175.

43. See Sixten Ringbom, 'Art in "The Epoch of the Great Spiritual"': Occult Elements in the Early Theory of Abstract Painting', *Journal of the Warburg and Courtauld Institutes*, XXIX (1966) 396. On the strikingly similar mysticism underlying Mondrian's adoption of abstraction, see Robert Rosenblum, *Modern Painting and the Northern Romantic Tradition: Friedrich to Rothko* (1975) 173–94.

44. Kandinsky, *Art of Spiritual Harmony*, 6, 28–40.

45. Kandinsky, in *Theories of Modern Art*, 156–8, 159; cf. his *Art of Spiritual Harmony*, 49–70.

46. Kandinsky, in *Theories of Modern Art*, 166–8.

47. Ibid., 161 (emphasis added). Cf. *infra*, n. 59, and the paragraph to which it refers.

48. Kandinsky, in *Theories of Modern Art*, 166, 162.

49. See Ringbom: 'Art in "The Epoch of the Great Spiritual"', *Journal of the Warburg and Courtauld Institutes*, XXIX, 399, 400, 401, 405; and *The Sounding Cosmos: A Study in the Spiritualism of Kandinsky and the Genesis of Abstract Painting* (Åbo, 1970) *passim*, particularly 49–56, 120–30. Cf. Annie Besant and C. W. Leadbeater, *Thought-Forms* (London and Benares, 1905) *passim*, particularly 12–15, 18–19, 23, 25–9, 31.

50. Kandinsky, *Art of Spiritual Harmony*, 49; cf. 52, 62–3, 91–2.

51. Cited in Dube, *The Expressionists*, 95.

52. Quotations ibid., 125; and in Selz, *German Expressionist Painting*, 239–40.

53. *Theories of Modern Art*, 182.

54. Selz, *German Expressionist Painting*, 201 (emphasis added).

55. *Theories of Modern Art*, 180.

56. Selz, *German Expressionist Painting*, 202.

57. Michael Sadler, 'After Gauguin', *Rhythm*, I. 4 (Spring 1912) 23–9. Kandinsky's works had been seen in England in 1909 and succeeding years in Allied Artists' Association exhibitions.

58. Ibid., 24, 29; cf. Kandinsky, *Art of Spiritual Harmony*, 91–2. Fry quoted by Cork, *Vorticism and Abstract Art*, 216.

59. Ramiro de Maeztu, 'Expressionism', *New Age*, XIV (27 Nov 1913) 122–3. The 'soul' of people and things was a word reiterated in Fry's striking comments on the 'visionary' van Gogh in 'Art', *Nation*; VIII (1910–11) 403. The Imagist John Cournos likewise contrasted Gaudier's early 'photographic' rendering with his later 'intensity of vision' which no longer reflected 'outward appearances' but instead 'the soul of things', their 'inner being'; see his 'Gaudier-Brzeska's Art', *Egoist*, II (1 Sep 1915) 137–8.

60. C. R. W. Nevinson, 'Vital English Art', *New Age*, XV (18 June 1914) 160–2. This is a reprint of a lecture delivered at the Doré Gallery.

61. *The Letters of Wyndham Lewis*, ed. W. K. Rose (1963) 62–3; Wees, *Vorticism and the English Avant-Garde*, 111–13.

62. See Wyndham Lewis, 'A Man of the Week. Marinetti', *New Weekly*, I (30 May 1914) 328–9; Pound, *Selected Prose*, 428.

63. Wees, *Vorticism and the English Avant-Garde*, 94–101; Cork, *Vorticism and Abstract Art*, 99–100.

64. *Poetry and Drama*, I (Sep, Dec 1913) 291–305, 319–26; 389–91 (quotation from 389).

65. *Futurist Manifestos*, 34; see also 25–6, 27, 33–4. On Pound's views see Chapter 7.

66. William Lipke, 'Futurism and the Development of Vorticism', *Studio International*, 173 (April 1967) 174–76; Cork, *Vorticism and Abstract Art*, 224–38; Wees, *Vorticism and the English Avant-Garde*, 87, 106, 108–9, 114–16; Wyndham Lewis, 'Automobilism', *New Weekly*, II (20 June 1914) 13; *Wyndham Lewis on Art: Collected Writings 1913–1956*, ed. Walter Michel and C. J. Fox (1969) 25, 26, 30–1, 46–9.

67. *Egoist*, I (15 Apr 1914) 160; cf. *Pound/Joyce*, 26. 'Cubism' was at that time the label for the group of painters who had exhibited in Lewis's 'Cubist Room' at the 'Camden Town Group and Others' show in Brighton from December 1913 to January 1914. Pound adopted Lewis's politically motivated anti-Futurist polemic: see his 'Vortex', *Blast*, I (20 June 1914) 154; and *Gaudier-Brzeska*, 82, 90.

68. See Pound, 'Vortex', *Blast*, I, 154; and *Lewis on Art*, 63–4, 72, 452, 455.

69. See Lewis, *Letters*, 488, 489.

70. *Lewis on Art*, 74; see also particularly 34, 60–1, 73–5. This and the other passages cited suggest the unacknowledged influence of Fry and MacCarthy. For an alternative interpretation of Lewis's views, stressing the romantic 'immediacy' of Impressionism, see Wagner, *Lewis: Portrait of the Artist*, 127–32.

71. *Lewis on Art*, 35; Pound, *Literary Essays*, 153, and *Gaudier-Brzeska*, 114–15. This section by Lewis, 'Futurism, Magic and Life' (*Lewis on Art*, 35–9) was even twenty years later singled out for praise by Pound: see *Selected Prose*, 425.

72. *Lewis on Art*, 88; Wadsworth, 'Inner Necessity', *Blast*, I, 119.

73. *Lewis on Art*, 70.

74. On Wadsworth, see Cork, *Vorticism and Abstract Art*, 350–76.

75. *Lewis on Art*, 96; see also 59, 61–2, 65–6, 339–40. Pound later echoed this view of Cubism: see *Literary Essays*, 424; and *Selected Prose*, 425.

# 258 *Notes*

76. *Lewis on Art*, 96–7; cf. 73–5.
77. Jacob Epstein, *Epstein. An Autobiography*, 2nd edn (1963) 60, 56. Pound implied as much in a letter to Patricia Hutchins, 11 Nov 1956: 'Epstein at Frith Street. Hulme boosting the Flenites. I doubt if anyone else would have at that time.' See Patricia Hutchins, *Ezra Pound's Kensington. An Exploration 1885–1913* (1965) 129. Pound clearly found Hulme's exposition of the new sculpture helpful, even if he did not fully grasp Hulme's theoretical as opposed to technical exposition.
78. He warned Hulme not to make his proposed *Blast* article an 'advertisement' for Epstein. Remark in TMS of talk between Samuel Hynes and Sir Jacob Epstein, 26 Feb 1954, in HRC, Texas.
79. Wyndham Lewis, *Blasting and Bombardiering* (1937; repr. 1961) 100–1 (quotation from 100).
80. Bomberg quoted in Jones, *Life and Opinions of Hulme*, 116; Cork, *Vorticism and Abstract Art*, 175; Pound, *Gaudier-Brzeska*, 25–6. Gaudier's attitude to abstraction provoked a heated posthumous debate; his personal dicta suggest that at his death his views remained undetermined. *Contra* Pound's belief that Gaudier had unreservedly embraced abstraction (see, for example, *Gaudier-Brzeska*, 78–9) see Roger Fry, 'Gaudier-Brzeska', *Burlington Magazine*, xxix (Aug 1916) 210; the partisan Horace Brodzky, *Henri Gaudier-Brzeska 1891–1915* (1933) 85–6, 88, 90–4, 96, 118, 174; and John Cournos, 'The Death of Vorticism', *Little Review*, vi (June 1919) 48.
81. Epstein, *Autobiography*, 56–7. Hynes's talks with Epstein and Kate Lechmere, 9 Jan 1954, TMSS in HRC, Texas. In 'Art Notes' (signed 'B. H. Dias'), *New Age*, xxii (22 Nov 1917) 75, Pound conceded that 'misguided and excessive modernity' 'never had any true place in [Epstein's] character'.
82. Wagner, *Lewis: Portrait of the Artist*, 126, 153. Lewis's latest biographer, Jeffrey Meyers, gives an absurdly inflated view of Lewis's innovative importance; see his *The Enemy: A Biography of Wyndham Lewis* (London and Henley, 1980) 67. For a generally noncommittal assessment, minimising Hulme's influence, see Walter Michel, *Wyndham Lewis: Paintings and Drawings* (1971) 75.
83. Wyndham Lewis: *Letters*, 491–2, 552–3; *Rude Assignment* (1950) 128–9; and cf. *Time and Western Man* (1927) 55–6.

NOTES TO CHAPTER 6: EZRA POUND: THE PRE-IMAGIST PHASE

1. See Thomas Parkinson, 'Yeats and Pound: The Illusion of Influence', *Comparative Literature*, vi. 3 (Summer 1954) 256–64; Richard Ellmann, 'Ez and Old Billyum', in *New Approaches to Ezra Pound*, ed. Eva Hesse (1969) 55–85; K. L. Goodwin, *The Influence of Ezra Pound* (1966) 75–105; N. Christoph de Nagy, *The Poetry of Ezra Pound: The Pre-Imagist Stage* (Bern, 1960); Thomas H. Jackson, *The Early Poetry of Ezra Pound* (Cambridge, Mass., 1968). For a different approach see Herbert N. Schneidau, 'Pound and Yeats: The Question of Symbolism', *ELH*, xxxii (1965) 220–37.
2. Pound: *Early Poems*, 313; *Selected Prose*, 116; *Early Poems*, 269–72, 209.
3. Yeats: *Uncollected Prose*, i, 187; *Letters*, 63, 106.
4. See Pound, 'Hilda's Book', in Hilda Doolittle, *End to Torment: A Memoir of*

*Ezra Pound*, ed. Norman Holmes Pearson and Michael King (New York, 1979) 73–4, 83, 84.

5. Ibid., 79–80, 12; Pound, *Early Poems*, 28; Doolittle, *End to Torment*, 23, 68.Cf. 'Threnos', *Early Poems*, 30, and Pound's transmogrification of fencing-lessons at Pennsylvania University in 'For E. McC.' (ibid., 39–40).

6. Ibid., 79–80, 26–7, 30–1, 295. Cf. the later Dantesque 'La Nuvoletta' ibid., (151–2); 'Scriptor Ignotus' (ibid., 24–6) similarly depicts Katherine Heyman as muse.

7. Doolittle, *End to Torment*, 83–4, 71–2; Pound, *Early Poems*, 236–7.

8. Ibid., 43, 52, 77. 'The Tree' and 'A Girl' further reveal Pound's sympathy with a desire to identify with a world of imaginative richness generally condemned as 'folly', while 'Planh' and 'An Idyl for Glaucus' are mythopoeic renderings of the need to escape into a form of alternative experience. The aspiration to escape from the phenomenal to the noumenal world inspires also the insipid 'Paracelsus in Excelsis'. See ibid., 35, 186, 126, 83–5, 148.

9. Yeats, *Letters*, 210–11.

10. Pater seems a plausible mediator for both Hegel and Schiller; see Ch. 2, n. 81. Yeats's comments in *Uncollected Prose*, I, 103, 113–14, 295, and *Explorations*, 148–9, 210–13, are particularly close to the Schillerian antithesis; Yeats defined *naïveté* in this sense in 1906 (*Explorations*, 203) but had employed it as early as 1889: see *Letters to the New Island*, 178.

11. Yeats, *Letters*, 31; cf. *Essays and Introductions*, 102–3.

12. Later defined by a control as 'Complete harmony between physical body, intellect & spiritual desire'; see *A Critical Edition of Yeats's 'A Vision' (1925)*, ed. George Mills Harper and Walter Kelly Hood (1978) Notes, 12. Its social ramifications were outlined in *Autobiographies*, 190–2.

13. On Ferguson see particularly *Uncollected Prose*, I, 81–2, 84, 90–1, 92, 159; *Letters to the New Island*, 177. By 1896 Yeats's fervour had abated somewhat; see *Uncollected Prose*, I, 404–5. Cf. also Yeats's comments on the 'bardic' quality of R. D. Joyce and his criticism of 'Michael Field' (ibid., I, 105, 109, 112–13, 225–6). Other favourite phrases for this quality were 'barbaric sincerity' or 'spontaneity', linking an idealised view of heroic antiquity with post-Romantic veneration for the childlike. Frank Kermode offers a seminal discussion of 'Unity of Being' in Yeats's poetry in *Romantic Image* (1971) particularly chs 3–5.

14. An account is repr. in *Uncollected Prose*, I, 266–75.

15. See also ibid., I, 147–8, 248–50; *Letters to the New Island*, 158–9, 190–2; *Autobiographies*, 189–95. Home Rule propagandism undoubtedly conditioned Yeats's distinction between the imaginative purity of Ireland and the vulgar commercialism of England and her literary realism. His aim was to shatter the distorted literary image of Ireland which existed in the popular 'West British' writers as an extension of England's political hegemony. See *Uncollected Prose*, I, 104, 255–6 and II, 240–1, 245–6, 321, 326; *Letters to the New Island*, 109–10, 153–4, 172–4.

16. Denis Donoghue, *Yeats* (1971) 14. See also T. R. Henn, *The Lonely Tower*, 2nd edn (1965) 105–6, 111, 128, 162, 276.

17. Yeats, *Autobiographies*, 355.

18. See *Uncollected Prose*, I, 137, 164–5; II, 119–21, 281–2.

19. See *Essays and Introductions*, 184–8; and *Uncollected Prose*, I, 382. Cf. Yeats's

argument that bereft of popular living (Irish) folklore Shelley was driven to a
factitious classical mythology to express his subjective inspiration, just as
Blake was forced to devise an esoteric system to clothe his imaginative
revelations: *Uncollected Prose*, I, 287–8; *Autobiographies*, 150; *Essays and
Introductions*, 111–15.

20. *Uncollected Prose*, I, 284. Cf. the vatic strains of I, 183, 322–3; II, 42–3, 44–5.
21. Ibid., I, 247.
22. See Yeats, *Essays and Introductions*, 189–94, and *Uncollected Prose*, I, 260, 367,
   374; George Mills Harper, *Yeats's Golden Dawn* (1974) 148.
23. Yeats, *Uncollected Prose*, I, 423.
24. Ibid., I, 336–7.
25. See, for example, Nagy, *Poetry of Pound: The Pre-Imagist Stage*, 36–52; Jackson,
   *Early Poetry of Pound*, 4–7, 63–72.
26. Pound, *Early Poems*, 61–2, 44, 37.
27. I ignore the widespread use in Pound's early poetry of *personae* in dramatic
   monologues. 'Masks', *Early Poems*, 34, defines 'myth' in the acceptation I
   intend.
28. *Early Poems*, 40–3, quotation on 42; 244–5, 321.
29. Pound, *The Spirit of Romance*, 92.
30. *Early Poems*, 10–12, 9–10, 86–7.
31. *Early Poems*, 36 and n. 296; 322 (variants omitted), my italics. Cf. Shelley's 'A
   Defence of Poetry' in *English Critical Essays: Nineteenth Century*, ed. Edmund D.
   Jones (1971) 110. Pound's essay explicates directly 'Aube of the West Dawn.
   Venetian June' (*Early Poems*, 63) which employs a trope similar to the
   transformation of the 'thaumaturgic' sky in Hulme's contemporaneous 'A
   City Sunset'. Cf. Pound's praise of Dante's use of the metamorphosis of
   Glaucus as a simile for the 'mystic ecstasy' Beatrice inspired; it was an
   expression of 'pantheism' or 'cosmic consciousness' more convincing than
   Wordsworth or Whitman (Dante, *Paradiso*, I, 67–9; Pound, *Spirit of Romance*,
   141, 155).
32. Pound, *Literary Essays*, 431 (emphasis added).
33. Yeats: *Memoirs*, 123–4; cf. *The Celtic Twilight* (1902) *passim*, particularly 45,
   106–8, 151–2.
34. *Uncollected Prose*, I, 287; cf. *Letters to the New Island*, 101.
35. For details see Richard Ellmann, *Yeats: The Man and the Masks* (1961) 118–
   30; Harper, *Yeats's Golden Dawn*, 18–19, 164–5; Virginia Moore, *The Unicorn:
   William Butler Yeats' Search for Reality* (New York, 1954) 66–82.
36. *Letters from AE*, ed. Alan Denson (London, New York and Toronto, 1961)
   17–18, 35, 46. See also Yeats, *Essays and Introductions*, 474–5.
37. The Rosicrucian details derive from Virginia Moore, *The Unicorn*, 140, 147,
   150.
38. Yeats: *Autobiographies*, 253–4; *Memoirs*, 123. Cf. Richard Ellmann, *The Identity
   of Yeats*, 2nd edn (1964) 305–6.
39. See *Some Passages from the Letters of AE to W. B. Yeats*, ed. E. C. Yeats (Dublin,
   1936) 1–3; *Letters to W. B. Yeats*, ed. Richard J. Finneran, George Mills
   Harper and William M. Murphy, 2 vols (1977) 27. For a less specific analogy
   with America see *Uncollected Prose*, I, 255–6.
40. Pound, *Selected Prose*, 53; see also 58, 290.
41. Hugh Kenner, *The Pound Era*, paperback edn (Berkeley, Calif., and Los

Angeles, 1973) 318–48. Yeats, *Memoirs*, 124; cf. *Essays and Introductions*, 475 and *Autobiographies*, 378.

42. Yeats, *Uncollected Prose*, II, 184–96; see particularly 190–6 (quotation from 195). Cf. *Uncollected Prose*, II, 55–7, 74, 127; *Essays and Introductions*, 205–6, 233; *Explorations*, 12–13.

43. Repr. in *Essays and Introductions*, 293–7 (quotation from 294). Cf. *Essays and Introductions*, 213–14 and the crucial comments in *Memoirs*, 184 and 185§96. See also *Autobiographies*, 295.

44. Pound, 'Letters to Viola Baxter Jordan', ed. with a commentary by Donald Gallup, *Paideuma*, I (1972) 109.

45. Pound, *Letters*, 3–4; see also *The Spirit of Romance*, 8, 82. For a fine analysis of Pound's 'expressive' poetry of the significant moment, see Jackson, *Early Poetry of Pound*, 14–28.

46. Yeats, *Essays and Introductions*, 174–6, 178–9 (quotations from 176, 178).

47. Pound, *Early Poems*, 8.

48. Ibid., 114–15, 115–16, 121, 126, 117–20; Yeats, *Variorum Poems*, 155–6.

49. Pound: *Early Poems*, 205; 'Raphaelite Latin', *Book News Monthly*, XXV (1906) 33, 34; 'M. Antonius Flamininus and John Keats: A Kinship in Genius', *Book News Monthly*, XXVI (1908) 447.

50. Pound, *The Spirit of Romance*, 223, 227 (emphasis added); see also 231.

51. Pound: 'M. Antonius Flamininus and John Keats', *Book News Monthly*, XXVI, 447; 'Three Cantos', *Poetry*, X (June 1917) 118–19. See also the reference to Metastasio and Lake Garda in 'Prolegomena' (1911), repr. in *Literary Essays*, 8–9.

52. See Pound: *Patria Mia* (first drafted early in 1911) 13–17, 26–7, 48–9; *Literary Essays*, 219.

53. Pound, 'Tagore's Poems', *Poetry*, I (Dec 1912) 93; cf. his 'Rabindranath Tagore', *Fortnightly Review*, n.s., XCIII (1 Mar 1913) 574, where a comparison with Dante's *Paradiso* is added, and 579, with 'Three Cantos', *Poetry*, X, 116.

54. Pound, 'Rabindranath Tagore', *Fortnightly Review*, n.s., XCIII, 571.

55. Ibid., 573. Pound employed this Juvenalian phrase elsewhere to characterise Stilnovist mysticism: see *The Spirit of Romance*, 94; and *Literary Essays*, 152.

56. Pound, 'Rabindranath Tagore', *Fortnightly Review*, n.s., XCIII, 574; cf. *The Spirit of Romance*, 92–3.

57. See *The Spirit of Romance*, 223–4; *Literary Essays*, 153; *The Cantos of Ezra Pound* (1964) 245. Pound's choice of 1527 presumably derives from the sack of Rome, which drastically reduced artistic patronage and constricted research into the Classical period, while the Reformation, Pound held, destroyed the habit of mystical 'contemplation' and fostered usury; see *Selected Prose*, 120, 243, 287. In art this resulted in the displacement of the medieval clean line in both painting and cut stone (synonymous for Pound with moral discrimination) by Mannerist exuberance and distortion.

58. Cf. his later description of 'totalitarian' mythology in Romantic organicist terms in *Selected Prose*, 101.

59. See Pound, *Translations*, 18; Noel Stock, *The Life of Ezra Pound* (Harmondsworth, Middx, 1974) 131.

60. Pound, *The Spirit of Romance*, 87, 18–21, 90; cf. *Selected Prose*, 53, 58–9.

61. See Pound, 'Interesting French Publications', *Book News Monthly*, XXV (1906) 54–5; Leon Surette, *A Light from Eleusis: A Study of Ezra Pound's Cantos*

(Oxford, 1979) 34–6; Pound, *The Spirit of Romance*, 90–2.
62. See Peter Makin, *Provence and Pound* (Berkeley, Calif., Los Angeles and London, 1978) 217–50, 168–75; the section summarised is 172–3.
63. Ibid., 351, 173, 246–7. Leon Surette, who believes that Pound's association of the Stilnovisti with the Eleusinian mysteries is unparalleled, also discusses the Albigensians and argues that a major structural pattern in the *Cantos* derives from the Eleusinian mysteries; see *A Light from Eleusis, passim*, particularly 34–80.
64. Pound: *The Spirit of Romance*, 94; *Guide to Kulchur*, 328, 77. Cf. *Spirit of Romance*, 22; and *Early Poems*, 99, where Pound adds that 'Poetry in its acme is expression from contemplation'. On Pound's limited acquaintance with Richard of St Victor, see *Letters*, 109; and Stock, *Life of Pound*, 80.
65. Pound: *Spirit of Romance*, 93–100; *Guide to Kulchur*, 299.
66. Pound, *Early Poems*, 89 (emphasis added). It is practically impossible to isolate the diverse sources of Pound's hermetic theories. In America he had read Swedenborg's *Heaven and Hell* and Balzac's *Séraphita* (see Doolittle, *End to Torment*, 23) and in London knew the Theosophist and occult expert G. R. S. Mead, but probably not very well before 1911 (see Stock, *Life of Pound*, 131, 141). The question is further complicated by Pound's reading of Plotinus and the Italian Renaissance Neoplatonists. I believe nevertheless that Pound's phraseology and line of argument is closest to Yeats's and probably indicates his influence. Compare Pound's well-known letter to Taupin: 'Symbole?? Je n'ai jamais lu "les idées des symbolistes" sur ce sujet. Dans ma jeunesse j'avais peut être quelqu'idée reçue du moyen âge. Dante, St Victor, dieu sais qui, des modifications via Yeats . . . mais je ne sais pas dénuder les traces' (*Letters*, 218).
67. Pound, *Spirit of Romance*, 14; see also 127.
68. See Yeats, *Essays and Introductions*, 28–52, particularly 28, 48–52; 78–80, 141–2, 156–60; and also *Autobiographies*, 183, 185–7, 258–65, 272, 371–5. Yeats later explained instinct as communication by association with the living memories of the dead, and inspiration as proceeding from one's spiritual Mask or Daimon; see *Mythologies* (1959) 359–63; *Explorations*, 330–2.
69. Repr. in Harper, *Yeats's Golden Dawn*, 259–68. See also 269–70, 244–5, 246–9, and Harper's comment on 99.
70. Ibid., 247–8, 263–4, 269–70, 54–6, 177. On 'energy' see also Yeats's 'Magic', *Essays and Introductions*, 28.
71. Yeats: *Uncollected Prose*, I, 367, 380, 394, 400–2, 408; *Essays and Introductions*, 116–20 (quotation from 116).
72. Ibid., 148; see also 140.
73. Pound, *Spirit of Romance*, 89.
74. Pound, *Literary Essays*, 162 (emphasis added). Kermode, *Romantic Image*, 150; cf. 159.
75. Pound: *Translations*, 18; *Literary Essays*, 154 (emphasis added). I suggest that the seemingly transparent phrase 'a definite meaning' carries in its context (ibid., 152–5) the same overtones as Pound's tantalising 'I mean or imply that certain truth exists' (*Guide to Kulchur*, 295), in which a plain, declarative statement implies an esoteric interpretation which it then withholds or merely alludes to obliquely.
76. *Literary Essays*, 154; cf. *ABC of Reading*, paperback edn (1961) 104.

77. *Spirit of Romance*, 105; *Literary Essays*, 344 (emphasis added).
78. *Spirit of Romance*, 96–7; *Selected Prose*, 390. Cf. the incantatory catalogue of 'The Alchemist' (*Early Poems*, 225–9).
79. For the connotations of this word see, for example, *Spirit of Romance*, 105, 145; *Translations*, 26, 46, 50–1, 118, 132–3, 136–7; 'The House of Splendour', 'Apparuit', 'A Virginal', *Early Poems*, 170–1, 182–3, 195.
80. *Spirit of Romance*, 90; cf. *Translations*, 106–7. See also *Spirit of Romance*, 106.
81. *Selected Prose*, 28–31; *Translations*, 18. Cf. Walter Pater, *The Renaissance: Studies in Art and Poetry* (1873), 5th edn (1910) VII–XI.
82. Yeats, *Essays and Introductions*, 121.
83. Pound, *Translations*, 18 (first emphasis added).
84. See also ibid., 19–20.
85. On Pound's occult interests from 1909 see Stock, *Life of Pound*, 92. On his praise for Mead, who appeared about twice monthly at Yeats's Mondays and whose lectures Pound attended in December 1911, see Schneidau, 'Pound and Yeats', *ELH*, XXXII, 226–7.
86. See Stock, *Life of Pound*, 103.
87. Pound, *Selected Prose*, 346. Cf. 'Through Alien Eyes, I', *New Age*, XII (16 Jan 1913) 252; 'Affirmations . . . II. Vorticism', *New Age*, XVI (14 Jan 1915) 277, 278; *Literary Essays*, 154; *Guide to Kulchur*, 152.
88. Annie Besant and C. W. Leadbeater, *Thought-Forms* (London and Benares, 1905) 11–14.
89. Ibid., 25; cf. 14.
90. For example in 'Rosa Alchemica' (1896), repr. in *The Secret Rose, Stories by W. B. Yeats*, ed. Phillip L. Marcus *et al.* (Ithaca, NY, and London, 1981) 142–4; 'The Moods' (1895), as repr. in *Uncollected Prose*, I, 367; 'The Autumn of the Body' (1898), repr. in *Essays and Introductions*, 189–94.
91. Yeats, *Letters*, 402; cf. letter to Quinn, ibid., 403.
92. See Pound: *Selected Prose*, 47–52 (quotations from 47, 49, 50); *Cantos*, 488 (cf. 465, 563, 653).
93. First used in 'Through Alien Eyes, I', *New Age*, XII, 252.
94. *Selected Prose*, 331 (emphasis added).
95. Besant and Leadbeater, *Thought-Forms*, 27–9 (quotation from 29); cf. 18.
96. Pound, *Selected Prose*, 331–2 (quotations from 332; emphasis added).
97. *Selected Prose*, 25.
98. *Literary Essays*, 443, 444.
99. See also *Spirit of Romance*, 127.
100. Yeats, *Essays and Introductions*, 157 (emphasis added).
101. T. S. Eliot, *Selected Essays*, 3rd edn (1951) 145.
102. The magical aspect of this symbolist theory is emphasised by Yeats in 'Rosa Alchemica', *The Secret Rose*, 142–4.
103. See Stéphane Mallarmé, *Propos sur la poésie*, ed. Henri Mondor, 2nd edn (Monaco, 1953) 65–6, 77, 78, 79–80, 81–3, 87–9, 91, 95, 97, 101–2. Hegelian influences on Mallarmé are assessed in Jean-Pierre Richard, *L'Univers imaginaire de Mallarmé* (Paris, 1961) 231–3; A. W. Raitt, *Villiers de l'Isle-Adam et le mouvement symboliste* (Paris, 1965) 282–6; D. J. Mossop, *Pure Poetry: Studies in French Poetic Theory and Practice 1746–1945* (Oxford, 1971) 131–42. More recently Malcolm Bowie has re-emphasised the (neo-) Platonic cast of

Mallarmé's thought; see *Mallarmé and the Art of Being Difficult* (Cambridge, 1978) 29–30 and *passim*.

104. Stéphane Mallarmé, *Œuvres complètes*, ed. Henri Mondor and G. Jean-Aubry (Paris, [1951]) 663; see also 875–6.

105. Ibid., 378; *Propos*, 82.

106. Ibid., 79–80. On correspondential aspects cf. ibid., 174, and the emphasis on seizing 'rapports' in *Œuvres complètes*, 647–8, 871. See also 'Le Démon de l'Analogie', ibid., 272–3.

107. Ibid., 363–4, 368, 375.

108. Ibid., 854; cf. the speculation on the evocative properties of individual letters in 'Les Mots anglais', ibid., 923–62, and the general comment on 920–1.

109. Otherwise inexpressible ideas were evoked by the suggestive, virginal whiteness of the spatial intervals of the *mise en page*, and the silence of the enforced pauses in the delivery of the poem (cf. the stimulating comments in *Œuvres complètes*, 310, 366–7, 379–81, 387; *Propos*, 207–8). Mallarmé's typographical experiments effectively transformed the book into a musical score, dictating the mode in which it must be *performed* rather than read. Language thus became a gestural vehicle as flexible, suggestive and aesthetically neutral as the dancer who represented another variety of Mallarmé's desired 'incorporation visuelle de l'idée'. On literature as performance see *Œuvres complètes*, 455–6, 369–72, and the comments on punctuation on 407.

110. See, for example, ibid., 662; *Propos*, 89, 91. Cf. Yeats's reference to 'the Great Work' in *Variorum Poems*, 849.

111. Mallarmé, *Œuvres complètes*, 646, 400. On poetry as creation see also 870. For comparable formulations of Mallarmé's aim of evocation see, for example, ibid., 365–6, 367–8, 868–9; *Propos*, 46–7.

112. *Œuvres complètes*, 462–4, 472–7. Cf. 'Ses purs ongles . . . ', ibid., 68–9.

113. See particularly 'Toast funèbre' and 'Prose pour des Esseintes', ibid., 54–7.

114. *The Complete Poems and Plays of T. S. Eliot* (1969) 172, 191. Cf. particularly the sonnet triptych in Mallarmé, *Œuvres complètes*, 73–4.

115. See Pound: *Letters*, 25, 140, 141; *Translations*, 222, 236.

116. Cf. *Selected Prose*, 47–8; and *Translations*, 325.

117. Ibid., 324: Yeats: 'Anima Mundi', *Mythologies*, 343–66; *A Vision* (1925) 224–8; *A Vision*, 2nd edn, reissued with Yeats's final revisions (New York, 1966) 223–31; *Variorum Plays*, 976.

118. Yeats, *Explorations*, 330–1; see also 35–6. Pound, *Translations*, 135 (cf. *Cantos*, 182, 370, 480); *Cantos*, 485 (cf. 474, 495, 556); Yeats, *Variorum Poems*, 350.

119. Pound, *Cantos*, 9.

120. Yeats, *Variorum Poems*, 270–6, 323–8, 470–4; Pound, *Early Poems*, 215–22.

121. Yeats, *Explorations*, 55–6; see also the references to 'drinking the blood' in *Variorum Plays*, 968–9, 976.

122. See, for example, *Explorations*, 330–2; 'The Curse of Cromwell', *Variorum Poems*, 580–1; *Purgatory, Variorum Plays*, 1041–9.

123. Pound: *Guide to Kulchur*, 57–8; *Cantos*, 457.

124. Cf. *Polite Essays* (1937) 51.

125. *Cantos*, 487.

126. See 'Victorian Eclogues' i and ii; 'Song in the Manner of Housman'; 'Translations from Heine'; 'Leviora' (*Early Poems*, 156–8, 163–7, 213–14). At

the other extreme: 'Canzon', stanza i; 'Canzone: Of Angels', stanzas iv and v; 'Sonnet: Chi è questa', ll. 3–4; 'Ballatetta', 'The House of Splendour', and 'The Flame' *(Early Poems*, 136, 140–1, 143, 147, 170–1, 171–2).
127. *Early Poems*, 167–74.
128. Nagy has indicated the refutation of Symons in the phrase 'of days and nights' in 'The Flame'; see *Poetry of Pound: The Pre-Imagist Stage*, 41.
129. Pound, *Early Poems*, 215–22; cf. the wry self-consciousness of 'N. Y.', ibid., 185.
130. Ibid., 218.

NOTES TO CHAPTER 7: THE LONDON VORTEX: POUND'S RENAISSANCE 'FORMA'

1. For details see my D Phil thesis, 'The Transition from Symbolism to Imagism, 1885–1914' (Oxford, 1982) 303–5; and Cyrena N. Pondrom (ed.), 'Selected Letters from H.D. to F. S. Flint: a Commentary on the Imagist Period', *Contemporary Literature*, 10 (Autumn 1969) 557–86.
2. See Pound, *Literary Essays*, 8–12. On the article's data see Noel Stock, *The Life of Ezra Pound*, 137.
3. See Hilda Doolittle, *End to Torment: A Memoir of Ezra Pound*, ed. Norman Holmes Pearson and Michael King (New York, 1979) 18; also Richard Aldington, *Life for Life's Sake* (1968), 122.
4. Pound, *Literary Essays*, 3.
5. Pound, *Letters*, 10.
6. 'Notes and Announcements' for Nov 1913, quoted in Stock, *Life of Pound*, 157; Pound, 'Status rerum', *Poetry*, I (Jan 1913) 126; Aldington, *Life for Life's Sake*, 123.
7. Pound, *Letters*, 18. In 'Documents on Imagism from the Papers of F. S. Flint', *Review*, xv (Apr 1965) 36–8, Christopher Middleton reprints the original draft for the interview with Pound's MS amendations. Peter Jones, in *Imagist Poetry* (Harmondsworth, 1972) 129–34, conveniently reprints the finished article.
8. ALI to Flint postmarked 20 Jan 1913, ALI to Flint postmarked 23 Jan 1913, in HRC, Texas.
9. Glenn Hughes, *Imagism and the Imagists* (1931; repr. New York, 1960) 35–6; S. Foster Damon, *Amy Lowell: A Chronicle* (Boston, Mass., and New York, 1935) 208; Stanley K. Coffman, *Imagism: A Chapter for the History of Modern Poetry* (1951; repr. New York, 1972), 16–17.
10. *Letters*, 213; *Literary Essays*, 80. Aldington, ALS to Flint 12 Sep 1913; Robert Frost, ALS to Flint 17 June 1913; both in HRC, Texas.
11. See J. G. Fletcher, *Life is my Song* (New York and Toronto, 1937) 62–3.
12. Pound: 'Peals of Iron', *Poetry*, III (Dec 1913) 112–13; *Letters*, 22; 'In Metre', *New Freewoman*, I (15 Sep 1913) 131–2.
13. Stock, *Life of Pound*, 173. This poem is presumably the one now printed as 'The Death of the Hired Man'.
14. See Charles Norman, *Ezra Pound* (New York, 1960) 110–11; Damon, *Amy Lowell*, 209–16; Hughes, *Imagism and the Imagists*, 130–1. Fletcher's account for public consumption, presenting himself more genially, is in *Life is my Song*, 80–2.

15. See *Pound/Joyce*, 18–19. Cf. Pound, *Letters*, 129–30, advising Margaret Anderson to make use of Lowell's capital.
16. Aldington, *Life for Life's Sake*, 124.
17. See Stock, *Life of Pound*, 182; and Pound, *Letters*, 27.
18. Pound, 'A Letter from London', *Little Review*, iii (Apr 1916) 8.
19. *Patria Mia*, 31, 34–5. (The 'Patria Mia' articles and 'America: Chances and Remedies' series were written by Pound early in 1911 shortly after his return from an extended visit to America. The book version often differs substantially from these. Where there is no difference I have referred to the book version; where the book omits significant passages or alters important readings, I have referred to the original articles.) See also 'Patria Mia, xi', *New Age*, xii (14 Nov 1912) 34; 'To Whistler, American' (1912), in *Shorter Poems*, 251; 'Letters from Ezra Pound', *Little Review*, iv (Oct 1917) 38.
20. For the primary sense see *Selected Prose*, 386. The quotation is from 'Through Alien Eyes, iii' *New Age*, xii (30 Jan 1913) 300. Cf. *Letters*, 28; *Gaudier-Brzeska*, 117; 'Pastiche. The Regional. ii', *New Age*, xxv (26 June 1919) 156.
21. See *Letters*, 7, 8, 25; *Literary Essays*, 214; *Selected Prose*, 169–73.
22. 'Patria Mia, i', *New Age*, xi (5 Sep 1912) 445. Cf. *Patria Mia*, 14, 16–17, with J. A. McN. Whistler, *The Gentle Art of Making Enemies*, 2nd, enlarged edn (1892; repr. New York, 1967) 144. Pound had alluded to this passage in 1910 in *The Spirit of Romance*, 154.
23. See 'Affirmations . . . . i. Arnold Dolmetsch', *New Age*, xvi (7 Jan 1915) 247; 'Pastiche. The Regional. ii', *New Age*, xxv (26 June 1919) 156; 'On Criticism in General', *Criterion*, i (Jan 1923) 143.
24. Quotation from *Literary Essays*, 220. Cf. *Gaudier-Brzeska*, 113; 'To a City Sending Him Advertisements', *Early Poems*, 287–8 and *Literary Essays*, 222; 'America: Chances and Remedies . . . v', *New Age*, xiii (29 May 1913) 115–16.
25. *Literary Essays*, 224–5.
26. 'Patria Mia, vii', *New Age*, xi (17 Oct 1912) 587–8, repr. as *Patria Mia*, 50–3 (emphasis added); 'America: Chances and Remedies . . . v. Proposition iii – The College of the Arts', *New Age*, xiii (29 May 1913) 115–16; *Patria Mia*, 70–3 (quotation from 73). cf. *Literary Essays*, 221–6.
27. See *Pound/Joyce*, 38–40; and *Letters*, 172–6, 182.
28. Cf. the crucial article 'Murder by Capital' (1933), repr. in *Selected Prose*, 197–202; *Letters*, 239; *Guide to Kulchur*, 62.
29. *Selected Prose*, 200–1.
30. Ford Madox Ford, Preface to *Collected Poems* (1914) 24–5. Cf. Pound: 'This Hulme Business', repr. in Hugh Kenner, *The Poetry of Ezra Pound* (1951) 308; *Selected Prose*, 433; *Letters*, 296.
31. On this publishers' conspiracy against genius see *Pound/Joyce*, 247, and 'Obstructivity', *The Apple*, i (1920) 168, 170, 172. For the Futurists and Storer see Ch. 5.
32. See Pound's remarks on John Quinn's purchase of work by living artists (*Gaudier-Brzeska*, 64) and letters to Quinn (particularly *Letters*, 51–4) and Simon Guggenheim (ibid., 196–7).
33. On Robert Frost see *Literary Essays*, 382, 384–5. For Upward see *Selected Prose*, 377–82; *Letters*, 22–3, 25; *Literary Essays*, 372. Michael Sheldon, 'Allen Upward: Some Biographical Notes', *Agenda*, xvi. 3–4 (Autumn–Winter 1978–

9) 108–21, provides a useful and suggestive summary of Upward's varied career and curious inability to capture public attention. See also Kenneth Cox, 'Allen Upward', ibid., 87–107.

34. On Epstein see particularly Pound, *Gaudier-Brzeska*, 95–6, 100–1. In a letter of November 1913 Pound termed Epstein 'a great sculptor' (*Letters*, 26). On Gaudier see *Gaudier-Brzeska*, 44–5, 47–50, 109, 141; and *Letters*, 27. Chronology established from Jacob Epstein, *Epstein. An Autobiography*, 2nd edn (1963) 56; and Richard Cork, *Vorticism and Abstract Art in the First Machine Age* (London, Berkeley, Calif., and Los Angeles, 1976), 179–83. Cf. also *Letters*, 36 (Apr 1914) on a writer and his family near starvation after attempting to run a magazine. A letter written by Gaudier in January 1913 gives a vivid idea of his penury; see H. S. Ede, *Savage Messiah* (1931) 225.

35. See Yeats: *Variorum Poems*, 818–20; and *Uncollected Prose*, II, 408–10.

36. See Yeats: *Memoirs*, 215; and *Autobiographies*, 518.

37. Pound, 'Affirmations . . . II. Vorticism', *New Age*, XVI (14 Jan 1915) 277; 'Affirmations . . . VII. The Non-existence of Ireland', *New Age*, XVI (25 Feb 1915) 451–3; 'The Rest', *Shorter Poems*, 101–2. Cf. Yeats, *Variorum Poems*, 287–8. 'Coole Park, 1929' and 'Coole Park and Ballylee, 1931' (ibid., 488–92) lend superb expression to the notion shared by Yeats and Pound of a 'vortex' on the Italian Renaissance model, here concentrated by the presiding energy of Lady Gregory. Cf. Pound's comment in 1918 that the secret of *quattrocento* aristocracy and hence the whole force of the Renaissance was 'the *personality* of its selection.' (*Literary Essays*, 319; emphasis added).

38. For the background see William C. Wees, *Vorticism and the English Avant-Garde* (Manchester, 1972), 58–72; and Cork, *Vorticism and Abstract Art*, 85–101, 146–61. Although Marinetti did appear there and Ford and Pound deliver lectures (the latter a version of 'Vorticism' published in the *Fortnightly Review*, Sep 1914) and some 'workshop' items were displayed at the Allied Artists' Association exhibition in June, the art-school never materialised. The most comprehensive account of the Omega Workshops feud is in Jeffrey Meyers, *The Enemy: A Biography of Wyndham Lewis* (London and Henley, 1980) 39–48.

39. For dating see Wees, *Vorticism and the English Arant-Garde*, 161–3.

40. See Pound, 'Preliminary Announcement of the College of Arts', *Egoist*, I (2 Nov 1914) 413–14.

41. Pound, ALS to Flint, datable only from attached envelope postmarked 25 Mar 1914, in HRC, Texas. On the 'germanic' system, see *supra*, p. 188; and 'The Logical Conclusion', *Early Poems*, 274. On these lectures see also Fletcher, *Life is my Song*, 136, 137. The identity between Pound's aspirations in spring and autumn 1914 is confirmed by an APCS (postmarked 23 Sep 1914, in HRC, Texas) to Flint requesting him, as he had in March, to give lectures on Contemporary French Poetry.

42. For a detailed examination of the Pound–Flint relationship see my D Phil thesis, 'The Transition from Symbolism to Imagism', 305–10, 313–22; and Middleton, 'Documents on Imagism', *Review*, XV, 33–51.

43. References to Arundell [*sic*] del Re, 'Georgian Reminiscences', *University of Tokyo Studies in English Literature*, XIV (1934) 33; *Pound/Joyce*, 19–20; *EP to LU*, ed. J. A. Robbins (Bloomington, Ind., 1963) 11.

44. See Pound, *Letters*, 31–4; and Coffman, *Imagism*, 17.

45. Richard Sieburth, *Instigations: Ezra Pound and Remy de Gourmont* (Cambridge,

Mass., and London, 1978) 20 (who, however, does not make any of my points) referring to Paige TS no. 323, 25 Mar 1914. On Pound's attempt in 1915, with John Quinn's finance, to take over the *Academy*, and in 1915–17 to establish a new international fortnightly or to infiltrate established magazines editorially, see B. L. Reid, *The Man from New York* (New York, 1968) 223–5, 248–9, 284–6.

46. Wees, *Vorticism and the English Avant-Garde*, 127–30. See Ronald Bush, *The Genesis of Ezra Pound's Cantos* (Princeton, NJ, 1976) 49–51, for an equally unsatisfactory explanation.

47. Pound: 'The New Sculpture', *Egoist*, I (16 Feb 1914) 67–8; 'Wyndham Lewis', *Egoist*, I (15 June 1914) 233–4.

48. *Selected Prose*, 386.

49. On *Tarr* see *Literary Essays*, 428–9. On *Ulysses* see *Literary Essays*, 416; *Guide to Kulchur*, 96; *Pound/Joyce*, 145. On Yeats see 'The Later Yeats' (May 1914), repr. in *Literary Essays*, 378–81; 'Mr Yeats' New Book', *Poetry*, IX (Dec 1916) 150–1.

50. See Yeats, *Variorum Poems*, 262, 289–90, 291. Cf. Pound: *Early Poems*, 284; *Letters*, 178; 'On Criticism in General', *Criterion*, I (1923) 144.

51. *Wyndham Lewis on Art: Collected Writings 1913–1956*, ed. Walter Michel and C. J. Fox (1969) 25. The title page of *Blast* states incorrectly '20 June 1914'.

52. See Wyndham Lewis, *Blasting and Bombardiering* (1937; repr. 1961), 32–6.

53. Lewis quoted in Douglas Goldring, *South Lodge* (1943) 65. See Wees, *Vorticism and the English Avant-Garde*, 165.

54. See William C. Wees, 'Ezra Pound as a Vorticist', *Wisconsin Studies in Contemporary Literature*, VI (1965) 56–72 (see particularly 57–67; the quotations here are from 57 and 59); William C. Lipke and Bernard W. Rozran, 'Ezra Pound and Vorticism: A Polite Blast', *Wisconsin Studies in Contemporary Literature*, VII (1966) 201–10.

55. Richard Aldington, '*Blast*', *Egoist*, I (15 July 1914) 273. Nevertheless Aldington signed the manifesto, and Lewis had intended to append Flint's name also, but with characteristic inefficiency forgot to ask permission in time. Lewis apparently intended to include some material by Flint in *Blast*, II; there was accordingly no straight-forward break with Imagism. (Aldington, TLS to Flint 4 July 1914, HRC, Texas.)

56. See Goldring, *South Lodge*, 67–8.

57. Quoted by Geoffrey Wagner, 'Wyndham Lewis and the Vorticist Aesthetic', *Journal of Aesthetics and Art Criticism*, XIII (1954–5) 17.

58. See Fletcher, *Life is my Song*, 146–7, 148–9.

59. See Aldington, *Life for Life's Sake*, 127; Damon, *Amy Lowell*, 237–40; Coffman, *Imagism*, 21–3; Hughes, *Imagism and the Imagists*, 36–7.

60. See Amy Lowell, ALS to Flint, 18 Aug 1914, in HRC, Texas.

61. Pound, *Letters*, 50. For a wholly partisan account from Pound's viewpoint see Kenner, *The Pound Era*, 291–2.

62. Cf. Yeats, 'Blood and the Moon', *Variorum Poems*, 482.

NOTES TO CHAPTER 8: IMAGISM

1. See, for example, comments by Edward Thomas, Rupert Brooke and J. C. Squire, repr. in *Ezra Pound: The Critical Heritage*, ed. Eric Homberger (London and Boston, Mass., 1972) 50–3, 58–9, 83–4.

2. Cf., for example, Pound's *Spirit of Romance*, 25, 126, *Selected Prose*, 28–9, 41, 42, and *Literary Essays*, 11–12, with Hulme, *FS*, 5, 9–14, 74–5. A detailed argument for Hulme's influence on Pound is provided in my D Phil thesis, 'The Transition from Symbolism to Imagism, 1885–1914' (Oxford, 1982) 326–34.

3. Pound, *Translations*, 23.

4. Cf. Pound, *Literary Essays*, 4.

5. See G. T. Tanselle, 'Two Early Letters of Ezra Pound', *American Literature*, 34 (1962–3) 116 (emphasis added); Pound, *Translations*, 24.

6. On Daniel see Pound: *Selected Prose*, 26–8; and *Literary Essays*, 112, 114, 115–16.

7. *Selected Prose*, 41. Pound is echoing Symons's criticism of Browning's partial grasp 'that verse must be like speech, without realising that it must be like dignified speech.'; see 'Mr W. B. Yeats', *Studies in Prose and Verse* (1904) 238, cf. 237. On Pound's high esteem in 1911 for Symons's criticism, see Tanselle, 'Two Early Letters of Pound', *American Literature*, 34, p. 118.

8. See Pound, *Literary Essays*, 49, 51–4.

9. Repr. from *Poetry Review*, Feb 1912, in *Literary Essays*, 9–12; see particularly 9.

10. *Literary Essays*, 5; cf. *Letters*, 90–1.

11. Herbert N. Schneidau, 'Pound and Yeats: The Question of Symbolism', *ELH*, xxxii (1965) 231, 232.

12. Ibid., 236. Cf. Ronald Bush, *The Genesis of Ezra Pound's Cantos* (Princeton, NJ, 1976), 104.

13. Pound, 'The Book of the Month', *Poetry Review*, i (Mar 1912) 133.

14. For an alternative discussion of Pound's views on literary impressionism, see Hugh Witemeyer, *The Poetry of Ezra Pound: Forms and Renewal, 1908–1920* (Berkeley, Calif., and Los Angeles, 1969) 176–83.

15. Pound, 'On Criticism in General', *Criterion*, i (Jan 1923) 144–6; quotations from 146.

16. Ford Madox Ford, 'On Impressionism', *Poetry and Drama*, ii (June, Dec 1914) 174, 323. Cf. his 'Joseph Conrad', *English Review*, x (Dec 1911) 76, 77. See also Herbert N. Schneidau, *Ezra Pound: The Image and the Real* (Baton Rouge, La., 1969) 26–7.

17. Richard Aldington, 'M. Marinetti's Lectures', *New Freewoman*, i (1 Dec 1913) 226; cf. his distinction between impressionism and impersonal 'presentation' in 'Books, Drawings, and Papers', *Egoist*, i (1 Jan 1914) 10; and his satire on Ford, 'Vates, the Social Reformer', in *Des Imagistes* (1914) 59–61.

18. Ford Madox Ford, *Collected Poems* (1914) 15–19 (quotation from 15). Cf. Pound, *Gaudier-Brzeska*, 86–7.

19. See *Literary Essays*, 4; and *Early Poems*, 171 (emphasis added).

20. *Selected Prose*, 402; *Gaudier-Brzeska*, 89.

21. *Poetry*, iv (June 1914) 120.

22. Ford Madox Ford: *Return to Yesterday* (New York, 1932) 400–1; 'Literary Portraits – xxxiii: Mr Sturge Moore and "The Sea is Kind" ', *Outlook*, xxxiii (25 Apr 1914) 560; 'Literary Portraits – xxxv: Les Jeunes and "Des Imagistes" ', *Outlook*, xxxiii (9 May 1914) 636, 653; 'Literary Portraits – xliii: Mr Wyndham Lewis and "Blast" ', *Outlook*, xxxiv (4 July 1914) 15–16; 'Those Were the Days', Preface to *Imagist Anthology 1930* (1930) ix–xvi.

23. Ford, 'Literary Portraits – xxxv', *Outlook*, xxxiii, 636. Ford's garbled eclecticism also echoes Pound in a parallel of the 'abstract beauty' of Imagist poetry with music (ibid., 653). Cf. M. T. H. Sadler's Introduction to his translation of

Wassily Kandinsky, *The Art of Spiritual Harmony* (1914) x, xvii; Roger Fry, 'Art. The Post-Impressionists. – II', *Nation*, VIII (1910–11) 403, who memorably discusses van Gogh as a visionary who painted the 'soul' of people and things in a 'deep submission to their essence'; and Ramiro de Maeztu, 'Expressionism', *New Age*, XIV (27 Nov 1913), quoted *supra*, pp. 139–40.

24. Ford Madox Ford, 'Literary Portraits – XXXVI: Les Jeunes and "Des Imagistes" (Second Notice)', *Outlook*, XXXIII (16 May 1914) 682. Cf. the whole of Kandinsky's introductory chapter in *The Art of Spiritual Harmony*, particularly his stress on the 'non-material' on 29–30, 40.

25. Ford, 'Literary Portraits – XXXVI', *Outlook*, XXXIII, 682. He insisted elsewhere that the Futurists paralleled on canvas his own literary endeavours and that he had been preaching Marinetti's doctrines since he was fifteen. Further similarities lay, he maintained with a characteristically light-hearted gibe at Pound, in their common concentration on rendering present-day life, not the Troubadours or Albigensians. See his 'On Impressionism', *Poetry and Drama*, II, 175; 'Literary Portraits – XLIV: Signor Marinetti, Mr Lloyd George, St Katharine, and Others', *Outlook*, XXXIV (11 July 1914) 46–7.

26. Ford, 'Literary Portraits – XXXVI', *Outlook*, XXXIII, 682; cf. Michael Sadler, 'After Gauguin', *Rhythm*, I. 4 (Spring 1912) 23–9 (quoted *supra*, p. 139).

27. Pound, 'Vorticism' (Sep 1914), repr. in *Gaudier-Brzeska*, 92.

28. Ibid., 89–90 (quotation from 90).

29. 'Vortex. Pound', *Blast*, I (20 June 1914) 154; unpublished letter from Pound to Harriet Monroe, 7 Aug 1914, quoted in J. B. Harmer, *Victory in Limbo: Imagism 1908–1917* (1975) 178; *Gaudier-Brzeska*, 81. Witemeyer, in ch. 2 of *The Poetry of Pound*, particularly 32–7, has also stressed most persuasively the essential continuity between Imagism and Vorticism, as has, from a different approach, Thomas H. Jackson in *The Early Poetry of Ezra Pound*, (Cambridge, Mass., 1968) 96–108.

30. Pound: 'The New Sculpture', *Egoist*, I (16 Feb 1914) 67–8; 'Exhibition at the Goupil Gallery', *Egoist*, I (16 Mar 1914) 109 (cf. *Letters*, 74). Yeats, *Uncollected Prose*, II, 134.

31. *Pound/Joyce*, 26. Cf. Pound, *Pavannes and Divisions* (New York, 1918) 245–6.

32. William C. Wees, 'Ezra Pound as a Vorticist', *Wisconsin Studies in Contemporary Literature*, VI (1965) 71–2, referring to *Gaudier-Brzeska*, 120–1. Cf. Hugh Kenner, *The Poetry of Ezra Pound* (1951) 73–5; and Donald Davie, *Ezra Pound: Poet as Sculptor* (1965) 54–5.

33. Pound: 'Affirmations . . . II. Vorticism', *New Age*, XVI (14 Jan 1915) 277, 278; *Gaudier-Brzeska*, 121, 127; 'The Caressability of the Greeks' (letter), *Egoist*, I (16 March 1914) 117; 'Vortex. Pound', *Blast*, I, 154; *Selected Prose*, 346–7.

34. *Gaudier-Brzeska*, 126; 'Affirmations . . . II. Vorticism', *New Age*, XVI, 278.

35. *Gaudier-Brzeska*, 121–2 (emphasis added).

36. 'Affirmations . . . II. Vorticism', *New Age*, XVI, 277; cf. 'Wyndham Lewis', *Egoist*, I (15 June 1914) 233.

37. 'Wyndham Lewis', *Egoist*, I, 233.

38. See 'Affirmations . . . II. Vorticism', *New Age*, XVI, 277, 278; and *Selected Prose*, 344–5.

39. See *Literary Essays*, 49, 52.

40. On Fenollosa's Romantic organicism and theory of language as process, see *The Chinese Written Character as a Medium for Poetry*, ed. Ezra Pound (1936) 13,

14, 15–16, 19, 21, 23. Kenner has an excellent, suggestive account of Fenollosa's lasting impact on Pound in *The Pound Era*, paperback edn (Berkeley, Calif., and Los Angeles, 1973) 157–61, 192–231, 289–91.

41. Cf. Pound: 'Vortex. Pound', *Blast*, i, 153–4; 'Affirmations . . . iii. Jacob Epstein' (1915) and 'Affirmations . . . v. Gaudier-Brzeska' (1915), repr. in *Gaudier-Brzeska*, 98, 109, 110.

42. See ibid., 84; and *Letters*, 210 (emphasis added).

43. For an alternative interpretation see Wallace Martin, 'The Sources of the Imagist Aesthetic', *PMLA*, 85 (1970) 201.

44. See Yeats, *Essays and Introductions*, 161. N. Christoph de Nagy, in *Ezra Pound's Poetics and Literary Tradition: The Critical Decade* (Bern, 1966) 82–3, also makes my general point, although with an inadequate account of Symbolist technique, while his rigid dichotomy between Imagism as phanopoeia and Symbolism as melopoeia totally falsifies Pound's position in its neglect of the importance of 'rhythm' and *melos*.

45. Pound, *Gaudier-Brzeska*, 85.

46. Ibid., 85–6; cf. 92. See Whistler's comments in *The Gentle Art of Making Enemies* 2nd, enlarged edn (1892; repr. New York, 1967) 126–8, 146–8. On programme music see Kandinsky, *The Art of Spiritual Harmony*, 42; Pound's comments on this subject in *Literary Essays*, 433–4, probably derive from Nietzsche's 'Der Fall Wagner', *WdB*, ii, 912–16, 919–20, 923–5.

47. Pound, *Gaudier-Brzeska*, 90–2.

48. Ibid., 91–2. Cf. ibid., 87 and 88, on the 'equation' of colours, which was Pound's first intuitive expression of the emotional experience underlying 'In a Station of the Metro'.

49. Ibid., 127 (emphasis added); see also 134. Cf. 'On the American Number', *Little Review*, v (Sep 1918) 62; 'Art Notes' [signed 'B. H. Dias'], *New Age*, xxvi (6 Nov 1919) 13; and the Neoplatonic interpretation of Epstein's sculpture in 'Exhibition at the Goupil Gallery', *Egoist*, i (16 Mar 1914) 109.

50. *Selected Prose*, 346–7.

51. *Guide to Kulchur*, 152. See also 'Through Alien Eyes, i', *New Age*, xii (16 Jan 1913) 252; 'Affirmations . . . ii. Vorticism', *New Age*, xvi, 277; *Literary Essays*, 154; *Selected Prose*, 346.

52. *The Complete Poems and Plays of T. S. Eliot* (1969) 175.

53. *Literary Essays*, 442. For a good exposition of this profoundly traditional symbolism see Giorgio Melchiori, *The Whole Mystery of Art* (1961; repr. Westport, Conn., 1979), ch. 5, 'The Mundane Egg', 164–99.

54. Pound, *Early Poems*, 58; cf. *Spirit of Romance*, 68.

55. *Early Poems*, 72.

56. See *Spirit of Romance*, 158–9.

57. *Early Poems*, 114–15. For this quality see also 'Portrait' and ' "Fair Helena" by Rackham', ibid., 115–16.

58. See particularly 'Canzon: The Spear', 'Canzon' and 'Canzon: Of Incense', ibid., 134–9.

59. Ibid., 193, 194.

60. Ibid., 9–10; 83–5, 300–1; 198.

61. Repr. in *Shorter Poems*, 91–3, 94–5, 97–8, 101–5, 109, 111, 114, 124, 253; and *Early Poems*, 278, 279.

62. *Shorter Poems*, 99, 101, 120.

63. Ibid., 101. Cf. *Selected Prose*, 377–8; *Shorter Poems*, 209; 'Three Cantos', *Poetry*, x (June 1917) 116.
64. See *Shorter Poems*, 80, 85, 118.
65. Ibid., 119.
66. Cf. Pound's early comment in *Spirit of Romance*, 31, on the 'proper place' of nature in poetry as 'a background to the action, an interpretation of the mood; an equation, in other terms, or a "metaphor by sympathy" for the mood of the poem'.
67. Quotations from Donald Davie: 'Pound and Eliot: a Distinction', in *Eliot in Perspective*, ed. Graham Martin (1970) 62; and *Pound* (1975) 43. See also Davie, *Pound: Poet as Sculptor*, 57, 73–5; and *Pound*, 42–4.
68. Tony Tanner, *The Reign of Wonder* (New York, 1967) 91–2. Schneidau, in *Pound: The Image and the Real*, particularly 27–9, 83–4, 93, perceptively associates Pound's 'image' with epiphanies and has some sensible comments on Symbolism. But I would disagree with his statement that the image is 'a kind of secular revelation' (28); I feel it was for Pound almost always mystical and spiritual. I also cannot agree with his praise along these lines of 'The Garden' (30–1), which I find an irredeemably weak poem.
69. Wallace Martin, 'The Sources of the Imagist Aesthetic', *PMLA*, 85 (1970) 204.
70. See *The Collected Earlier Poems of William Carlos Williams* (New York, 1966) 277, 96–7, 408, 449, 343.
71. See Louis Zukofsky, *All: The Collected Short Poems 1956–64* (1967) 53–5; cf. 'The Ways', ibid., 88. Again this forms merely one mode in Zukofsky's total *oeuvre*, which is most obviously characterised by interest in the lyrical interplay of sounds.
72. Williams, *Collected Earlier Poems*, 142, 159, 241–2.
73. Ibid., 332.
74. Pound: *Shorter Poems*, 119; *Gaudier-Brzeska*, 85; letter to Homer L. Pound, 12 Oct 1916, quoted in Jackson, *Early Poetry of Pound*, 249.
75. *Shorter Poems*, 118, 119.
76. Ibid., 118; Witemeyer, *Poetry of Pound*, 142–3, prints Giles's versions of this and of 'Liu Ch'e'.
77. *Shorter Poems*, 118.
78. Ibid., 119.
79. Ibid., 131, 187.
80. Ibid., 171–7, 131–3.
81. *Des Imagistes*, 21–3.
82. Ibid., 28–9, 30, 20, 24–5, 26–7.
83. *Some Imagist Poets: An Anthology* (Boston, Mass., and New York, 1915) 21; *Some Imagist Poets 1916: An Annual Anthology* (Boston, Mass., and New York, 1916) 17–20, 21–5 (quotation from 23), 26–9.
84. *Collected Poems of H.D.* (New York, 1925) 52.
85. *Some Imagist Poets*, 24, 25–6, 27.
86. 'Choricos', in *Des Imagistes*, 7–9. The same stricture applies to 'Beauty Thou Hast Hurt Me Overmuch' and 'The River' (ibid., 13, 16).
87. Ibid., 12, 10, 19, 14.
88. Ibid., 11.
89. The same comment could be applied to Flint's Imagist version of 'The Swan'

(ibid., 35), which subordinates the creature itself to a surrounding landscape which appears like a Symbolist painting.

90. 'The Poetry of F. S. Flint', *Egoist*, II (1 May 1915) 80. In this respect compare Flint's 'London, my beautiful', *Des Imagistes*, 31.

91. See 'Trees' and 'Lunch', *Some Imagist Poets*, 53–5; 'Hallucination', *Des Imagistes*, 32; 'Accident', *Some Imagist Poets*, 58–9; 'Gloom', *Some Imagist Poets 1916*, 57–9.

92. Untitled poem beginning 'Immortal? . . . No', *Des Imagistes*, 33. Cf. the different ending printed in 'Three Poems', *Poetry and Drama*, I (Sep 1913) 307.

93. *Some Imagist Poets*, 62. See also 'Cones', *Some Imagist Poets, 1916*, 56.

94. Eliot, *Complete Poems and Plays*, 22.

95. See Davie, *Pound*, 65ff.

# Index